ASSASSINATION CLASSROOM

YUSEI MATSUI

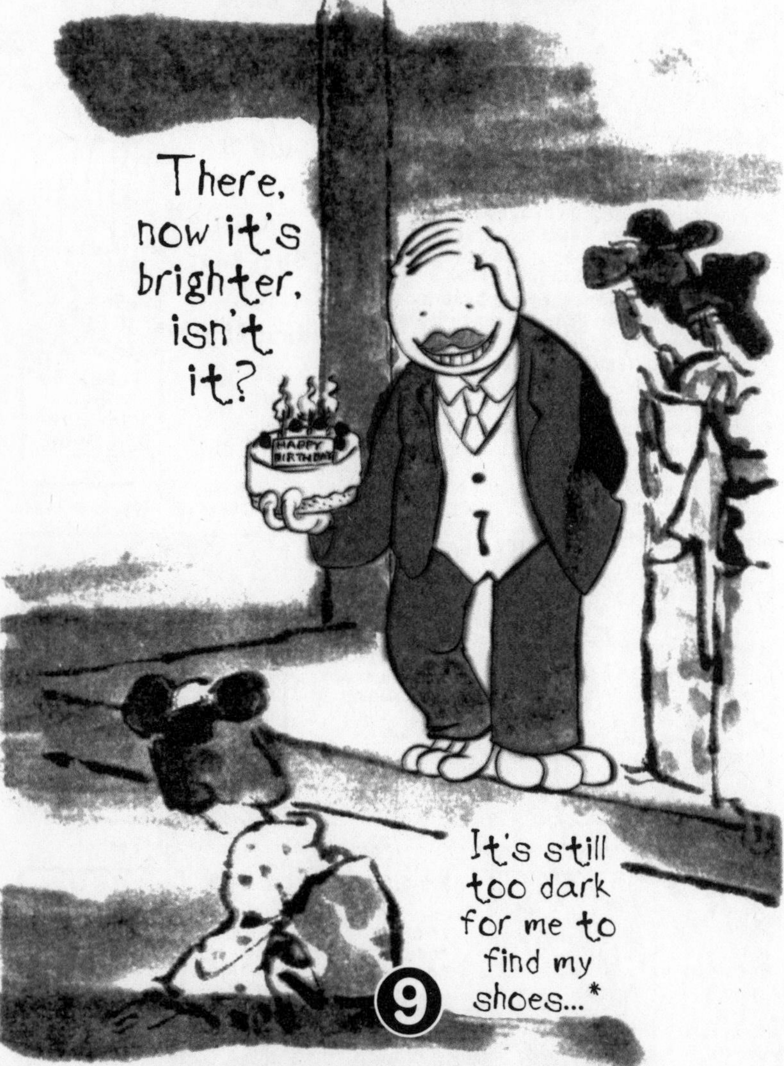
There, now it's brighter, isn't it?
HAPPY BIRTHDAY
It's still too dark for me to find my shoes...*
9

A SHOCKING TIME

SHONEN JUMP ADVANCED

*A parody of Kunibo Wada's famous satirical World War I illustration of a war profiteer lighting up a 100 yen note (worth about a million yen in the present day) to help a geisha search for her shoes.

Koro Tribune

August Issue

Published by: Class 3-E Newspaper Staff

Although we have a lot of data on his weaknesses, we are still far from successfully assassinating Koro Sensei...

Story Thus Far

I EXPECT TO SEE YOU EXECUTE THE BEST ASSASSINATION ATTEMPT YOU ARE CAPABLE OF.
MAKE THE MOST OF YOUR KNOWLEDGE, INGENUITY AND HARD WORK.
THIS IS MY IDEA OF THE MOST FUN EVER.

Kunugigaoka Junior High, Class 3-E is led by a monster who has disintegrated the moon and is planning to do the same to the Earth next March.

Even the armies of the world, with the latest technology, can't kill the super-creature Koro Sensei and collect the bounty of 100 million dollars! So it comes down to his students in the so-called "End Class." Thanks to Koro Sensei's dedication, they are becoming fine students who can academically outshine the top-ranking students at their school. Likewise, their assassination skills are rapidly improving under the tutelage of Mr. Karasuma of the Ministry of Defense, who is molding them into a professional team of assassins. The first semester is over and the clock is ticking. Will the students of 3-E successfully assassinate Koro Sensei?!

Koro Sensei

A mysterious, man-made creature with versatile tentacles capable of flying at Mach 20. His name is a play on the words "koro senai," which means "can't kill." Nobody knows who created him or why he wants to teach Class 3-E.

The distance he traveled by himself in volume 8: zero.

Nagisa Shiota

Class E student. Skilled at information gathering, he has been taking notes on Koro Sensei's weaknesses. Everyone is beginning to realize that he has a hidden talent for assassination.

He looked so natural in that outfit...

Kaede Kayano

Class E student. A kind and gentle student with an antipathy to large bosoms.

Kotaro Takebayashi

pick up!

He has an excellent knowledge of medicine for a student his age. He is giving his all to help the students infected with the virus, but hopes they will all recover by eleven o'clock because there's an anime on then that he wants to watch.

Karma Akabane

Class E student. A natural genius who earns top grades. His failure in the final exam of the first semester has forced him to grow up and take things a bit more seriously.

Tadaomi Karasuma

Member of the Ministry of Defense and the Class E students' P.E. teacher. Though serious about his duties, he is successfully building good relationships with his students.

Ryoma Terasaka

Class E student. Once a rebel and an outcast, he has gradually begun to fit in and is now a dependable assassin due to his great physical strength.

Okajima is in Critical condition!

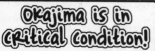

Just don't tell them he keeps mumbling "booty." Those could be his final words!

What should we tell his parents?

Irina Jelavich

A sexy assassin hired as an English teacher. She's known for using her "womanly charms" to get close to a target. She often flirts with Karasuma, but hasn't had any success so far.

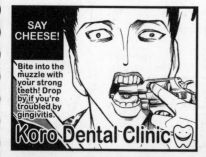

SAY CHEESE!

Bite into the muzzle with your strong teeth! Drop by if you're troubled by gingivitis.

Koro Dental Clinic

Gakuho Asano

The principal of Kunugigaoka Academy, who built this academically competitive school based on his faith in rationality and hierarchy.

Assassination Class Roster

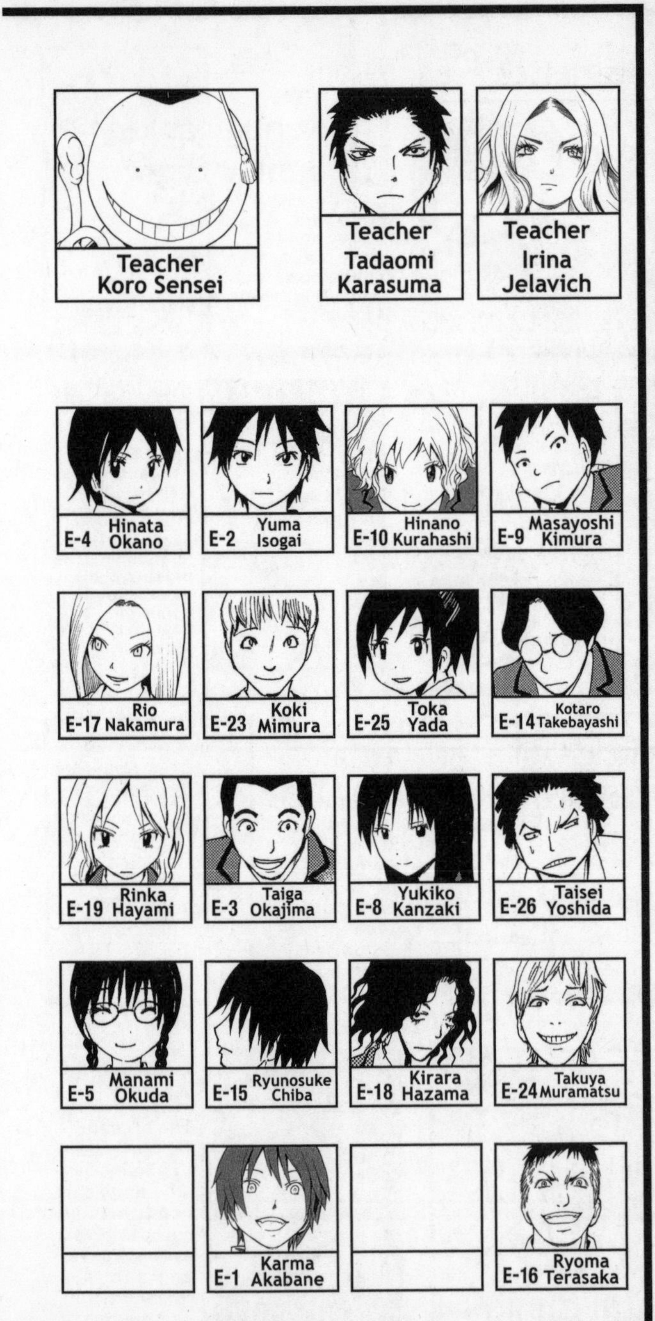
Teacher Koro Sensei
Teacher Tadaomi Karasuma
Teacher Irina Jelavich
E-4 Hinata Okano
E-2 Yuma Isogai
E-10 Hinano Kurahashi
E-9 Masayoshi Kimura
E-17 Rio Nakamura
E-23 Koki Mimura
E-25 Toka Yada
E-14 Kotaro Takebayashi
E-19 Rinka Hayami
E-3 Taiga Okajima
E-8 Yukiko Kanzaki
E-26 Taisei Yoshida
E-5 Manami Okuda
E-15 Ryunosuke Chiba
E-18 Kirara Hazama
E-24 Takuya Muramatsu
E-1 Karma Akabane
E-16 Ryoma Terasaka

Always assassinate your target using a method that brings a smile to your face.

I'm open for assassinations any time. But don't let them get in the way of your studies.

I won't harm students who try to assassinate me. But if your skills are rusty, expect a good polishing!

Individual Statistics

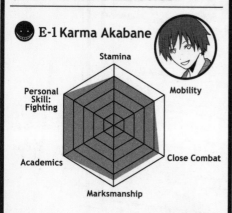

E-1 Karma Akabane

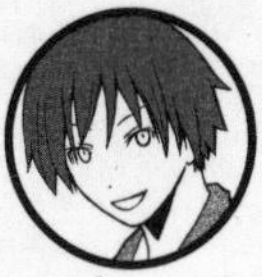

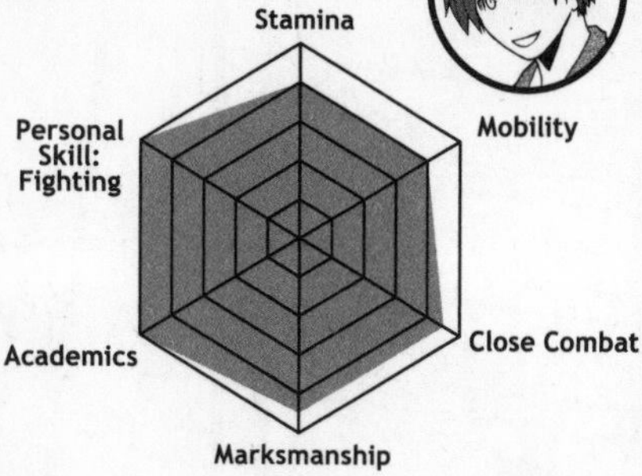
Stamina
Mobility
Close Combat
Marksmanship
Academics
Personal Skill: Fighting

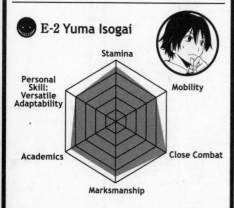

E-2 Yuma Isogai

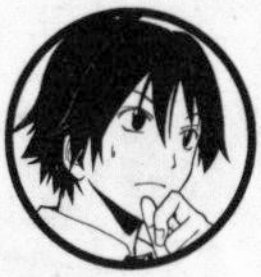

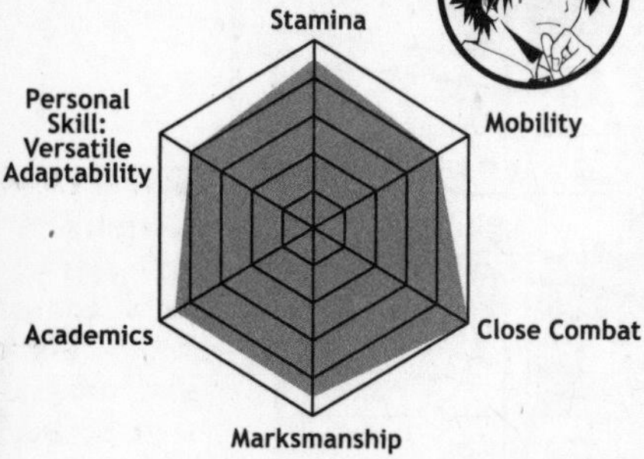
Stamina
Mobility
Close Combat
Marksmanship
Academics
Personal Skill: Versatile Adaptability

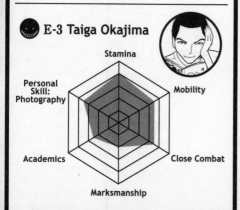

E-3 Taiga Okajima

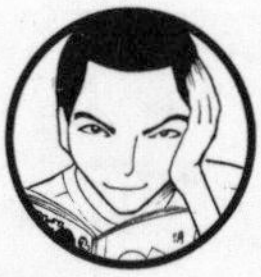

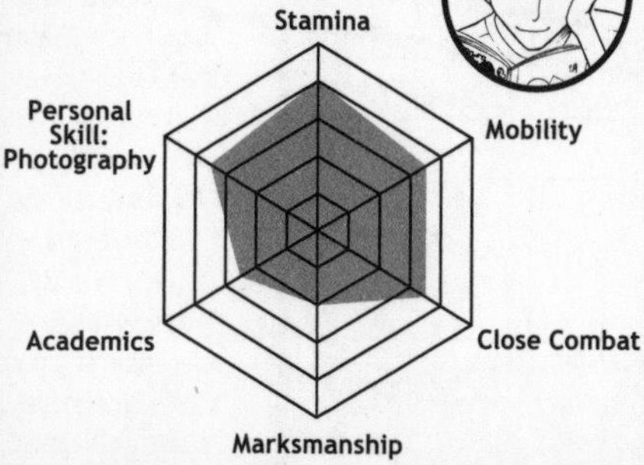
Stamina
Mobility
Close Combat
Marksmanship
Academics
Personal Skill: Photography

Kunugigaoka Junior High

3-E

Koro Sensei Class

Seating Arrangement

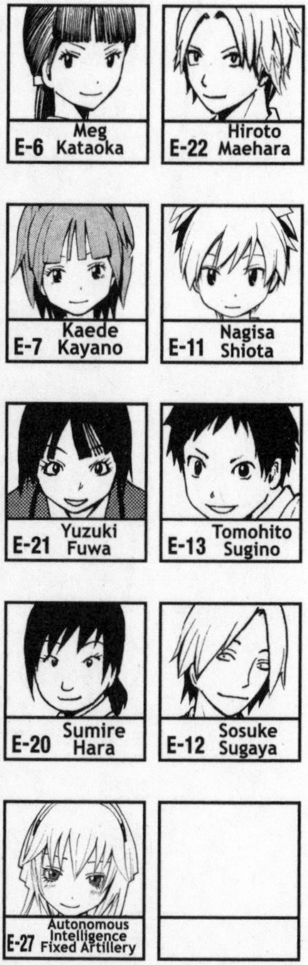
E-6 Meg Kataoka
E-22 Hiroto Maehara
E-7 Kaede Kayano
E-11 Nagisa Shiota
E-21 Yuzuki Fuwa
E-13 Tomohito Sugino
E-20 Sumire Hara
E-12 Sosuke Sugaya
E-27 Autonomous Intelligence Fixed Artillery

ASSASSINATION CLASSROOM 9 CONTENTS

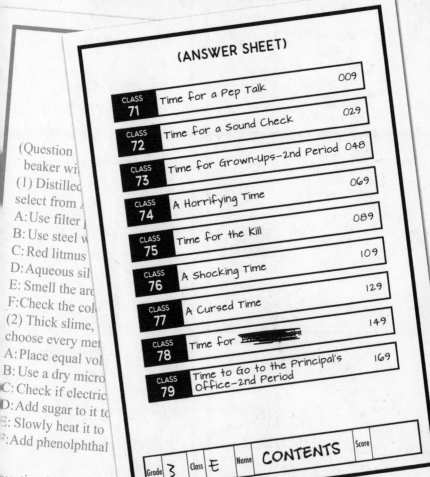

(ANSWER SHEET)

Grade	3	Class	E	Name	CONTENTS	Score	

(Question
beaker wi
(1) Distilled
select from A
A: Use filter
B: Use steel w
C: Red litmus
D: Aqueous sil
E: Smell the ar
F: Check the col
(2) Thick slime,
choose every met
A: Place equal vol
B: Use a dry micro
C: Check if electric
D: Add sugar to it to
E: Slowly heat it to
F: Add phenolphthal

uestion 2.) Illustratio
e Earth is revolving in ... depicts
swer the following question. ... direction of the arrow.
ges 1 to 3 from Illustration 2
mages of Planet Koro from
J of Illustration 3. ① Of Planet
1, 2, and 3 which one seems
rgest? ② Where
l it be located?

Illustration 2

1
2
3

Illustration 1

Earth's orbit
A
B
C
D
E
F
G
H
I
J
Sun
Planet Koro's Orbit
Earth

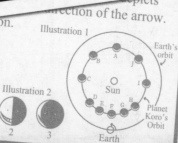

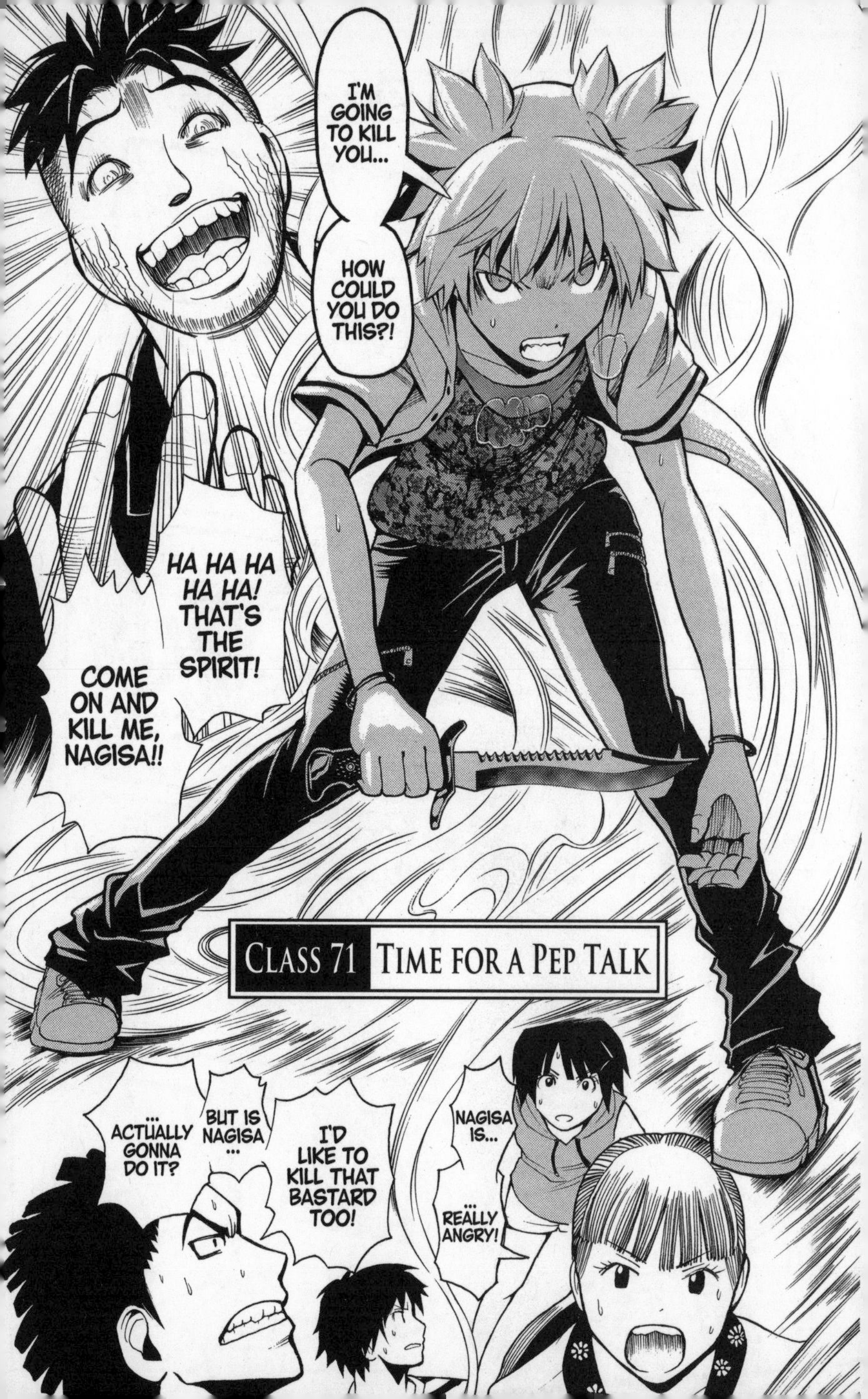
I'M GOING TO KILL YOU...
HOW COULD YOU DO THIS?!
HA HA HA HA HA! THAT'S THE SPIRIT!
COME ON AND KILL ME, NAGISA!!
CLASS 71 TIME FOR A PEP TALK
NAGISA IS...
...REALLY ANGRY!
I'D LIKE TO KILL THAT BASTARD TOO!
BUT IS NAGISA...
...ACTUALLY GONNA DO IT?

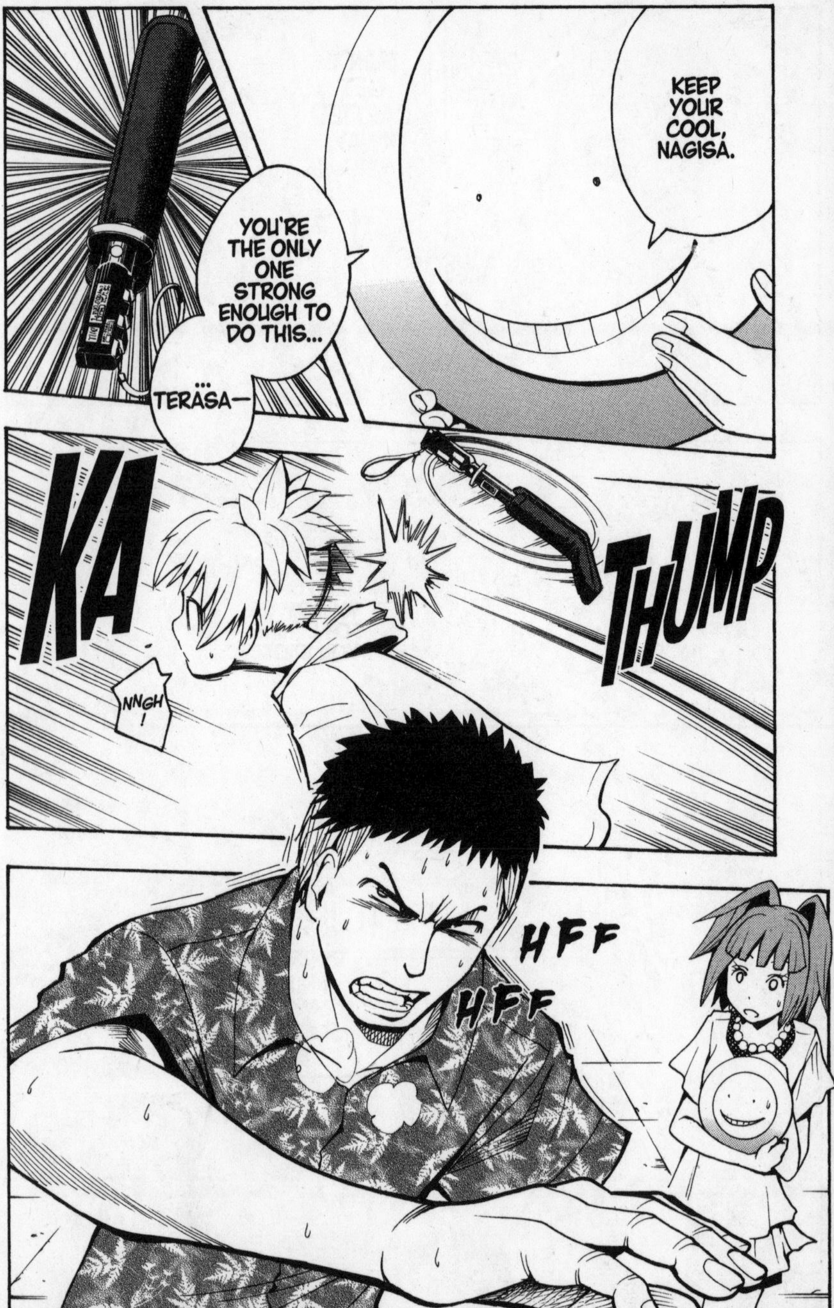
KEEP YOUR COOL, NAGISA.
YOU'RE THE ONLY ONE STRONG ENOUGH TO DO THIS...
...TERASA—
THUMP
KA
NNGH!
HFF
HFF

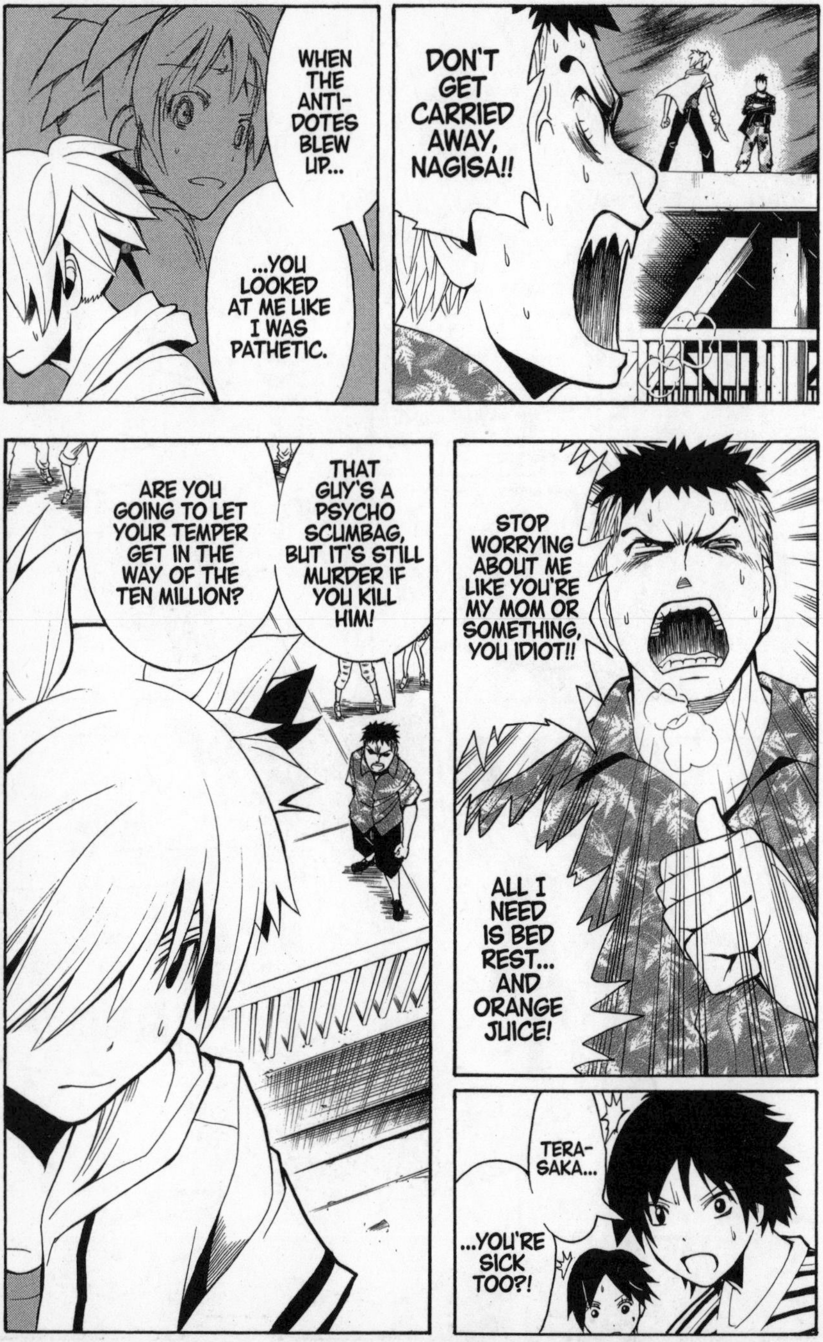
DON'T GET CARRIED AWAY, NAGISA!!
WHEN THE ANTI-DOTES BLEW UP...
...YOU LOOKED AT ME LIKE I WAS PATHETIC.
STOP WORRYING ABOUT ME LIKE YOU'RE MY MOM OR SOMETHING, YOU IDIOT!!
ALL I NEED IS BED REST... AND ORANGE JUICE!
TERA-SAKA...
...YOU'RE SICK TOO?!
THAT GUY'S A PSYCHO SCUMBAG, BUT IT'S STILL MURDER IF YOU KILL HIM!
ARE YOU GOING TO LET YOUR TEMPER GET IN THE WAY OF THE TEN MILLION?

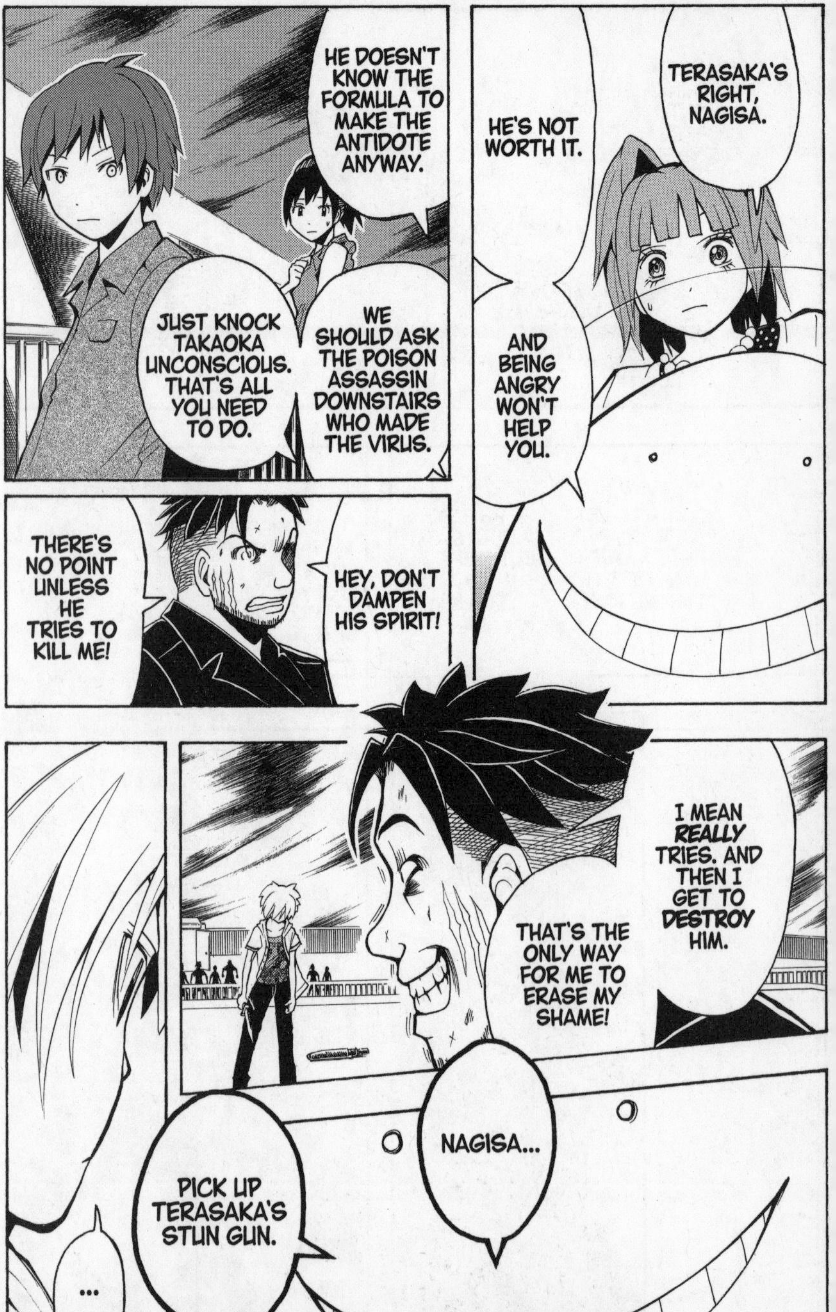
TERASAKA'S RIGHT, NAGISA.
HE'S NOT WORTH IT.
AND BEING ANGRY WON'T HELP YOU.
HE DOESN'T KNOW THE FORMULA TO MAKE THE ANTIDOTE ANYWAY.
WE SHOULD ASK THE POISON ASSASSIN DOWNSTAIRS WHO MADE THE VIRUS.
JUST KNOCK TAKAOKA UNCONSCIOUS. THAT'S ALL YOU NEED TO DO.
HEY, DON'T DAMPEN HIS SPIRIT!
THERE'S NO POINT UNLESS HE TRIES TO KILL ME!
I MEAN REALLY TRIES. AND THEN I GET TO DESTROY HIM.
THAT'S THE ONLY WAY FOR ME TO ERASE MY SHAME!
NAGISA...
PICK UP TERASAKA'S STUN GUN.
...

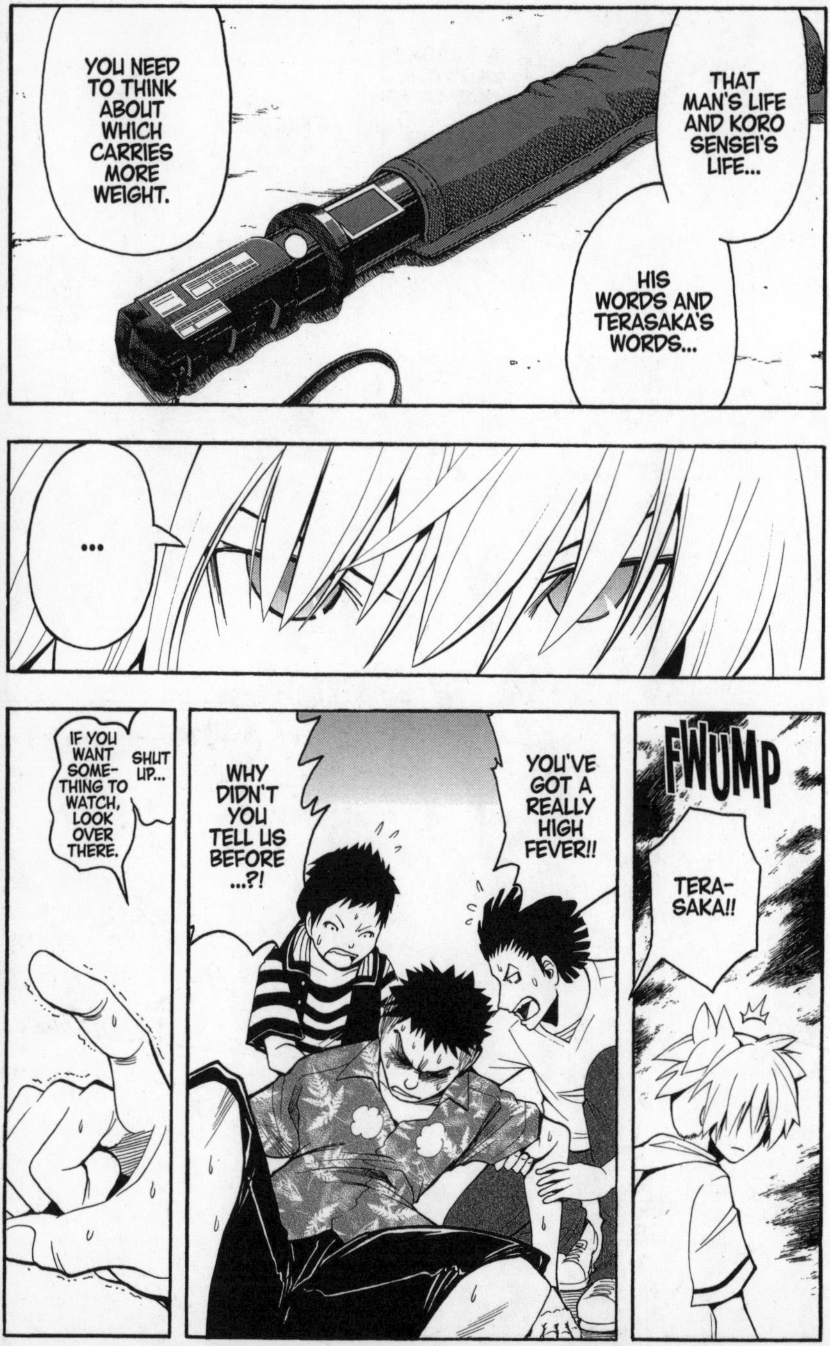
THAT MAN'S LIFE AND KORO SENSEI'S LIFE...
HIS WORDS AND TERASAKA'S WORDS...
YOU NEED TO THINK ABOUT WHICH CARRIES MORE WEIGHT.
...
FWUMP
TERA-SAKA!!
YOU'VE GOT A REALLY HIGH FEVER!!
WHY DIDN'T YOU TELL US BEFORE ...?!
SHUT UP...
IF YOU WANT SOME-THING TO WATCH, LOOK OVER THERE.

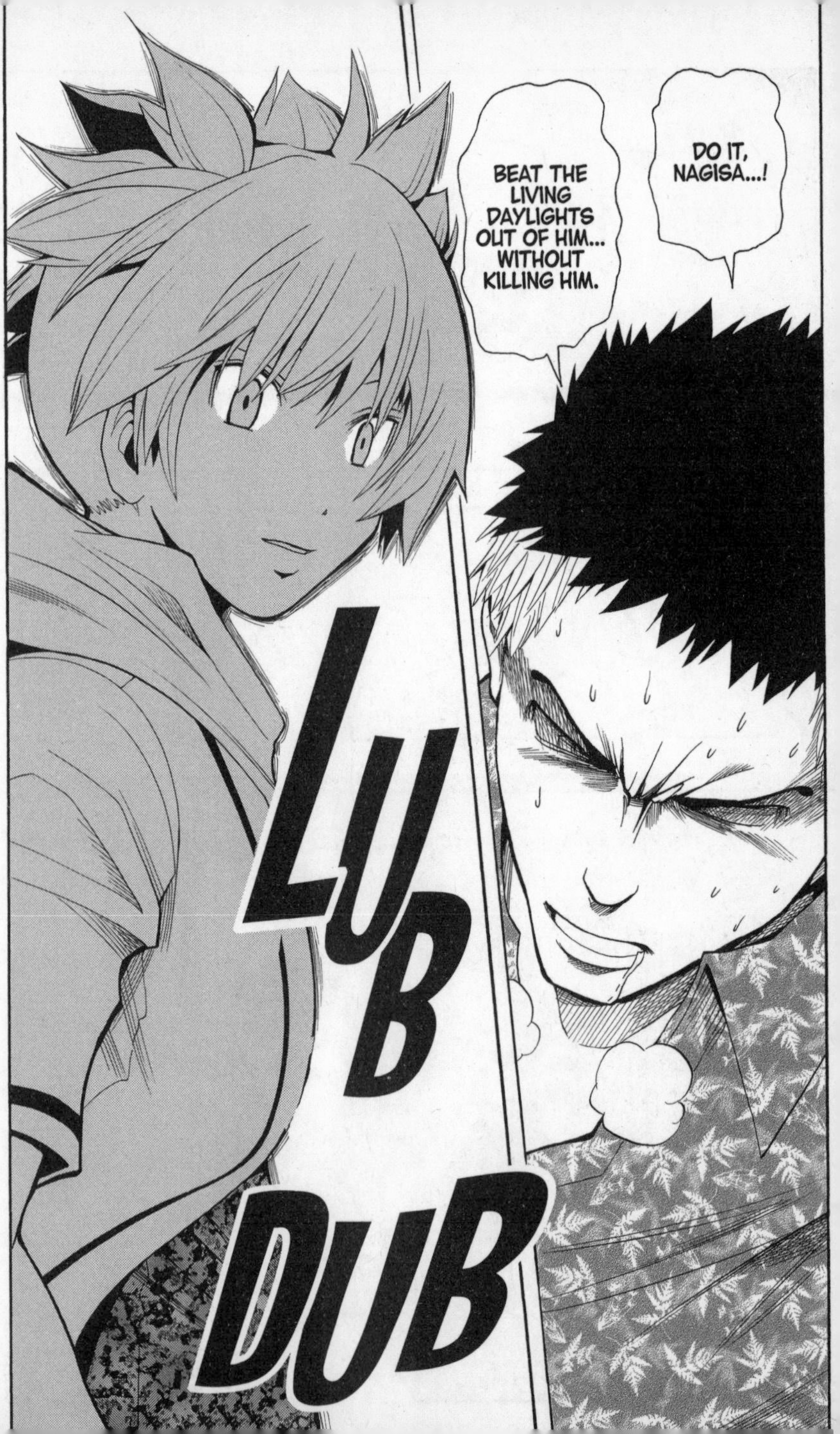
DO IT, NAGISA...!
BEAT THE LIVING DAYLIGHTS OUT OF HIM... WITHOUT KILLING HIM.
LUB DUB

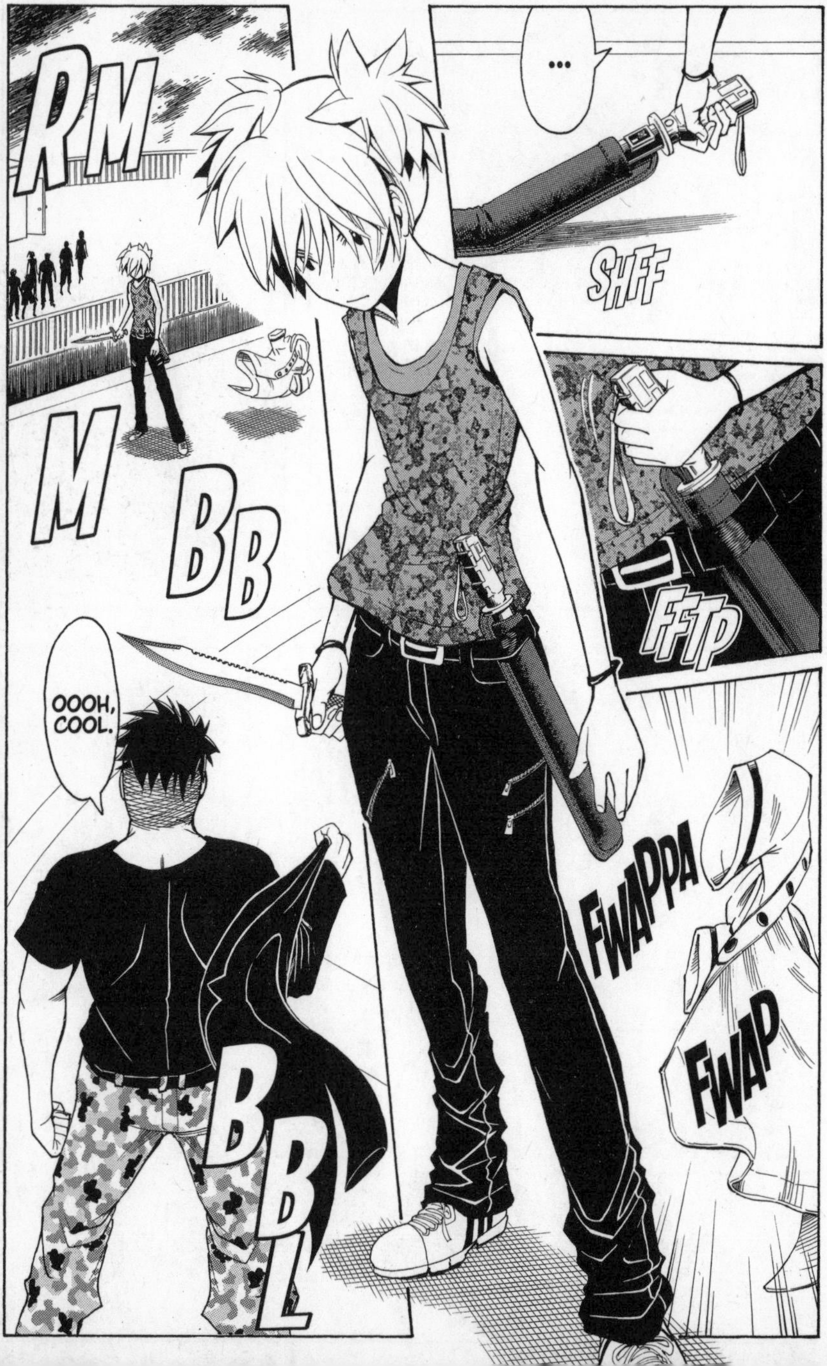
...
SHFF
FFTP
FWAPPA
FWAP
RM
M
BB
OOOH, COOL.
BBL

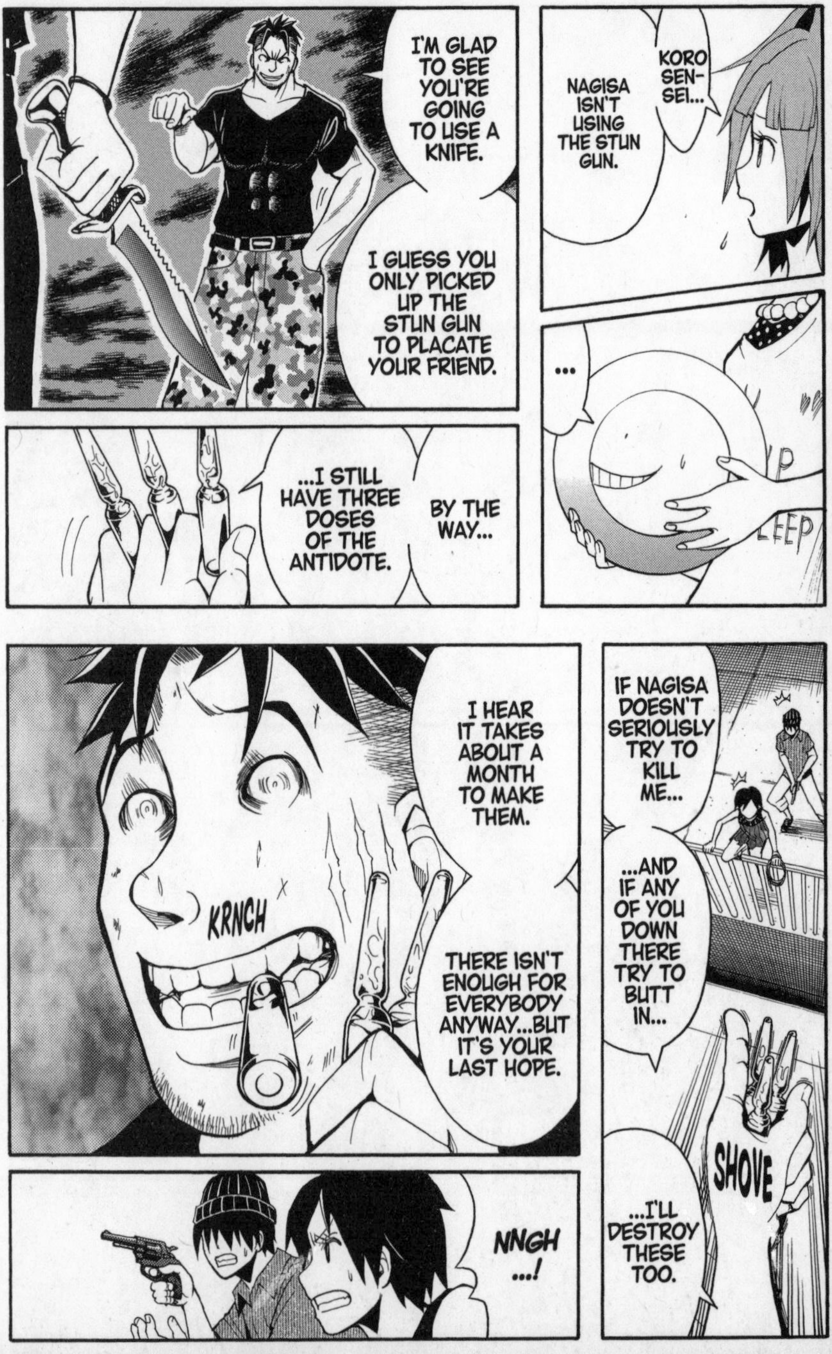
KORO SENSEI...
NAGISA ISN'T USING THE STUN GUN.
...
I'M GLAD TO SEE YOU'RE GOING TO USE A KNIFE.
I GUESS YOU ONLY PICKED UP THE STUN GUN TO PLACATE YOUR FRIEND.
BY THE WAY...
...I STILL HAVE THREE DOSES OF THE ANTIDOTE.
IF NAGISA DOESN'T SERIOUSLY TRY TO KILL ME...
...AND IF ANY OF YOU DOWN THERE TRY TO BUTT IN...
SHOVE
...I'LL DESTROY THESE TOO.
I HEAR IT TAKES ABOUT A MONTH TO MAKE THEM.
KRNCH
THERE ISN'T ENOUGH FOR EVERYBODY ANYWAY...BUT IT'S YOUR LAST HOPE.
NNGH ...!

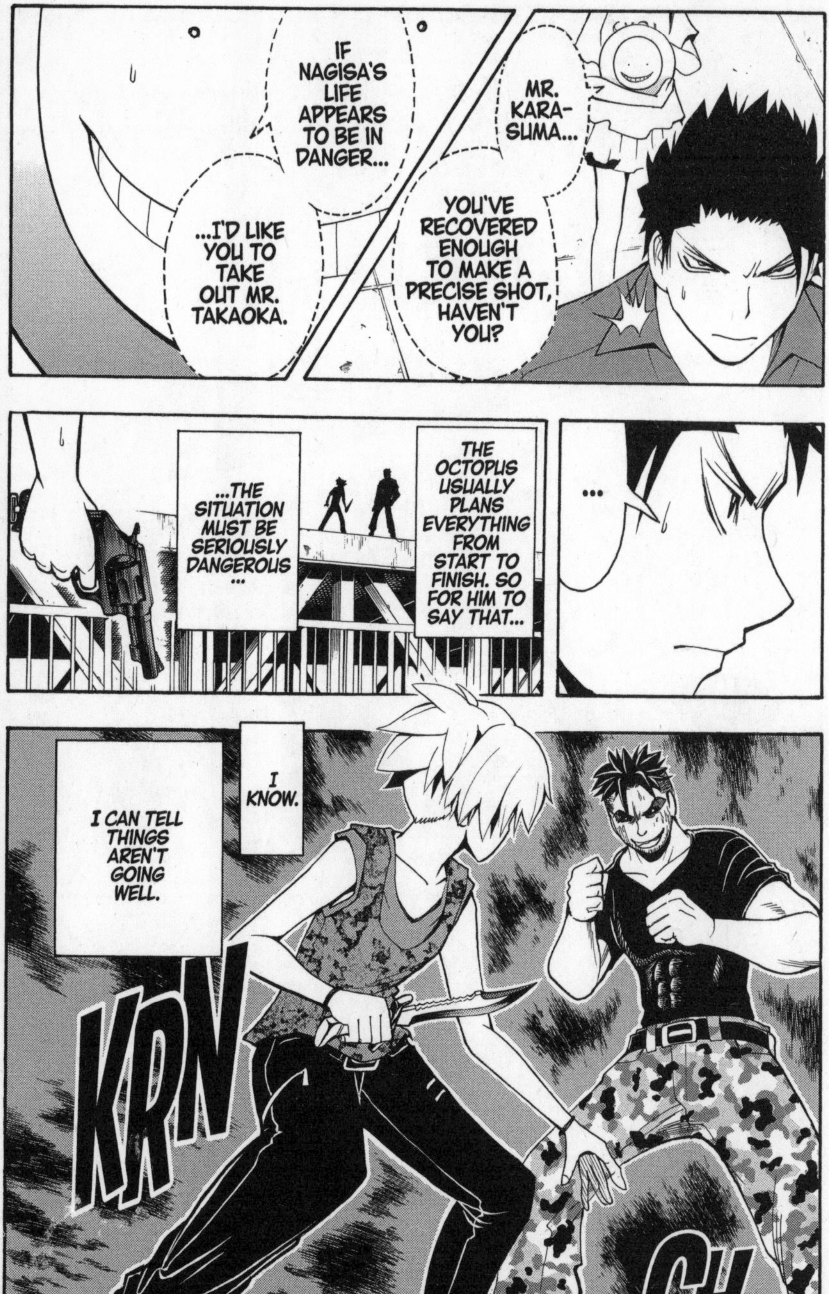
MR. KARA-SUMA...
YOU'VE RECOVERED ENOUGH TO MAKE A PRECISE SHOT, HAVEN'T YOU?
IF NAGISA'S LIFE APPEARS TO BE IN DANGER...
...I'D LIKE YOU TO TAKE OUT MR. TAKAOKA.
...
THE OCTOPUS USUALLY PLANS EVERYTHING FROM START TO FINISH. SO FOR HIM TO SAY THAT...
...THE SITUATION MUST BE SERIOUSLY DANGEROUS...
I KNOW.
I CAN TELL THINGS AREN'T GOING WELL.
KRN
CH

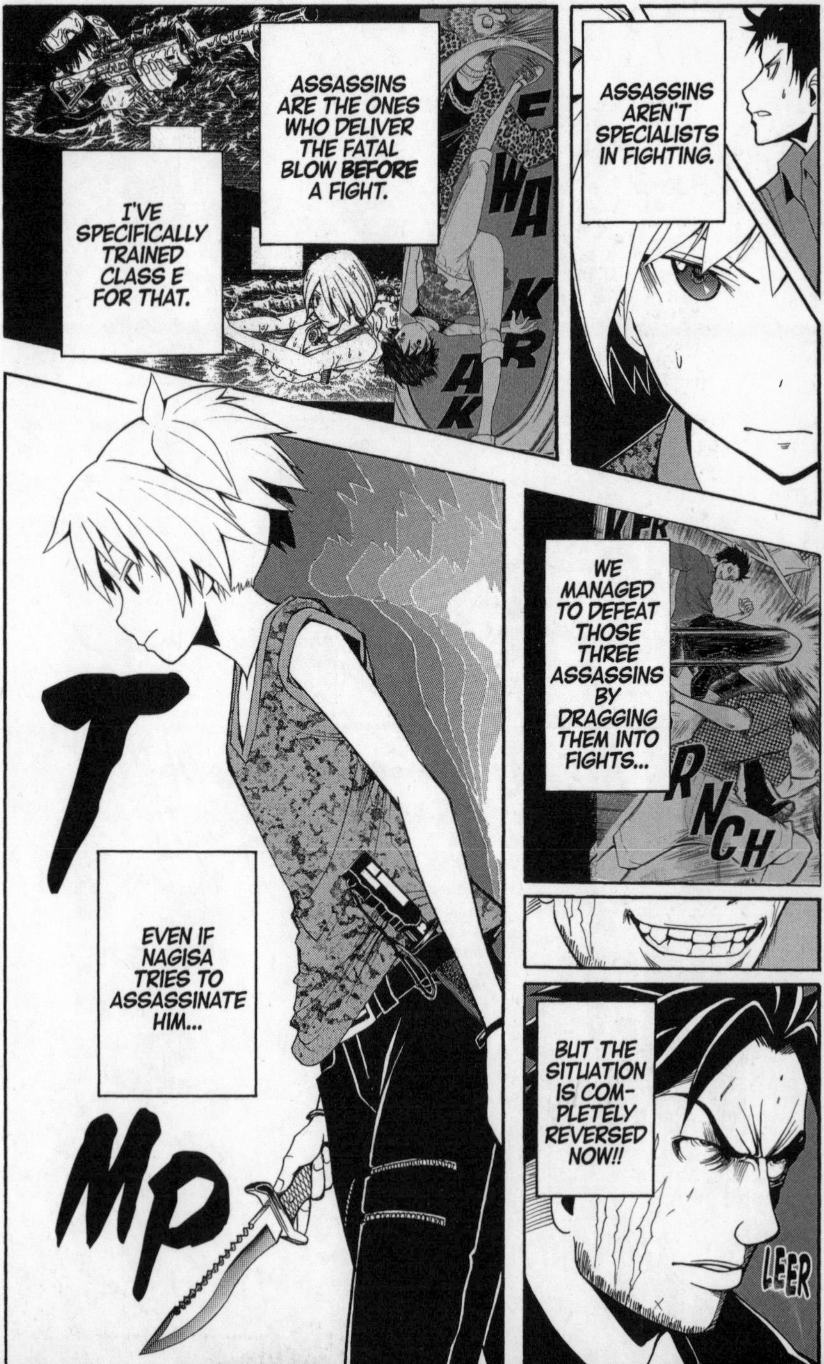
ASSASSINS AREN'T SPECIALISTS IN FIGHTING.
ASSASSINS ARE THE ONES WHO DELIVER THE FATAL BLOW BEFORE A FIGHT.
FWAK
KRAK
I'VE SPECIFICALLY TRAINED CLASS E FOR THAT.
WE MANAGED TO DEFEAT THOSE THREE ASSASSINS BY DRAGGING THEM INTO FIGHTS...
RNCH
BUT THE SITUATION IS COM-PLETELY REVERSED NOW!!
LEER
T
MP
EVEN IF NAGISA TRIES TO ASSASSINATE HIM...

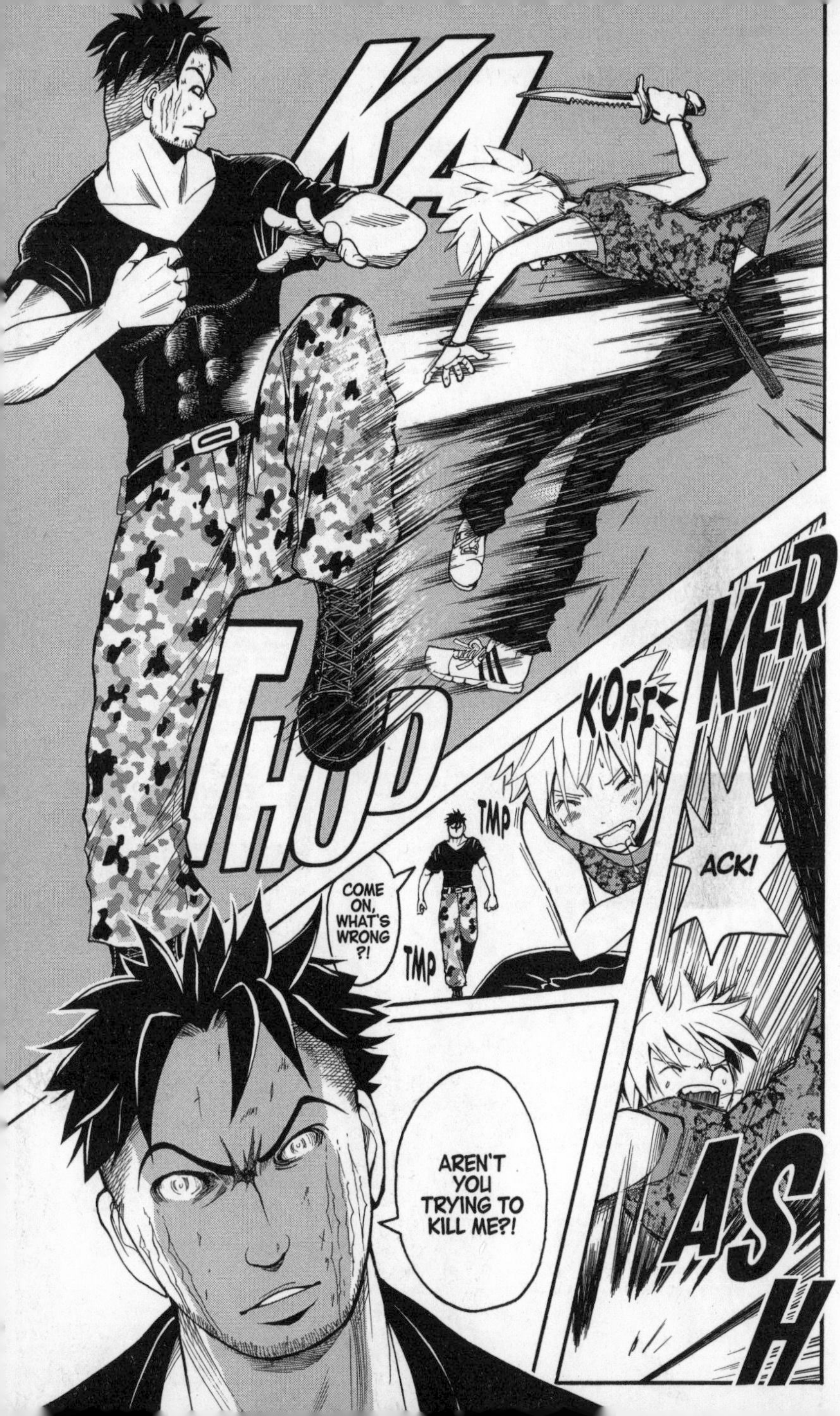
KA
THUD
KER
ACK!
ASH
KOFF
TMP
COME ON, WHAT'S WRONG?!
TMP
AREN'T YOU TRYING TO KILL ME?!

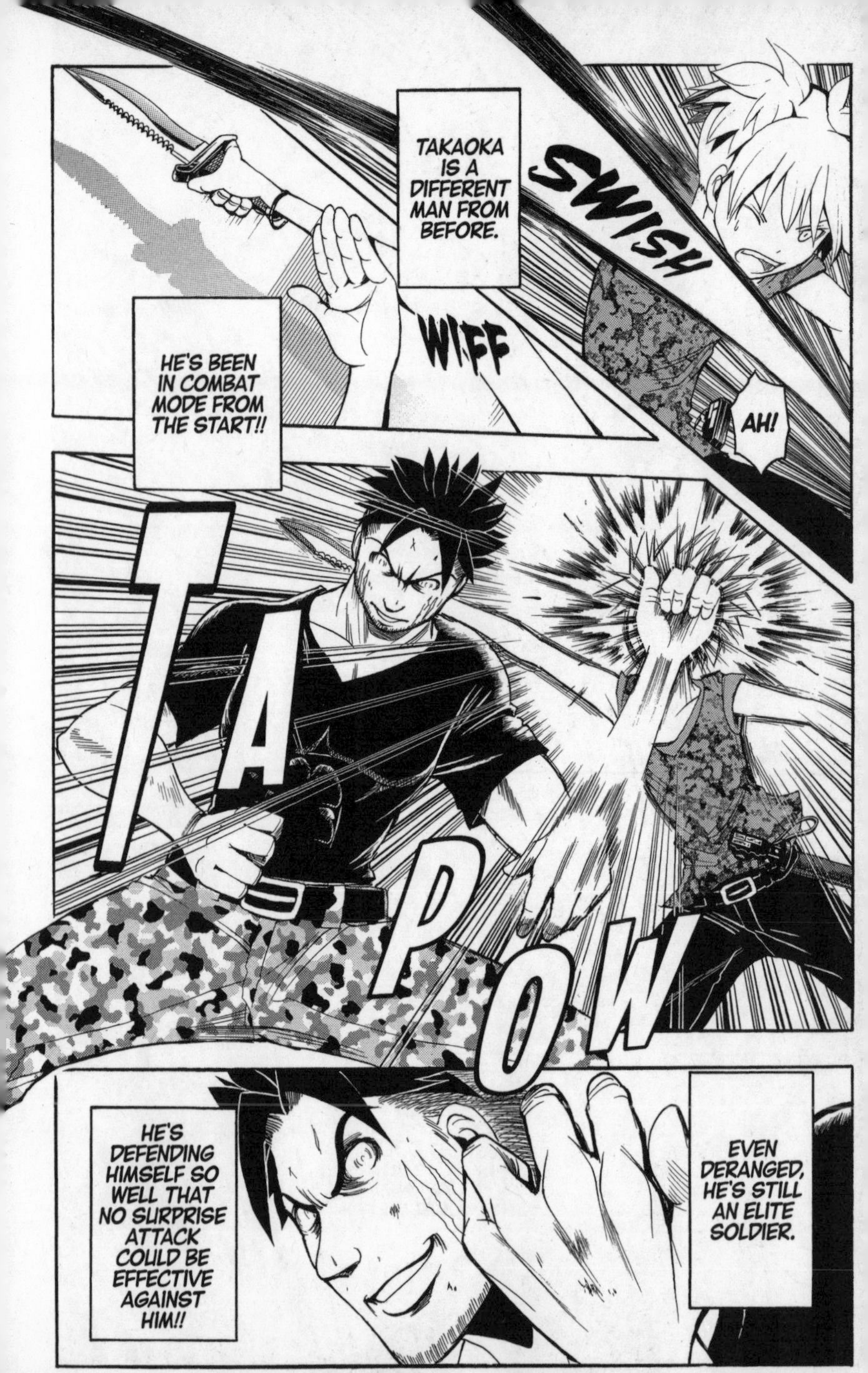
SWISH
TAKAOKA IS A DIFFERENT MAN FROM BEFORE.
AH!
WIFF
HE'S BEEN IN COMBAT MODE FROM THE START!!
TAPOW
EVEN DERANGED, HE'S STILL AN ELITE SOLDIER.
HE'S DEFENDING HIMSELF SO WELL THAT NO SURPRISE ATTACK COULD BE EFFECTIVE AGAINST HIM!!

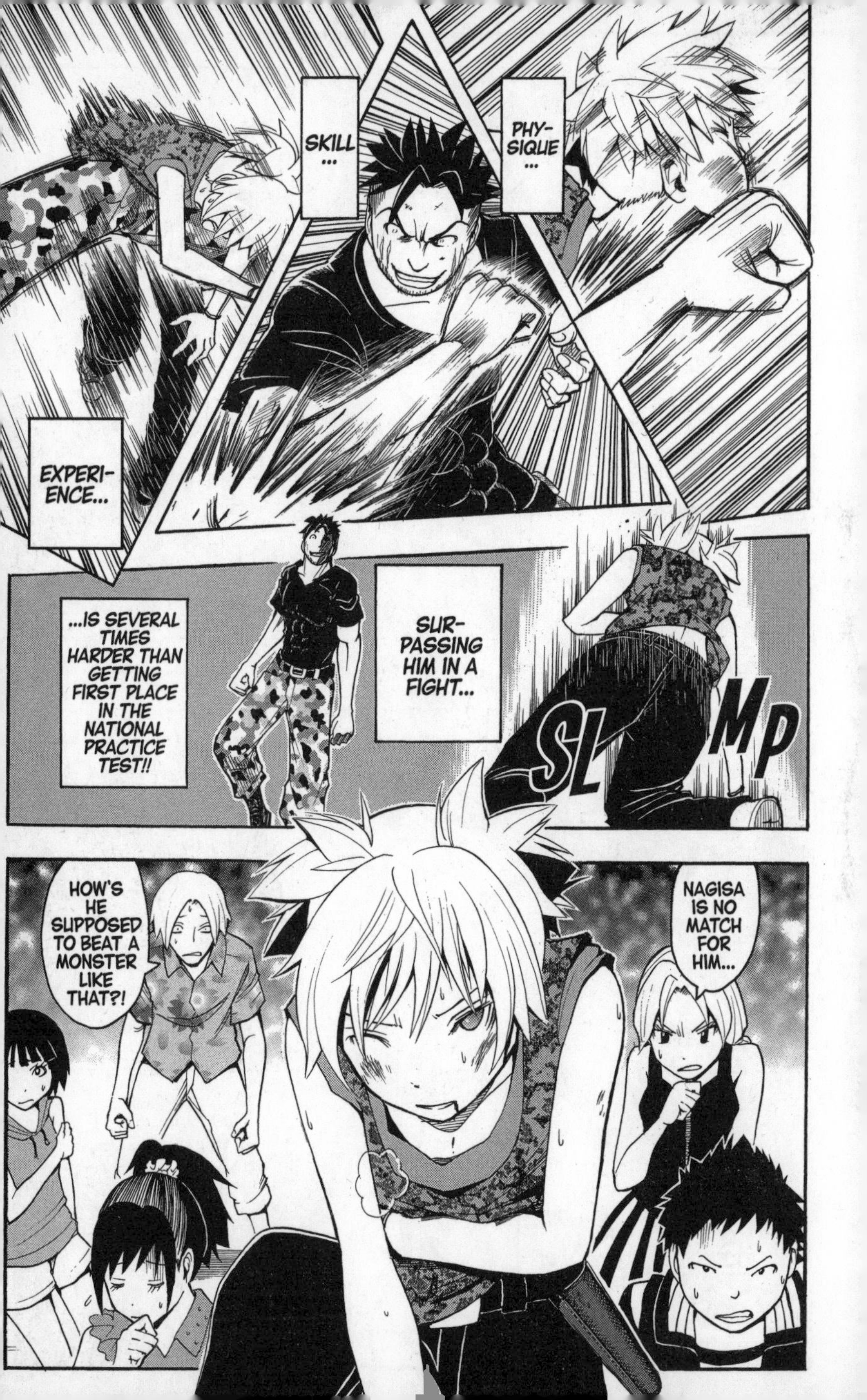
PHY-SIQUE...
SKILL...
EXPERI-ENCE...
SL MP
SUR-PASSING HIM IN A FIGHT...
...IS SEVERAL TIMES HARDER THAN GETTING FIRST PLACE IN THE NATIONAL PRACTICE TEST!!
NAGISA IS NO MATCH FOR HIM...
HOW'S HE SUPPOSED TO BEAT A MONSTER LIKE THAT?!

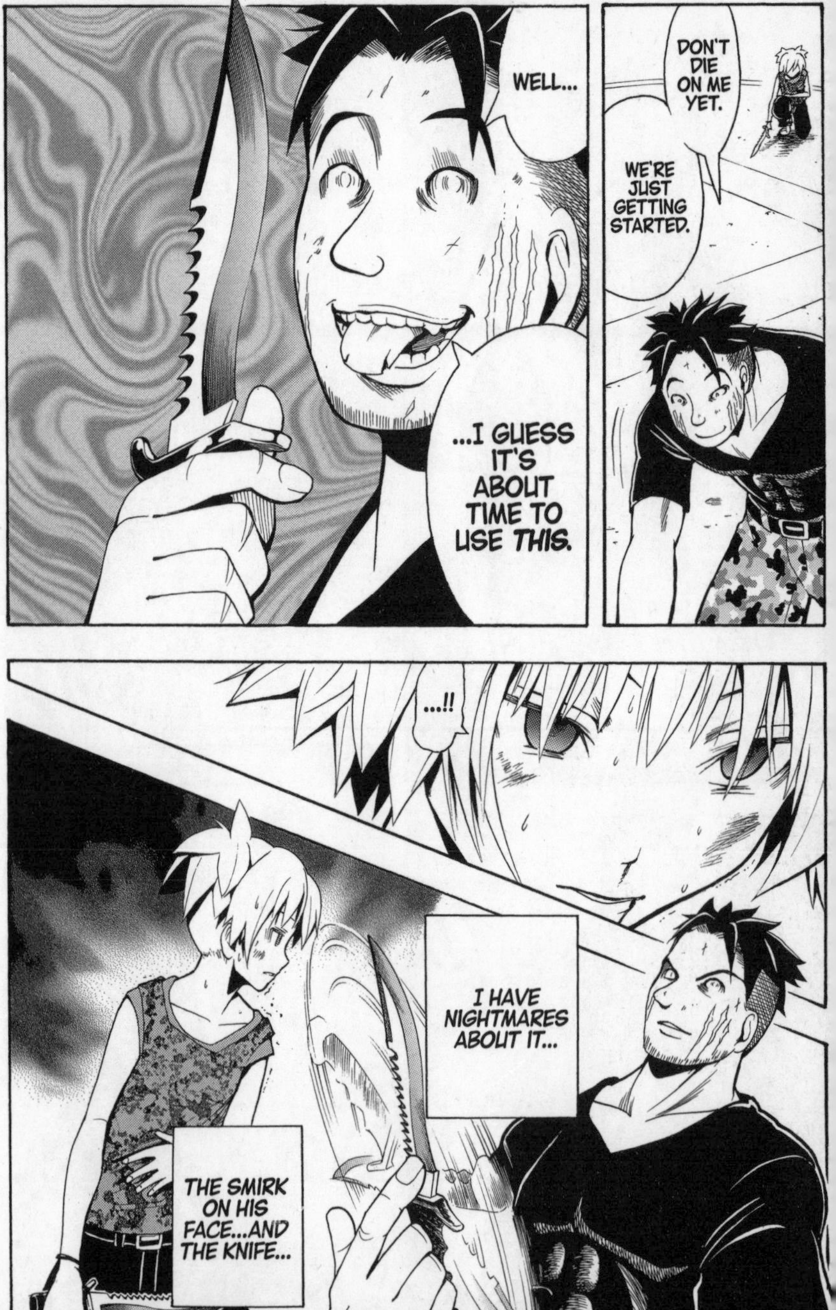
DON'T DIE ON ME YET.
WE'RE JUST GETTING STARTED.
WELL...
...I GUESS IT'S ABOUT TIME TO USE THIS.
...!!
I HAVE NIGHTMARES ABOUT IT...
THE SMIRK ON HIS FACE...AND THE KNIFE...

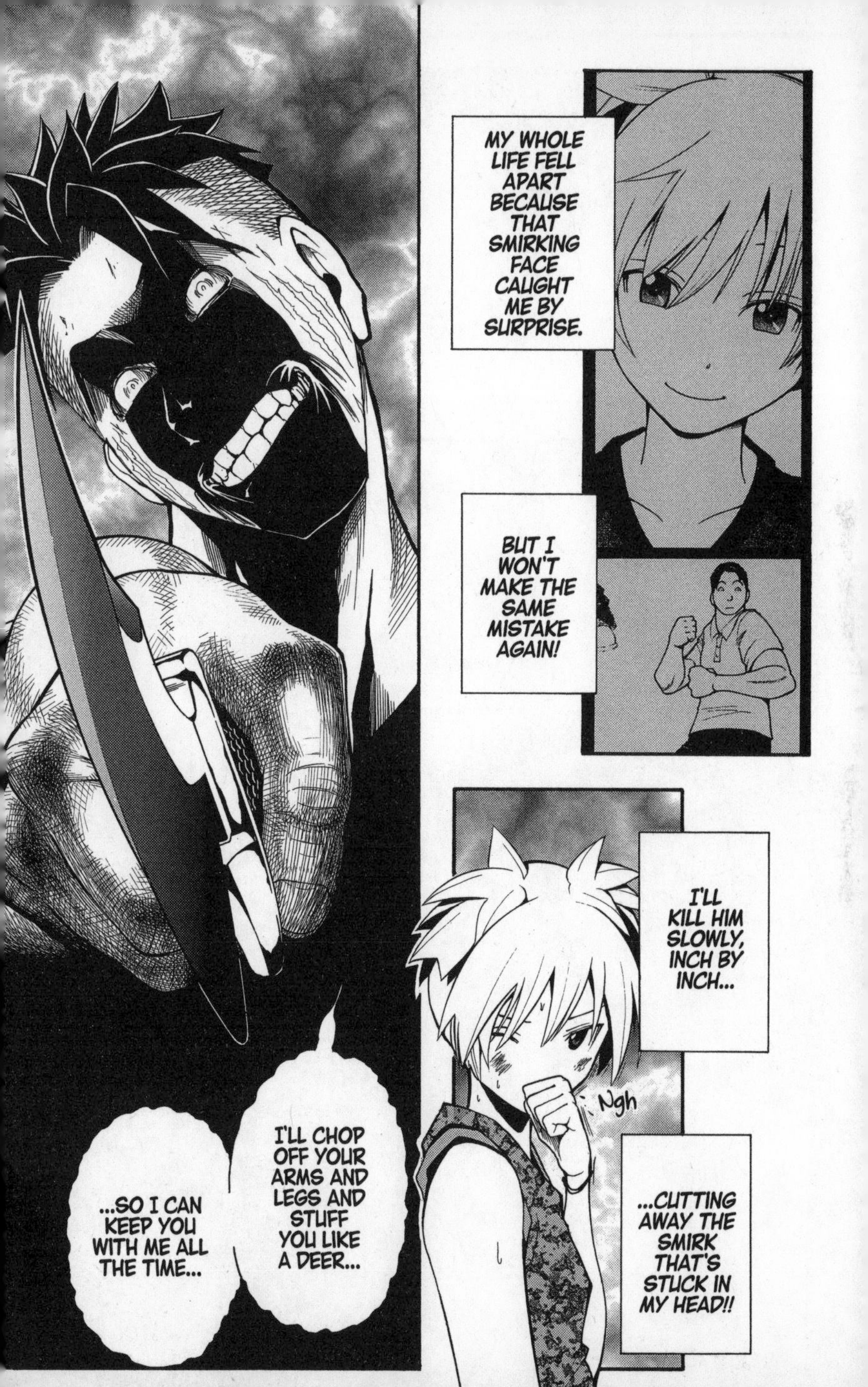
MY WHOLE LIFE FELL APART BECAUSE THAT SMIRKING FACE CAUGHT ME BY SURPRISE.
BUT I WON'T MAKE THE SAME MISTAKE AGAIN!
I'LL KILL HIM SLOWLY, INCH BY INCH...
Ngh
...CUTTING AWAY THE SMIRK THAT'S STUCK IN MY HEAD!!
I'LL CHOP OFF YOUR ARMS AND LEGS AND STUFF YOU LIKE A DEER...
...SO I CAN KEEP YOU WITH ME ALL THE TIME...

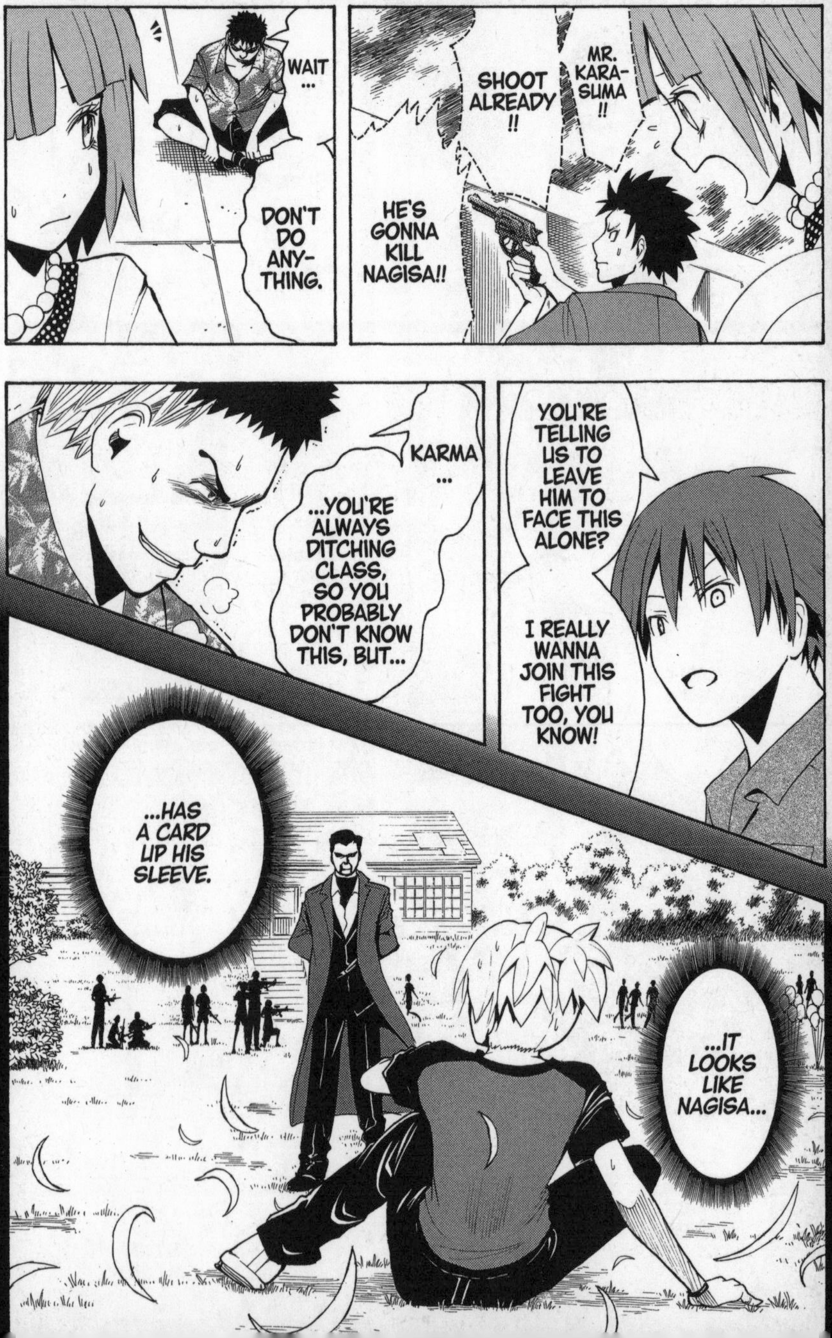
MR. KARASUMA!!
SHOOT ALREADY!!
HE'S GONNA KILL NAGISA!!
WAIT...
DON'T DO ANYTHING.
YOU'RE TELLING US TO LEAVE HIM TO FACE THIS ALONE?
I REALLY WANNA JOIN THIS FIGHT TOO, YOU KNOW!
KARMA...
...YOU'RE ALWAYS DITCHING CLASS, SO YOU PROBABLY DON'T KNOW THIS, BUT...
...IT LOOKS LIKE NAGISA...
...HAS A CARD UP HIS SLEEVE.

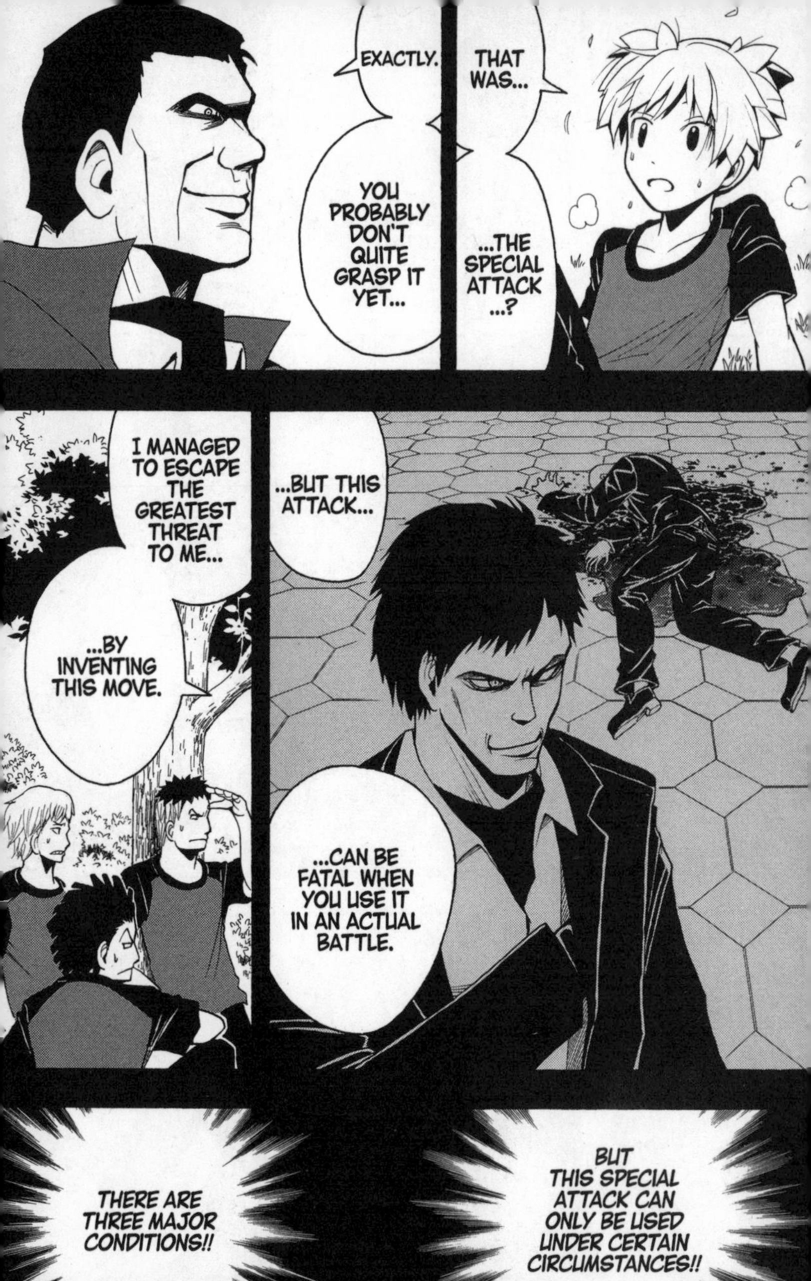
THAT WAS...
...THE SPECIAL ATTACK ...?
EXACTLY.
YOU PROBABLY DON'T QUITE GRASP IT YET...
...BUT THIS ATTACK...
...CAN BE FATAL WHEN YOU USE IT IN AN ACTUAL BATTLE.
I MANAGED TO ESCAPE THE GREATEST THREAT TO ME...
...BY INVENTING THIS MOVE.
BUT THIS SPECIAL ATTACK CAN ONLY BE USED UNDER CERTAIN CIRCUMSTANCES!!
THERE ARE THREE MAJOR CONDITIONS!!

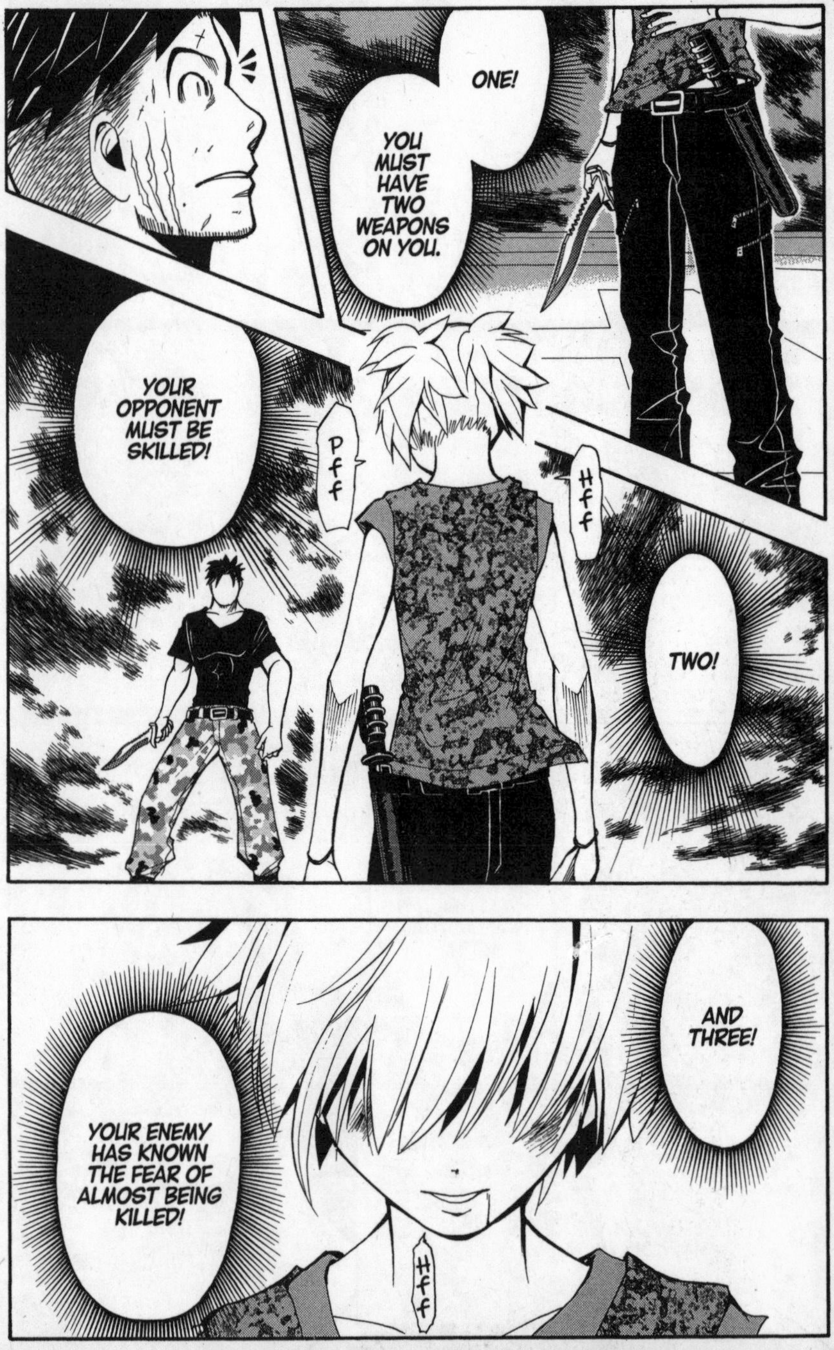
ONE!
YOU MUST HAVE TWO WEAPONS ON YOU.
TWO!
Hff
Pff
YOUR OPPONENT MUST BE SKILLED!
AND THREE!
Hff
YOUR ENEMY HAS KNOWN THE FEAR OF ALMOST BEING KILLED!

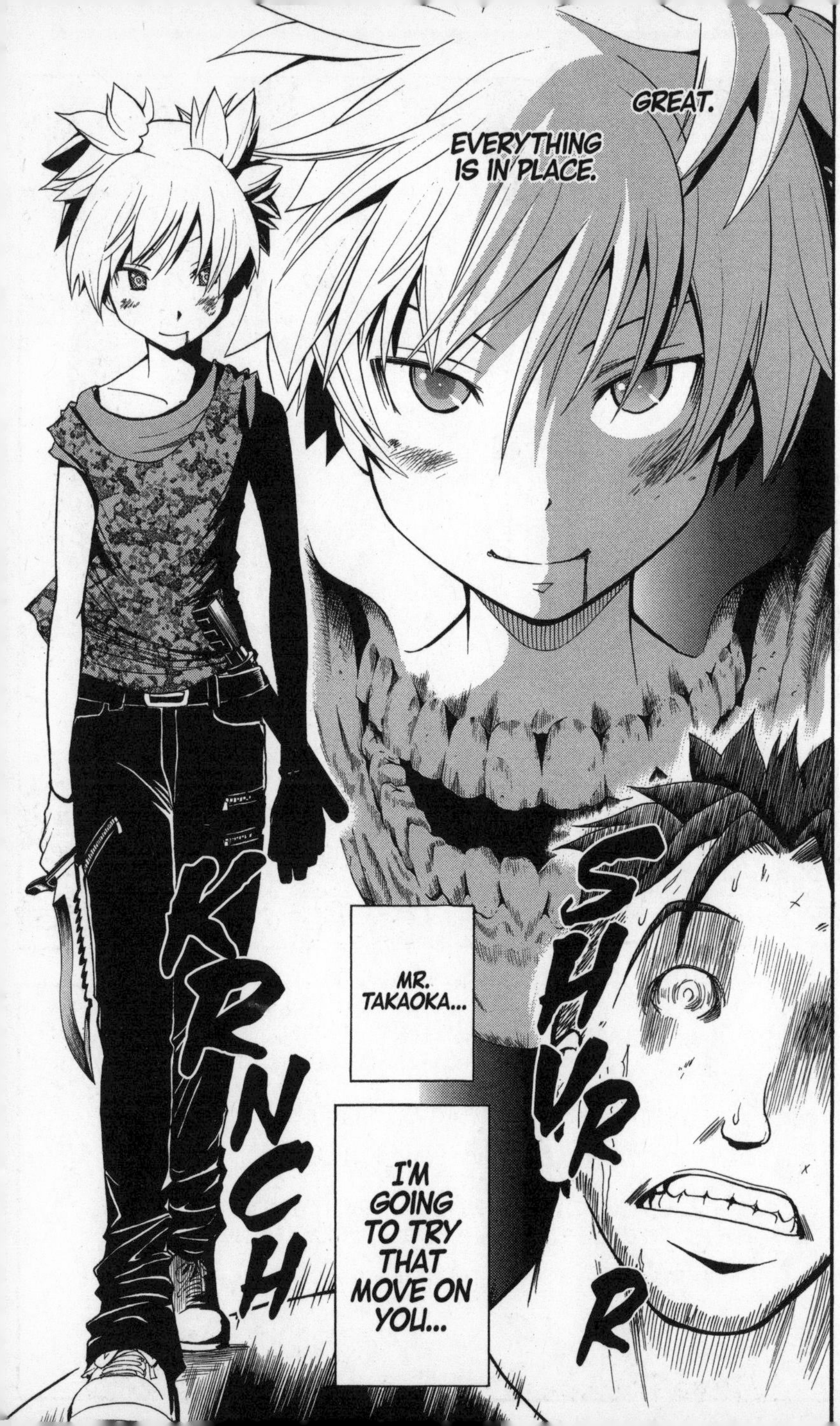
GREAT.
EVERYTHING IS IN PLACE.
SHVRR
SKRNCH
MR. TAKAOKA...
I'M GOING TO TRY THAT MOVE ON YOU...

LOVRO BROVSKI

- ☺ BIRTHDAY: APRIL 7 (59 YEARS OLD)

- ☺ HEIGHT: 5' 7"

- ☺ WEIGHT: 176 LBS.

- ☺ CAREER HISTORY: OFFICE WORKER → MERCENARY
  → PROFESSIONAL ASSASSIN
  → ASSASSIN TRAINING/
  ASSASSIN BROKERING

- ☺ HOBBY/SKILL: ASSASSINATION TECHNIQUES

- ☺ MOTTO: DEAD IS ALIVE

- ☺ CONFIRMED KILLS: 191 (COUNTLESS IF YOU
  INCLUDE THE TALLY HIS PUPILS HAVE RACKED UP)

- ☺ HOW HIS GRANDCHILDREN SEE HIM: KINDLY GRANDPA

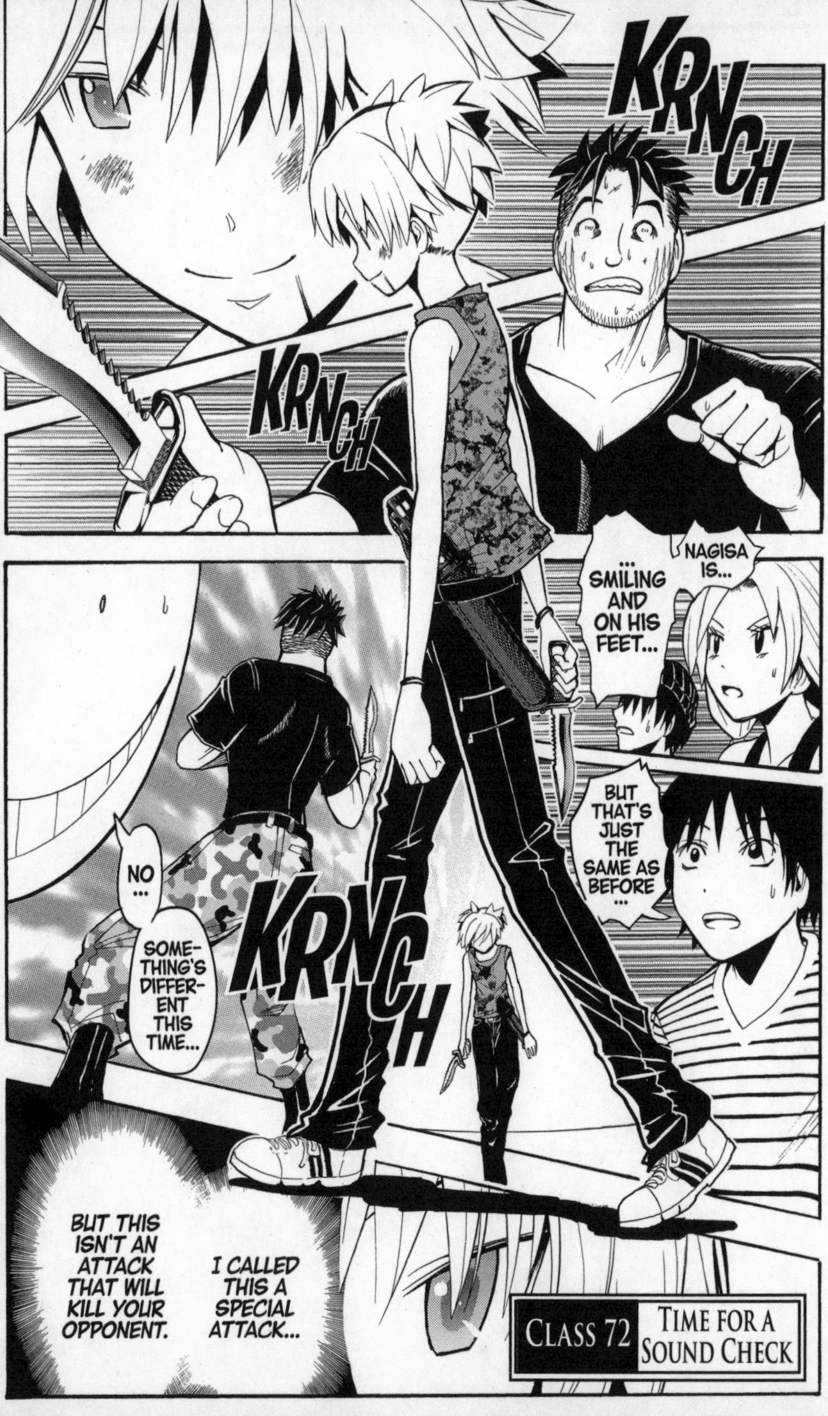
KRNCH
KRNCH
NAGISA IS...
...SMILING AND ON HIS FEET...
BUT THAT'S JUST THE SAME AS BEFORE...
NO...
SOMETHING'S DIFFERENT THIS TIME...
KRNCH
I CALLED THIS A SPECIAL ATTACK...
BUT THIS ISN'T AN ATTACK THAT WILL KILL YOUR OPPONENT.
CLASS 72
TIME FOR A SOUND CHECK

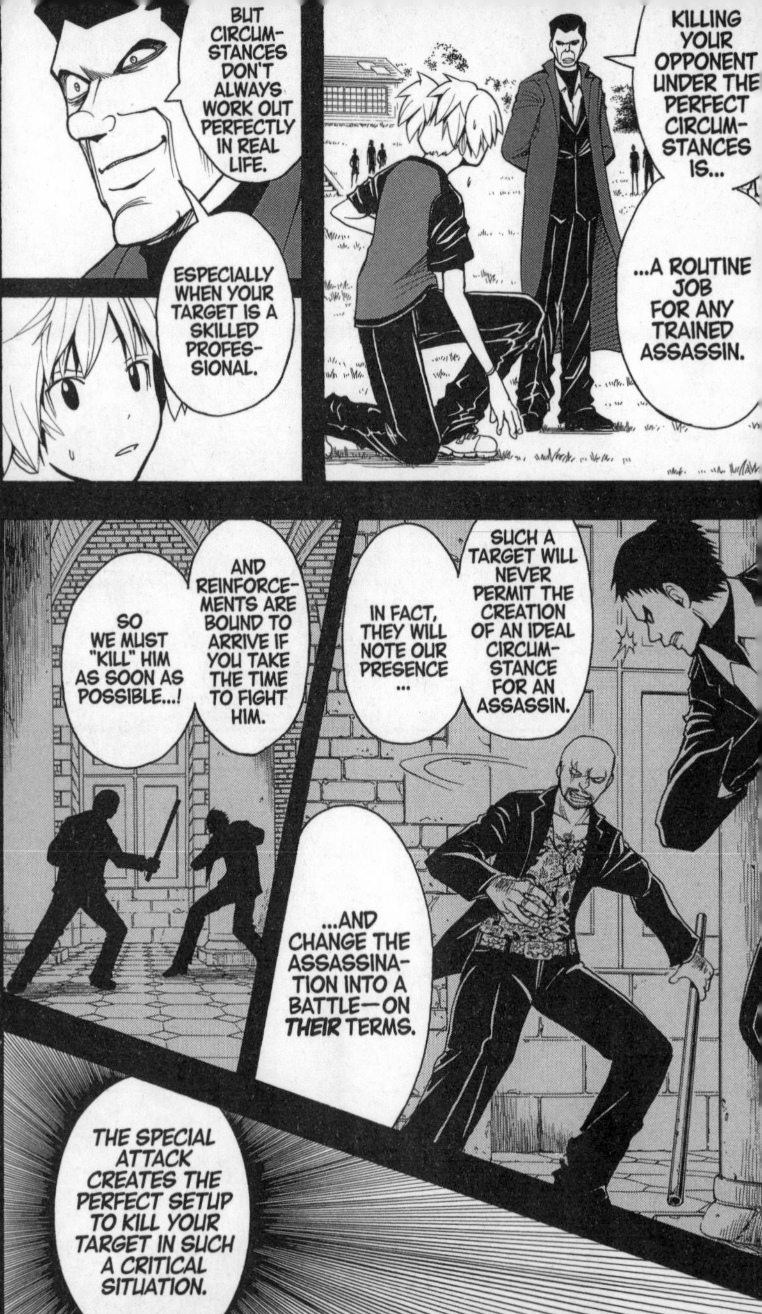
KILLING YOUR OPPONENT UNDER THE PERFECT CIRCUMSTANCES IS...
...A ROUTINE JOB FOR ANY TRAINED ASSASSIN.
BUT CIRCUMSTANCES DON'T ALWAYS WORK OUT PERFECTLY IN REAL LIFE.
ESPECIALLY WHEN YOUR TARGET IS A SKILLED PROFESSIONAL.
SUCH A TARGET WILL NEVER PERMIT THE CREATION OF AN IDEAL CIRCUMSTANCE FOR AN ASSASSIN.
IN FACT, THEY WILL NOTE OUR PRESENCE...
...AND CHANGE THE ASSASSINATION INTO A BATTLE—ON THEIR TERMS.
AND REINFORCEMENTS ARE BOUND TO ARRIVE IF YOU TAKE THE TIME TO FIGHT HIM.
SO WE MUST "KILL" HIM AS SOON AS POSSIBLE...!
THE SPECIAL ATTACK CREATES THE PERFECT SETUP TO KILL YOUR TARGET IN SUCH A CRITICAL SITUATION.

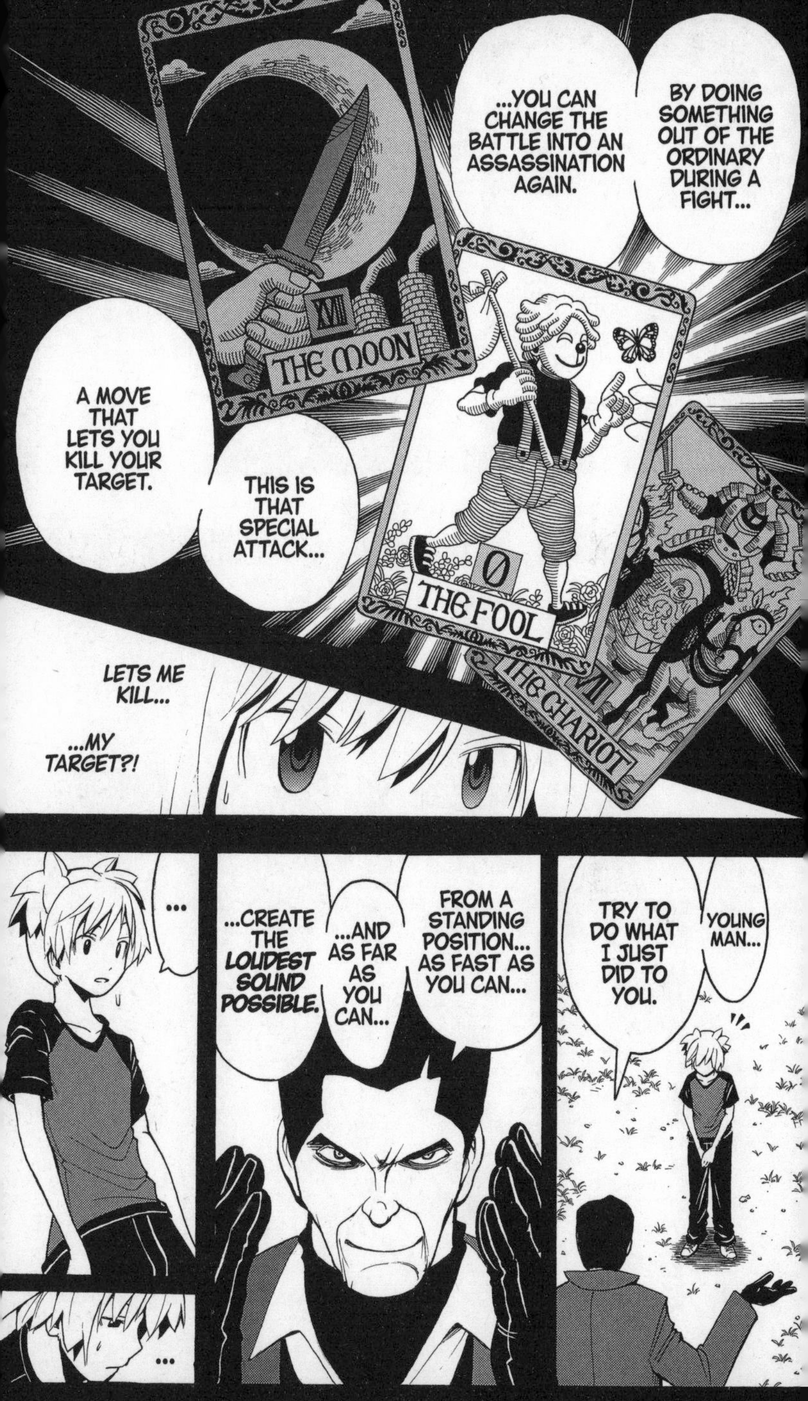
BY DOING SOMETHING OUT OF THE ORDINARY DURING A FIGHT...
...YOU CAN CHANGE THE BATTLE INTO AN ASSASSINATION AGAIN.
XVIII
THE MOON
0
THE FOOL
VII
THE CHARIOT
THIS IS THAT SPECIAL ATTACK...
A MOVE THAT LETS YOU KILL YOUR TARGET.
LETS ME KILL...
...MY TARGET?!
YOUNG MAN...
TRY TO DO WHAT I JUST DID TO YOU.
FROM A STANDING POSITION... AS FAST AS YOU CAN...
...AND AS FAR AS YOU CAN...
...CREATE THE LOUDEST SOUND POSSIBLE.
...
...

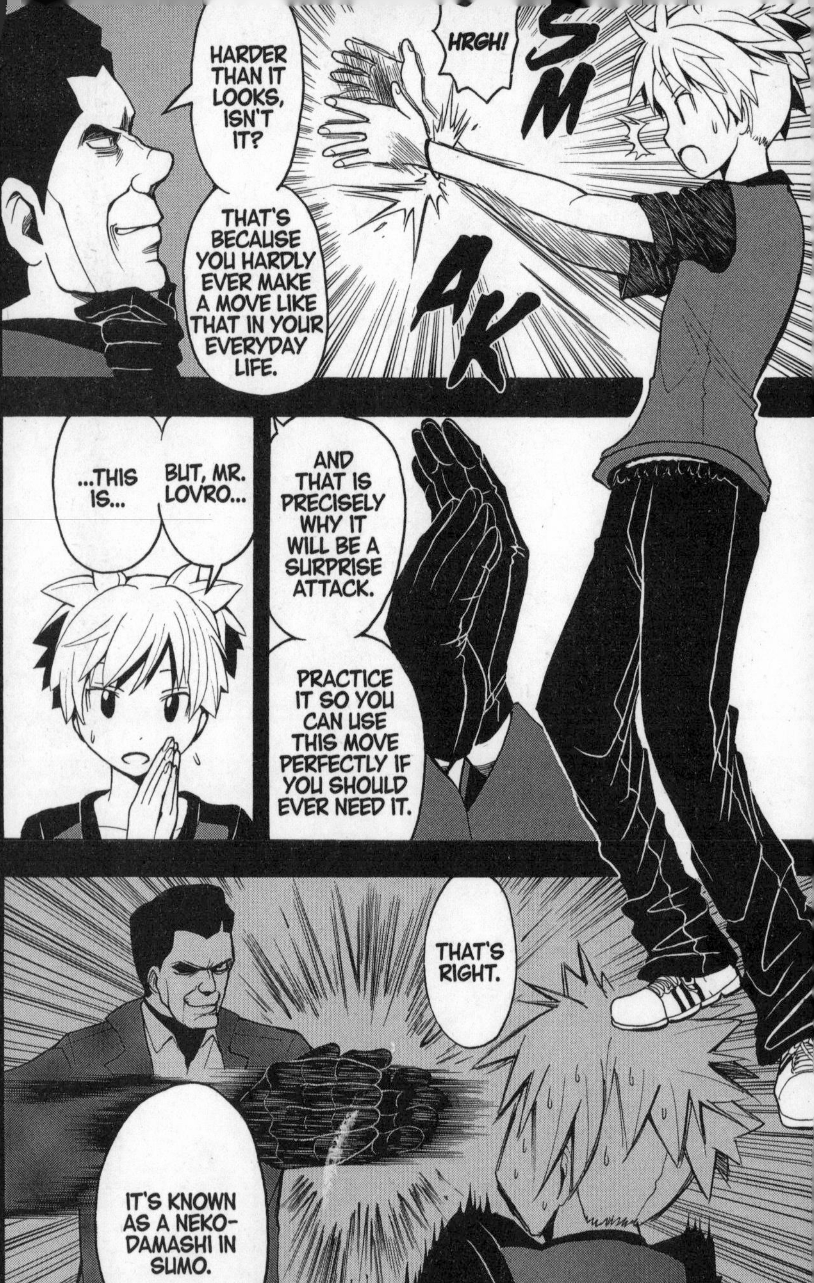
HRGH!
SMAK
HARDER THAN IT LOOKS, ISN'T IT?
THAT'S BECAUSE YOU HARDLY EVER MAKE A MOVE LIKE THAT IN YOUR EVERYDAY LIFE.
AND THAT IS PRECISELY WHY IT WILL BE A SURPRISE ATTACK.
PRACTICE IT SO YOU CAN USE THIS MOVE PERFECTLY IF YOU SHOULD EVER NEED IT.
BUT, MR. LOVRO...
...THIS IS...
THAT'S RIGHT.
IT'S KNOWN AS A NEKO-DAMASHI IN SUMO.

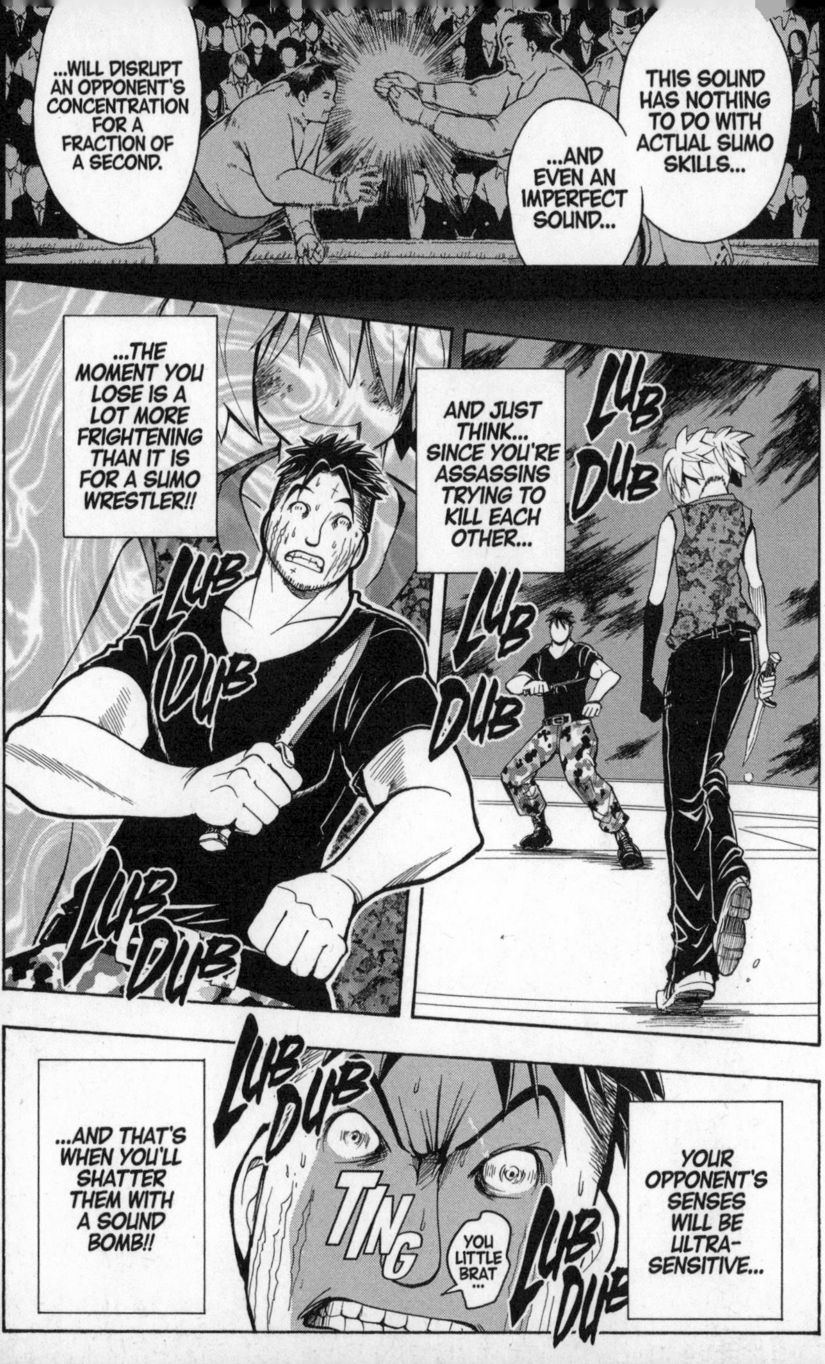
THIS SOUND HAS NOTHING TO DO WITH ACTUAL SUMO SKILLS...
...AND EVEN AN IMPERFECT SOUND...
...WILL DISRUPT AN OPPONENT'S CONCENTRATION FOR A FRACTION OF A SECOND.
LUB DUB
AND JUST THINK... SINCE YOU'RE ASSASSINS TRYING TO KILL EACH OTHER...
LUB DUB
...THE MOMENT YOU LOSE IS A LOT MORE FRIGHTENING THAN IT IS FOR A SUMO WRESTLER!!
LUB DUB
LUB DUB
YOUR OPPONENT'S SENSES WILL BE ULTRA-SENSITIVE...
LUB DUB
YOU LITTLE BRAT...
TING
LUB DUB
...AND THAT'S WHEN YOU'LL SHATTER THEM WITH A SOUND BOMB!!

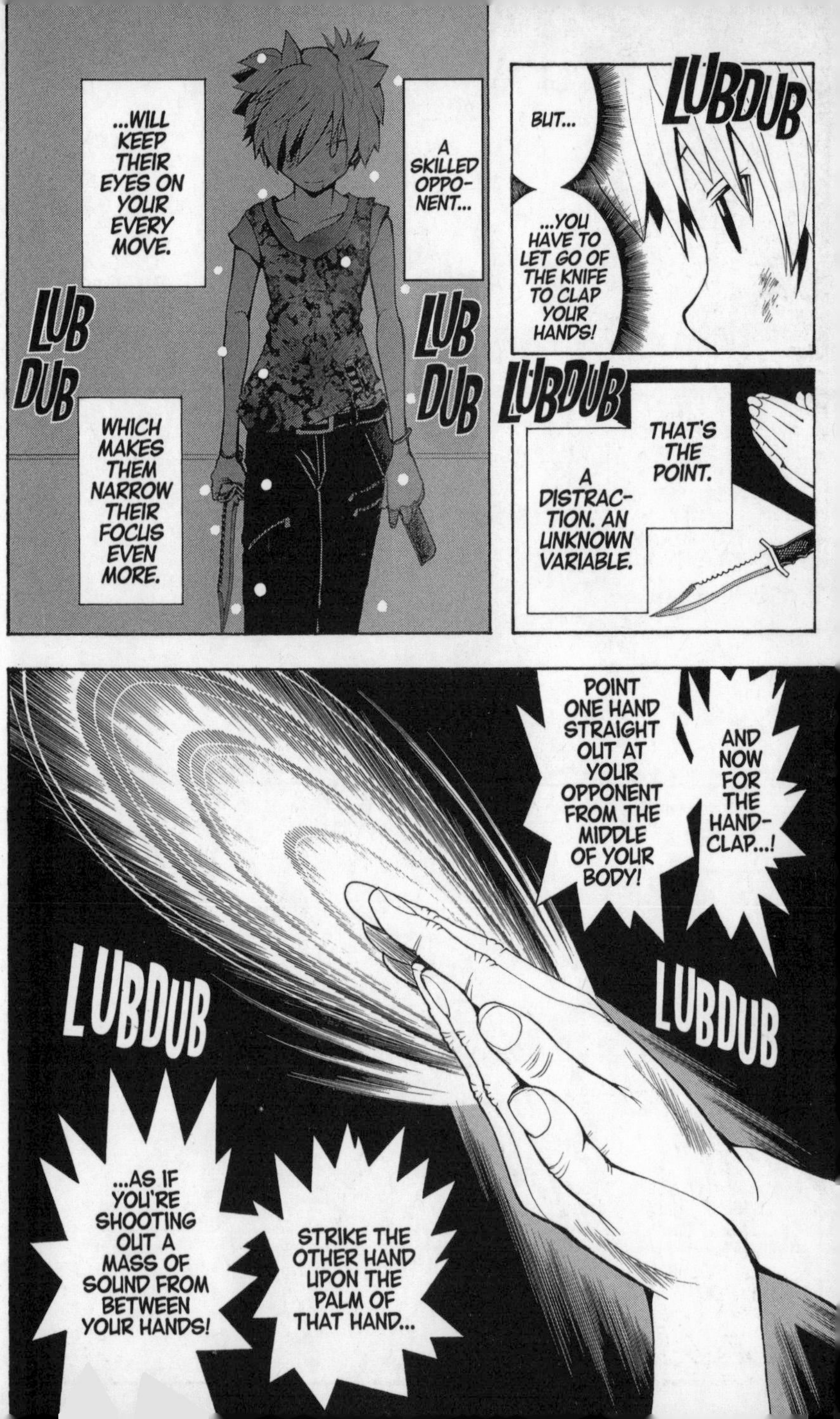
LUBDUB
BUT...
...YOU HAVE TO LET GO OF THE KNIFE TO CLAP YOUR HANDS!
LUBDUB
THAT'S THE POINT.
A DISTRACTION. AN UNKNOWN VARIABLE.
A SKILLED OPPONENT...
...WILL KEEP THEIR EYES ON YOUR EVERY MOVE.
LUB DUB
LUB DUB
WHICH MAKES THEM NARROW THEIR FOCUS EVEN MORE.
AND NOW FOR THE HAND-CLAP...!
POINT ONE HAND STRAIGHT OUT AT YOUR OPPONENT FROM THE MIDDLE OF YOUR BODY!
LUBDUB
LUBDUB
STRIKE THE OTHER HAND UPON THE PALM OF THAT HAND...
...AS IF YOU'RE SHOOTING OUT A MASS OF SOUND FROM BETWEEN YOUR HANDS!

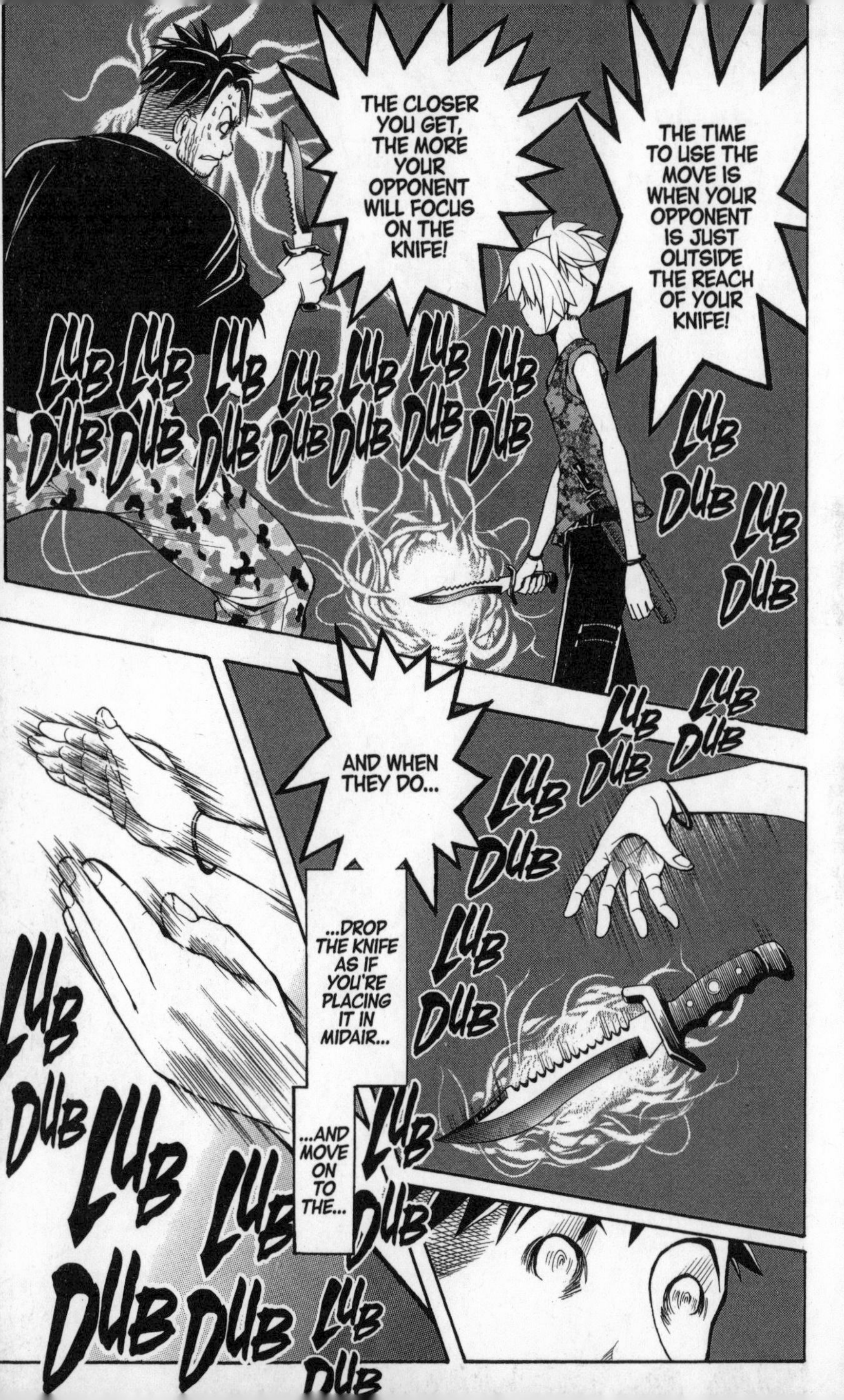
THE TIME TO USE THE MOVE IS WHEN YOUR OPPONENT IS JUST OUTSIDE THE REACH OF YOUR KNIFE!
THE CLOSER YOU GET, THE MORE YOUR OPPONENT WILL FOCUS ON THE KNIFE!
LUB DUB LUB DUB
LUB DUB LUB DUB LUB DUB LUB DUB LUB DUB LUB DUB LUB DUB
LUB DUB LUB DUB
AND WHEN THEY DO...
LUB DUB LUB DUB
...DROP THE KNIFE AS IF YOU'RE PLACING IT IN MIDAIR...
...AND MOVE ON TO THE...
LUB DUB LUB DUB
LUB DUB LUB DUB LUB DUB

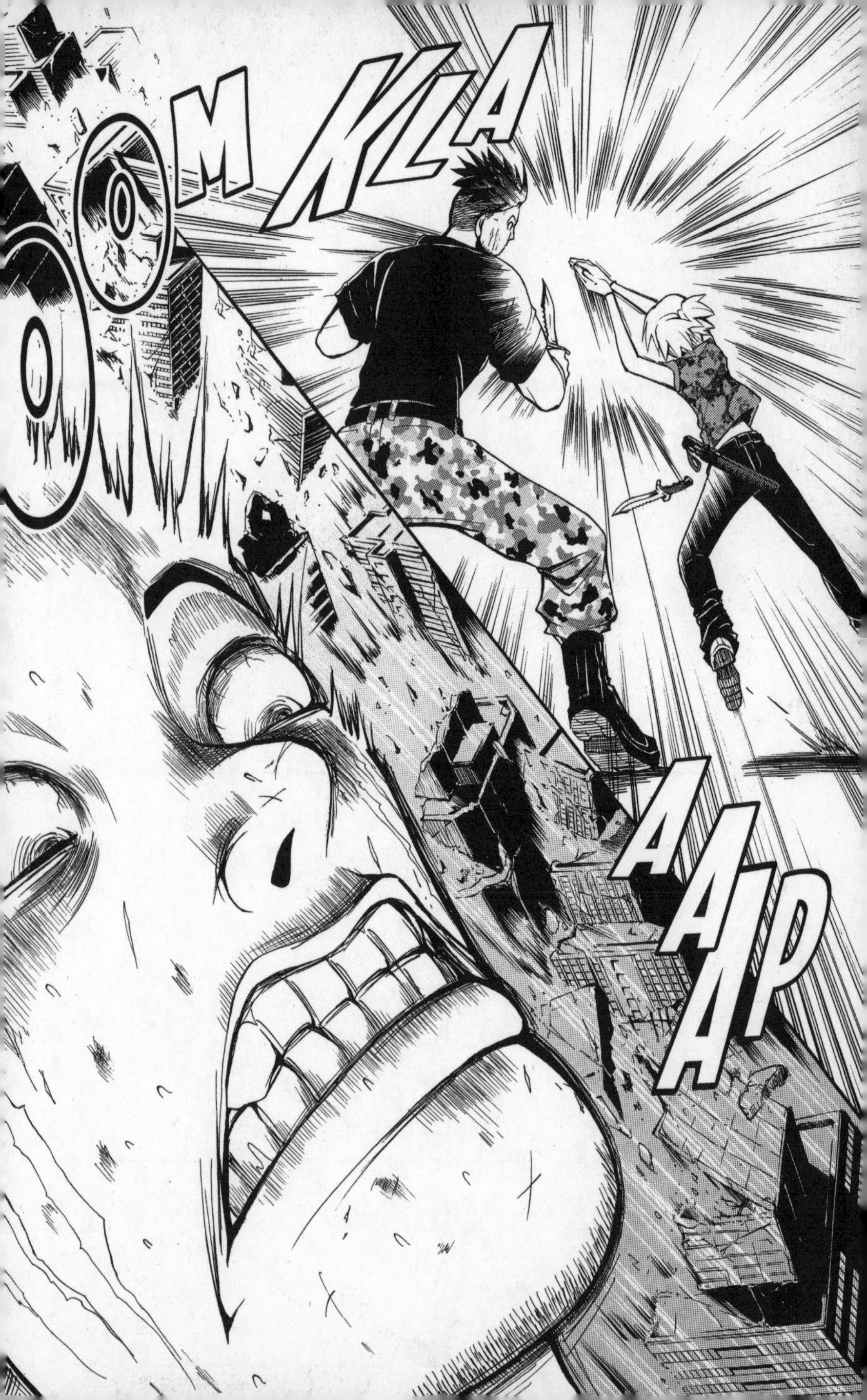
OOOM
KLA
AAAP

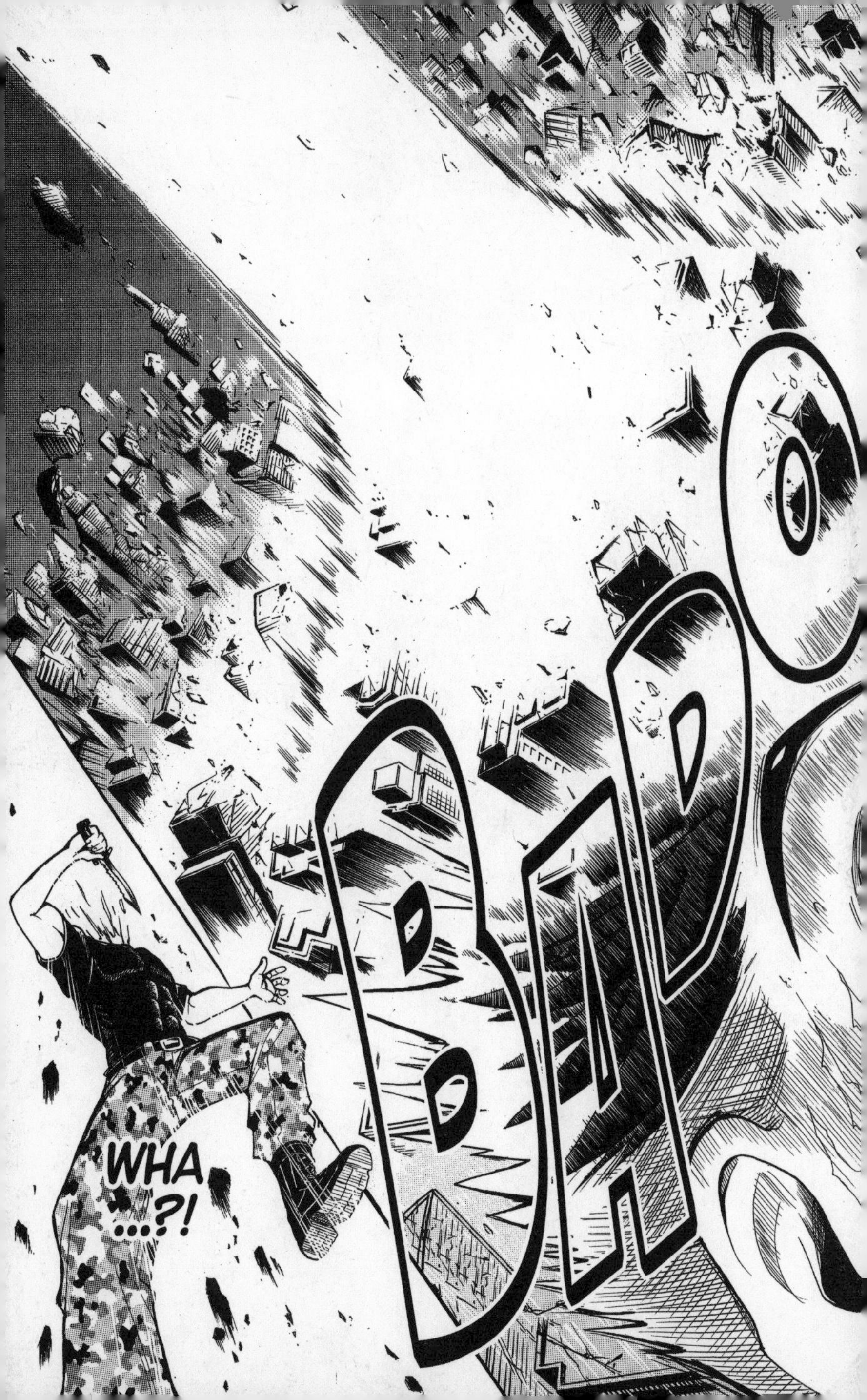
WHA ...?!

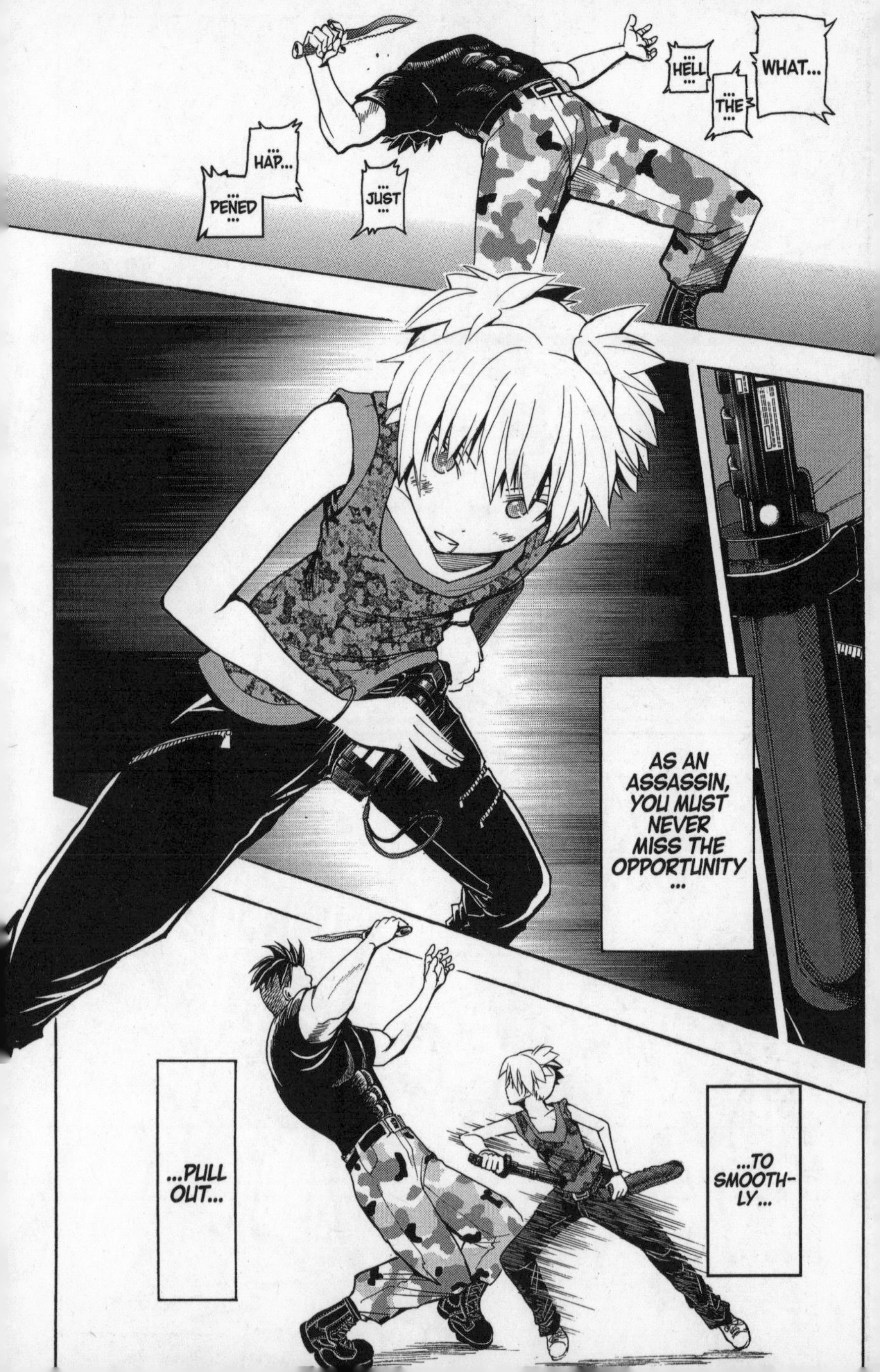
WHAT...
...THE...
...HELL...
...JUST...
HAP... ...PENED...
AS AN ASSASSIN, YOU MUST NEVER MISS THE OPPORTUNITY...
...TO SMOOTH-LY...
...PULL OUT...

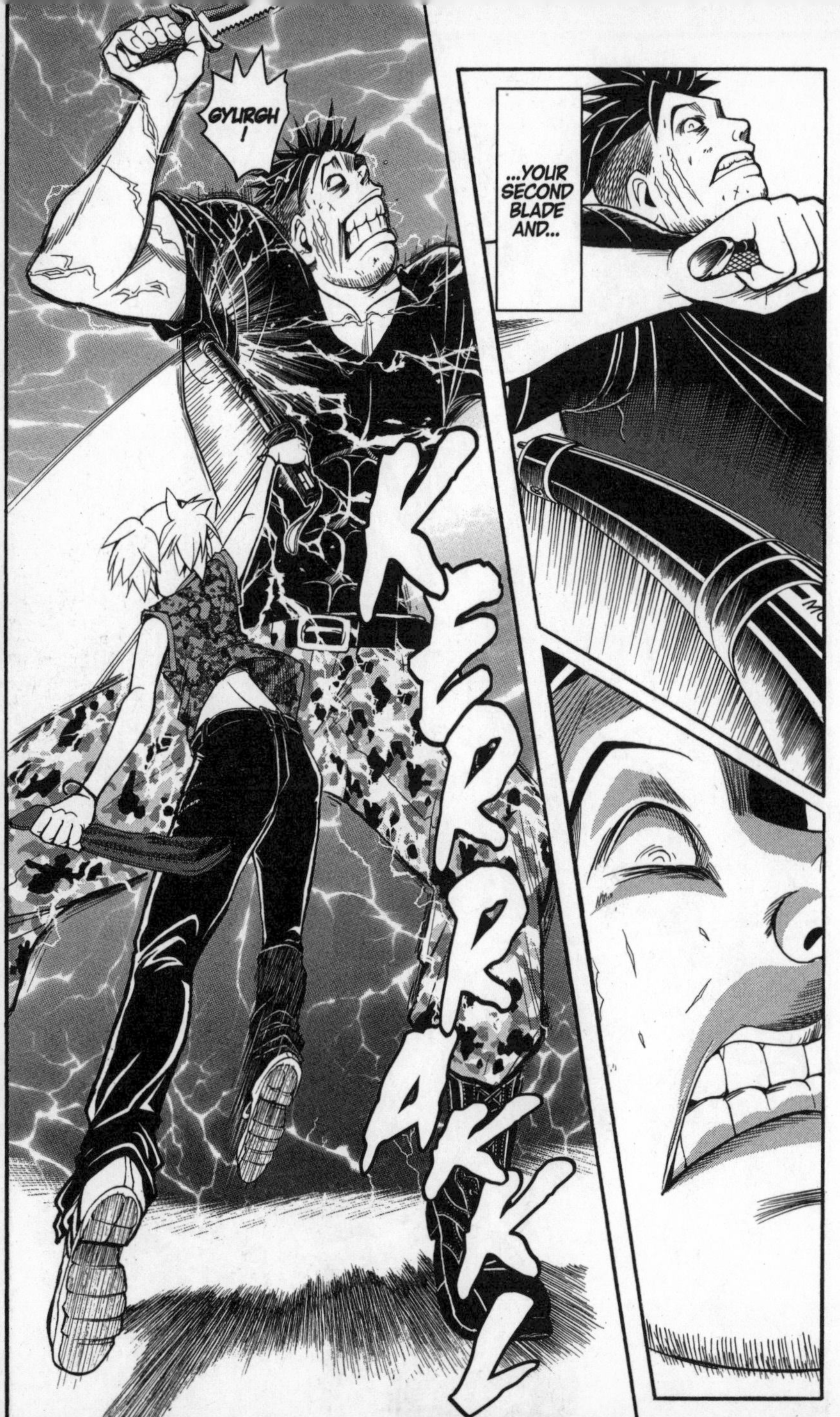
...YOUR SECOND BLADE AND...
GYURGH!
KERRAKK

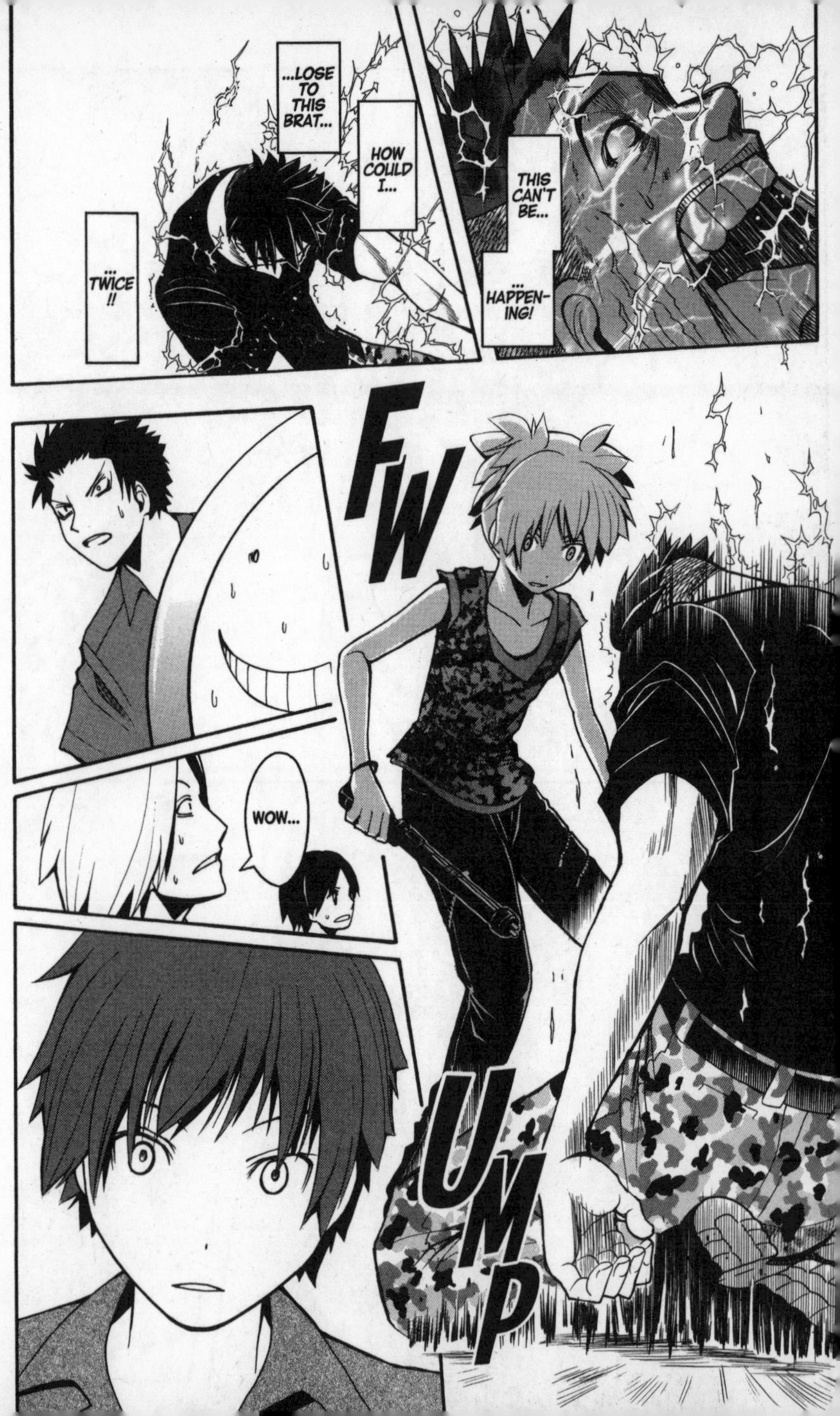
THIS CAN'T BE...
...HAPPENING!
HOW COULD I...
...LOSE TO THIS BRAT...
...TWICE!!
FWUMP
WOW...

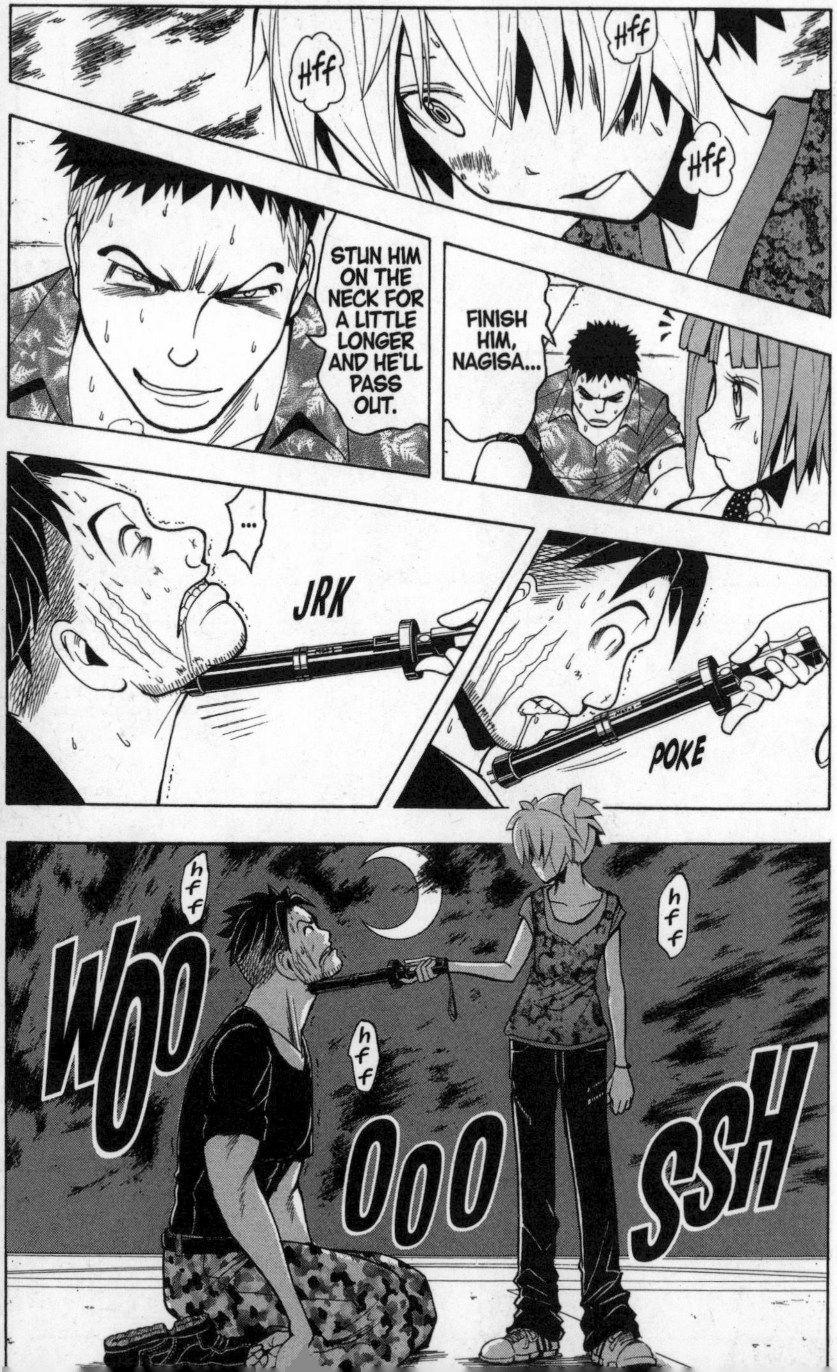
Hff
Hff
Hff
FINISH HIM, NAGISA...
STUN HIM ON THE NECK FOR A LITTLE LONGER AND HE'LL PASS OUT.
POKE
...
JRK
hff
hff
hff
WOO
OOO
SSH

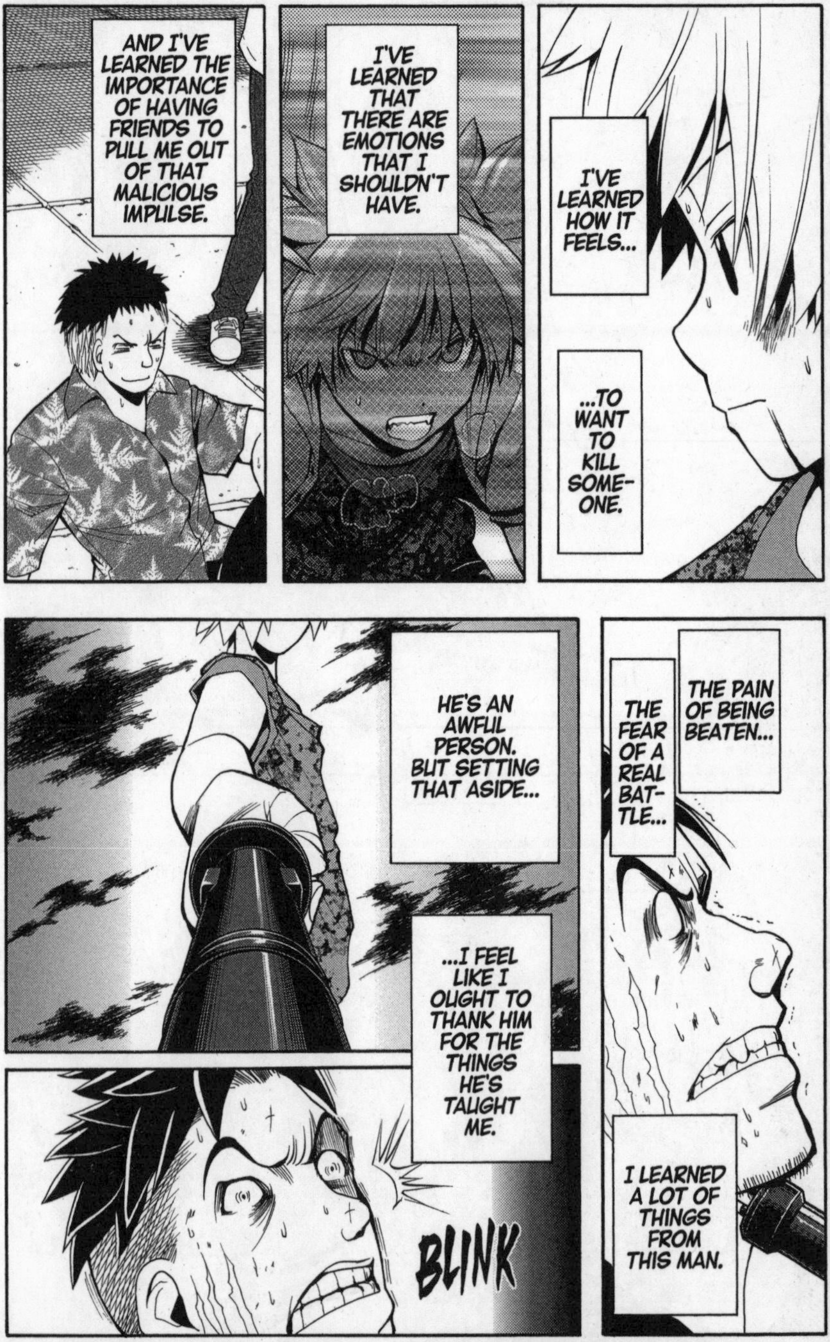
I'VE LEARNED HOW IT FEELS...
...TO WANT TO KILL SOMEONE.
I'VE LEARNED THAT THERE ARE EMOTIONS THAT I SHOULDN'T HAVE.
AND I'VE LEARNED THE IMPORTANCE OF HAVING FRIENDS TO PULL ME OUT OF THAT MALICIOUS IMPULSE.
THE PAIN OF BEING BEATEN...
THE FEAR OF A REAL BATTLE...
I LEARNED A LOT OF THINGS FROM THIS MAN.
HE'S AN AWFUL PERSON. BUT SETTING THAT ASIDE...
...I FEEL LIKE I OUGHT TO THANK HIM FOR THE THINGS HE'S TAUGHT ME.
BLINK

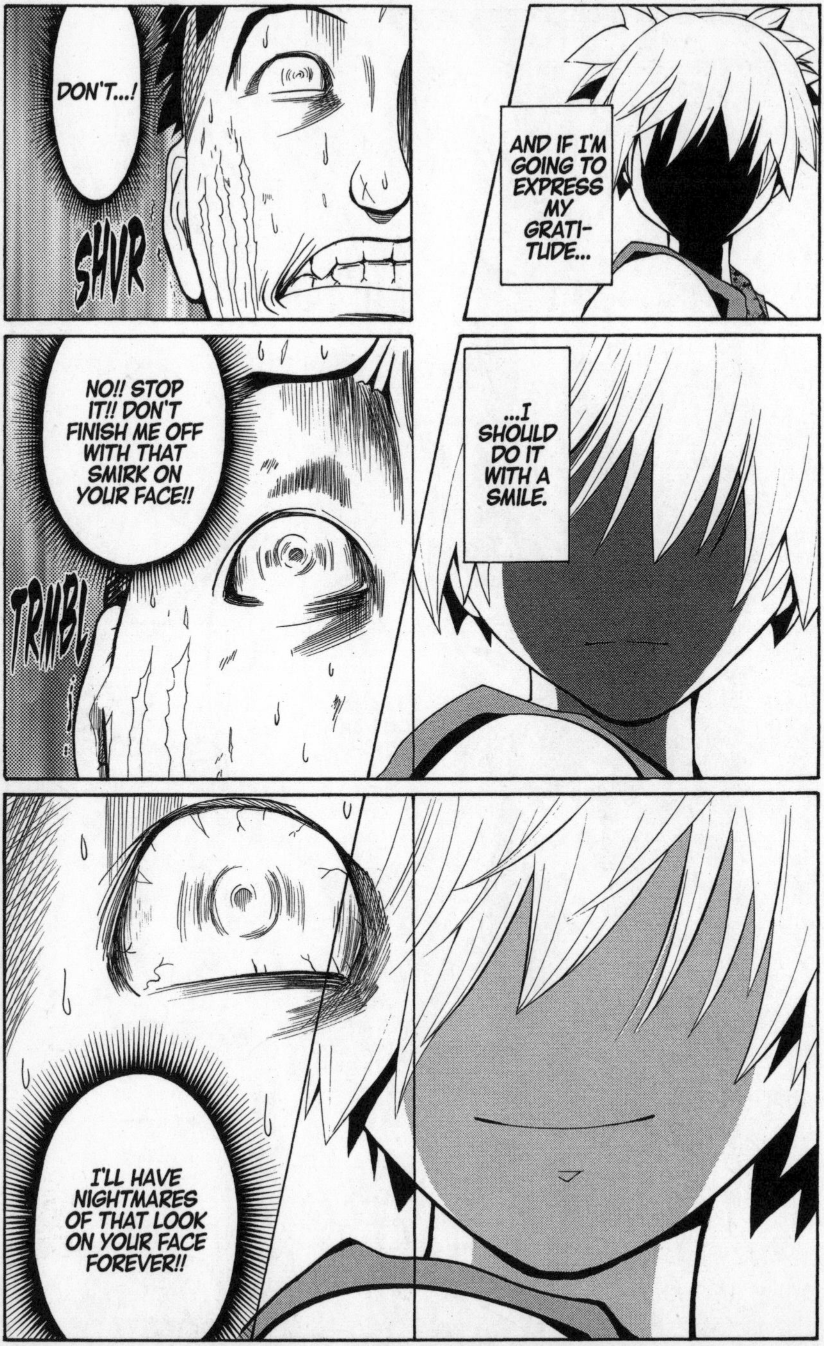
AND IF I'M GOING TO EXPRESS MY GRATITUDE...
DON'T...!
SHVR
...I SHOULD DO IT WITH A SMILE.
NO!! STOP IT!! DON'T FINISH ME OFF WITH THAT SMIRK ON YOUR FACE!!
TRMBL
I'LL HAVE NIGHTMARES OF THAT LOOK ON YOUR FACE FOREVER!!

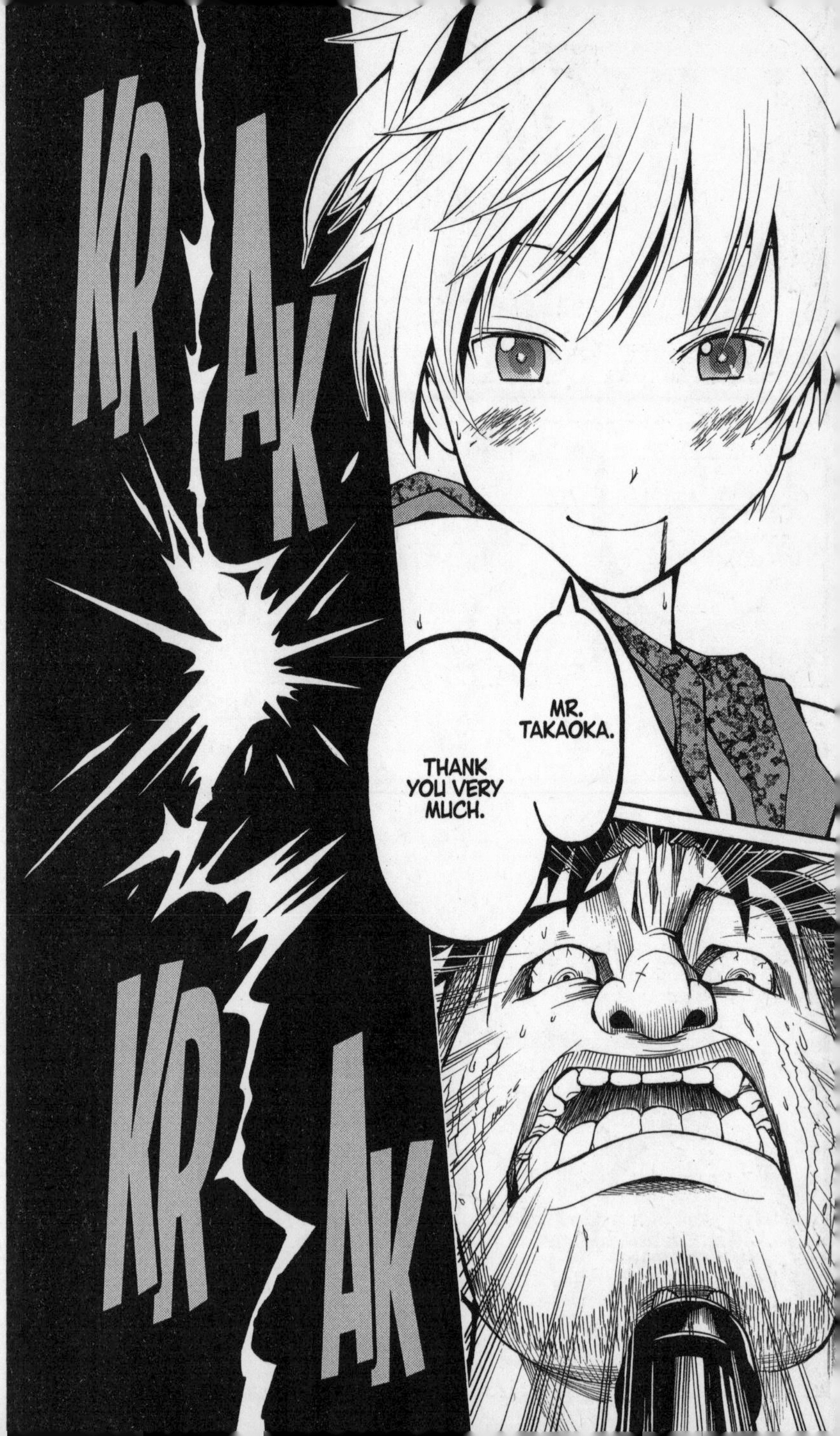
KRAK
MR. TAKAOKA.
THANK YOU VERY MUCH.
KRAK

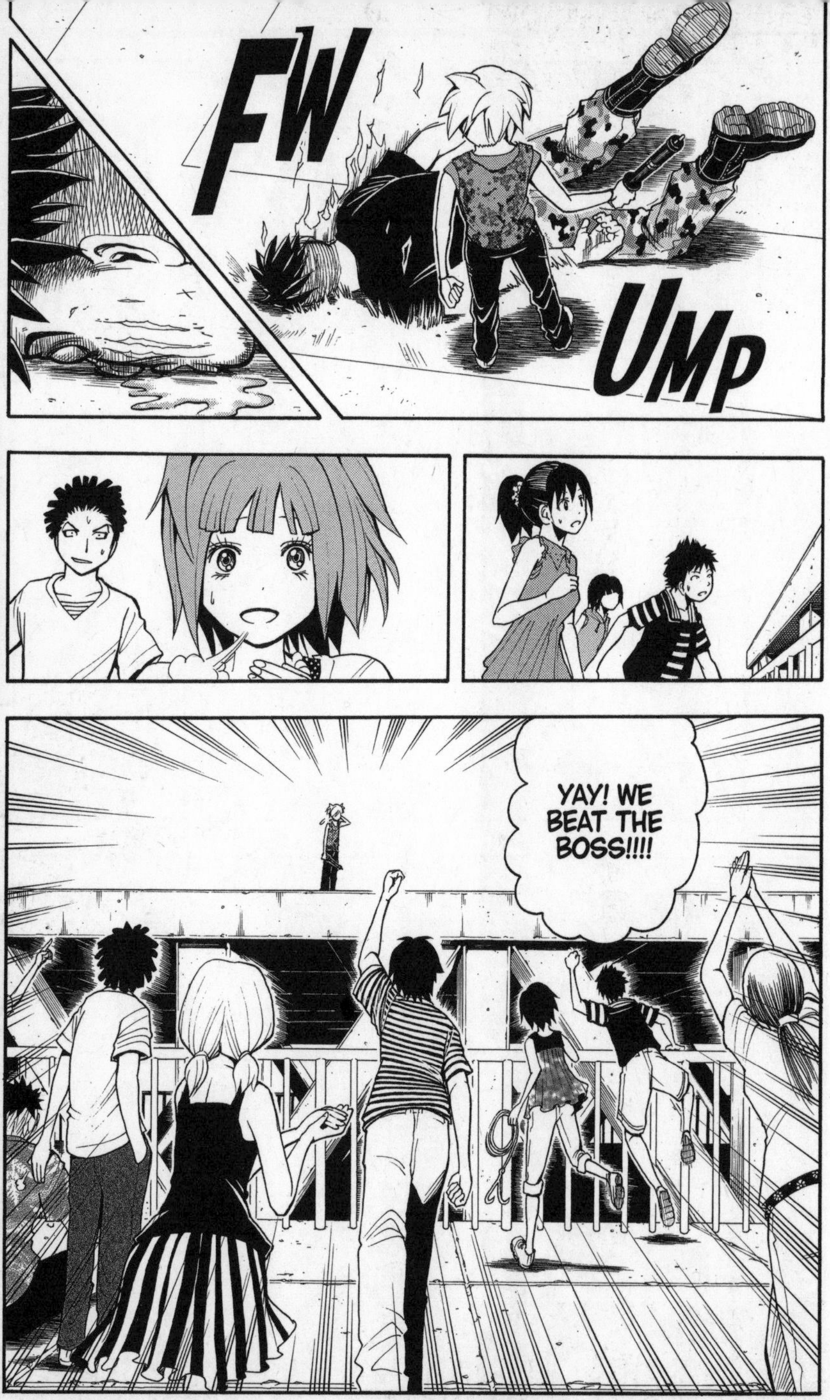
FWUMP
YAY! WE BEAT THE BOSS!!!!

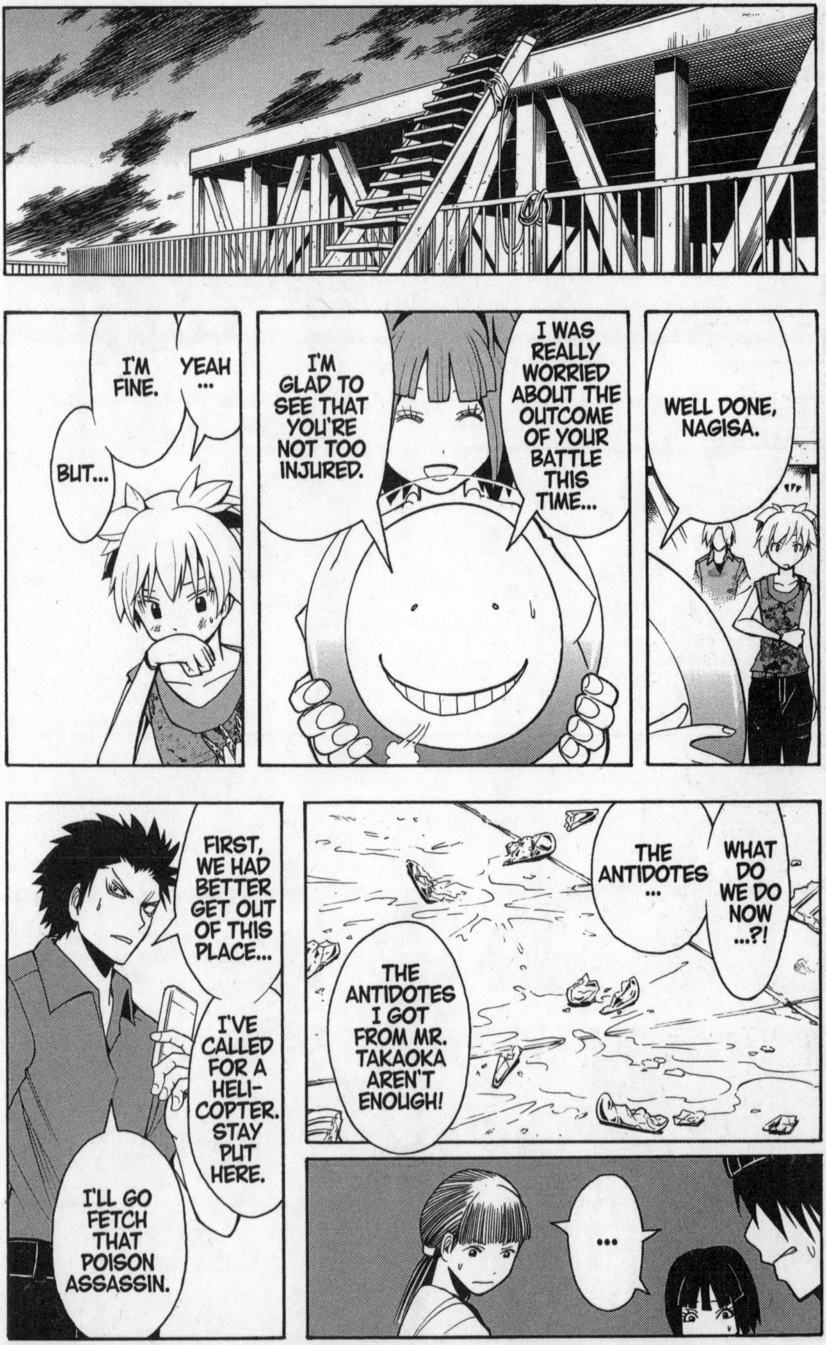

WELL DONE, NAGISA.
I WAS REALLY WORRIED ABOUT THE OUTCOME OF YOUR BATTLE THIS TIME...
I'M GLAD TO SEE THAT YOU'RE NOT TOO INJURED.
YEAH ...
I'M FINE.
BUT...
WHAT DO WE DO NOW ...?!
THE ANTIDOTES ...
THE ANTIDOTES I GOT FROM MR. TAKAOKA AREN'T ENOUGH!
...
FIRST, WE HAD BETTER GET OUT OF THIS PLACE...
I'VE CALLED FOR A HELI-COPTER. STAY PUT HERE.
I'LL GO FETCH THAT POISON ASSASSIN.

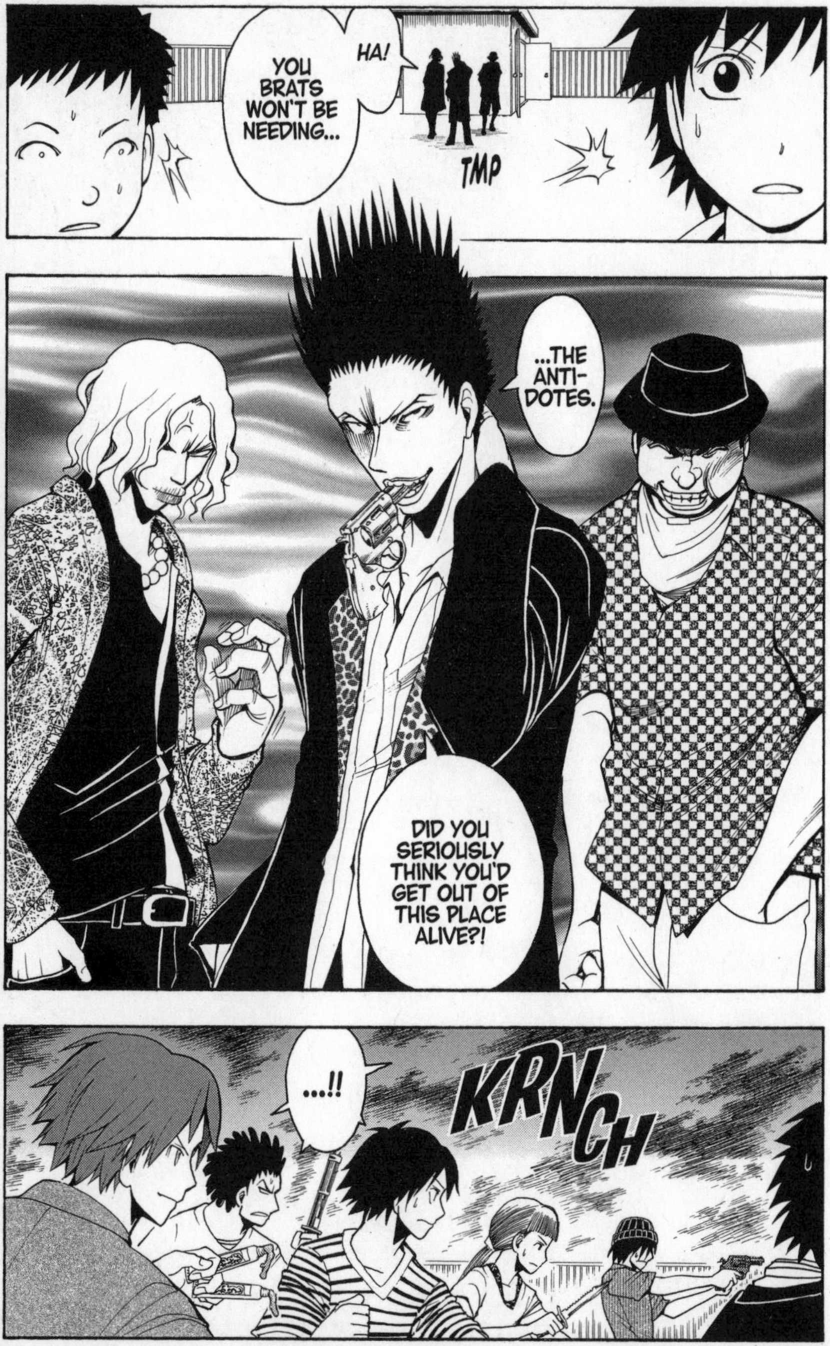
HA!
YOU BRATS WON'T BE NEEDING...
TMP
...THE ANTI-DOTES.
DID YOU SERIOUSLY THINK YOU'D GET OUT OF THIS PLACE ALIVE?!
KRNCH
...!!

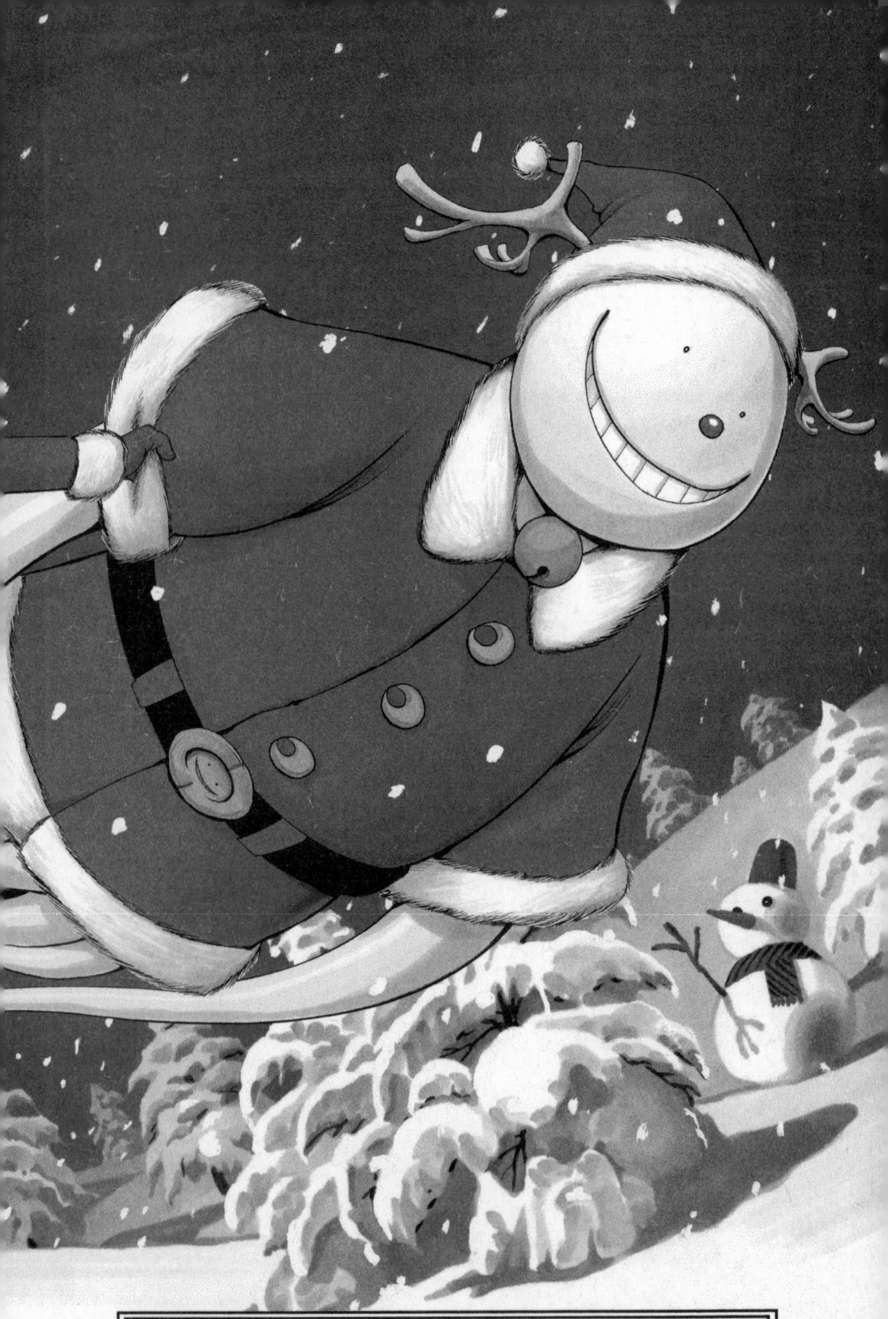

CLASS 73 TIME FOR GROWN-UPS—2ND PERIOD

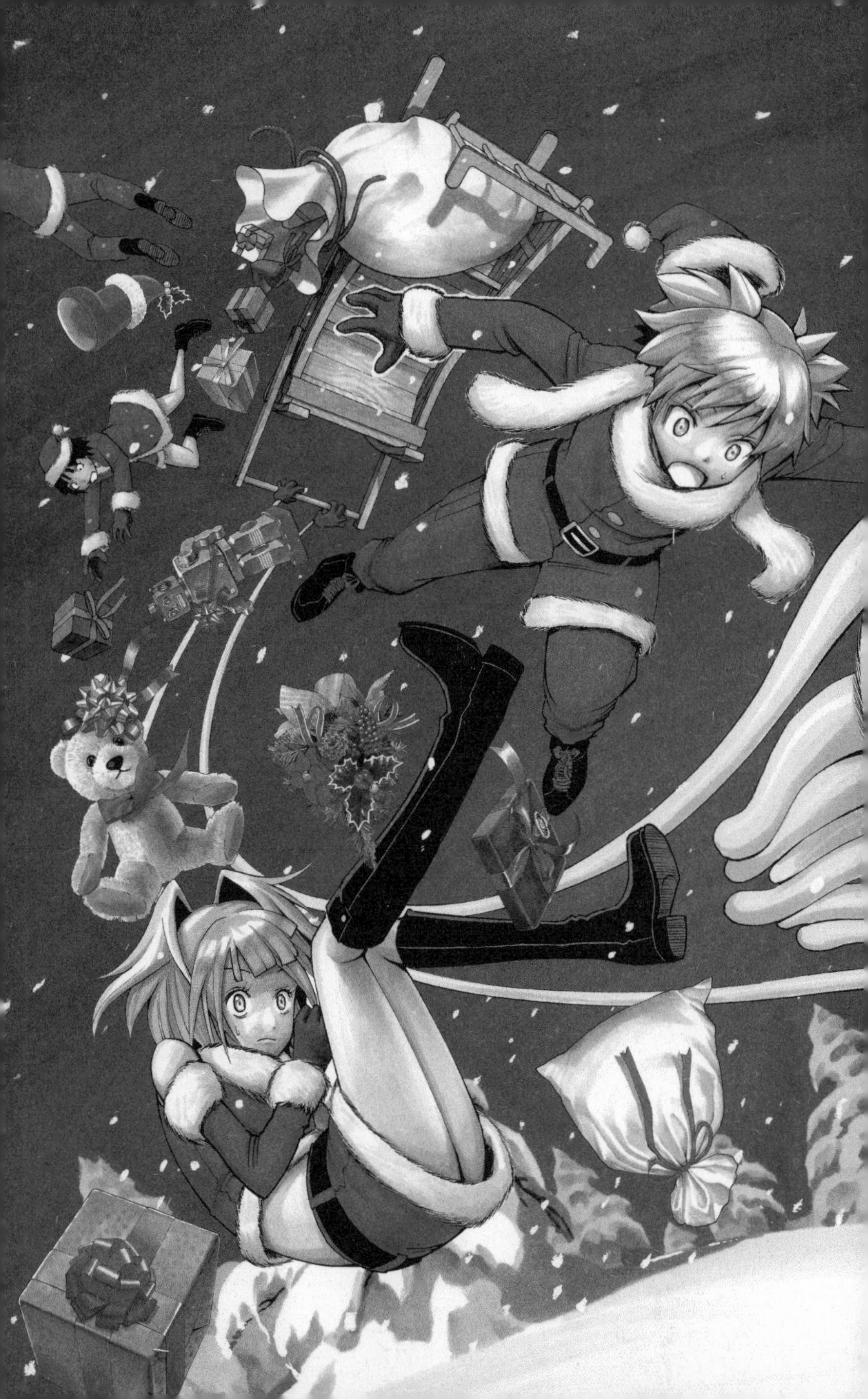

Christmas Eve Challenge

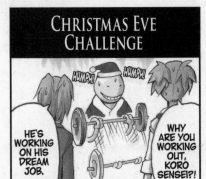

WHY ARE YOU WORKING OUT, KORO SENSEI?!
HUMPH!
HUMPH!
HE'S WORKING ON HIS DREAM JOB.
THE "ACTUALLY-DELIVERING-A-PRESENT-TO-EVERY-CHILD-IN-THE-WORLD-IN-ONE-NIGHT" CHALLENGE?
NUURGH
HE WON'T LISTEN TO ME. HE SAYS HE'S FAST ENOUGH TO PULL IT OFF!!
BUT HOW ARE YOU GOING TO BUY ALL THOSE PRESENTS?!
PLOP

Koro Sensei's Weakness 24
Quickly gives up on his dreams.

SHONEN JUMP 2014 ISSUE 4/5 JOINT ISSUE

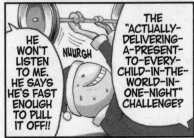

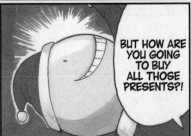

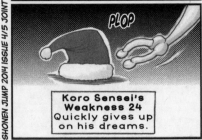

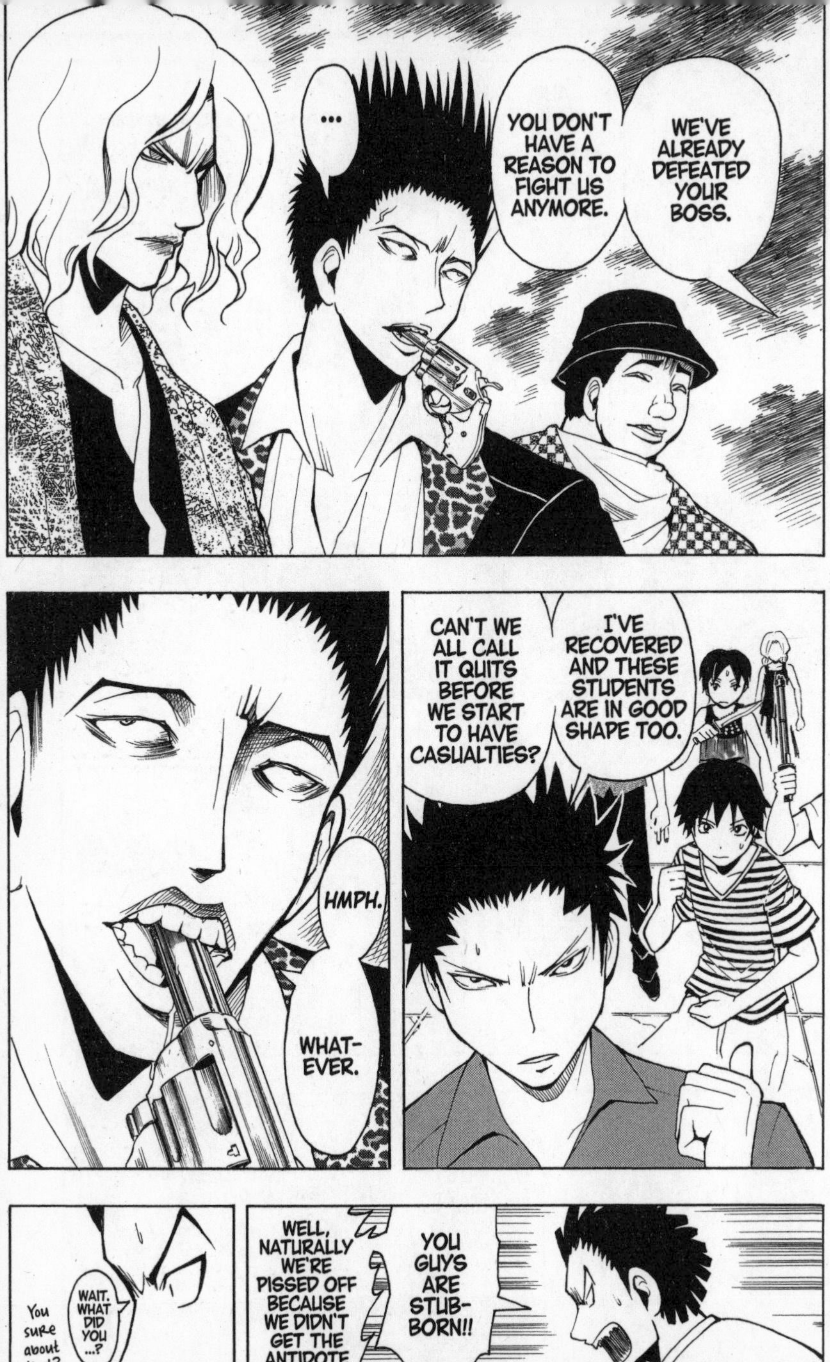
WE'VE ALREADY DEFEATED YOUR BOSS.
YOU DON'T HAVE A REASON TO FIGHT US ANYMORE.
...
I'VE RECOVERED AND THESE STUDENTS ARE IN GOOD SHAPE TOO.
CAN'T WE ALL CALL IT QUITS BEFORE WE START TO HAVE CASUALTIES?
HMPH.
WHAT-EVER.
YOU GUYS ARE STUB-BORN!!
WELL, NATURALLY WE'RE PISSED OFF BECAUSE WE DIDN'T GET THE ANTIDOTE AND...
WAIT. WHAT DID YOU ...?
You sure about that?

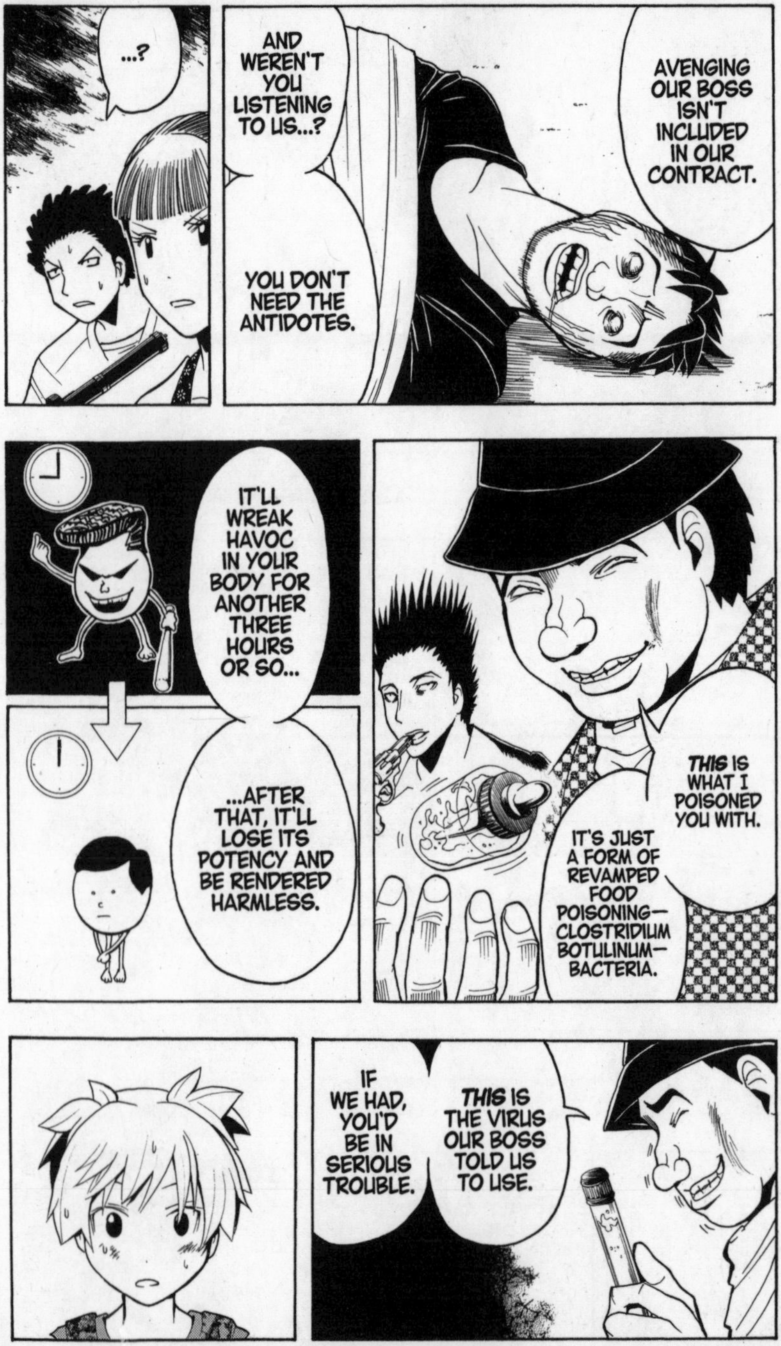
AVENGING OUR BOSS ISN'T INCLUDED IN OUR CONTRACT.
AND WEREN'T YOU LISTENING TO US...?
YOU DON'T NEED THE ANTIDOTES.
...?
THIS IS WHAT I POISONED YOU WITH.
IT'S JUST A FORM OF REVAMPED FOOD POISONING—CLOSTRIDIUM BOTULINUM—BACTERIA.
IT'LL WREAK HAVOC IN YOUR BODY FOR ANOTHER THREE HOURS OR SO...
...AFTER THAT, IT'LL LOSE ITS POTENCY AND BE RENDERED HARMLESS.
THIS IS THE VIRUS OUR BOSS TOLD US TO USE.
IF WE HAD, YOU'D BE IN SERIOUS TROUBLE.

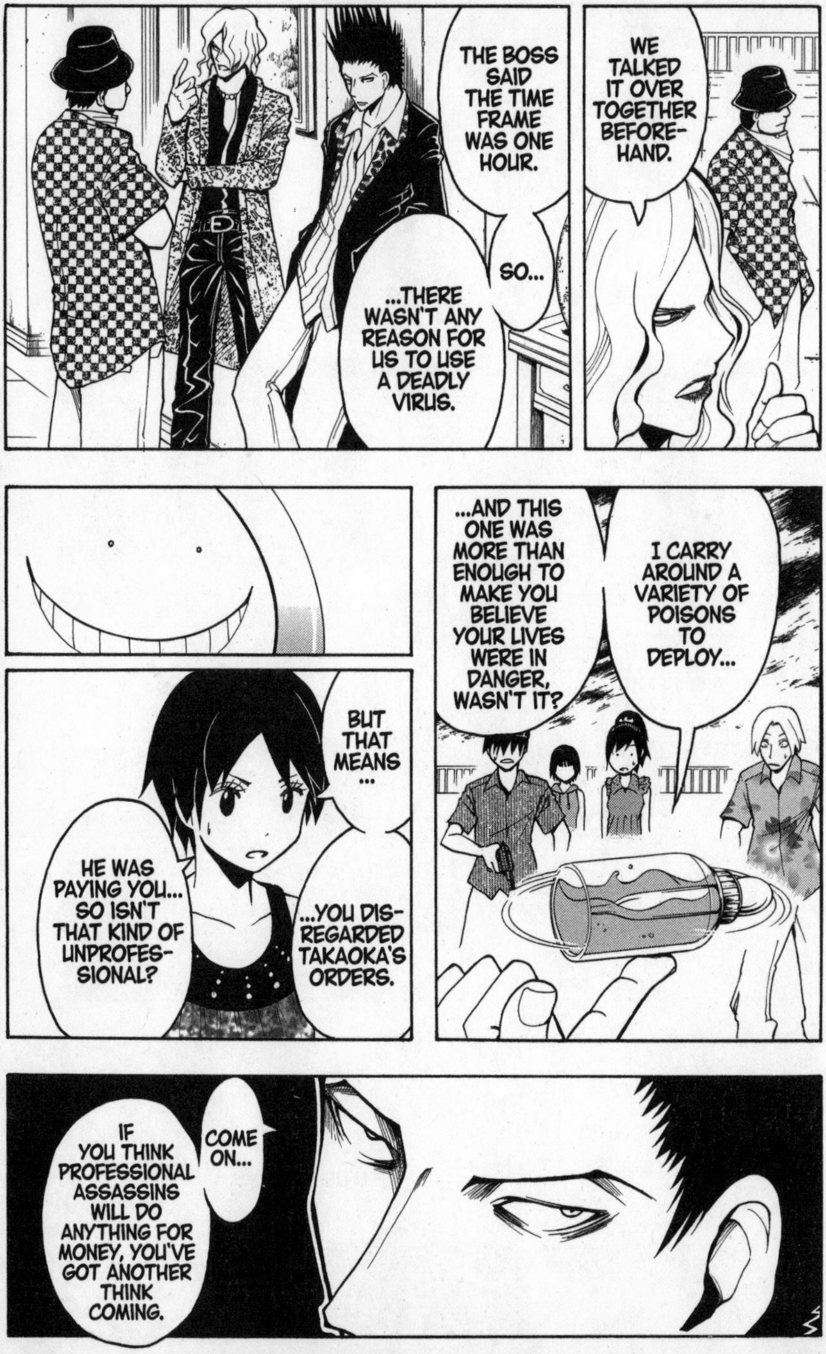
WE TALKED IT OVER TOGETHER BEFOREHAND.
THE BOSS SAID THE TIME FRAME WAS ONE HOUR.
SO...
...THERE WASN'T ANY REASON FOR US TO USE A DEADLY VIRUS.
I CARRY AROUND A VARIETY OF POISONS TO DEPLOY...
...AND THIS ONE WAS MORE THAN ENOUGH TO MAKE YOU BELIEVE YOUR LIVES WERE IN DANGER, WASN'T IT?
BUT THAT MEANS...
...YOU DISREGARDED TAKAOKA'S ORDERS.
HE WAS PAYING YOU... SO ISN'T THAT KIND OF UNPROFESSIONAL?
COME ON...
IF YOU THINK PROFESSIONAL ASSASSINS WILL DO ANYTHING FOR MONEY, YOU'VE GOT ANOTHER THINK COMING.

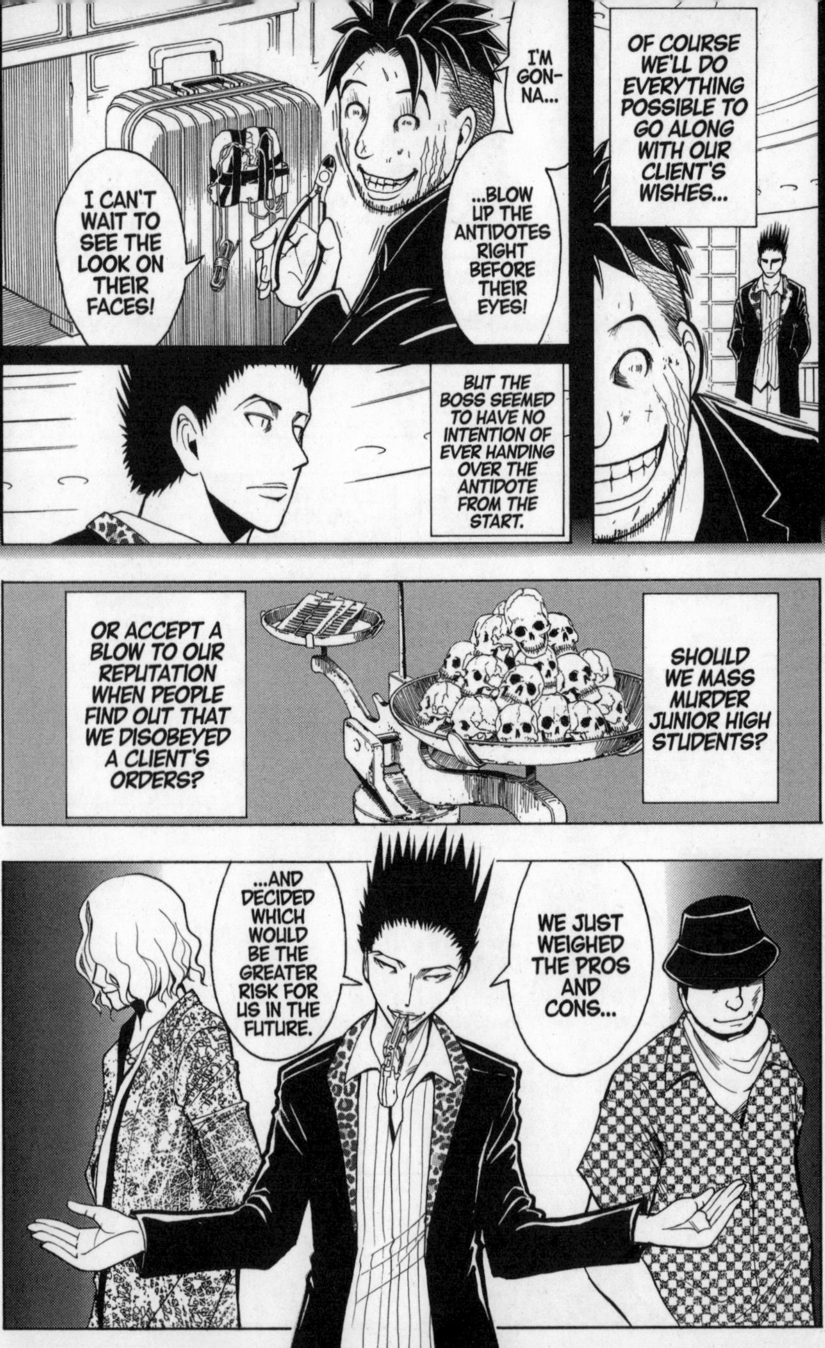
OF COURSE WE'LL DO EVERYTHING POSSIBLE TO GO ALONG WITH OUR CLIENT'S WISHES...
I'M GONNA...
...BLOW UP THE ANTIDOTES RIGHT BEFORE THEIR EYES!
I CAN'T WAIT TO SEE THE LOOK ON THEIR FACES!
BUT THE BOSS SEEMED TO HAVE NO INTENTION OF EVER HANDING OVER THE ANTIDOTE FROM THE START.
SHOULD WE MASS MURDER JUNIOR HIGH STUDENTS?
OR ACCEPT A BLOW TO OUR REPUTATION WHEN PEOPLE FIND OUT THAT WE DISOBEYED A CLIENT'S ORDERS?
WE JUST WEIGHED THE PROS AND CONS...
...AND DECIDED WHICH WOULD BE THE GREATER RISK FOR US IN THE FUTURE.

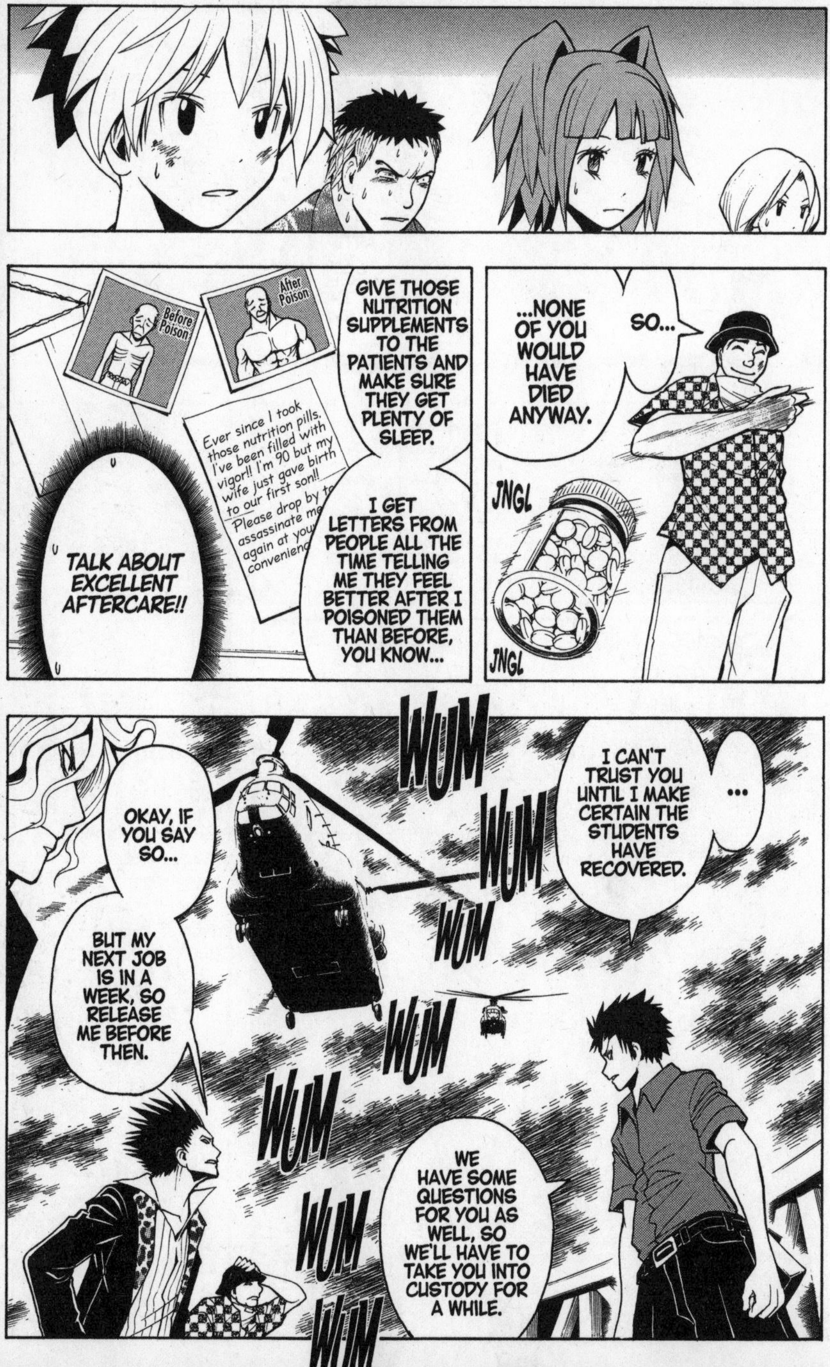
SO...
...NONE OF YOU WOULD HAVE DIED ANYWAY.
JNGL
JNGL
GIVE THOSE NUTRITION SUPPLEMENTS TO THE PATIENTS AND MAKE SURE THEY GET PLENTY OF SLEEP.
I GET LETTERS FROM PEOPLE ALL THE TIME TELLING ME THEY FEEL BETTER AFTER I POISONED THEM THAN BEFORE, YOU KNOW...
After Poison
Before Poison
Ever since I took those nutrition pills, I've been filled with vigor!! I'm 90 but my wife just gave birth to our first son!! Please drop by to assassinate me again at your
TALK ABOUT EXCELLENT AFTERCARE!!
...
I CAN'T TRUST YOU UNTIL I MAKE CERTAIN THE STUDENTS HAVE RECOVERED.
WUM
WUM
WUM
WUM
OKAY, IF YOU SAY SO...
BUT MY NEXT JOB IS IN A WEEK, SO RELEASE ME BEFORE THEN.
WUM
WUM
WE HAVE SOME QUESTIONS FOR YOU AS WELL, SO WE'LL HAVE TO TAKE YOU INTO CUSTODY FOR A WHILE.
WUM

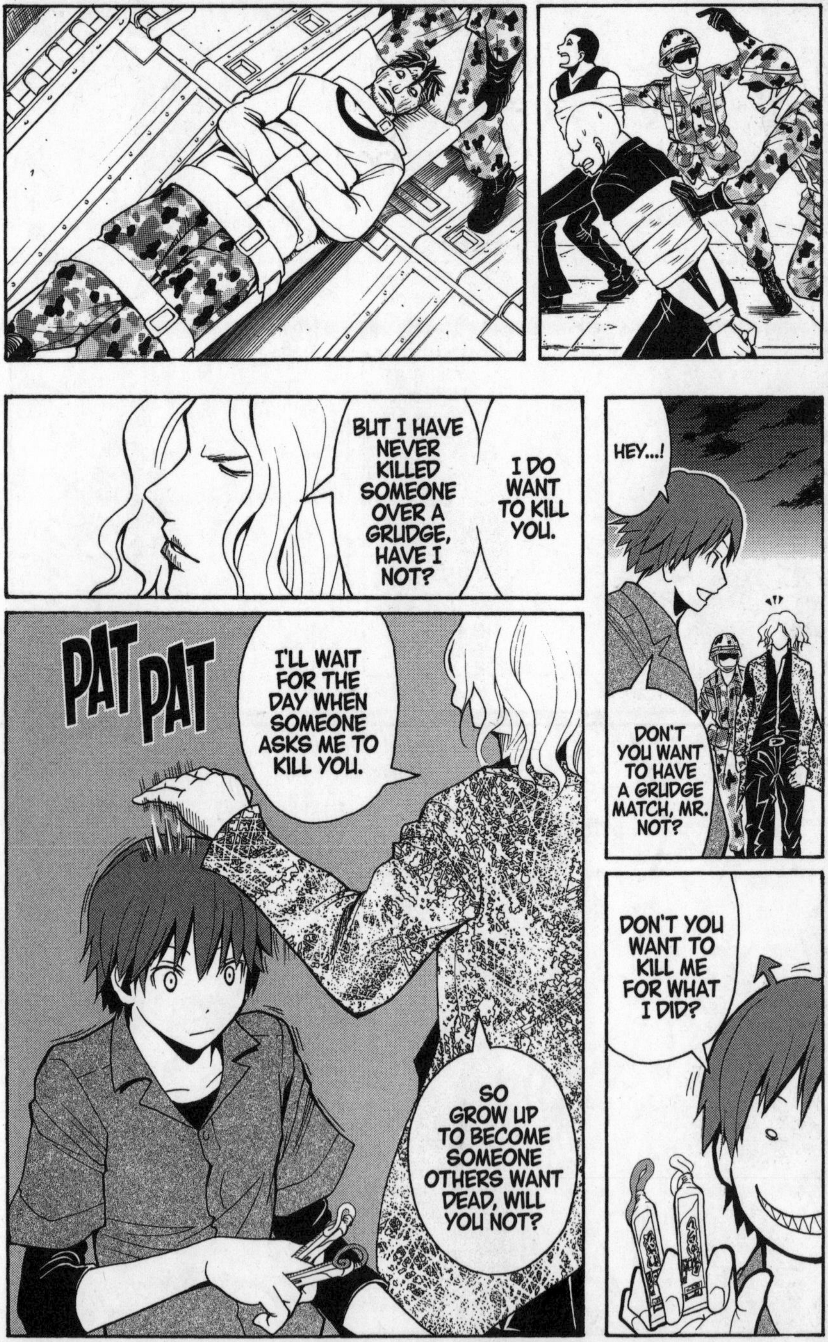
HEY...!
DON'T YOU WANT TO HAVE A GRUDGE MATCH, MR. NOT?
I DO WANT TO KILL YOU.
BUT I HAVE NEVER KILLED SOMEONE OVER A GRUDGE, HAVE I NOT?
PAT PAT
I'LL WAIT FOR THE DAY WHEN SOMEONE ASKS ME TO KILL YOU.
SO GROW UP TO BECOME SOMEONE OTHERS WANT DEAD, WILL YOU NOT?
DON'T YOU WANT TO KILL ME FOR WHAT I DID?

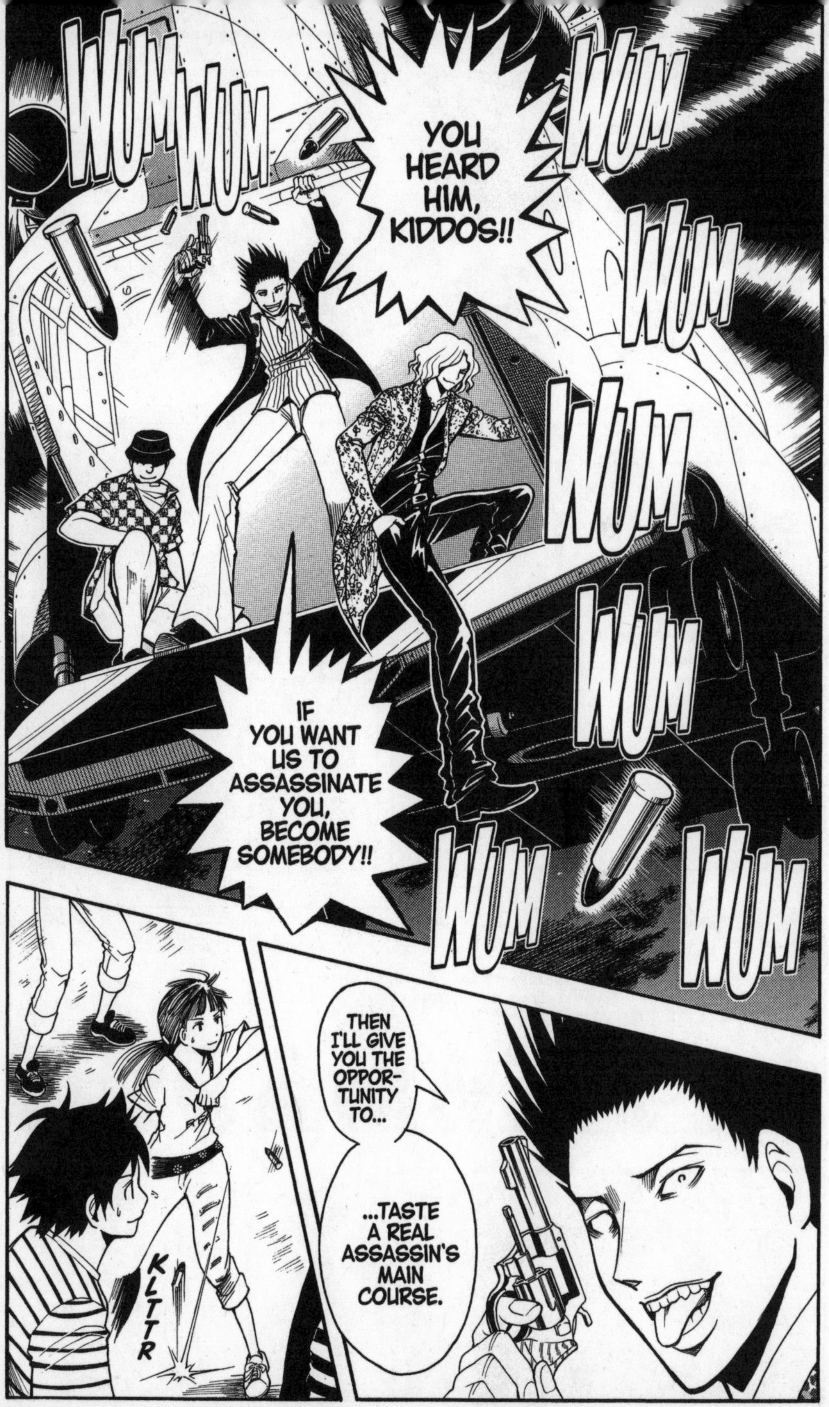
WUM WUM
WUM
WUM
YOU HEARD HIM, KIDDOS!!
WUM
WUM
IF YOU WANT US TO ASSASSINATE YOU, BECOME SOMEBODY!!
WUM
WUM
THEN I'LL GIVE YOU THE OPPOR-TUNITY TO...
...TASTE A REAL ASSASSIN'S MAIN COURSE.
KLTTR

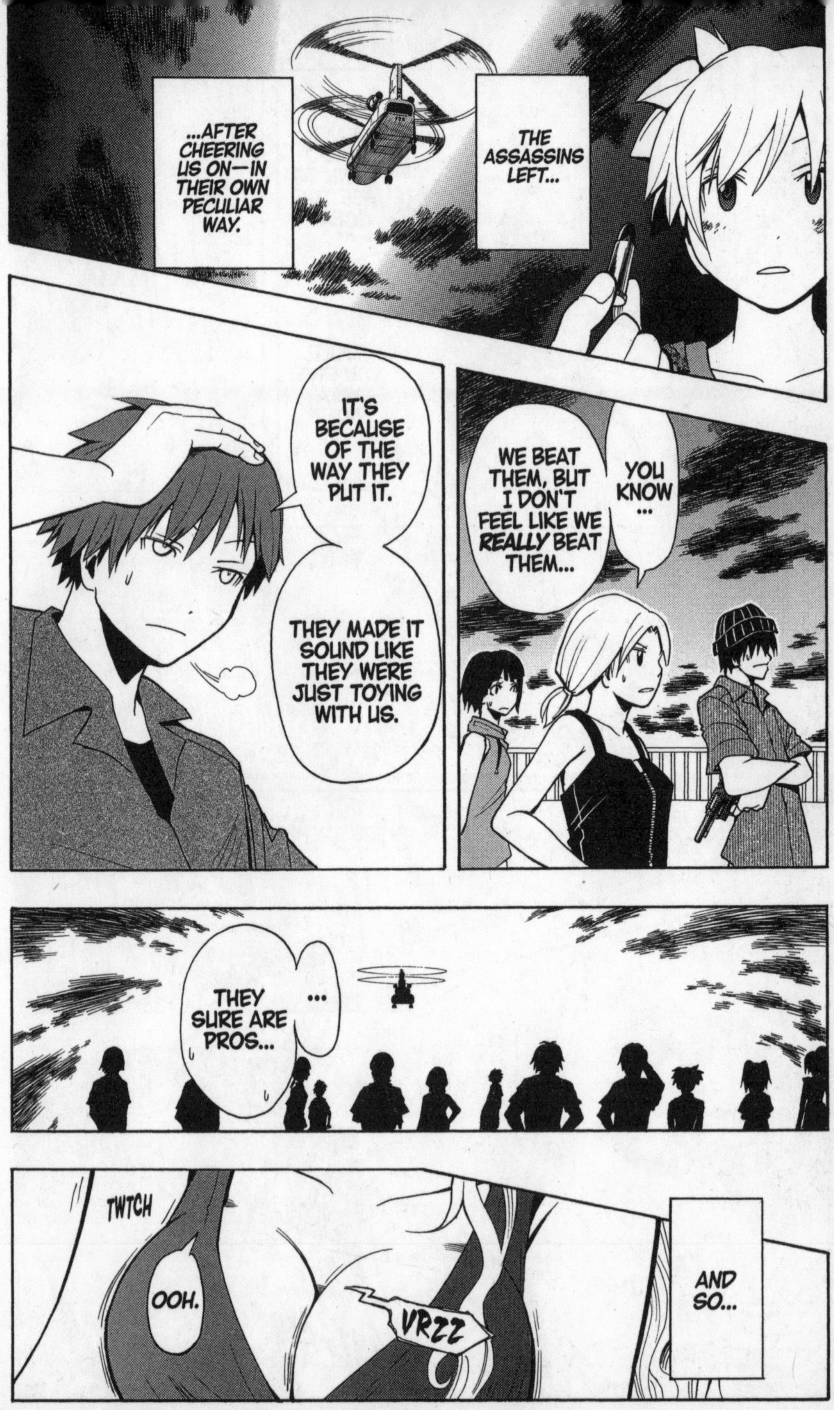
THE ASSASSINS LEFT...
...AFTER CHEERING US ON—IN THEIR OWN PECULIAR WAY.
YOU KNOW...
WE BEAT THEM, BUT I DON'T FEEL LIKE WE *REALLY* BEAT THEM...
IT'S BECAUSE OF THE WAY THEY PUT IT.
THEY MADE IT SOUND LIKE THEY WERE JUST TOYING WITH US.
...
THEY SURE ARE PROS...
AND SO...
VRZZ
OOH.
TWTCH

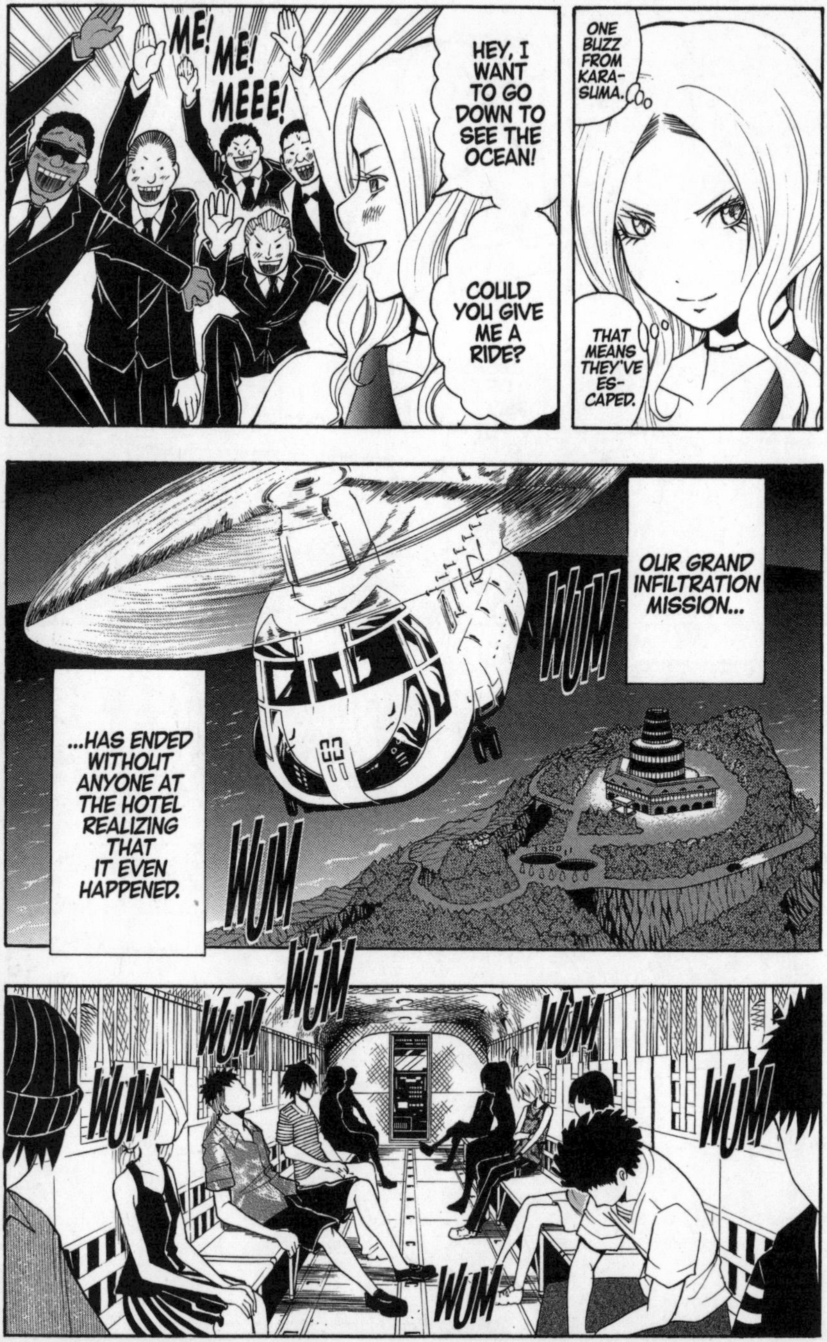
ONE BUZZ FROM KARASUMA.
THAT MEANS THEY'VE ES-CAPED.
HEY, I WANT TO GO DOWN TO SEE THE OCEAN!
COULD YOU GIVE ME A RIDE?
ME!
ME!
MEEE!
OUR GRAND INFILTRATION MISSION...
WUM
...HAS ENDED WITHOUT ANYONE AT THE HOTEL REALIZING THAT IT EVEN HAPPENED.
WUM
WUM
WUM
WUM
WUM
WUM
WUM
WUM

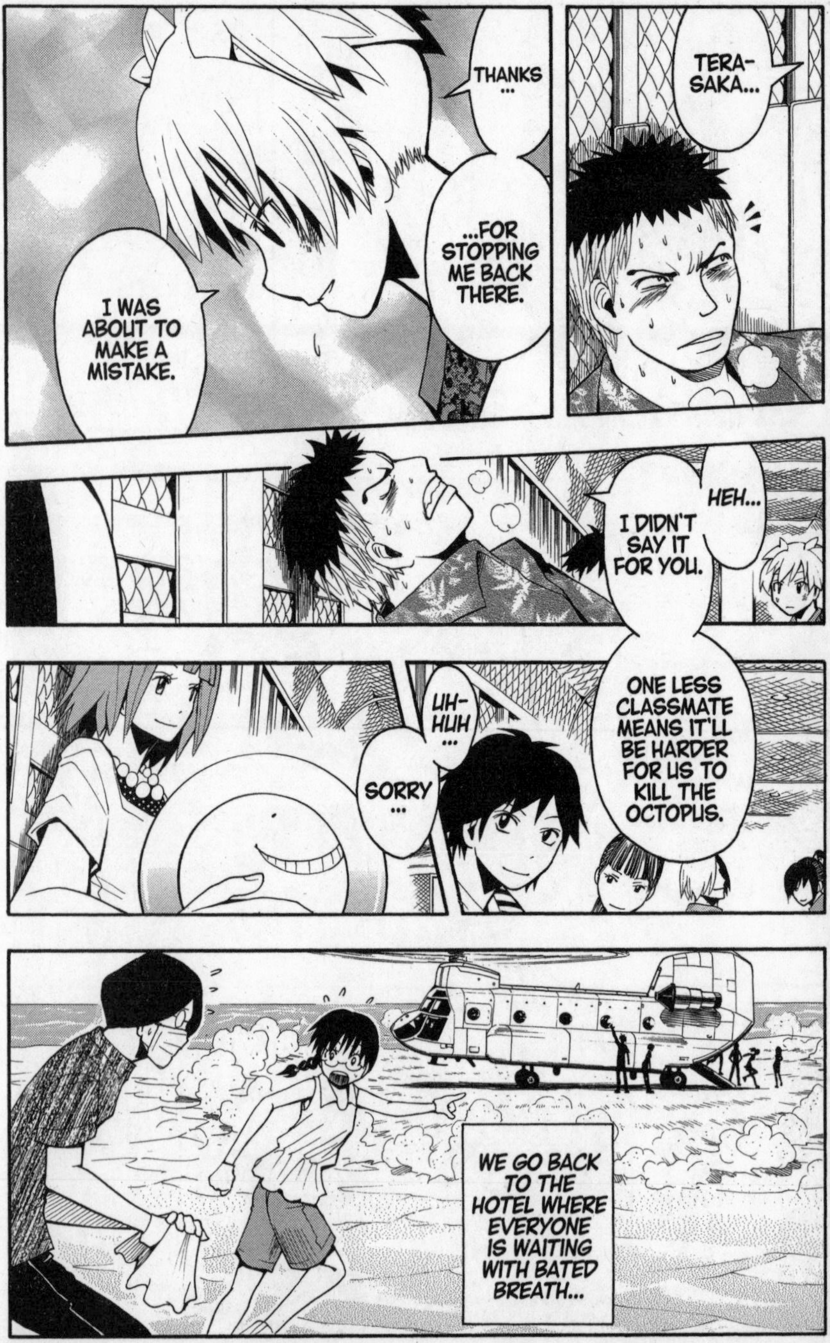
TERA-SAKA...
THANKS...
...FOR STOPPING ME BACK THERE.
I WAS ABOUT TO MAKE A MISTAKE.
HEH... I DIDN'T SAY IT FOR YOU.
ONE LESS CLASSMATE MEANS IT'LL BE HARDER FOR US TO KILL THE OCTOPUS.
UH-HUH...
SORRY...
WE GO BACK TO THE HOTEL WHERE EVERYONE IS WAITING WITH BATED BREATH...

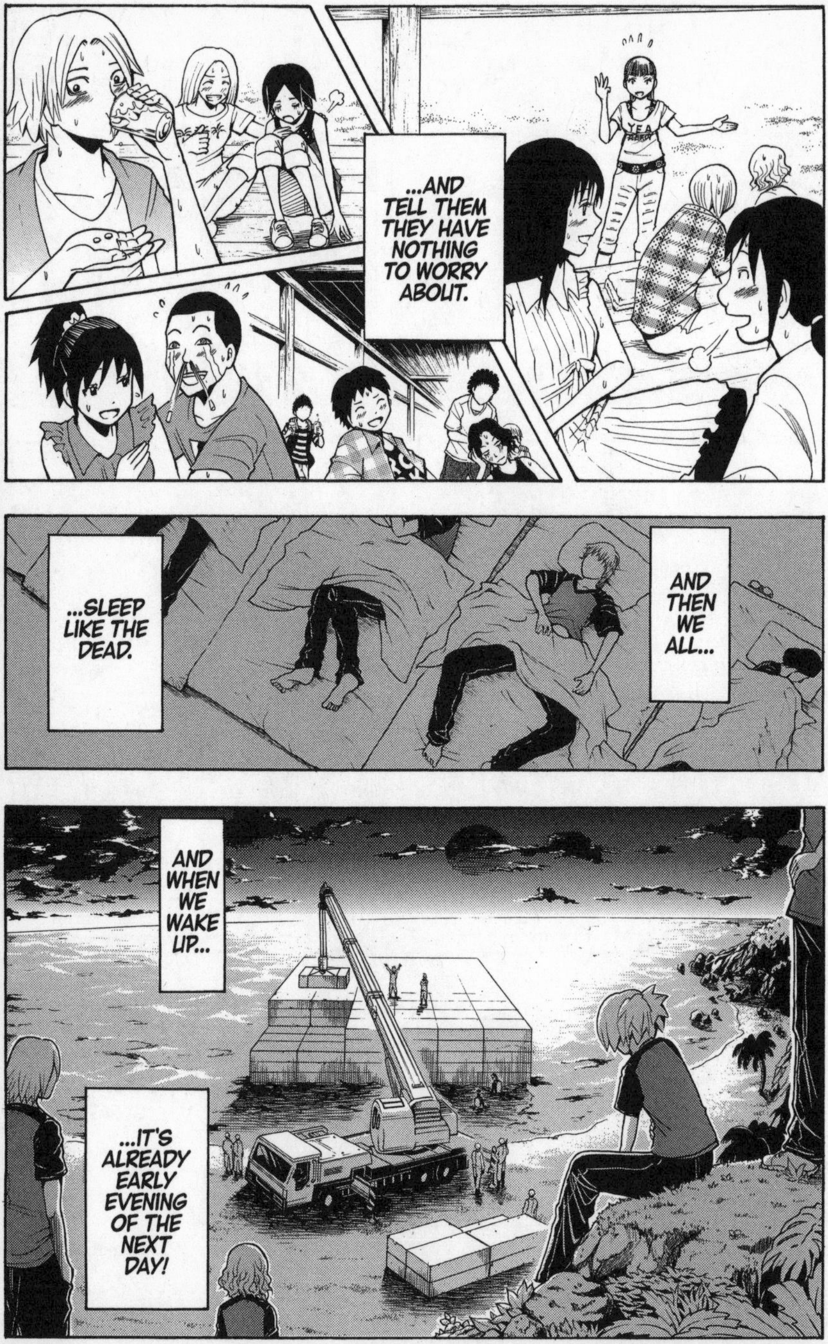
...AND TELL THEM THEY HAVE NOTHING TO WORRY ABOUT.
AND THEN WE ALL...
...SLEEP LIKE THE DEAD.
AND WHEN WE WAKE UP...
...IT'S ALREADY EARLY EVENING OF THE NEXT DAY!

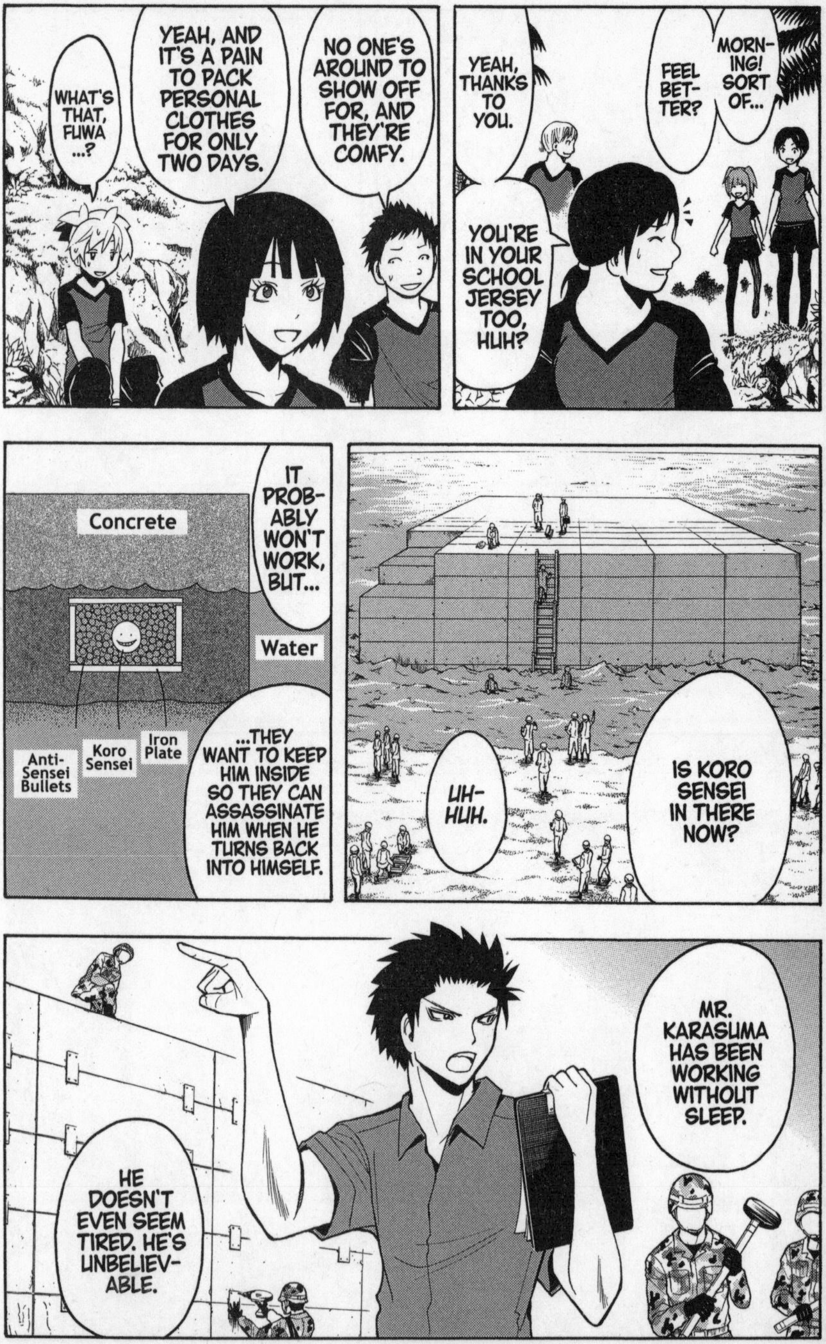
MORNING! SORT OF...
FEEL BETTER?
YEAH, THANKS TO YOU.
YOU'RE IN YOUR SCHOOL JERSEY TOO, HUH?
NO ONE'S AROUND TO SHOW OFF FOR, AND THEY'RE COMFY.
YEAH, AND IT'S A PAIN TO PACK PERSONAL CLOTHES FOR ONLY TWO DAYS.
WHAT'S THAT, FUWA...?
IS KORO SENSEI IN THERE NOW?
UH-HUH.
IT PROBABLY WON'T WORK, BUT...
Concrete
Water
Iron Plate
Koro Sensei
Anti-Sensei Bullets
...THEY WANT TO KEEP HIM INSIDE SO THEY CAN ASSASSINATE HIM WHEN HE TURNS BACK INTO HIMSELF.
MR. KARASUMA HAS BEEN WORKING WITHOUT SLEEP.
HE DOESN'T EVEN SEEM TIRED. HE'S UNBELIEVABLE.

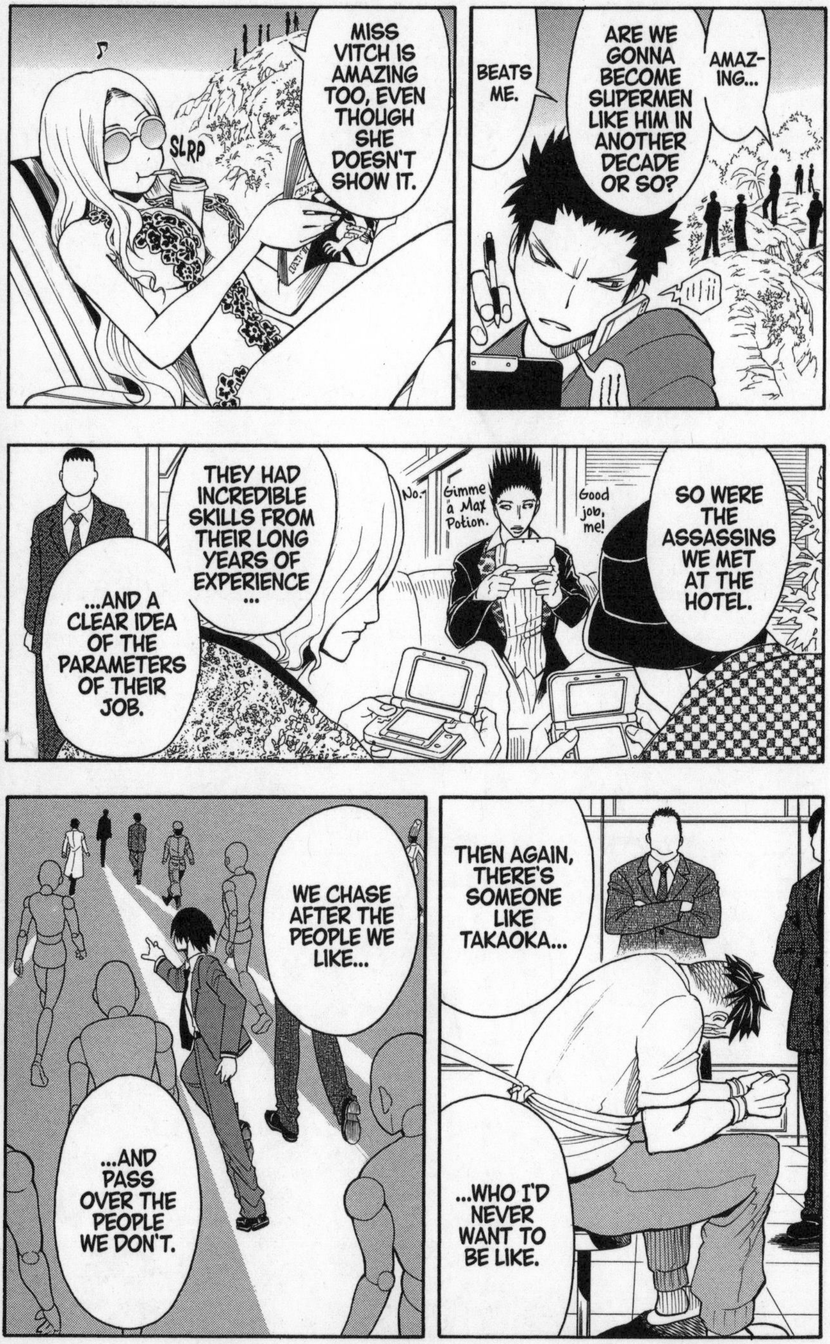
AMAZ-ING...
ARE WE GONNA BECOME SUPERMEN LIKE HIM IN ANOTHER DECADE OR SO?
BEATS ME.
MISS VITCH IS AMAZING TOO, EVEN THOUGH SHE DOESN'T SHOW IT.
SLRP
SO WERE THE ASSASSINS WE MET AT THE HOTEL.
Good job, me!
Gimme a Max Potion.
No.
THEY HAD INCREDIBLE SKILLS FROM THEIR LONG YEARS OF EXPERIENCE ...
...AND A CLEAR IDEA OF THE PARAMETERS OF THEIR JOB.
THEN AGAIN, THERE'S SOMEONE LIKE TAKAOKA...
...WHO I'D NEVER WANT TO BE LIKE.
WE CHASE AFTER THE PEOPLE WE LIKE...
...AND PASS OVER THE PEOPLE WE DON'T.

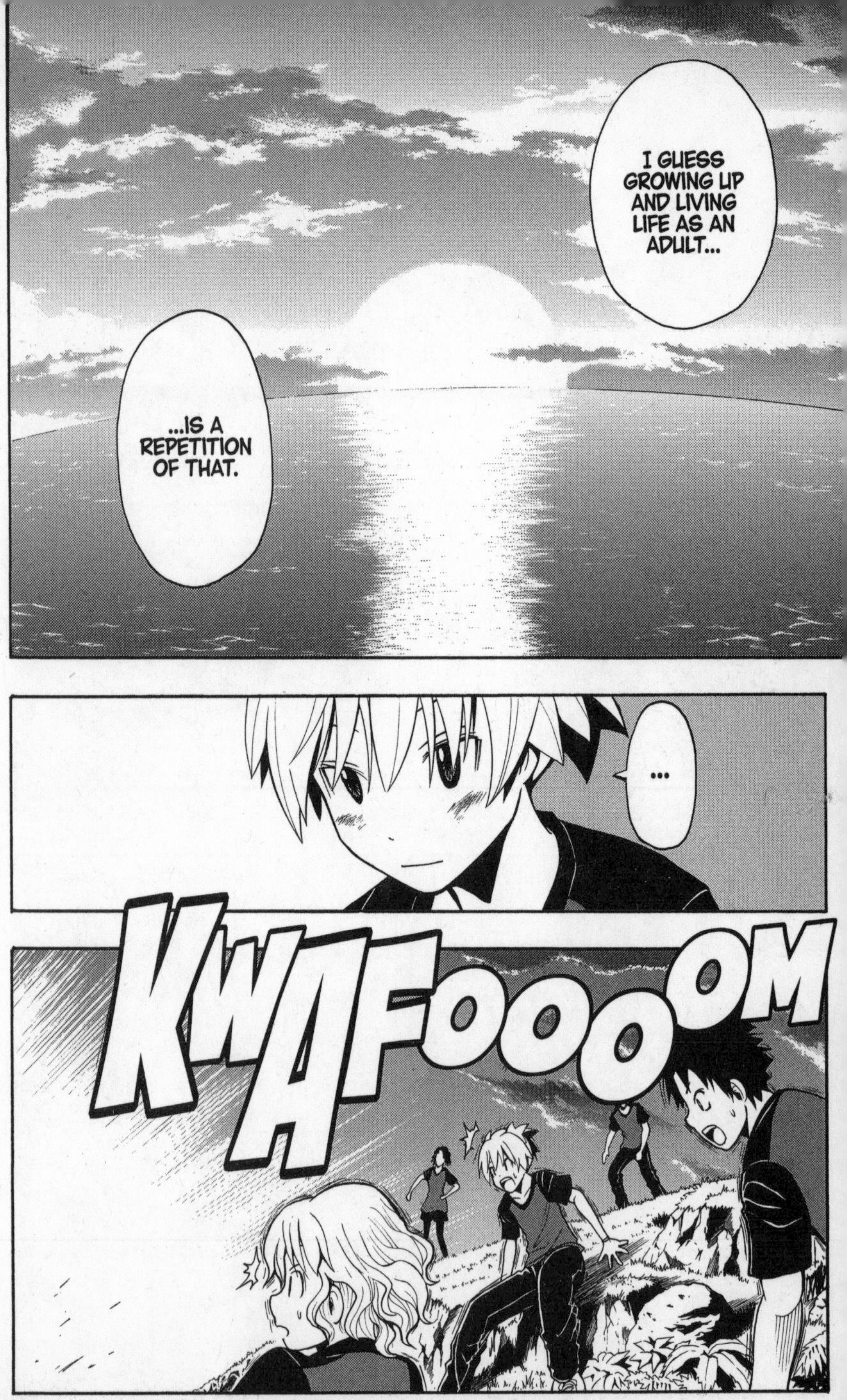
I GUESS GROWING UP AND LIVING LIFE AS AN ADULT...
...IS A REPETITION OF THAT.
...
KWAFOOOOM

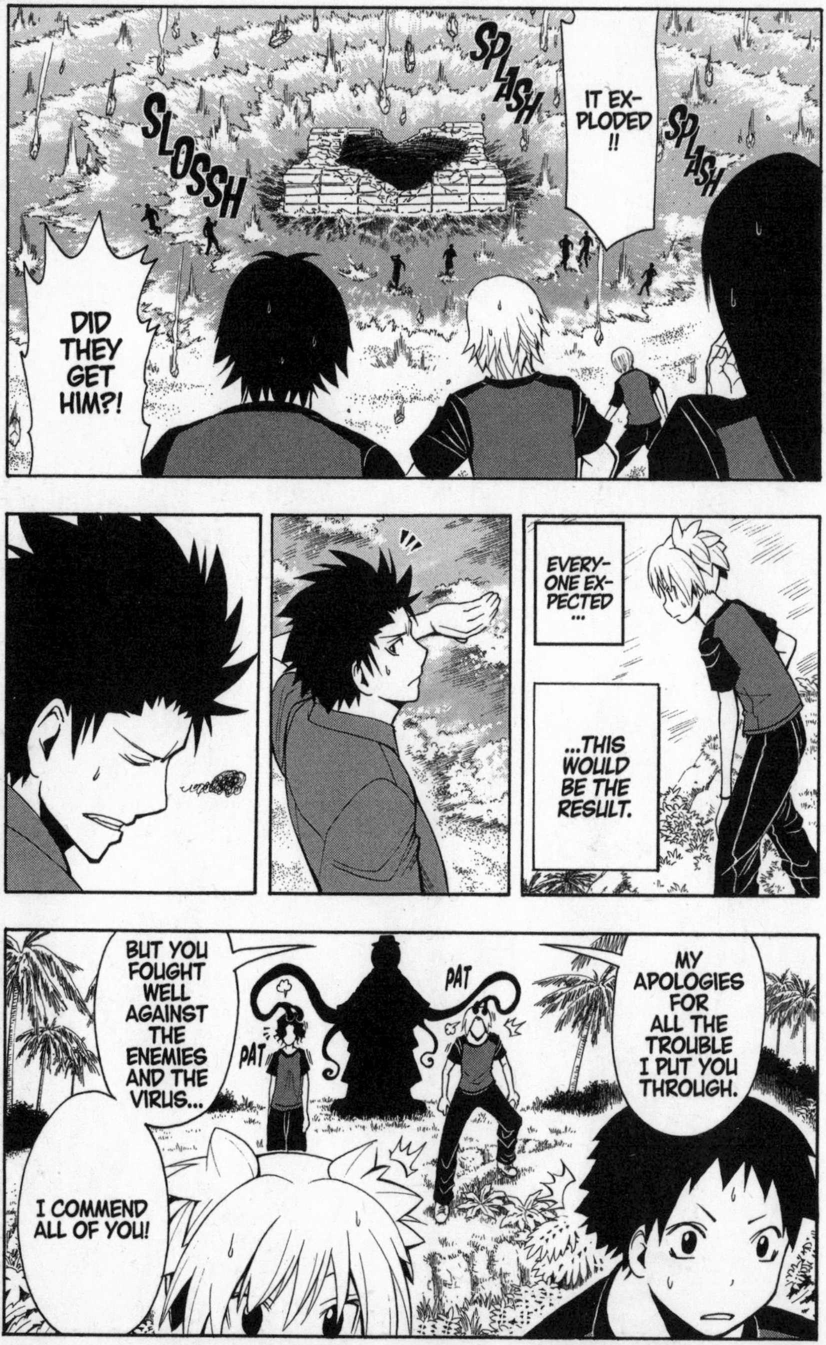
SPLASH
IT EXPLODED!!
SPLASH
SLOSSH
DID THEY GET HIM?!
EVERYONE EXPECTED...
...THIS WOULD BE THE RESULT.
!!
MY APOLOGIES FOR ALL THE TROUBLE I PUT YOU THROUGH.
PAT
PAT
BUT YOU FOUGHT WELL AGAINST THE ENEMIES AND THE VIRUS...
I COMMEND ALL OF YOU!

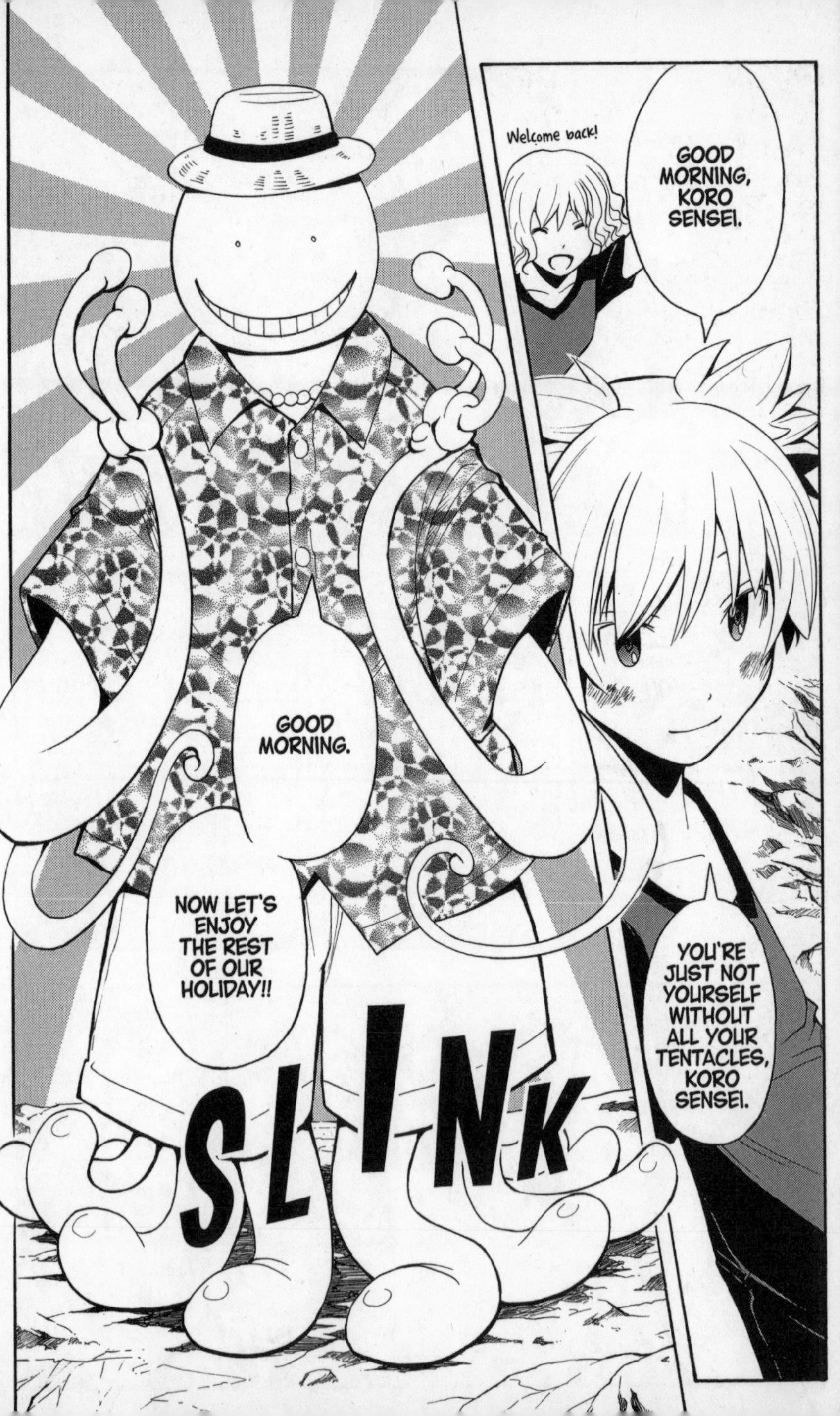
Welcome back!
GOOD MORNING, KORO SENSEI.
YOU'RE JUST NOT YOURSELF WITHOUT ALL YOUR TENTACLES, KORO SENSEI.
GOOD MORNING.
NOW LET'S ENJOY THE REST OF OUR HOLIDAY!!
SLINK

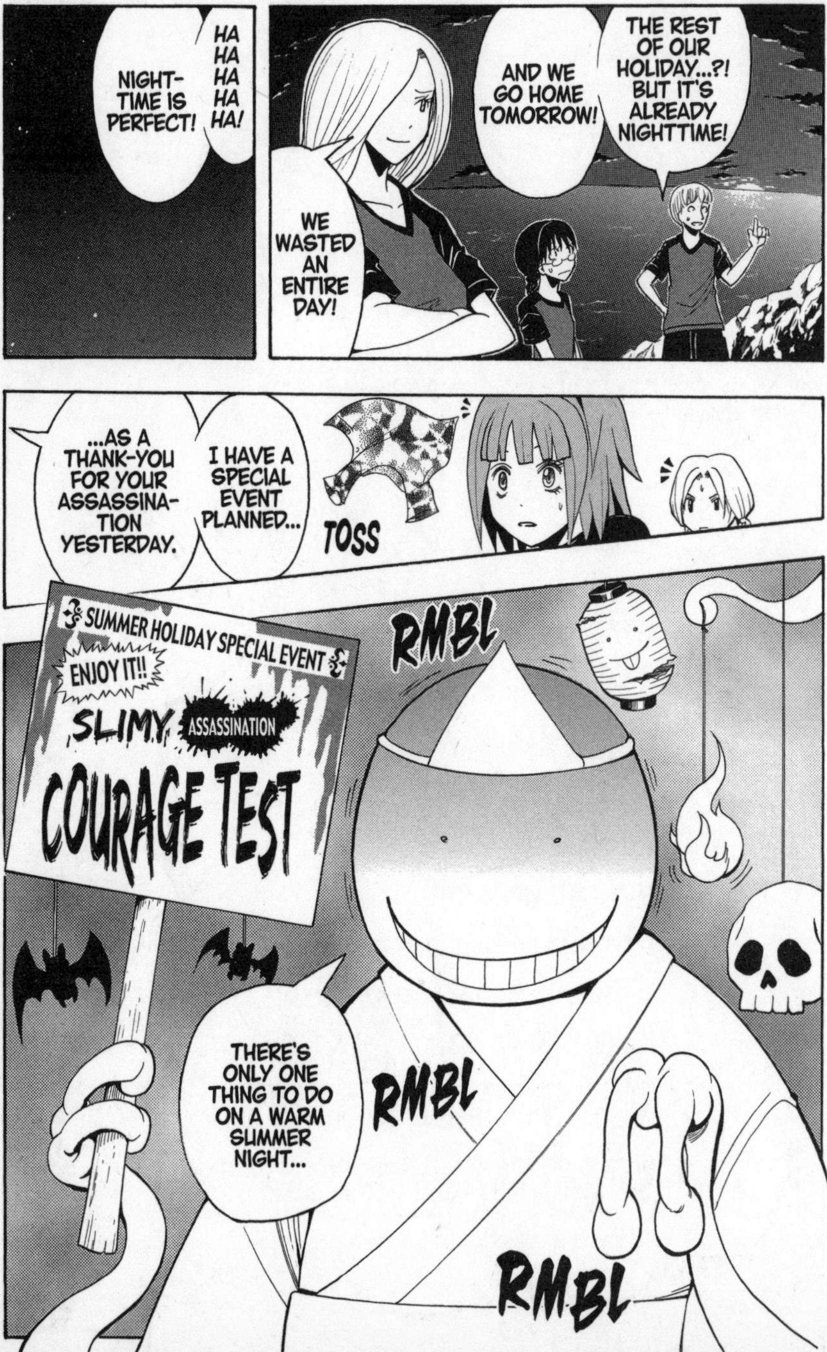
THE REST OF OUR HOLIDAY...?! BUT IT'S ALREADY NIGHTTIME!
AND WE GO HOME TOMORROW!
WE WASTED AN ENTIRE DAY!
HA HA HA HA HA!
NIGHT-TIME IS PERFECT!
TOSS
I HAVE A SPECIAL EVENT PLANNED...
...AS A THANK-YOU FOR YOUR ASSASSINATION YESTERDAY.
RMBL
SUMMER HOLIDAY SPECIAL EVENT
ENJOY IT!!
SLIMY ASSASSINATION
COURAGE TEST
THERE'S ONLY ONE THING TO DO ON A WARM SUMMER NIGHT...
RMBL
RMBL

E-21 YUZUKI FUWA

- 😊 BIRTHDAY: FEBRUARY 9

- 😊 HEIGHT: 5' 3"

- 😊 WEIGHT: 99 LBS.

- 😊 FAVORITE SUBJECT: HISTORY

- 😊 LEAST FAVORITE SUBJECT: MATHEMATICS

- 😊 HOBBY/SKILL: READING SHONEN MANGA

- 😊 FUTURE GOAL: EDITOR

- 😊 UPON READING A BOY'S MANGA MAGAZINE..SHE IS OVERCOME WITH THE URGE TO ADD SPEED LINES.

- 😊 UPON READING A MANGA MAGAZINE FOR YOUNG MEN... SHE TURNS BRIGHT RED AND STOPS TALKING.

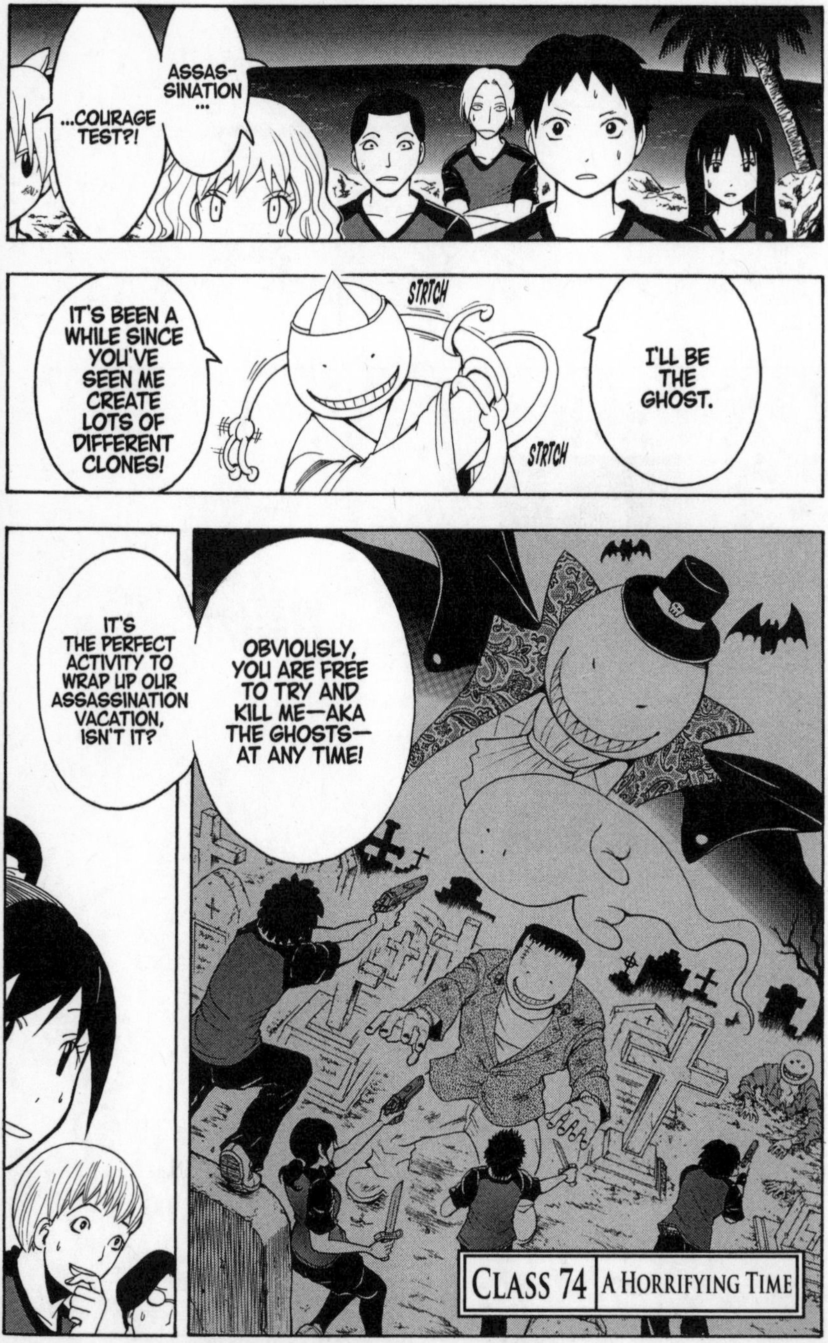
ASSAS-SINATION...
...COURAGE TEST?!
I'LL BE THE GHOST.
STRTCH
STRTCH
IT'S BEEN A WHILE SINCE YOU'VE SEEN ME CREATE LOTS OF DIFFERENT CLONES!
OBVIOUSLY, YOU ARE FREE TO TRY AND KILL ME—AKA THE GHOSTS—AT ANY TIME!
IT'S THE PERFECT ACTIVITY TO WRAP UP OUR ASSASSINATION VACATION, ISN'T IT?

CLASS 74 A HORRIFYING TIME

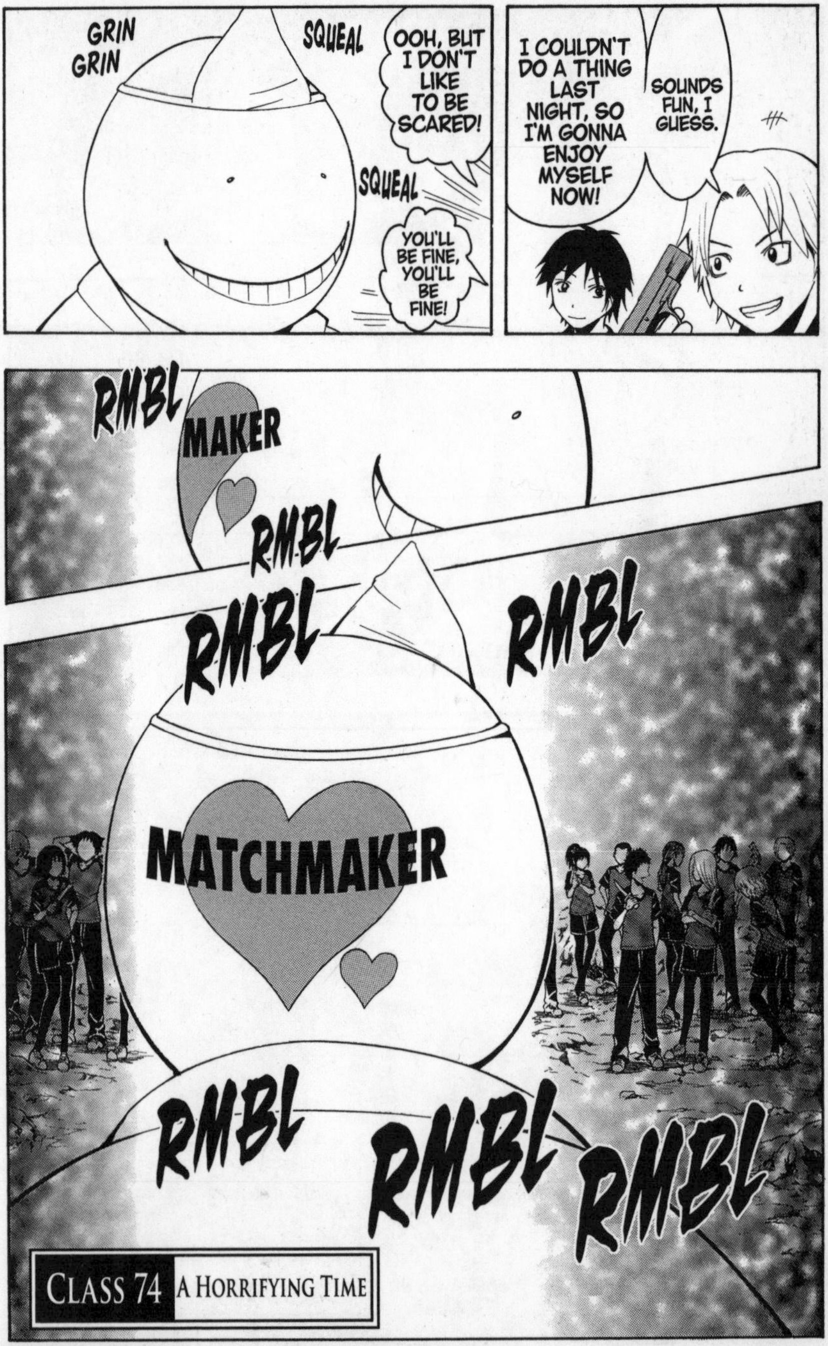
SOUNDS FUN, I GUESS.
I COULDN'T DO A THING LAST NIGHT, SO I'M GONNA ENJOY MYSELF NOW!
OOH, BUT I DON'T LIKE TO BE SCARED!
SQUEAL
SQUEAL
YOU'LL BE FINE, YOU'LL BE FINE!
GRIN GRIN
RMBL
MAKER
RMBL
RMBL
RMBL
MATCHMAKER
RMBL
RMBL
RMBL

CLASS 74 A HORRIFYING TIME

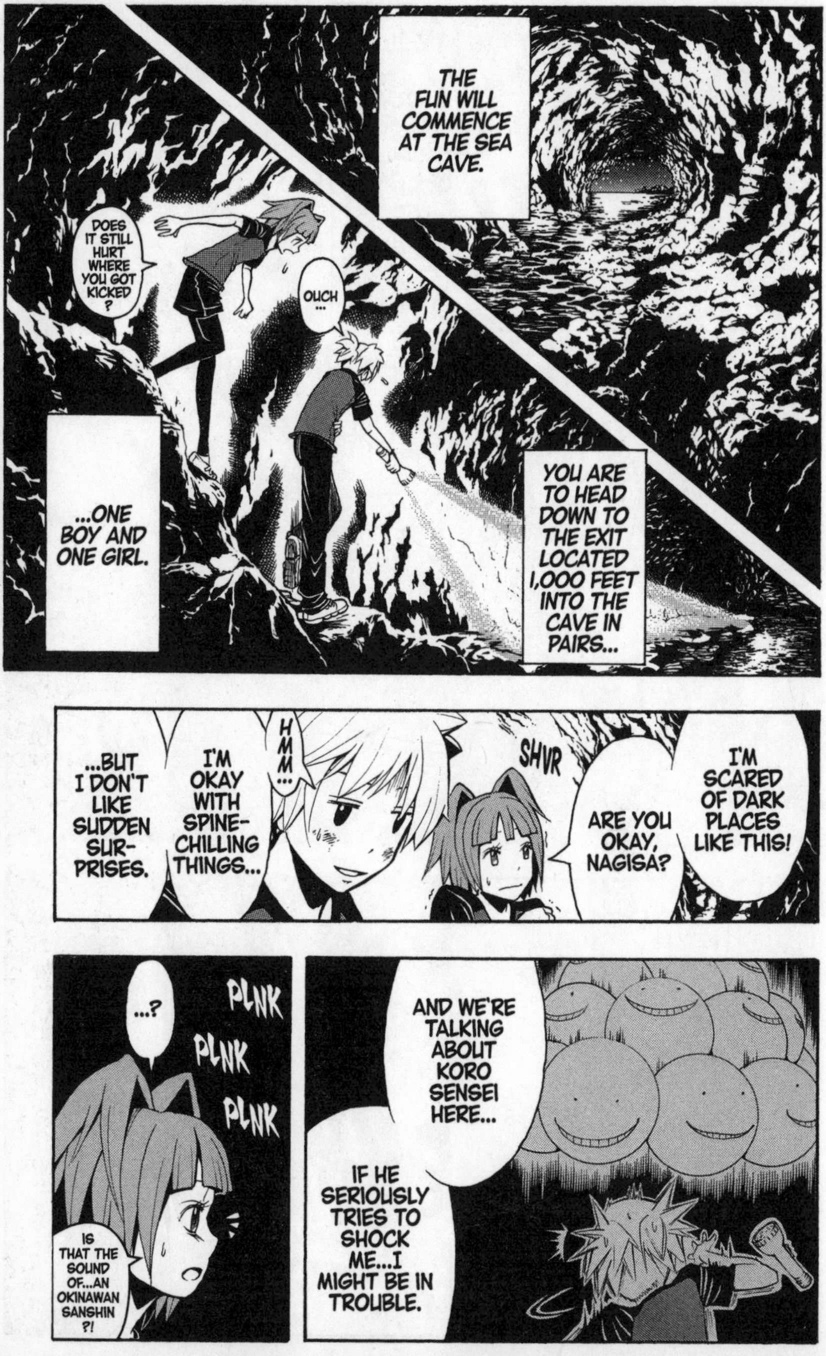
THE FUN WILL COMMENCE AT THE SEA CAVE.
YOU ARE TO HEAD DOWN TO THE EXIT LOCATED 1,000 FEET INTO THE CAVE IN PAIRS...
...ONE BOY AND ONE GIRL.
DOES IT STILL HURT WHERE YOU GOT KICKED?
OUCH...
I'M SCARED OF DARK PLACES LIKE THIS!
SHVR
ARE YOU OKAY, NAGISA?
HMM...
I'M OKAY WITH SPINE-CHILLING THINGS...
...BUT I DON'T LIKE SUDDEN SURPRISES.
AND WE'RE TALKING ABOUT KORO SENSEI HERE...
IF HE SERIOUSLY TRIES TO SHOCK ME...I MIGHT BE IN TROUBLE.
PLNK
PLNK
PLNK
...?
IS THAT THE SOUND OF...AN OKINAWAN SANSHIN?!

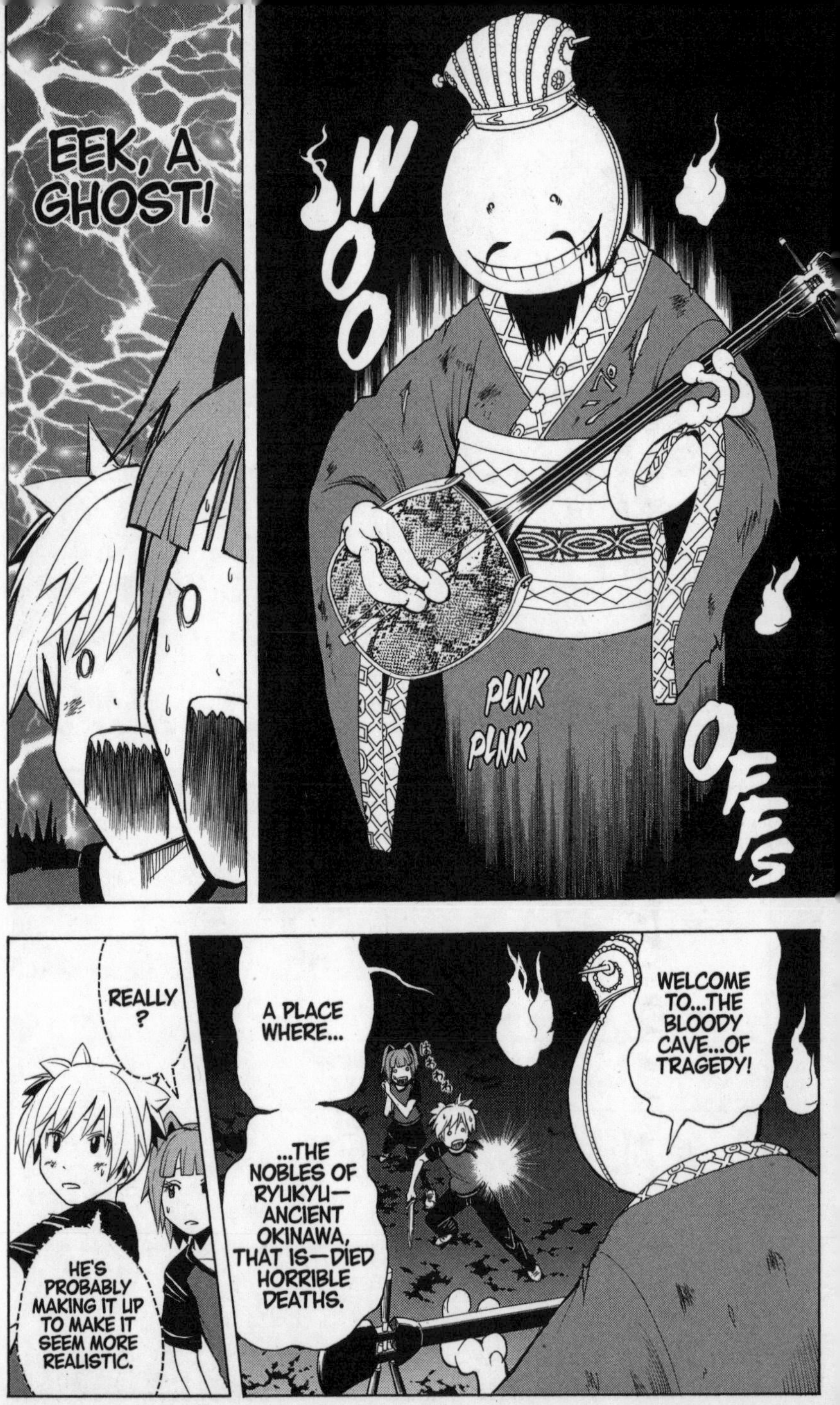
WOOO
PLNK
PLNK
OFFS
EEK, A GHOST!
WELCOME TO...THE BLOODY CAVE...OF TRAGEDY!
A PLACE WHERE...
...THE NOBLES OF RYUKYU—ANCIENT OKINAWA, THAT IS—DIED HORRIBLE DEATHS.
REALLY?
HE'S PROBABLY MAKING IT UP TO MAKE IT SEEM MORE REALISTIC.

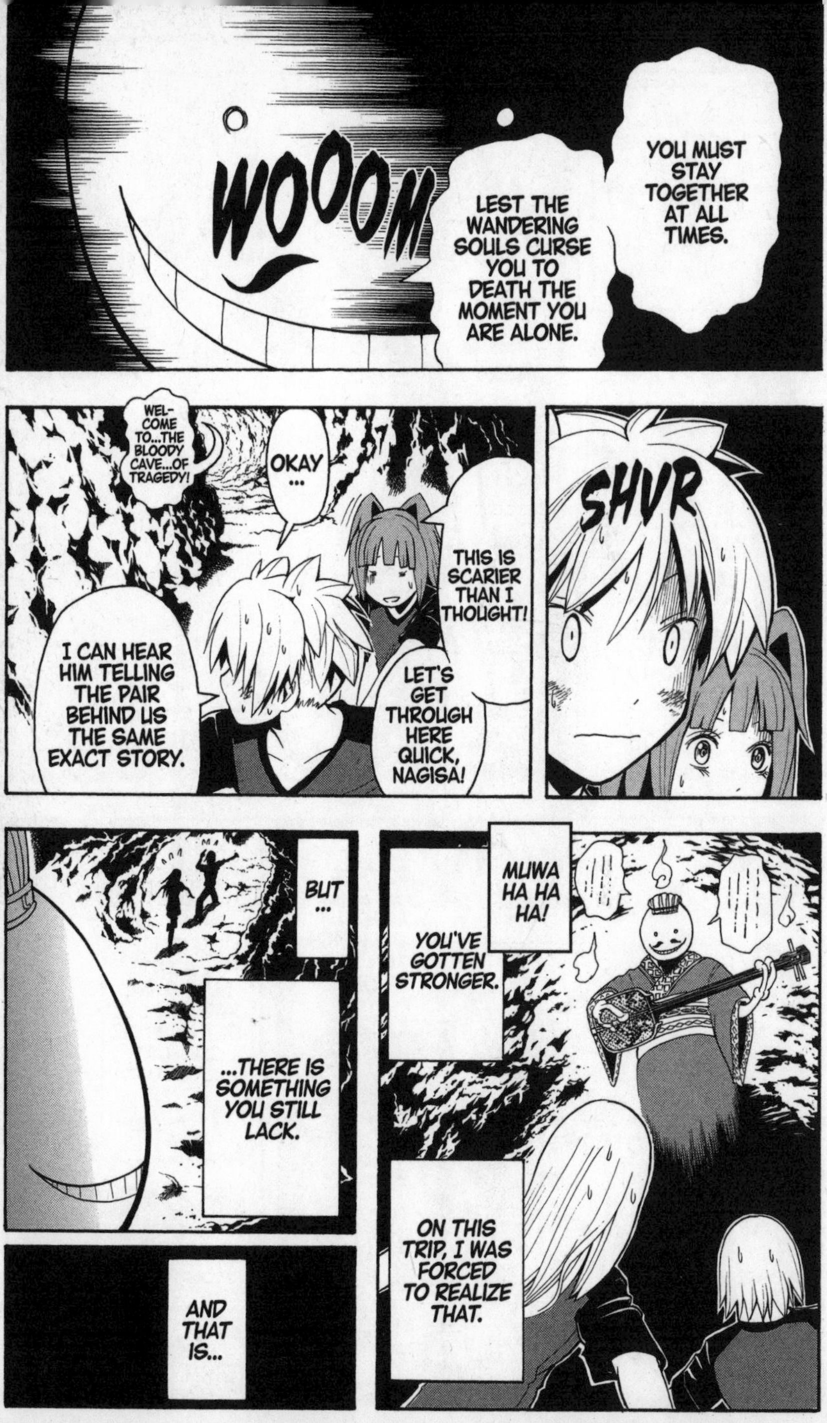
WOOOM
YOU MUST STAY TOGETHER AT ALL TIMES.
LEST THE WANDERING SOULS CURSE YOU TO DEATH THE MOMENT YOU ARE ALONE.
SHVR
THIS IS SCARIER THAN I THOUGHT!
LET'S GET THROUGH HERE QUICK, NAGISA!
OKAY...
WEL-COME TO...THE BLOODY CAVE...OF TRAGEDY!
I CAN HEAR HIM TELLING THE PAIR BEHIND US THE SAME EXACT STORY.
MUWA HA HA HA!
YOU'VE GOTTEN STRONGER.
ON THIS TRIP, I WAS FORCED TO REALIZE THAT.
BUT...
...THERE IS SOMETHING YOU STILL LACK.
AND THAT IS...

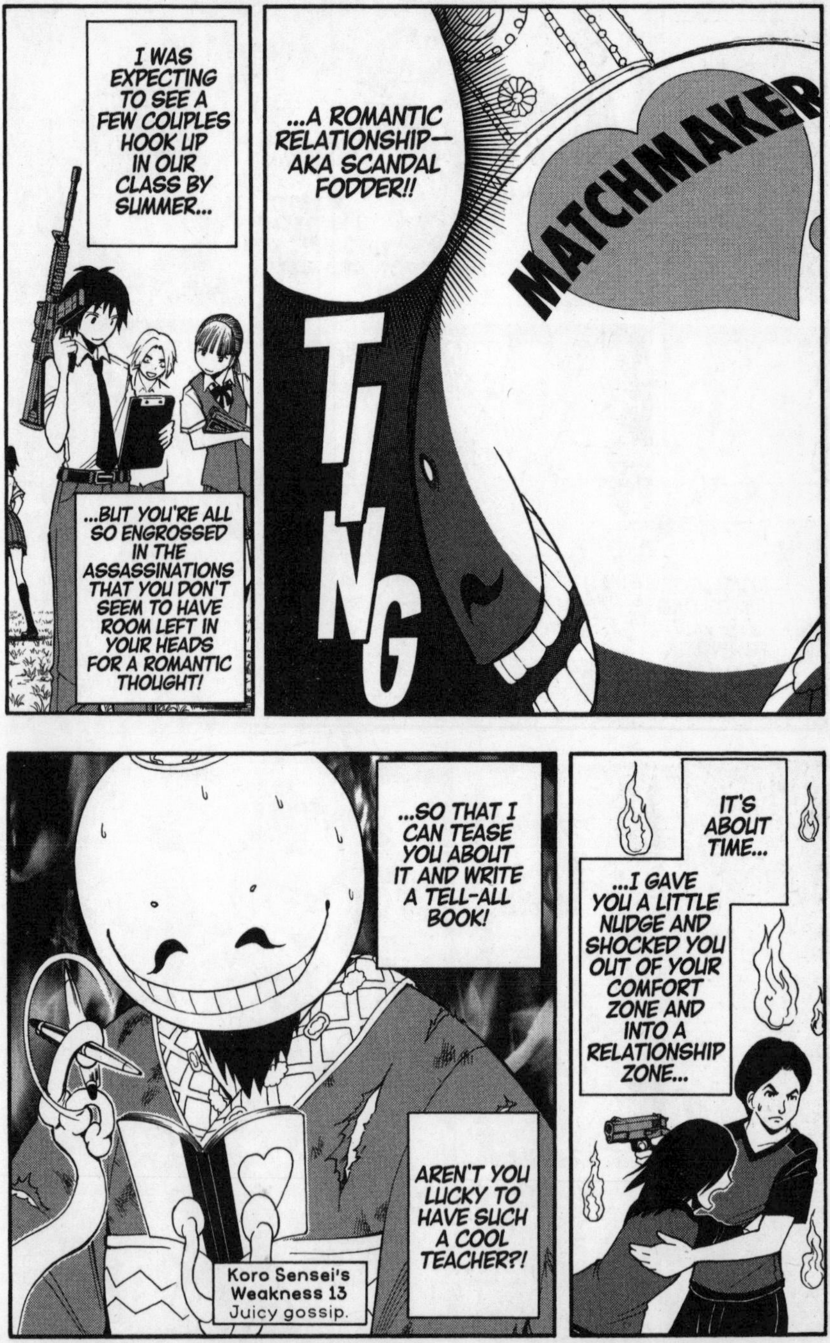
...A ROMANTIC RELATIONSHIP—AKA SCANDAL FODDER!!
MATCHMAKER
TING
I WAS EXPECTING TO SEE A FEW COUPLES HOOK UP IN OUR CLASS BY SUMMER...
...BUT YOU'RE ALL SO ENGROSSED IN THE ASSASSINATIONS THAT YOU DON'T SEEM TO HAVE ROOM LEFT IN YOUR HEADS FOR A ROMANTIC THOUGHT!
IT'S ABOUT TIME...
...I GAVE YOU A LITTLE NUDGE AND SHOCKED YOU OUT OF YOUR COMFORT ZONE AND INTO A RELATIONSHIP ZONE...
...SO THAT I CAN TEASE YOU ABOUT IT AND WRITE A TELL-ALL BOOK!
AREN'T YOU LUCKY TO HAVE SUCH A COOL TEACHER?!
Koro Sensei's Weakness 13
Juicy gossip.

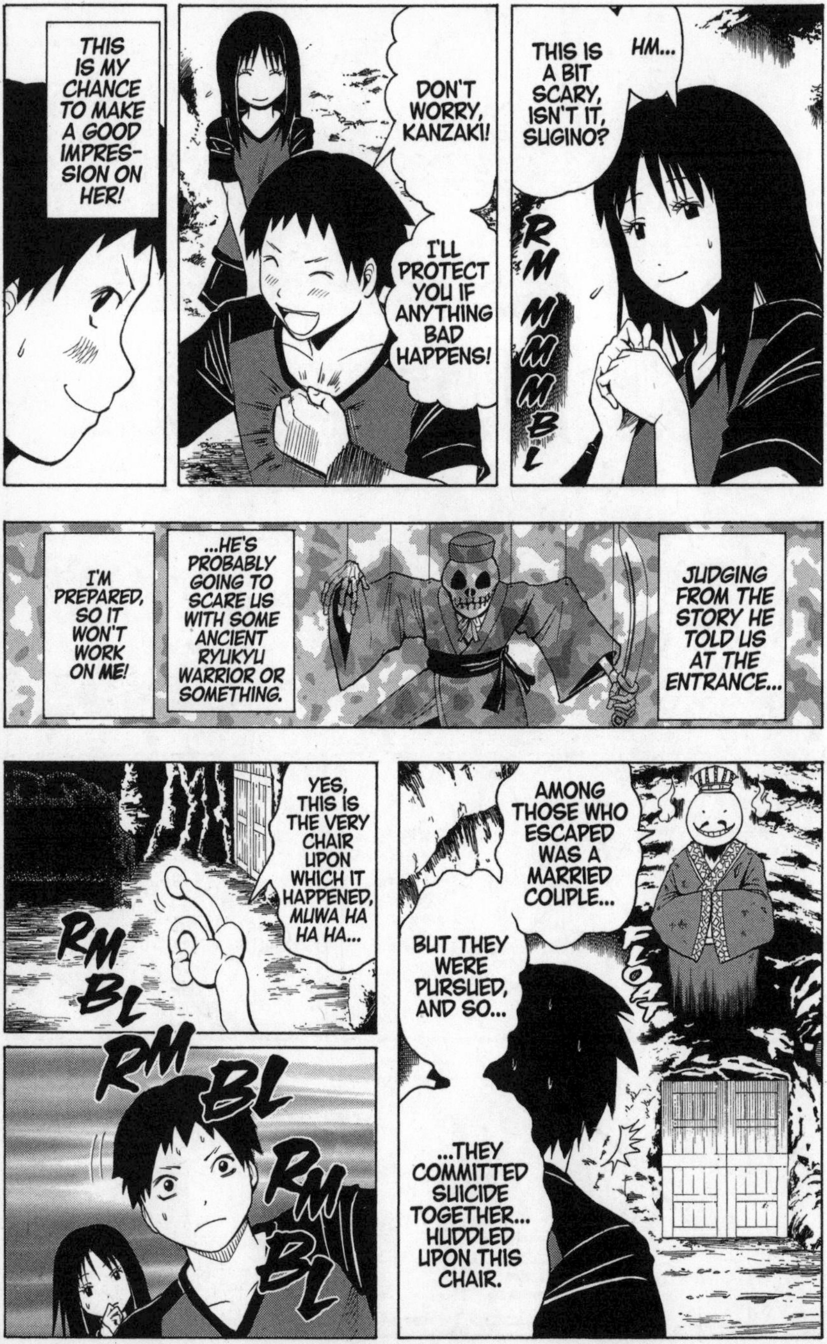
HM...
THIS IS A BIT SCARY, ISN'T IT, SUGINO?
RMMMMMBL
DON'T WORRY, KANZAKI!
I'LL PROTECT YOU IF ANYTHING BAD HAPPENS!
THIS IS MY CHANCE TO MAKE A GOOD IMPRESSION ON HER!
JUDGING FROM THE STORY HE TOLD US AT THE ENTRANCE...
...HE'S PROBABLY GOING TO SCARE US WITH SOME ANCIENT RYUKYU WARRIOR OR SOMETHING.
I'M PREPARED, SO IT WON'T WORK ON ME!
AMONG THOSE WHO ESCAPED WAS A MARRIED COUPLE...
FLOAT
BUT THEY WERE PURSUED, AND SO...
...THEY COMMITTED SUICIDE TOGETHER... HUDDLED UPON THIS CHAIR.
YES, THIS IS THE VERY CHAIR UPON WHICH IT HAPPENED, MUWA HA HA HA...
RM BL
RM BL
RM BL

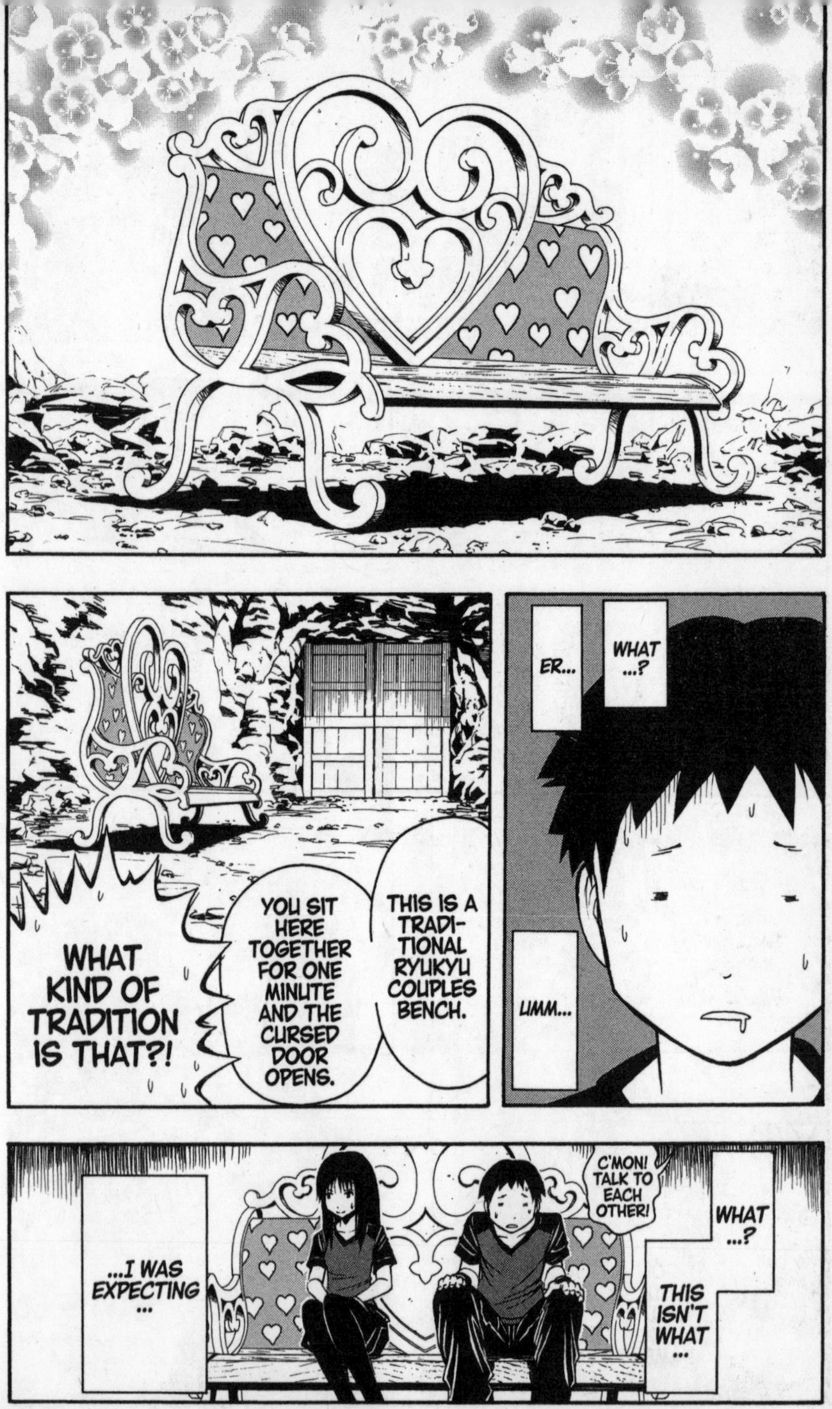
WHAT ...?
ER...
UMM...
THIS IS A TRADI- TIONAL RYUKYU COUPLES BENCH.
YOU SIT HERE TOGETHER FOR ONE MINUTE AND THE CURSED DOOR OPENS.
WHAT KIND OF TRADITION IS THAT?!
C'MON! TALK TO EACH OTHER!
WHAT ...?
THIS ISN'T WHAT ...
...I WAS EXPECTING ...

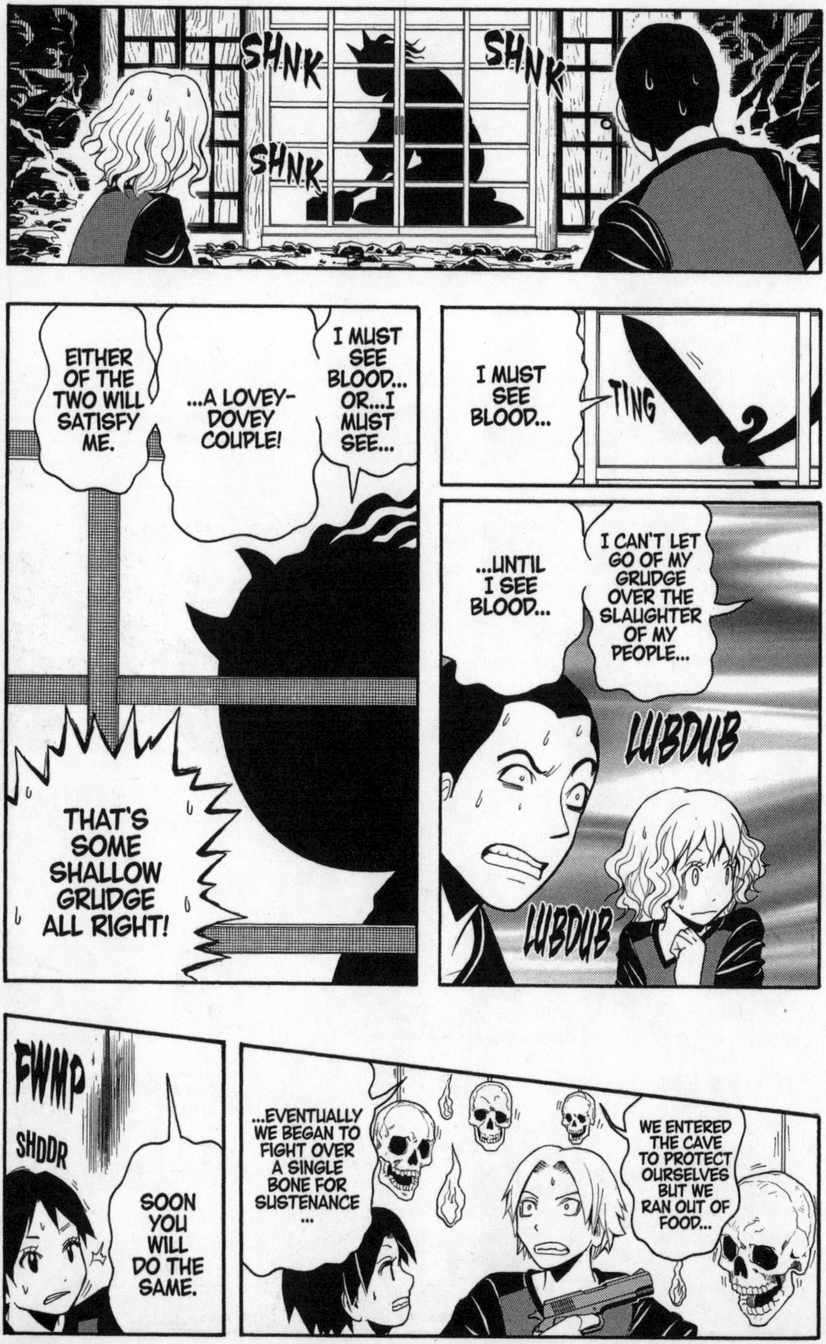
SHNK
SHNK
SHNK
I MUST SEE BLOOD...
TING
I CAN'T LET GO OF MY GRUDGE OVER THE SLAUGHTER OF MY PEOPLE...
...UNTIL I SEE BLOOD...
LUBDUB
LUBDUB
I MUST SEE BLOOD... OR...I MUST SEE...
...A LOVEY-DOVEY COUPLE!
EITHER OF THE TWO WILL SATISFY ME.
THAT'S SOME SHALLOW GRUDGE ALL RIGHT!
WE ENTERED THE CAVE TO PROTECT OURSELVES BUT WE RAN OUT OF FOOD...
...EVENTUALLY WE BEGAN TO FIGHT OVER A SINGLE BONE FOR SUSTENANCE...
FWMP
SHDDR
SOON YOU WILL DO THE SAME.

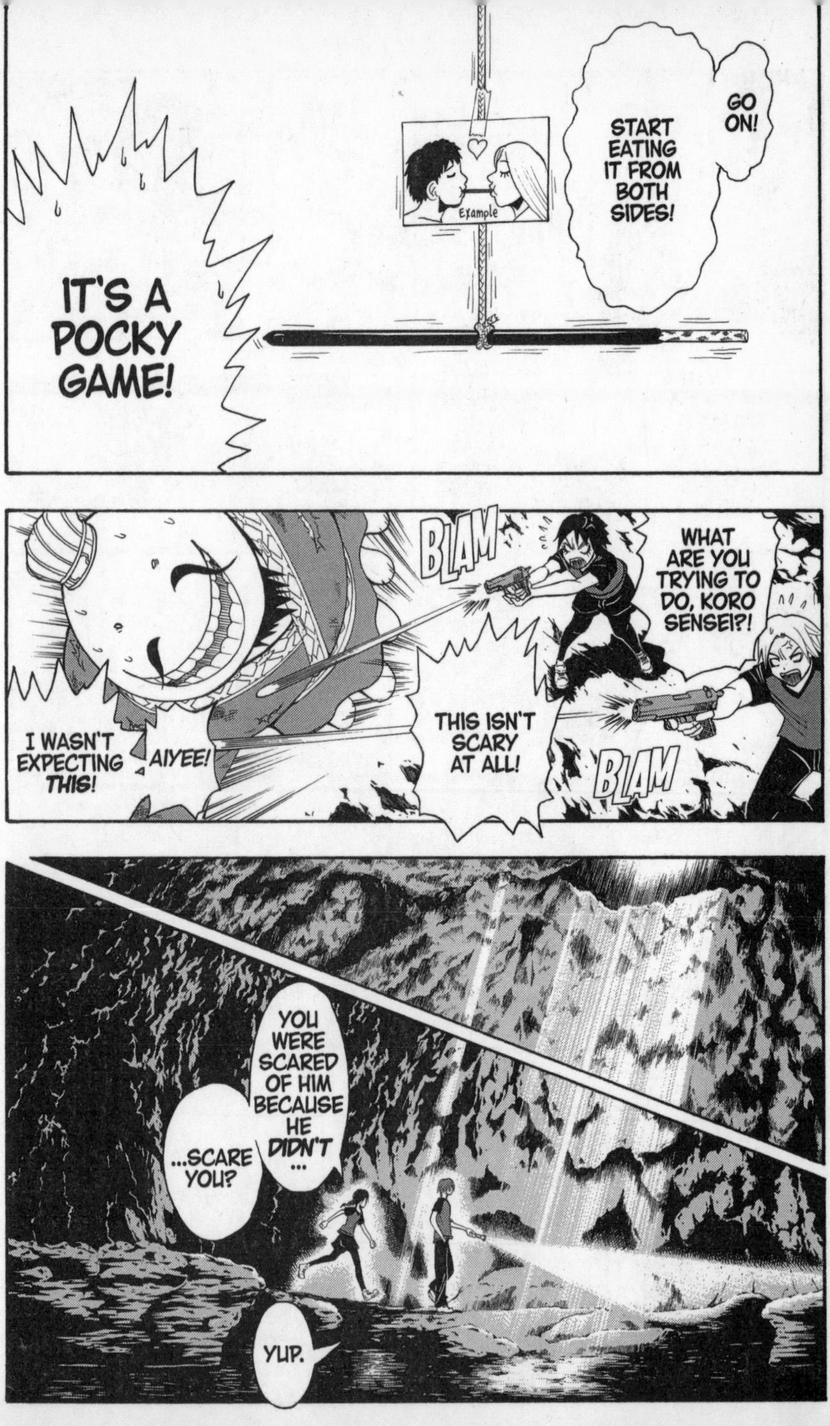
START EATING IT FROM BOTH SIDES! GO ON!
Example
IT'S A POCKY GAME!
WHAT ARE YOU TRYING TO DO, KORO SENSEI?!
BLAM
BLAM
THIS ISN'T SCARY AT ALL!
AIYEE!
I WASN'T EXPECTING THIS!
YOU WERE SCARED OF HIM BECAUSE HE DIDN'T ...
...SCARE YOU?
YUP.

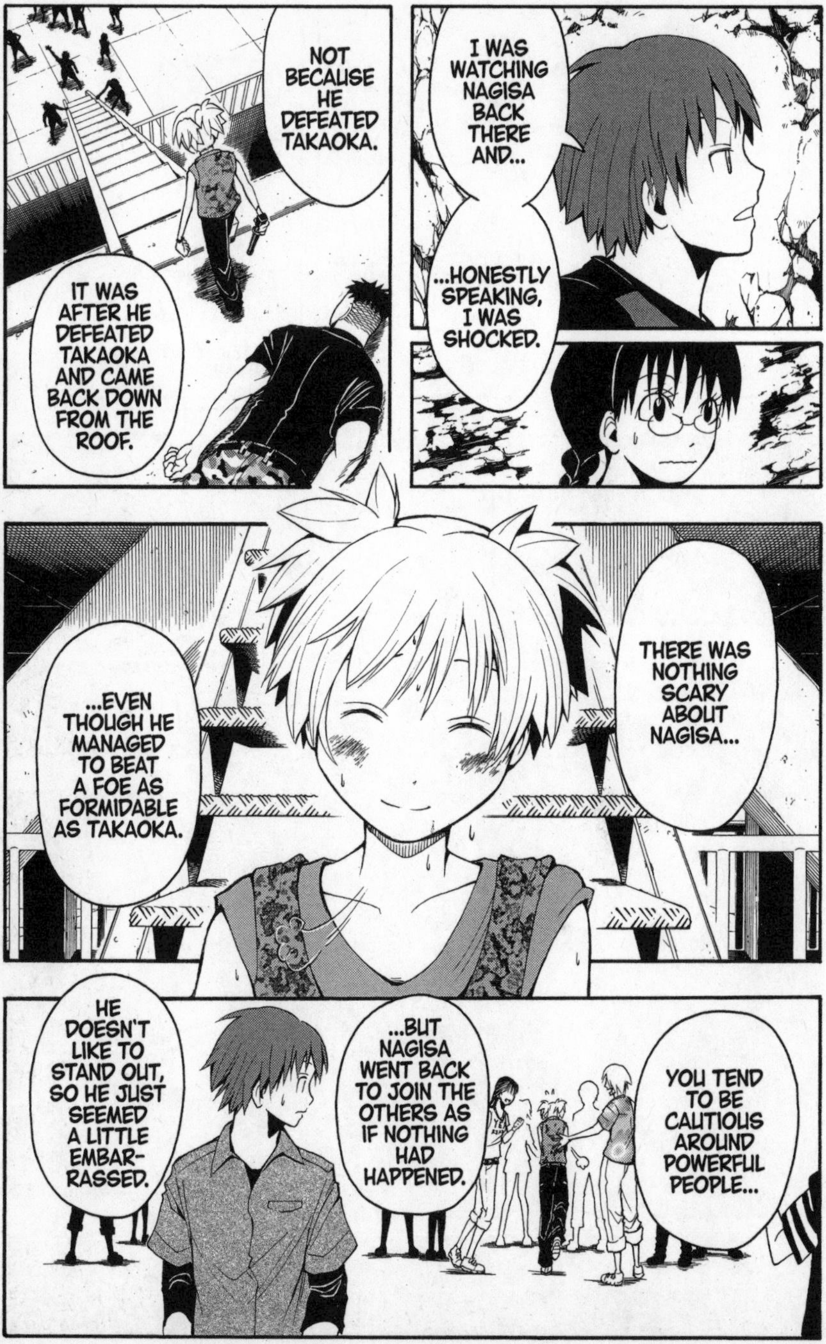
I WAS WATCHING NAGISA BACK THERE AND...
...HONESTLY SPEAKING, I WAS SHOCKED.
NOT BECAUSE HE DEFEATED TAKAOKA.
IT WAS AFTER HE DEFEATED TAKAOKA AND CAME BACK DOWN FROM THE ROOF.
THERE WAS NOTHING SCARY ABOUT NAGISA...
...EVEN THOUGH HE MANAGED TO BEAT A FOE AS FORMIDABLE AS TAKAOKA.
YOU TEND TO BE CAUTIOUS AROUND POWERFUL PEOPLE...
...BUT NAGISA WENT BACK TO JOIN THE OTHERS AS IF NOTHING HAD HAPPENED.
HE DOESN'T LIKE TO STAND OUT, SO HE JUST SEEMED A LITTLE EMBARRASSED.

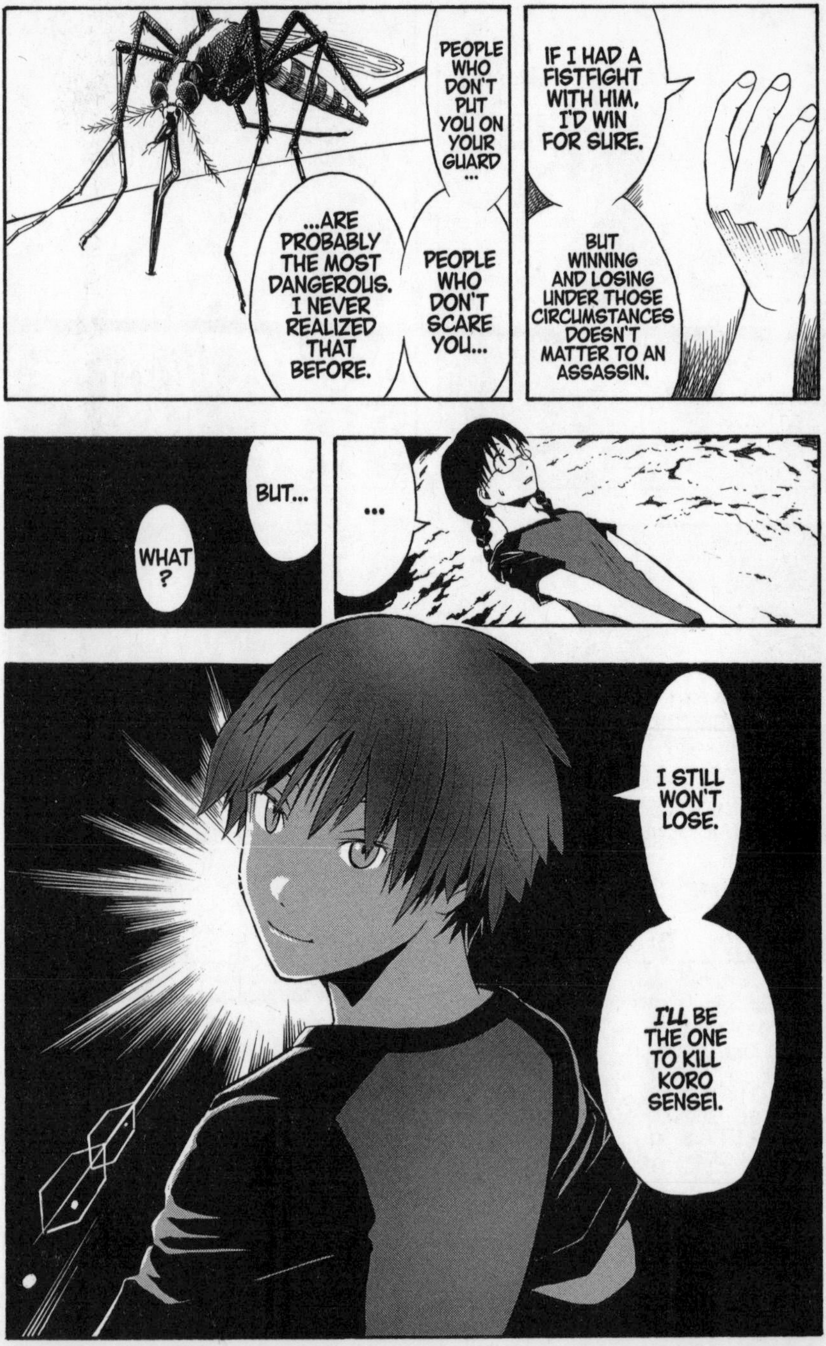
IF I HAD A FISTFIGHT WITH HIM, I'D WIN FOR SURE.
BUT WINNING AND LOSING UNDER THOSE CIRCUMSTANCES DOESN'T MATTER TO AN ASSASSIN.
PEOPLE WHO DON'T PUT YOU ON YOUR GUARD...
PEOPLE WHO DON'T SCARE YOU...
...ARE PROBABLY THE MOST DANGEROUS. I NEVER REALIZED THAT BEFORE.
...
BUT...
WHAT?
I STILL WON'T LOSE.
I'LL BE THE ONE TO KILL KORO SENSEI.

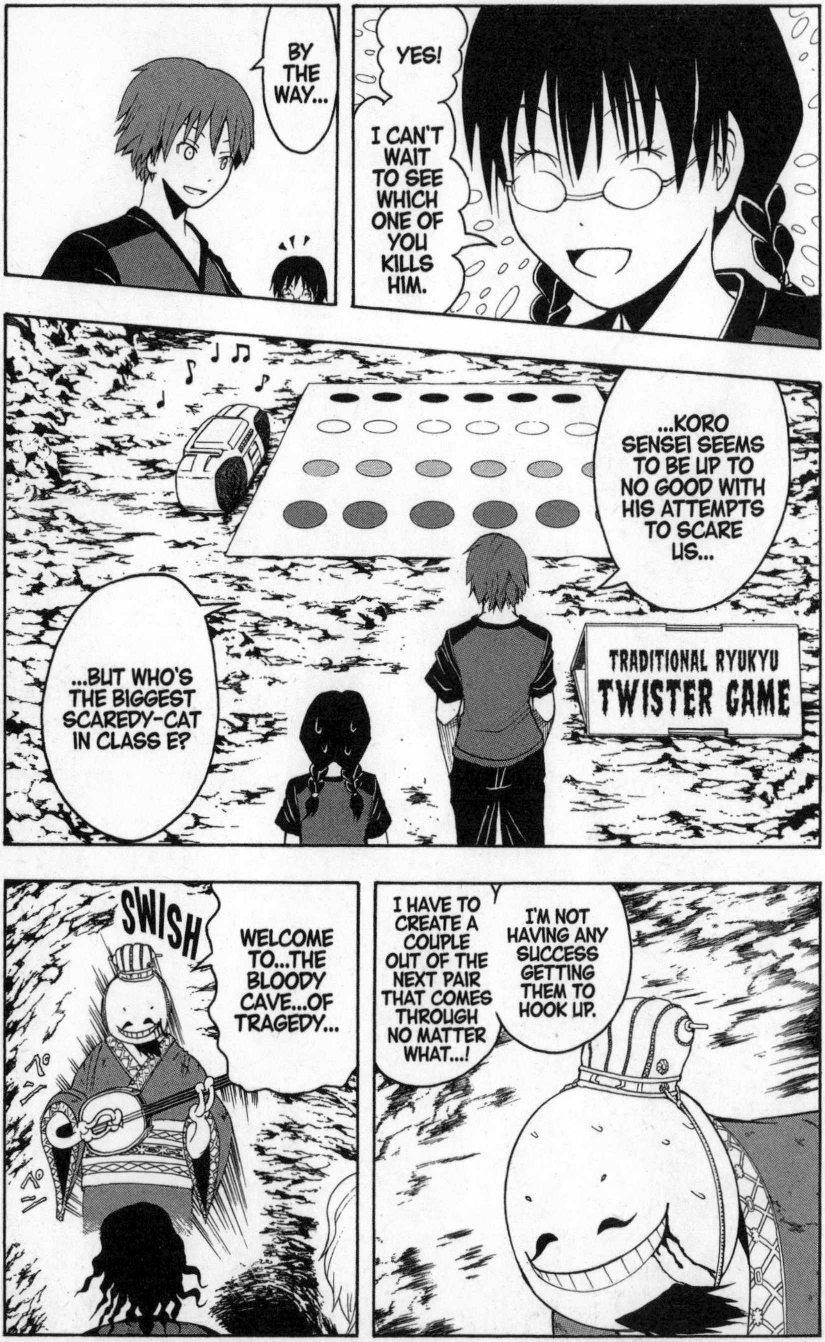
YES!
I CAN'T WAIT TO SEE WHICH ONE OF YOU KILLS HIM.
BY THE WAY...
...KORO SENSEI SEEMS TO BE UP TO NO GOOD WITH HIS ATTEMPTS TO SCARE US...
TRADITIONAL RYUKYU TWISTER GAME
...BUT WHO'S THE BIGGEST SCAREDY-CAT IN CLASS E?
I'M NOT HAVING ANY SUCCESS GETTING THEM TO HOOK UP.
I HAVE TO CREATE A COUPLE OUT OF THE NEXT PAIR THAT COMES THROUGH NO MATTER WHAT...!
SWISH
WELCOME TO...THE BLOODY CAVE...OF TRAGEDY...

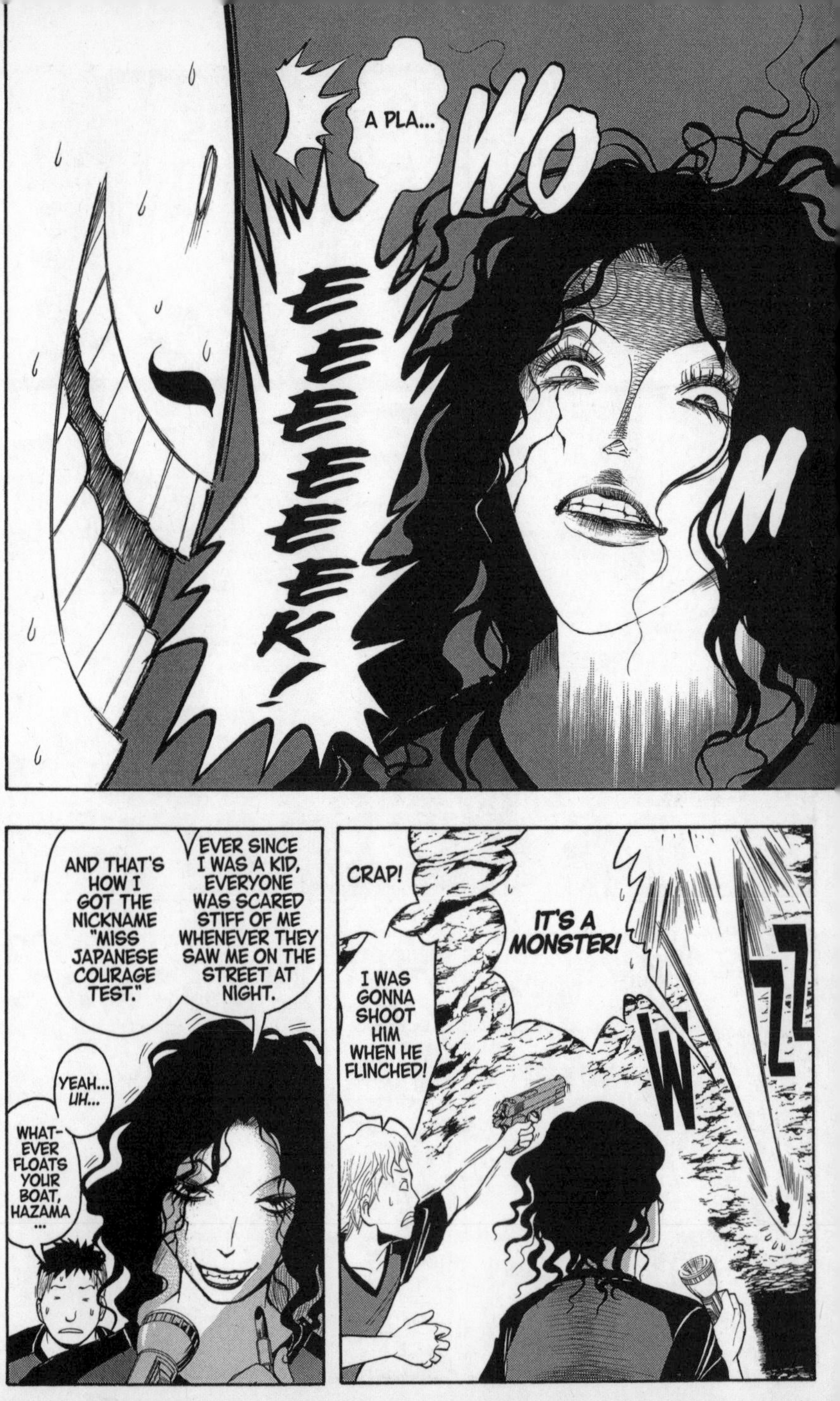
WO
M
A PLA...
EEEEEEK!
ZZ
IT'S A MONSTER!
CRAP!
I WAS GONNA SHOOT HIM WHEN HE FLINCHED!
W
EVER SINCE I WAS A KID, EVERYONE WAS SCARED STIFF OF ME WHENEVER THEY SAW ME ON THE STREET AT NIGHT.
AND THAT'S HOW I GOT THE NICKNAME "MISS JAPANESE COURAGE TEST."
YEAH... UH...
WHAT-EVER FLOATS YOUR BOAT, HAZAMA...

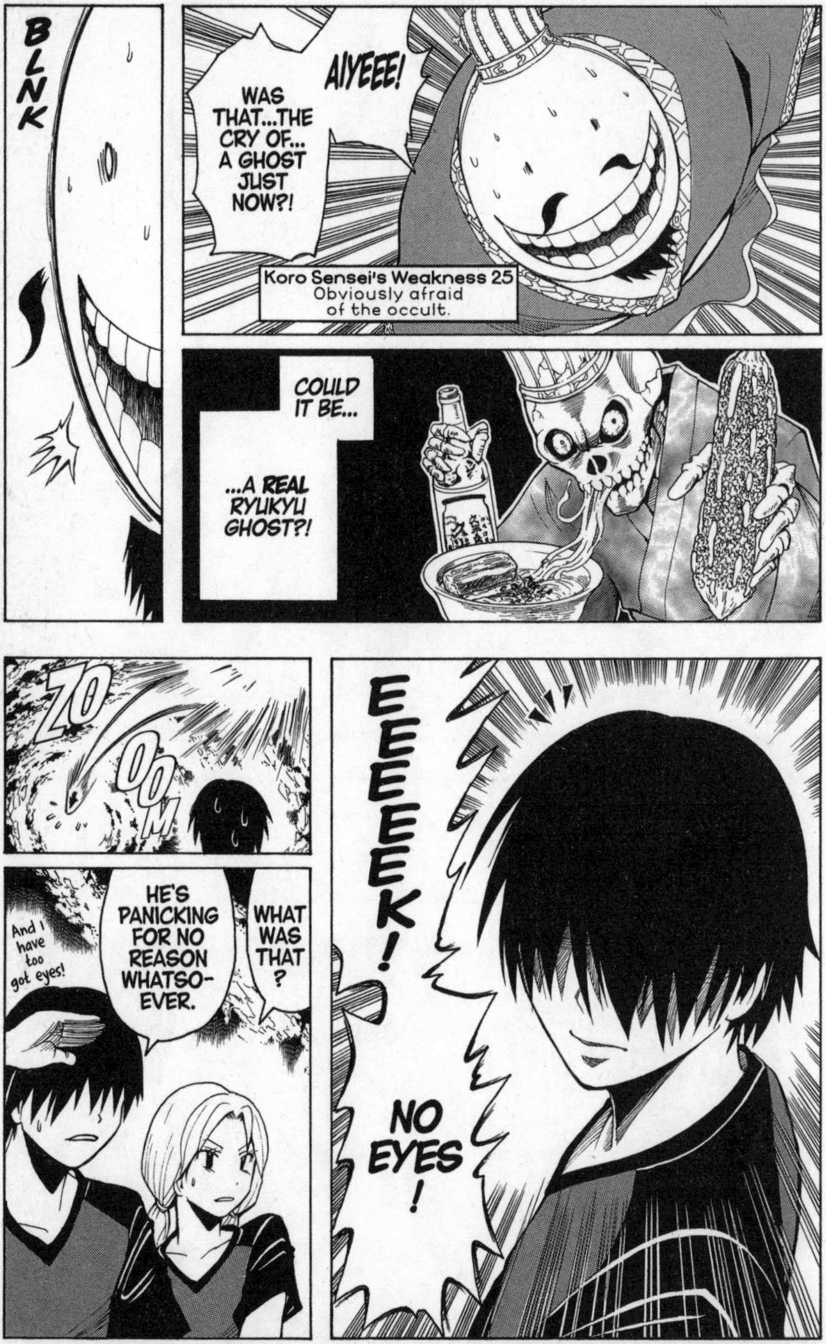
AIYEEE!
WAS THAT...THE CRY OF... A GHOST JUST NOW?!
Koro Sensei's Weakness 25 Obviously afraid of the occult.
COULD IT BE...
...A REAL RYUKYU GHOST?!
BLNK
EEEEEK!
NO EYES!
ZOOOOM
WHAT WAS THAT?
HE'S PANICKING FOR NO REASON WHATSO-EVER.
And I have too got eyes!

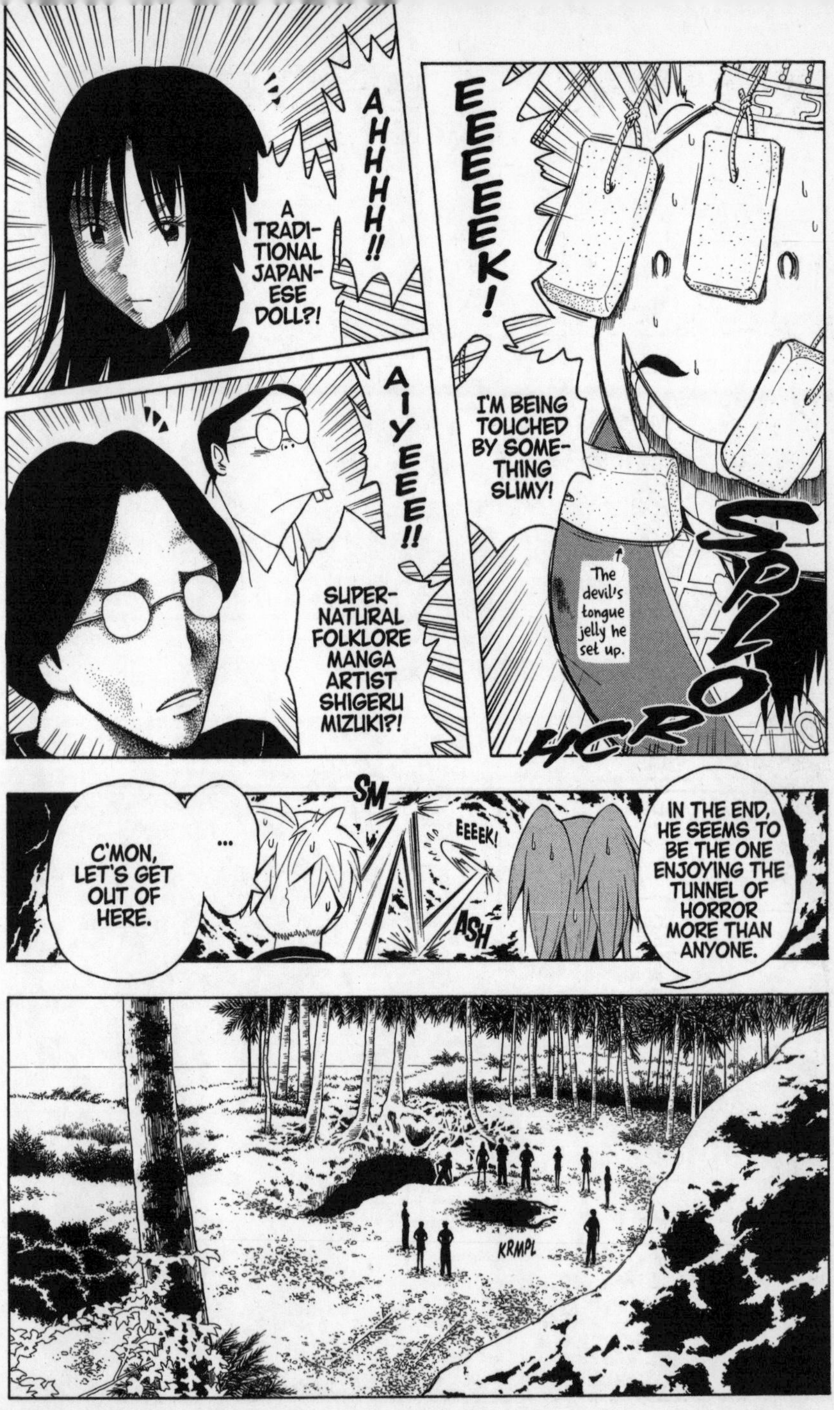
EEEEEEK!
I'M BEING TOUCHED BY SOME-THING SLIMY!
The devil's tongue jelly he set up.
SPLORCH
AHHHHH!!
A TRADI-TIONAL JAPAN-ESE DOLL?!
AIYEEEE!!
SUPER-NATURAL FOLKLORE MANGA ARTIST SHIGERU MIZUKI?!
IN THE END, HE SEEMS TO BE THE ONE ENJOYING THE TUNNEL OF HORROR MORE THAN ANYONE.
EEEEK!
SMASH
...
C'MON, LET'S GET OUT OF HERE.
KRMPL

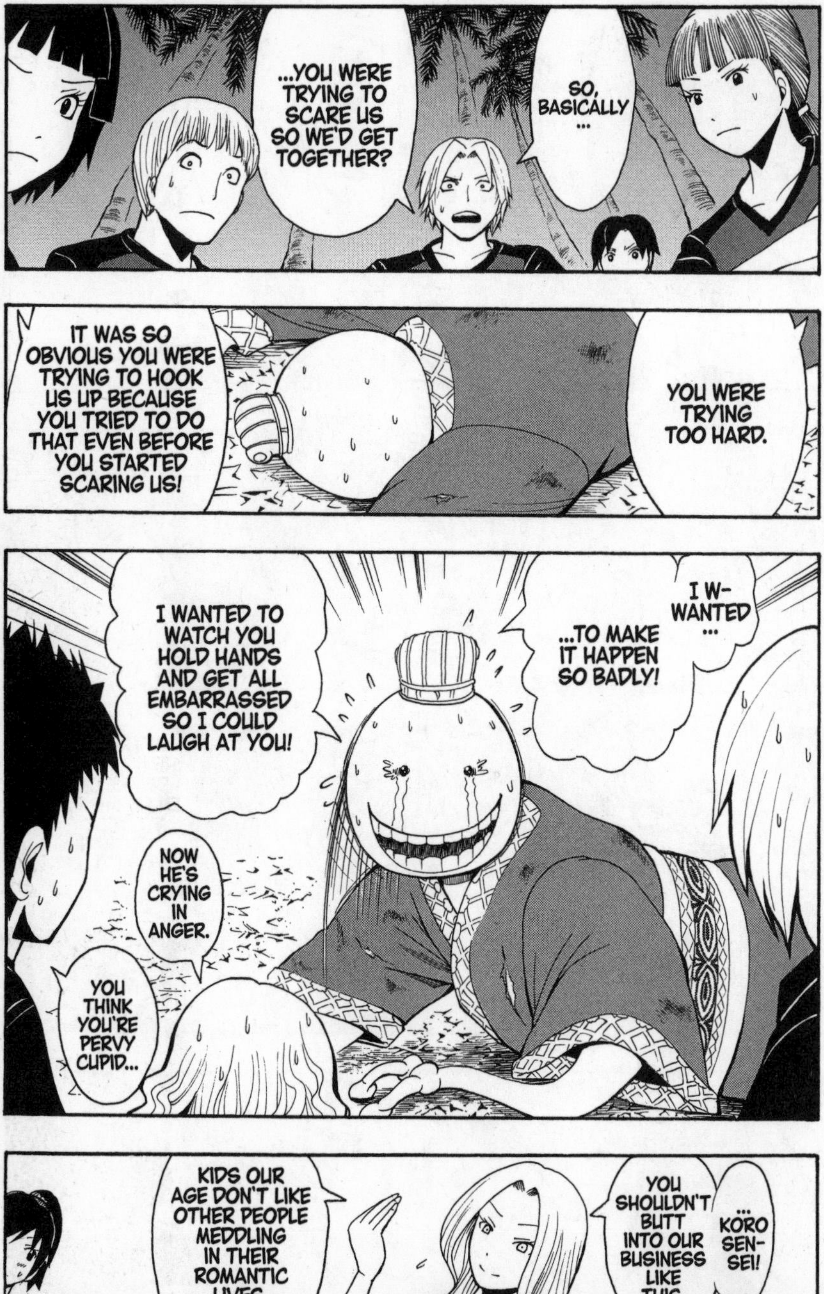
SO, BASICALLY...
...YOU WERE TRYING TO SCARE US SO WE'D GET TOGETHER?
YOU WERE TRYING TOO HARD.
IT WAS SO OBVIOUS YOU WERE TRYING TO HOOK US UP BECAUSE YOU TRIED TO DO THAT EVEN BEFORE YOU STARTED SCARING US!
I W-WANTED...
...TO MAKE IT HAPPEN SO BADLY!
I WANTED TO WATCH YOU HOLD HANDS AND GET ALL EMBARRASSED SO I COULD LAUGH AT YOU!
NOW HE'S CRYING IN ANGER.
YOU THINK YOU'RE PERVY CUPID...
...KORO SENSEI!
YOU SHOULDN'T BUTT INTO OUR BUSINESS LIKE THIS.
KIDS OUR AGE DON'T LIKE OTHER PEOPLE MEDDLING IN THEIR ROMANTIC LIVES, YOU KNOW.

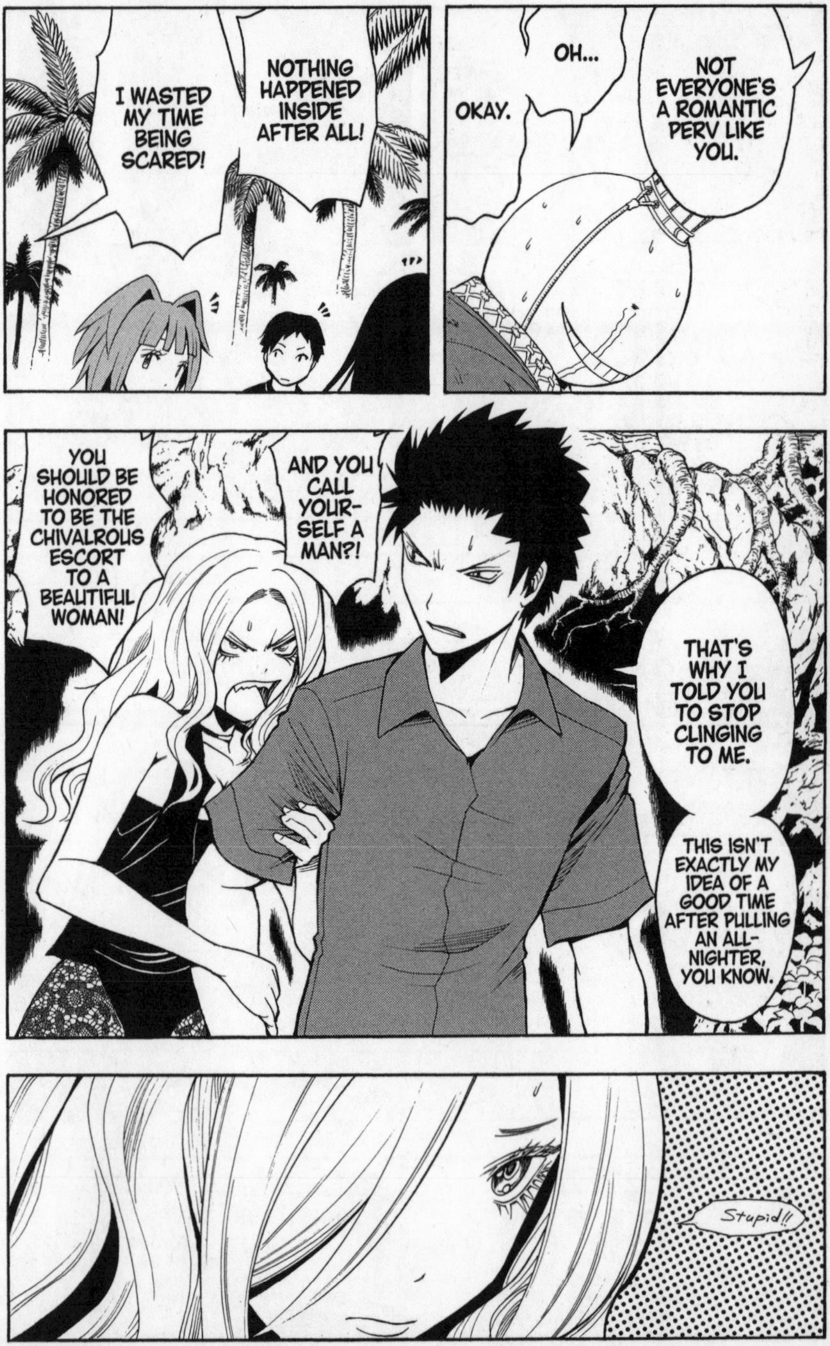
NOT EVERYONE'S A ROMANTIC PERV LIKE YOU.
OH... OKAY.
NOTHING HAPPENED INSIDE AFTER ALL!
I WASTED MY TIME BEING SCARED!
THAT'S WHY I TOLD YOU TO STOP CLINGING TO ME.
THIS ISN'T EXACTLY MY IDEA OF A GOOD TIME AFTER PULLING AN ALL-NIGHTER, YOU KNOW.
AND YOU CALL YOUR-SELF A MAN?!
YOU SHOULD BE HONORED TO BE THE CHIVALROUS ESCORT TO A BEAUTIFUL WOMAN!
Stupid!!

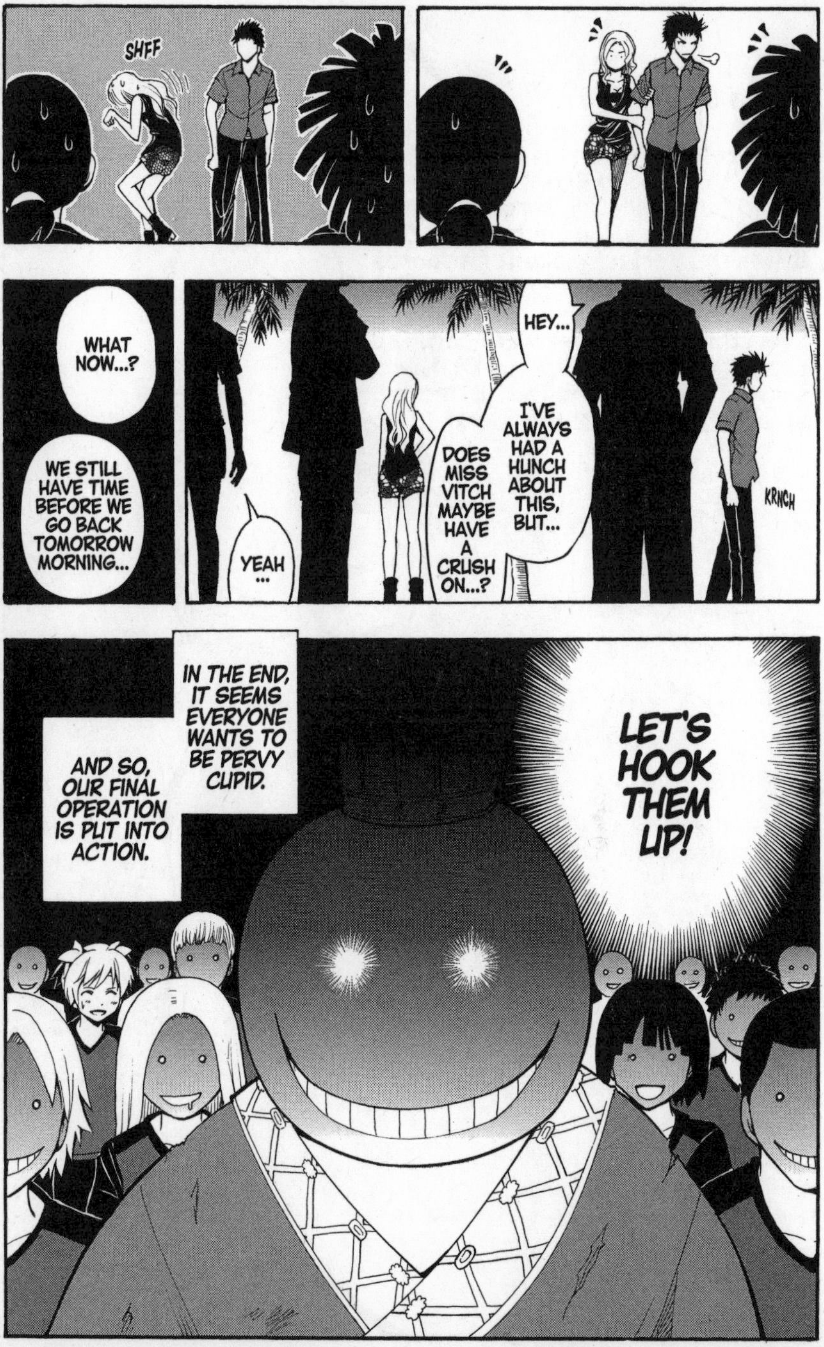
SHFF
HEY...
I'VE ALWAYS HAD A HUNCH ABOUT THIS, BUT...
KRNCH
DOES MISS VITCH MAYBE HAVE A CRUSH ON...?
YEAH ...
WHAT NOW...?
WE STILL HAVE TIME BEFORE WE GO BACK TOMORROW MORNING...
LET'S HOOK THEM UP!
IN THE END, IT SEEMS EVERYONE WANTS TO BE PERVY CUPID.
AND SO, OUR FINAL OPERATION IS PUT INTO ACTION.

Okinawa Island

After getting my driver's license, I found the time to drive around the island for a four-day, three-night trip. Everybody drove so courteously that it was the perfect place for a rookie driver to practice.

Everything I ate there was good. I still can't forget the traditional Okinawan soki soba I had in the mountainous area in the north of the island.

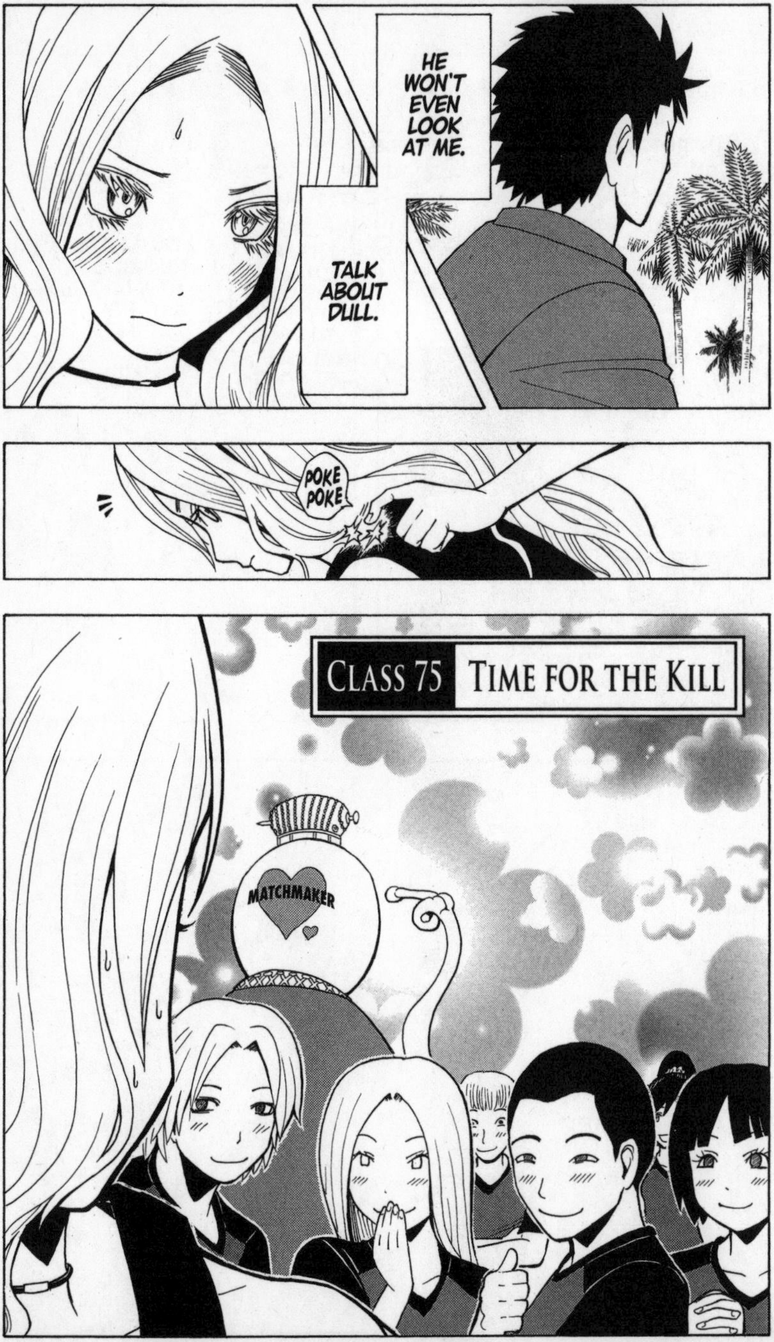
HE WON'T EVEN LOOK AT ME.
TALK ABOUT DULL.
POKE POKE
CLASS 75 TIME FOR THE KILL
MATCHMAKER

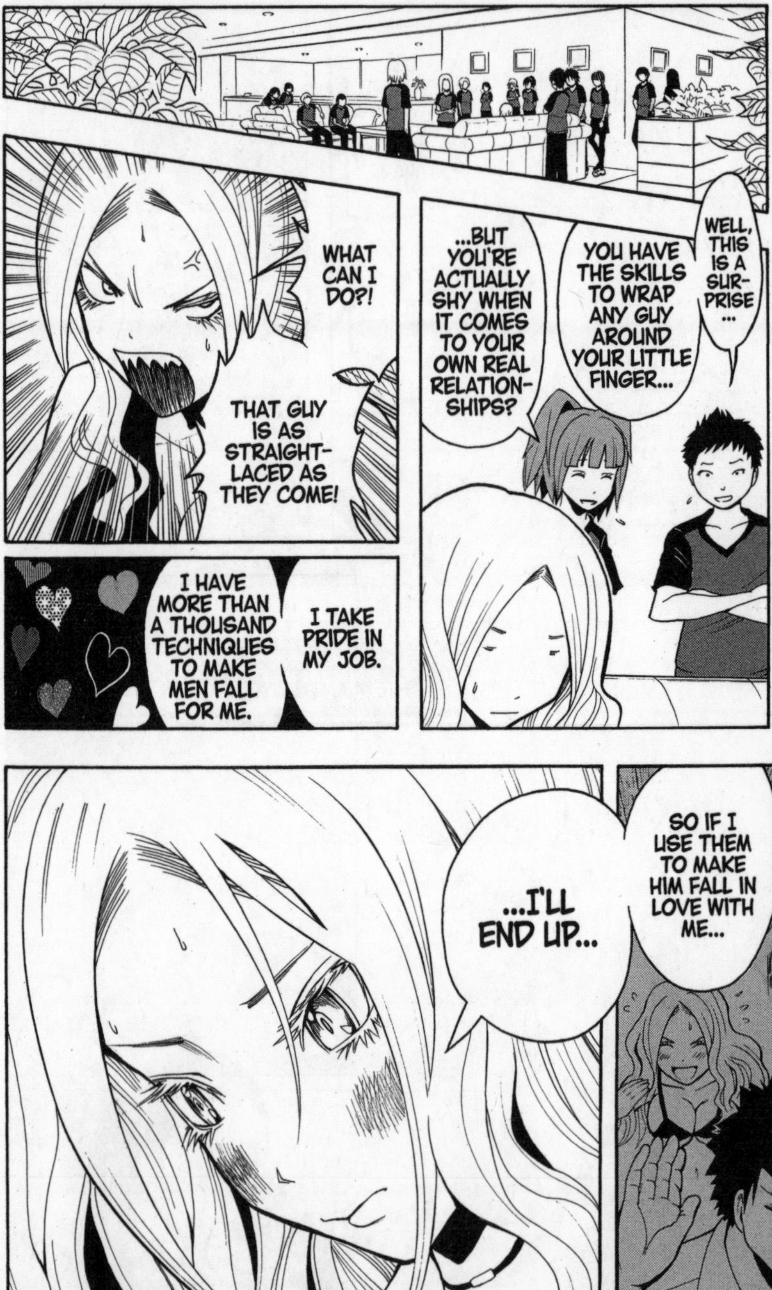
WELL, THIS IS A SURPRISE...
YOU HAVE THE SKILLS TO WRAP ANY GUY AROUND YOUR LITTLE FINGER...
...BUT YOU'RE ACTUALLY SHY WHEN IT COMES TO YOUR OWN REAL RELATIONSHIPS?
WHAT CAN I DO?!
THAT GUY IS AS STRAIGHT-LACED AS THEY COME!
I TAKE PRIDE IN MY JOB.
I HAVE MORE THAN A THOUSAND TECHNIQUES TO MAKE MEN FALL FOR ME.
SO IF I USE THEM TO MAKE HIM FALL IN LOVE WITH ME...
...I'LL END UP...

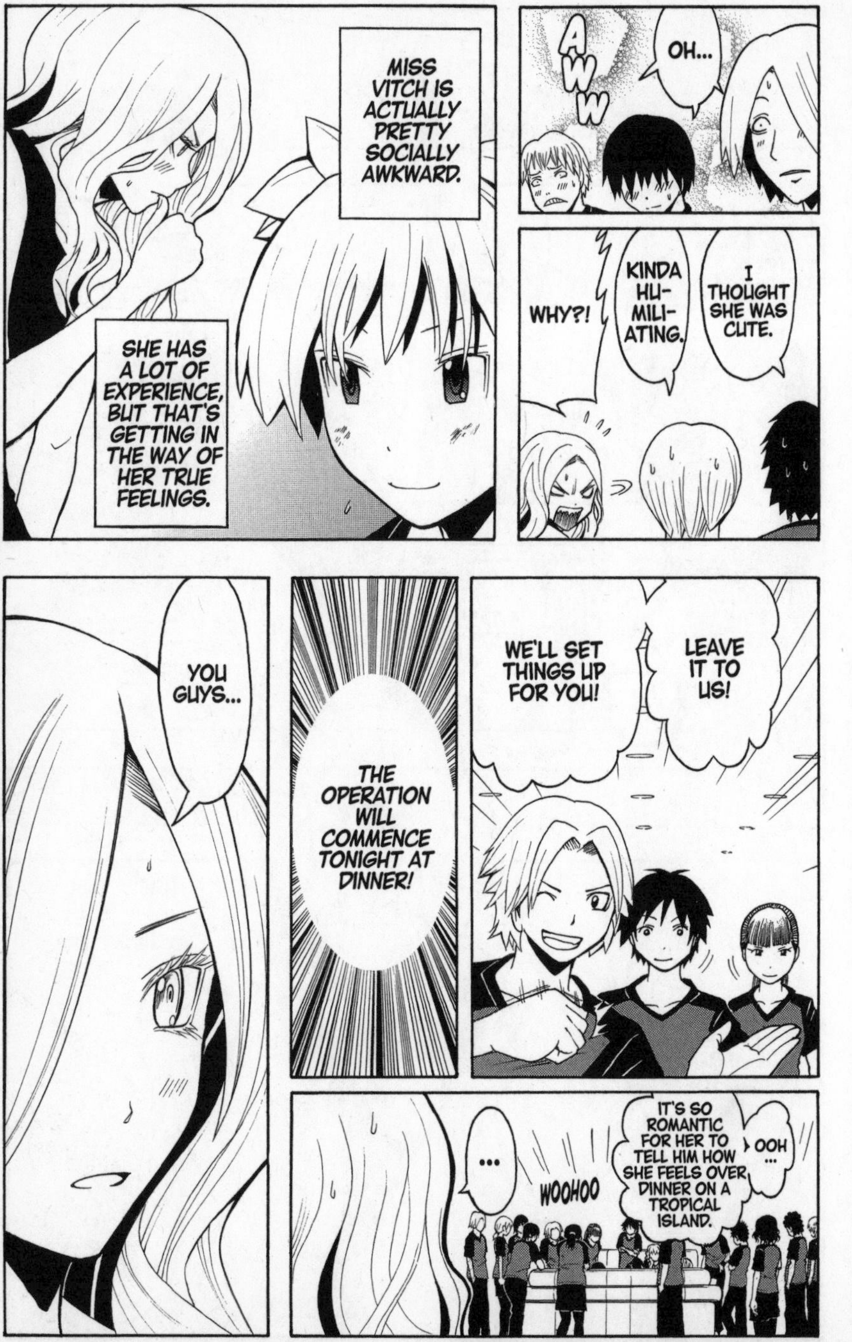
OH...
AWWW
I THOUGHT SHE WAS CUTE.
KINDA HUMILIATING.
WHY?!
MISS VITCH IS ACTUALLY PRETTY SOCIALLY AWKWARD.
SHE HAS A LOT OF EXPERIENCE, BUT THAT'S GETTING IN THE WAY OF HER TRUE FEELINGS.
LEAVE IT TO US!
WE'LL SET THINGS UP FOR YOU!
THE OPERATION WILL COMMENCE TONIGHT AT DINNER!
OOH ...
IT'S SO ROMANTIC FOR HER TO TELL HIM HOW SHE FEELS OVER DINNER ON A TROPICAL ISLAND.
WOOHOO
...
YOU GUYS...

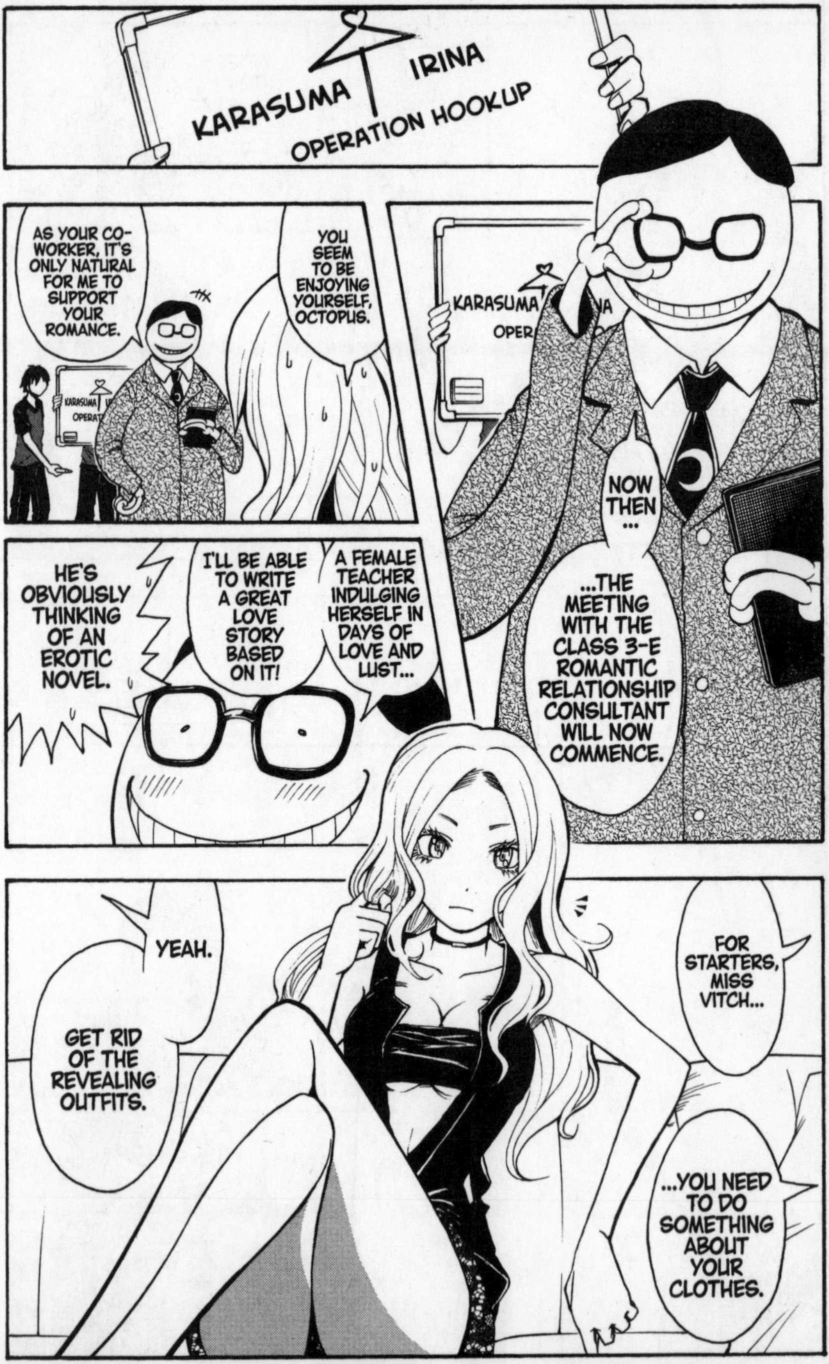
KARASUMA IRINA
OPERATION HOOKUP
NOW THEN...
...THE MEETING WITH THE CLASS 3-E ROMANTIC RELATIONSHIP CONSULTANT WILL NOW COMMENCE.
YOU SEEM TO BE ENJOYING YOURSELF, OCTOPUS.
AS YOUR CO-WORKER, IT'S ONLY NATURAL FOR ME TO SUPPORT YOUR ROMANCE.
A FEMALE TEACHER INDULGING HERSELF IN DAYS OF LOVE AND LUST...
I'LL BE ABLE TO WRITE A GREAT LOVE STORY BASED ON IT!
HE'S OBVIOUSLY THINKING OF AN EROTIC NOVEL.
FOR STARTERS, MISS VITCH...
...YOU NEED TO DO SOMETHING ABOUT YOUR CLOTHES.
YEAH.
GET RID OF THE REVEALING OUTFITS.

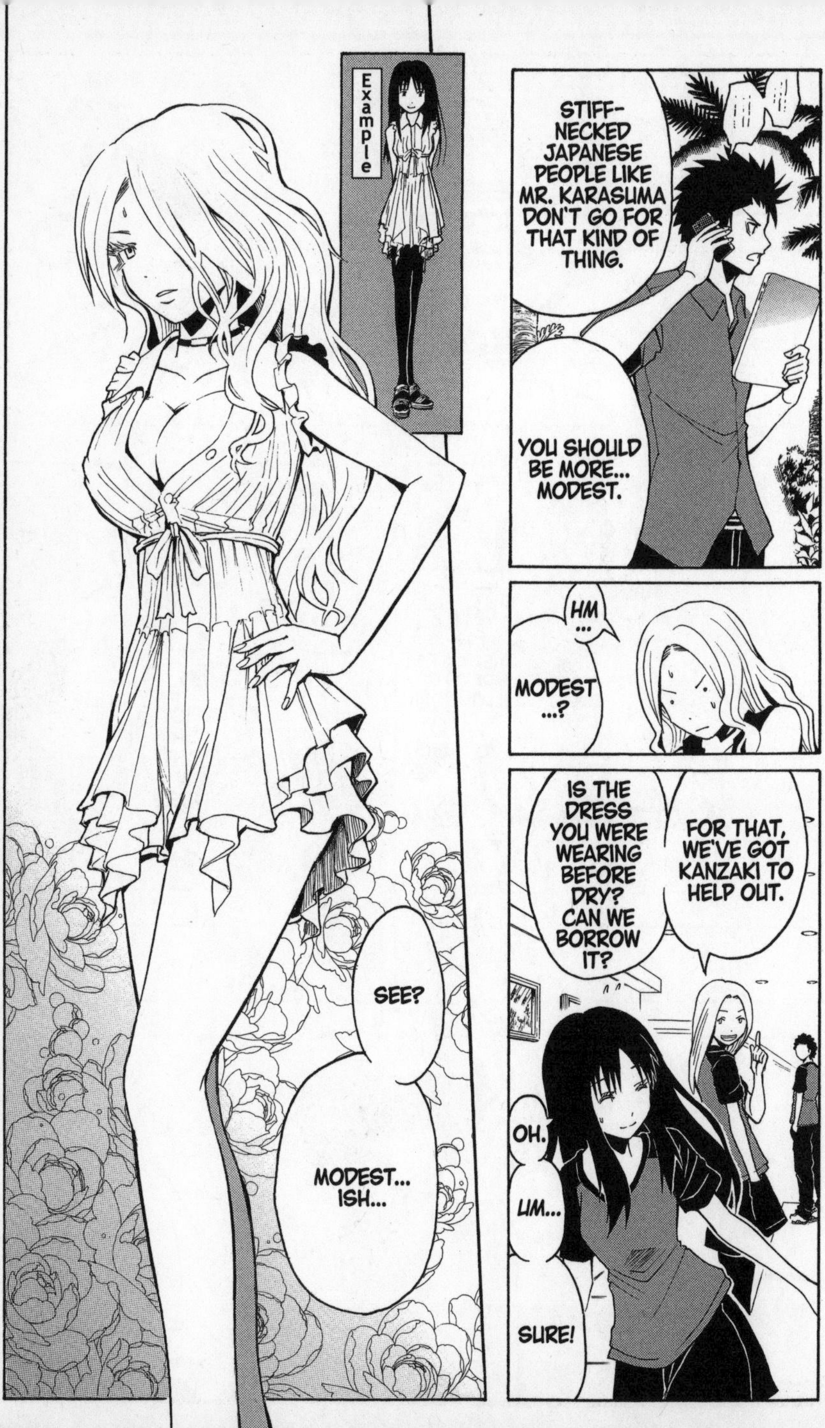
STIFF-NECKED JAPANESE PEOPLE LIKE MR. KARASUMA DON'T GO FOR THAT KIND OF THING.
YOU SHOULD BE MORE... MODEST.
HM...
MODEST...?
FOR THAT, WE'VE GOT KANZAKI TO HELP OUT.
IS THE DRESS YOU WERE WEARING BEFORE DRY? CAN WE BORROW IT?
OH.
UM...
SURE!
Example
SEE?
MODEST... ISH...

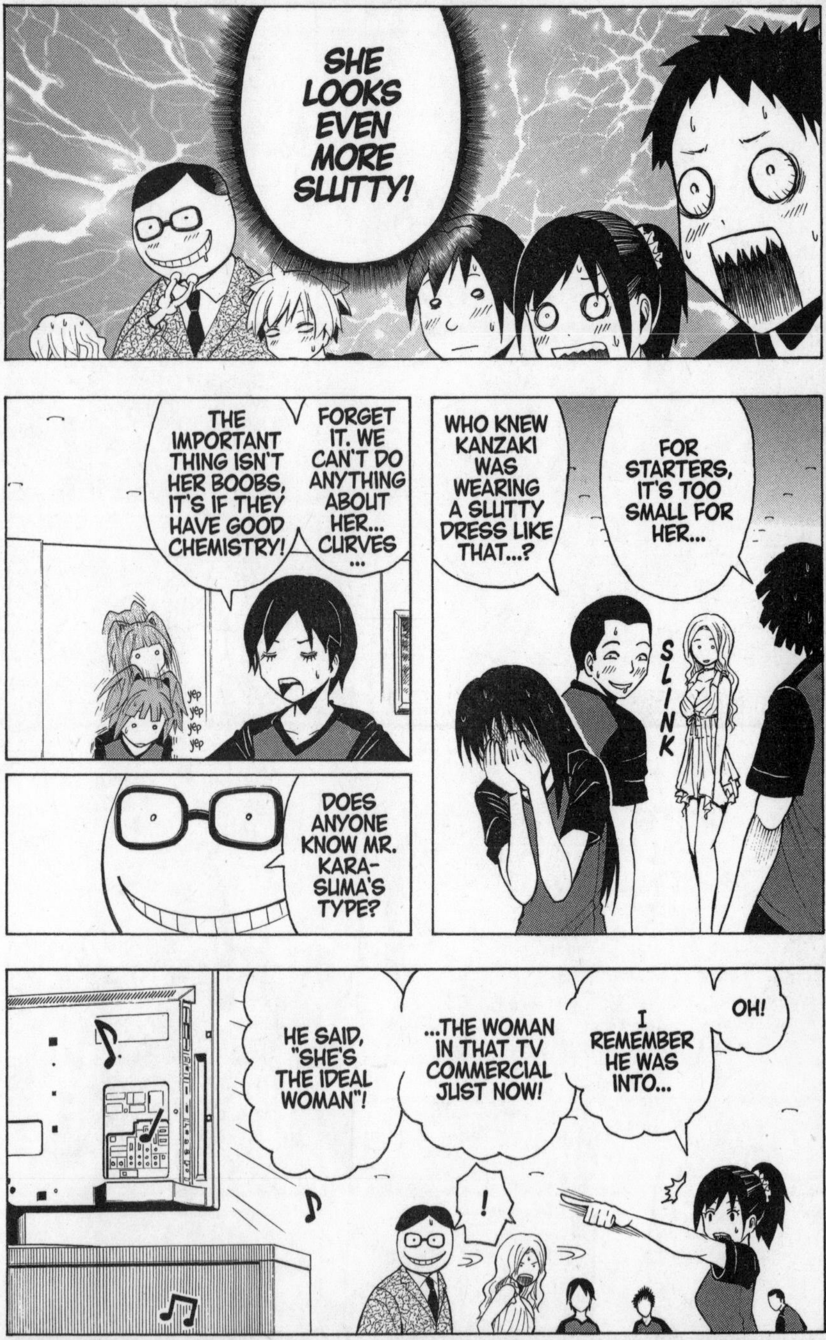
SHE LOOKS EVEN MORE SLUTTY!
FOR STARTERS, IT'S TOO SMALL FOR HER...
WHO KNEW KANZAKI WAS WEARING A SLUTTY DRESS LIKE THAT...?
SLINK
FORGET IT. WE CAN'T DO ANYTHING ABOUT HER... CURVES ...
THE IMPORTANT THING ISN'T HER BOOBS, IT'S IF THEY HAVE GOOD CHEMISTRY!
yep yep yep yep
DOES ANYONE KNOW MR. KARA-SUMA'S TYPE?
OH!
I REMEMBER HE WAS INTO...
...THE WOMAN IN THAT TV COMMERCIAL JUST NOW!
HE SAID, "SHE'S THE IDEAL WOMAN"!
!

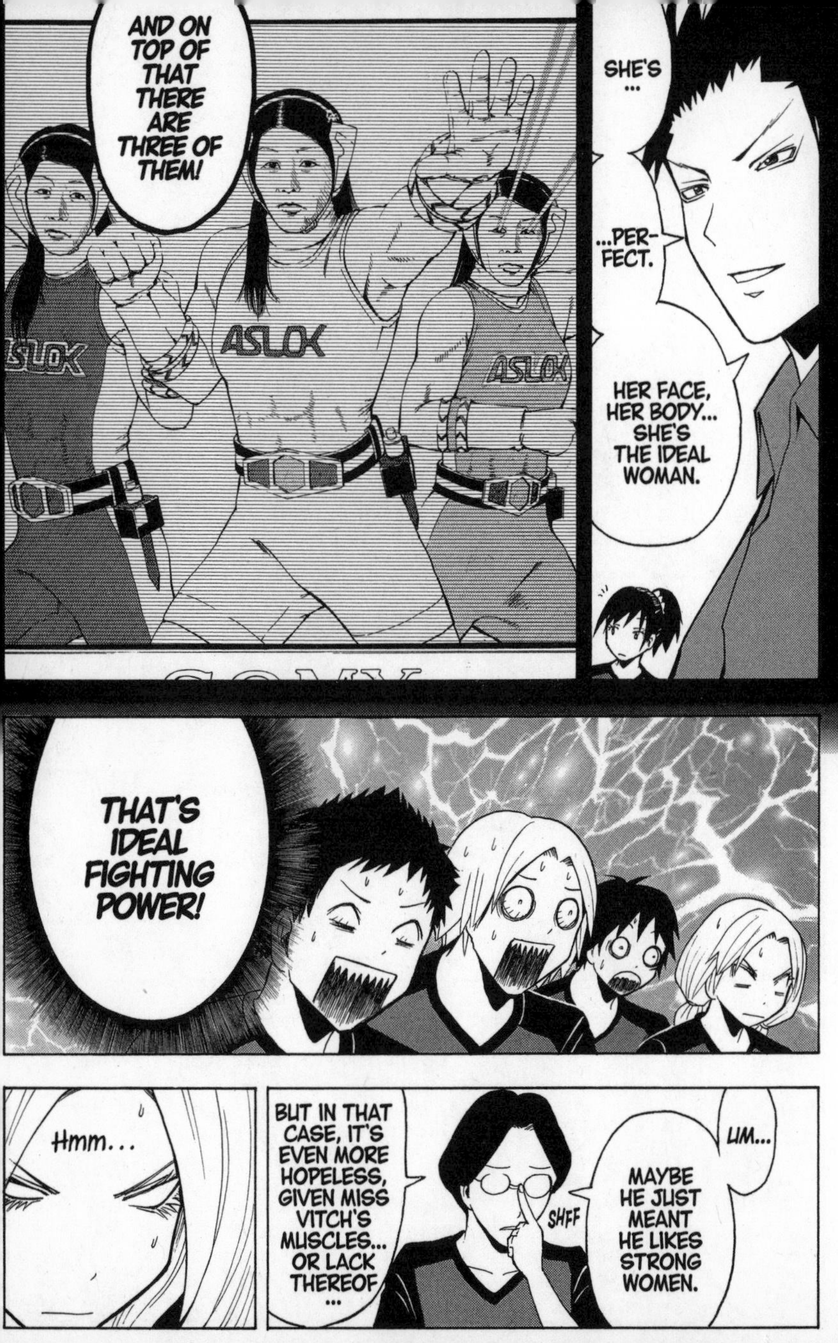

SHE'S ...
...PER-FECT.
HER FACE, HER BODY... SHE'S THE IDEAL WOMAN.
AND ON TOP OF THAT THERE ARE THREE OF THEM!
ASLOK
ASLOK
ASLOK
THAT'S IDEAL FIGHTING POWER!
UM...
MAYBE HE JUST MEANT HE LIKES STRONG WOMEN.
SHFF
BUT IN THAT CASE, IT'S EVEN MORE HOPELESS, GIVEN MISS VITCH'S MUSCLES... OR LACK THEREOF ...
Hmm...

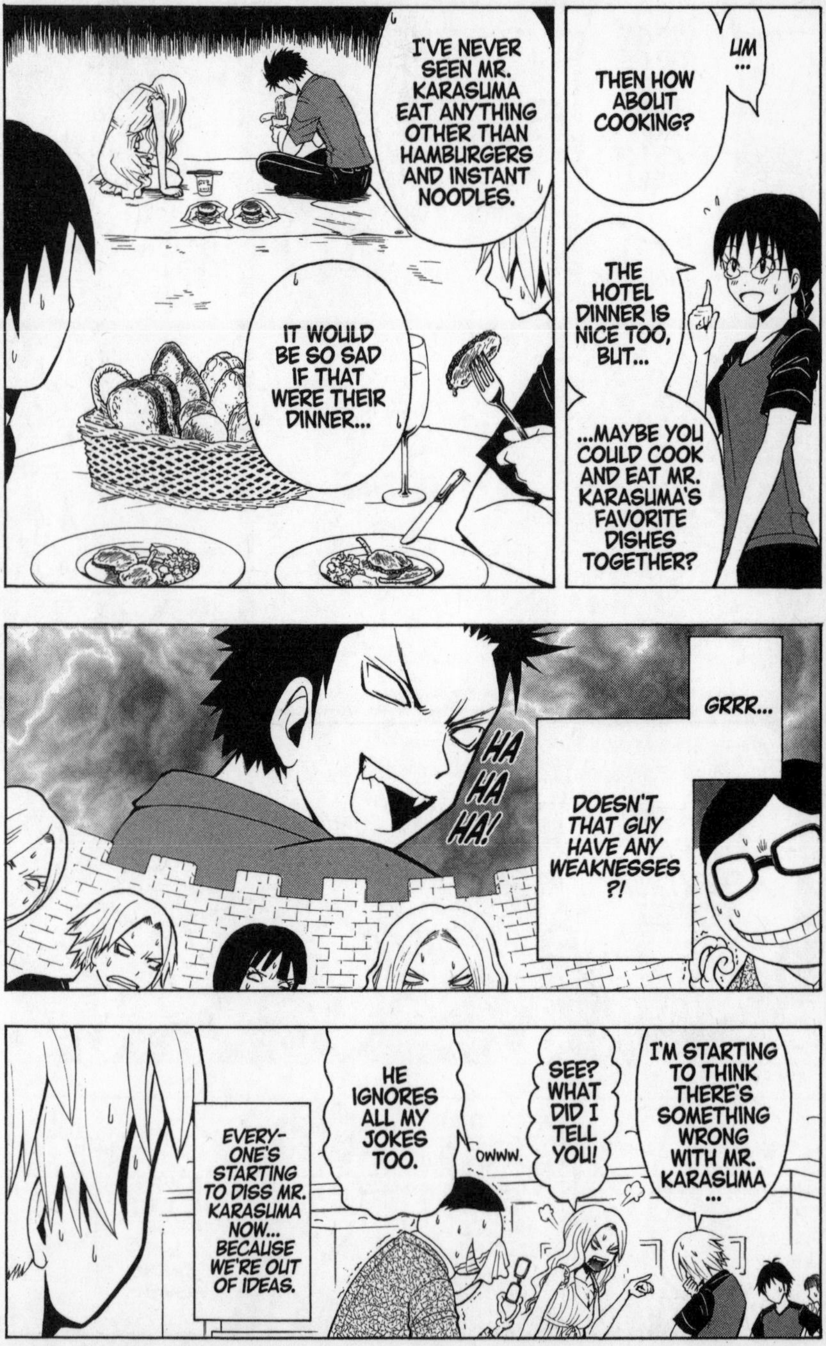
UM...
THEN HOW ABOUT COOKING?
THE HOTEL DINNER IS NICE TOO, BUT...
...MAYBE YOU COULD COOK AND EAT MR. KARASUMA'S FAVORITE DISHES TOGETHER?
I'VE NEVER SEEN MR. KARASUMA EAT ANYTHING OTHER THAN HAMBURGERS AND INSTANT NOODLES.
IT WOULD BE SO SAD IF THAT WERE THEIR DINNER...
GRRR...
HA HA HA HA!
DOESN'T THAT GUY HAVE ANY WEAKNESSES?!
I'M STARTING TO THINK THERE'S SOMETHING WRONG WITH MR. KARASUMA...
SEE? WHAT DID I TELL YOU!
OWWW.
HE IGNORES ALL MY JOKES TOO.
EVERYONE'S STARTING TO DISS MR. KARASUMA NOW... BECAUSE WE'RE OUT OF IDEAS.

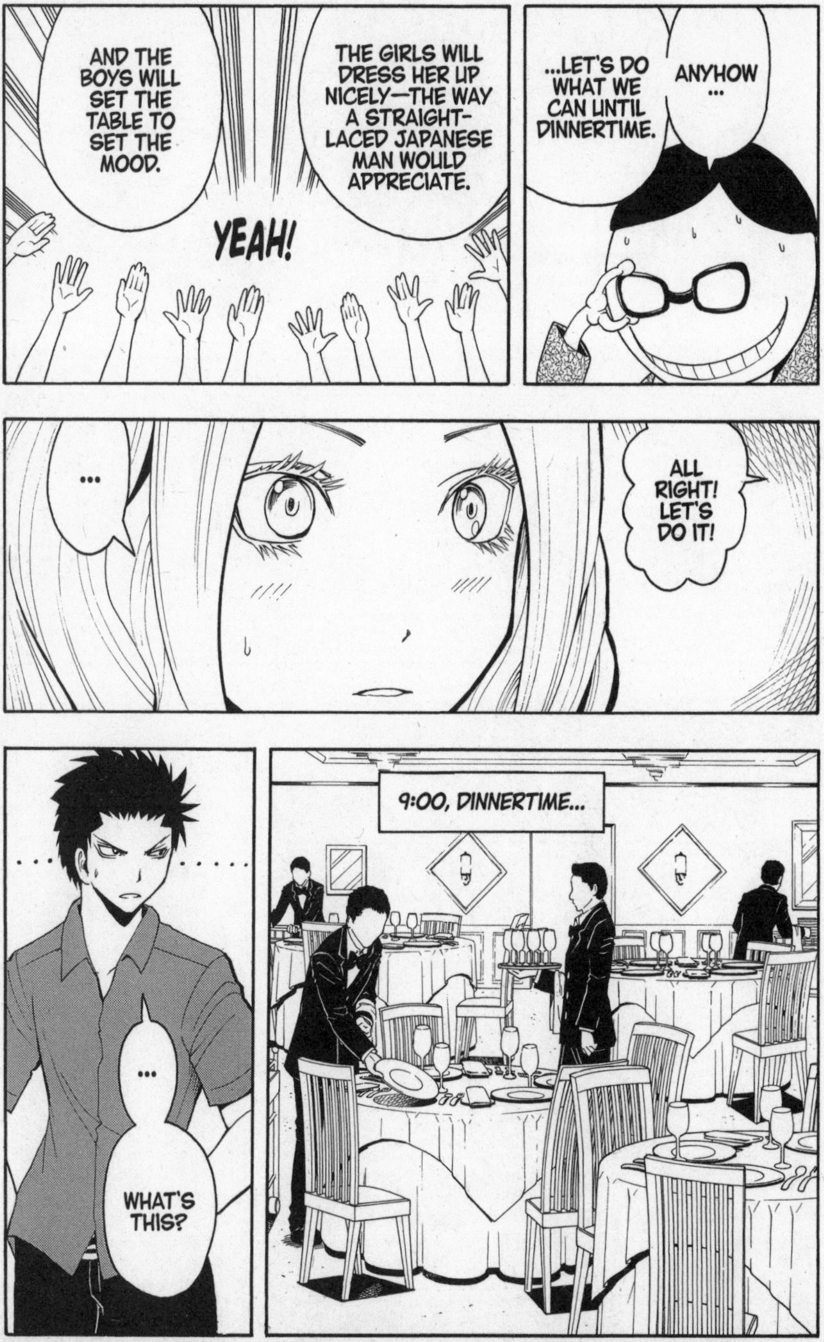
ANYHOW...
...LET'S DO WHAT WE CAN UNTIL DINNERTIME.
THE GIRLS WILL DRESS HER UP NICELY—THE WAY A STRAIGHT-LACED JAPANESE MAN WOULD APPRECIATE.
AND THE BOYS WILL SET THE TABLE TO SET THE MOOD.
YEAH!
ALL RIGHT! LET'S DO IT!
...
9:00, DINNERTIME...
...
WHAT'S THIS?

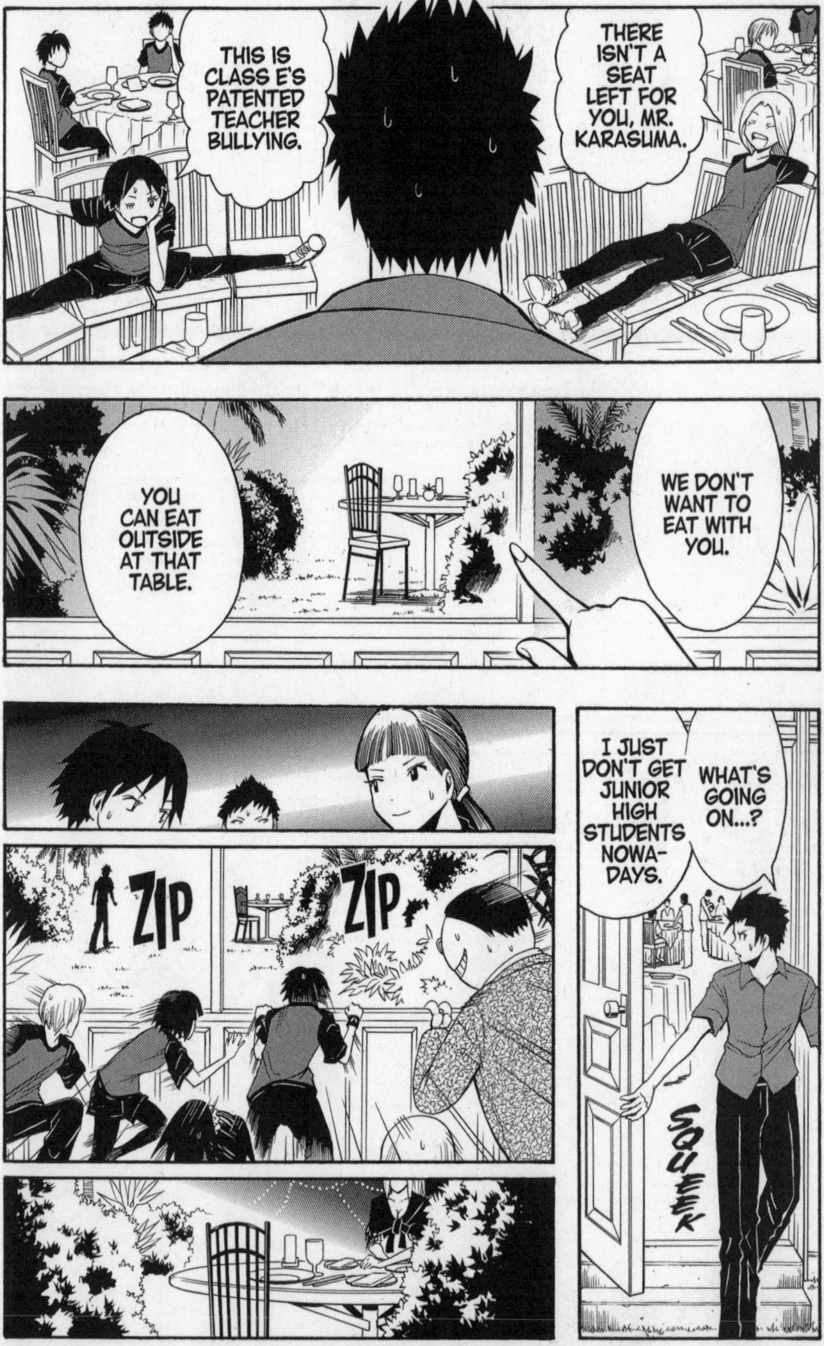
THERE ISN'T A SEAT LEFT FOR YOU, MR. KARASUMA.
THIS IS CLASS E'S PATENTED TEACHER BULLYING.
WE DON'T WANT TO EAT WITH YOU.
YOU CAN EAT OUTSIDE AT THAT TABLE.
WHAT'S GOING ON...?
I JUST DON'T GET JUNIOR HIGH STUDENTS NOWA-DAYS.
SQUEEK
ZIP
ZIP

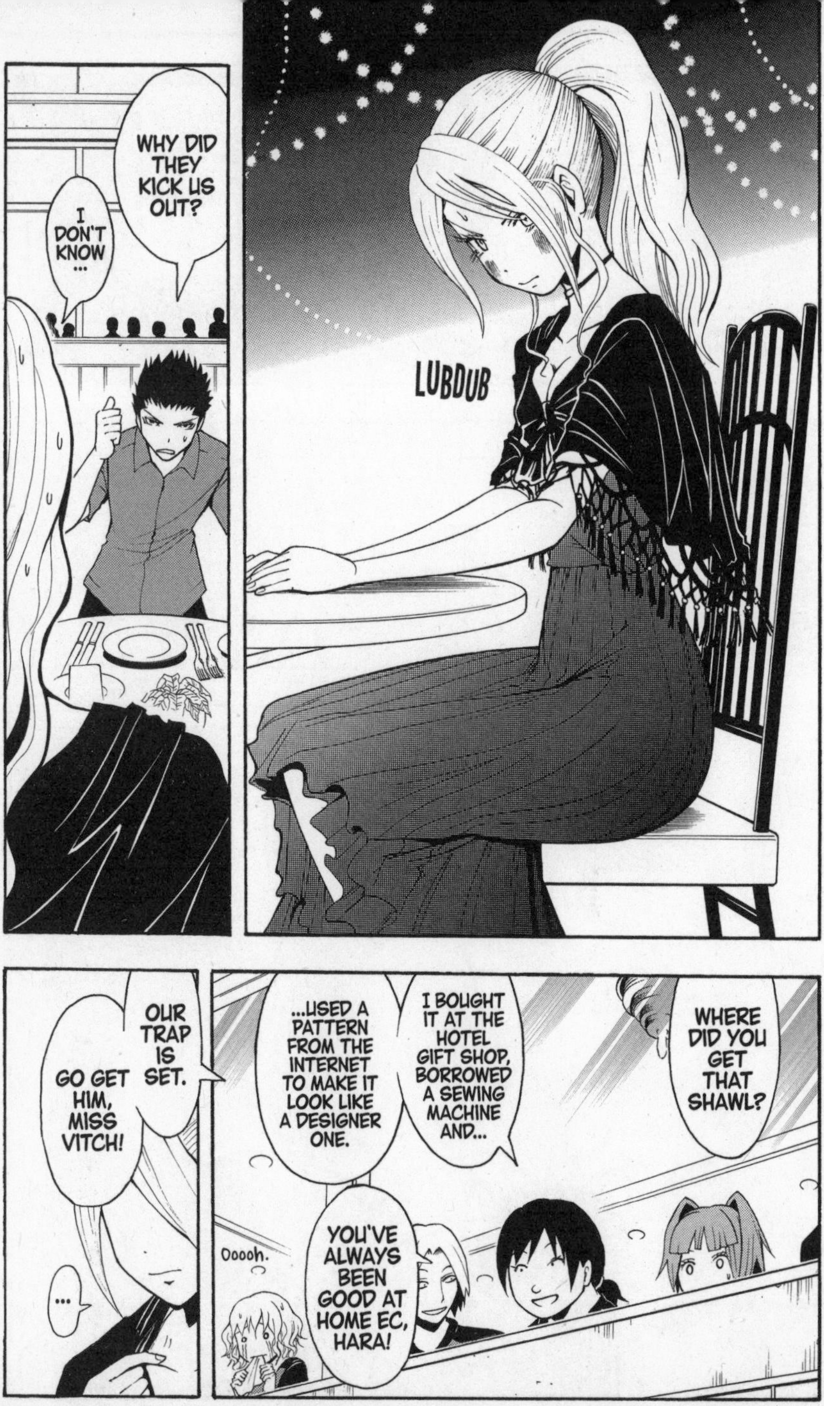
LUBDUB
WHY DID THEY KICK US OUT?
I DON'T KNOW...
WHERE DID YOU GET THAT SHAWL?
I BOUGHT IT AT THE HOTEL GIFT SHOP, BORROWED A SEWING MACHINE AND...
...USED A PATTERN FROM THE INTERNET TO MAKE IT LOOK LIKE A DESIGNER ONE.
YOU'VE ALWAYS BEEN GOOD AT HOME EC, HARA!
Ooooh.
OUR TRAP IS SET.
GO GET HIM, MISS VITCH!
...

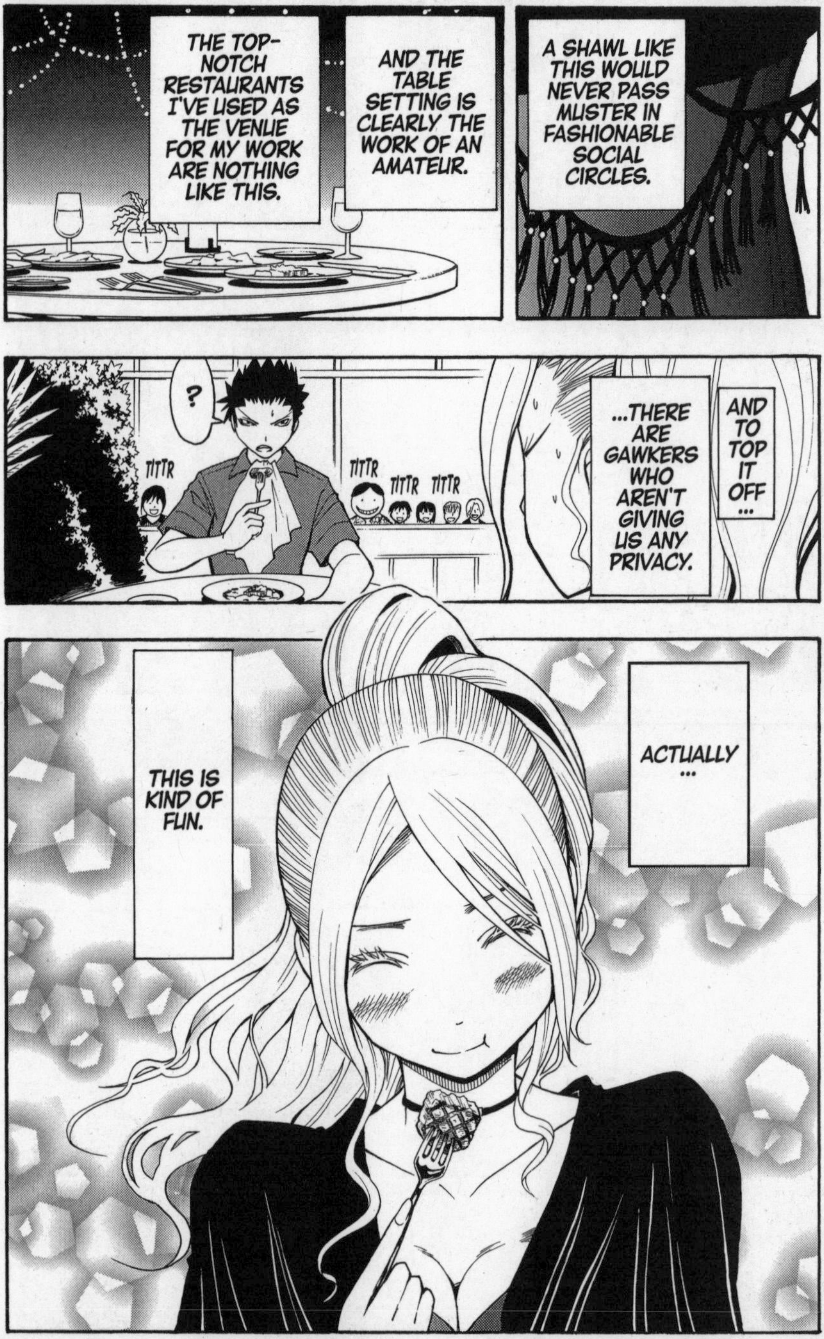
A SHAWL LIKE THIS WOULD NEVER PASS MUSTER IN FASHIONABLE SOCIAL CIRCLES.
AND THE TABLE SETTING IS CLEARLY THE WORK OF AN AMATEUR.
THE TOP-NOTCH RESTAURANTS I'VE USED AS THE VENUE FOR MY WORK ARE NOTHING LIKE THIS.
AND TO TOP IT OFF...
...THERE ARE GAWKERS WHO AREN'T GIVING US ANY PRIVACY.
?
TITTR
TITTR
TITTR
TITTR
ACTUALLY...
THIS IS KIND OF FUN.

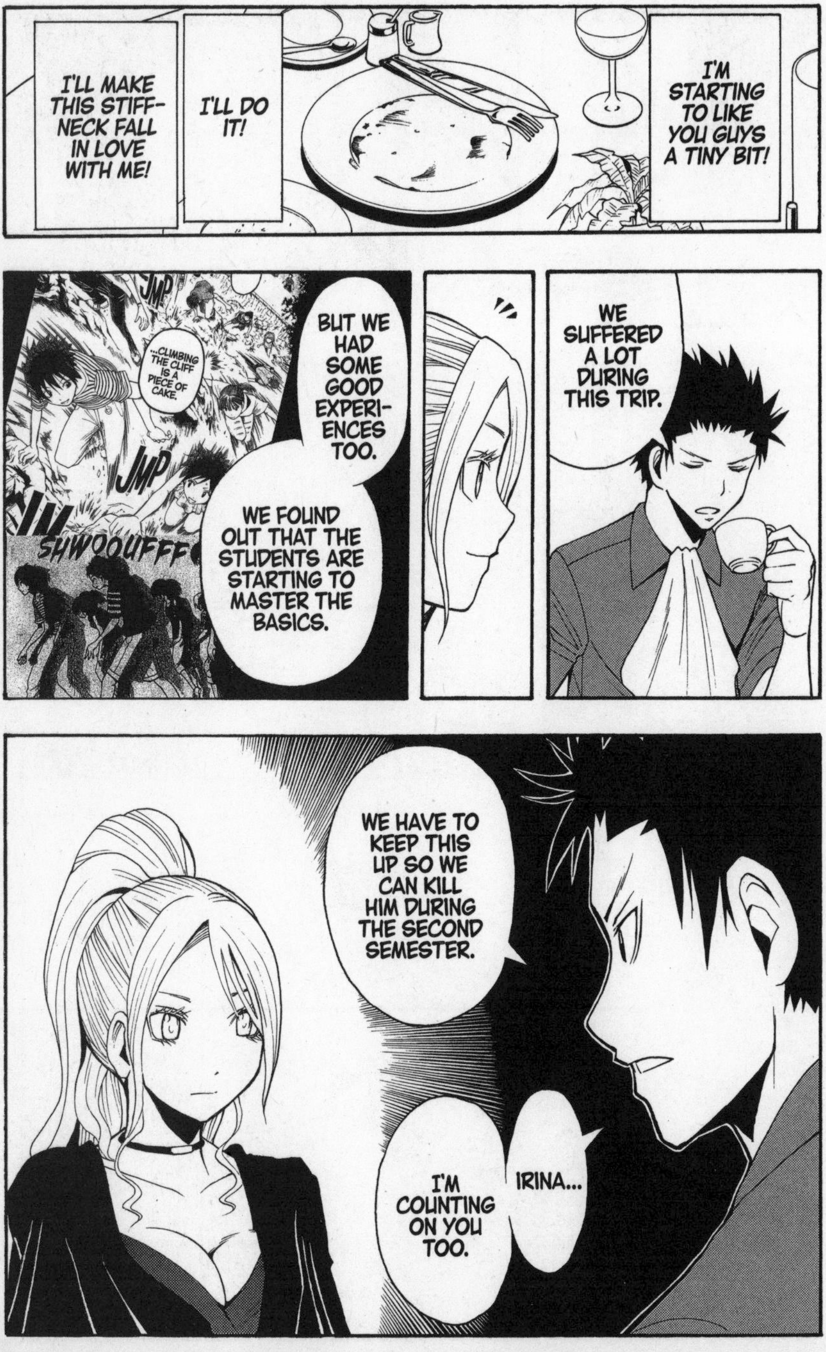

I'M STARTING TO LIKE YOU GUYS A TINY BIT!
I'LL DO IT!
I'LL MAKE THIS STIFF-NECK FALL IN LOVE WITH ME!
WE SUFFERED A LOT DURING THIS TRIP.
BUT WE HAD SOME GOOD EXPERIENCES TOO.
JMP
...CLIMBING THE CLIFF IS A PIECE OF CAKE.
JMP
JM
SHWOOUFFF
WE FOUND OUT THAT THE STUDENTS ARE STARTING TO MASTER THE BASICS.
WE HAVE TO KEEP THIS UP SO WE CAN KILL HIM DURING THE SECOND SEMESTER.
IRINA...
I'M COUNTING ON YOU TOO.

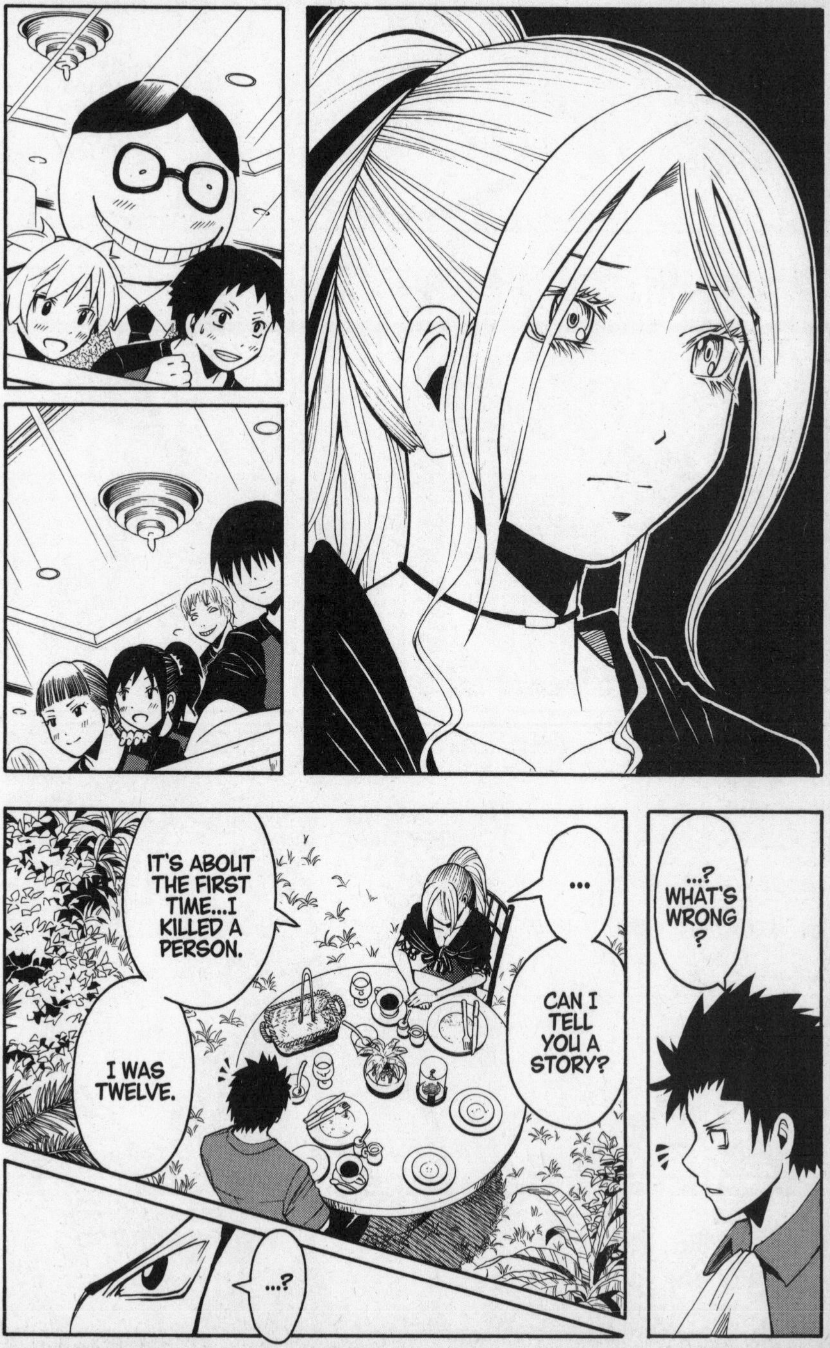
...? WHAT'S WRONG?
...
CAN I TELL YOU A STORY?
IT'S ABOUT THE FIRST TIME...I KILLED A PERSON.
I WAS TWELVE.
...?

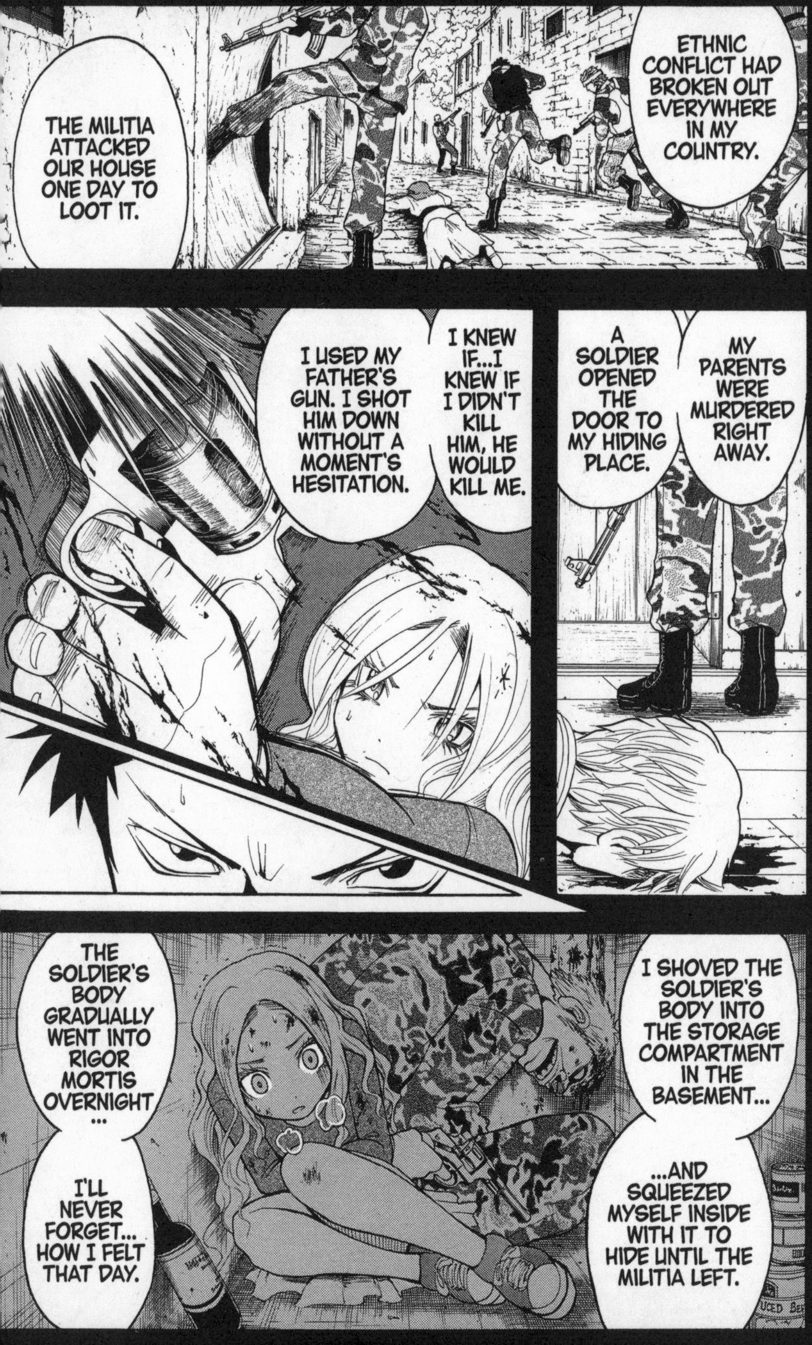
ETHNIC CONFLICT HAD BROKEN OUT EVERYWHERE IN MY COUNTRY.
THE MILITIA ATTACKED OUR HOUSE ONE DAY TO LOOT IT.
MY PARENTS WERE MURDERED RIGHT AWAY.
A SOLDIER OPENED THE DOOR TO MY HIDING PLACE.
I KNEW IF...I KNEW IF I DIDN'T KILL HIM, HE WOULD KILL ME.
I USED MY FATHER'S GUN. I SHOT HIM DOWN WITHOUT A MOMENT'S HESITATION.
I SHOVED THE SOLDIER'S BODY INTO THE STORAGE COMPARTMENT IN THE BASEMENT...
...AND SQUEEZED MYSELF INSIDE WITH IT TO HIDE UNTIL THE MILITIA LEFT.
THE SOLDIER'S BODY GRADUALLY WENT INTO RIGOR MORTIS OVERNIGHT...
I'LL NEVER FORGET... HOW I FELT THAT DAY.

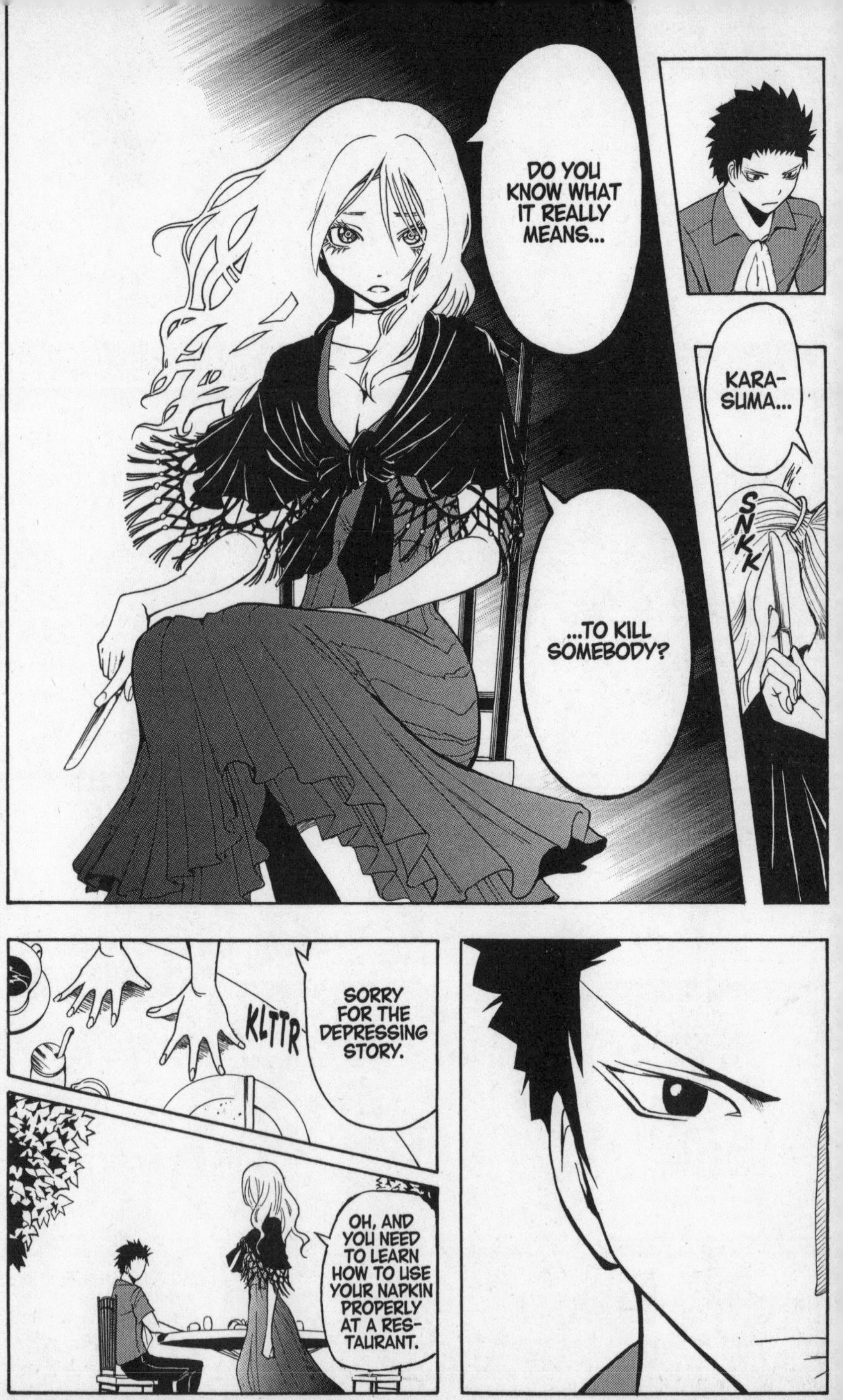
KARA-SUMA...
SNKK
DO YOU KNOW WHAT IT REALLY MEANS...
...TO KILL SOMEBODY?
SORRY FOR THE DEPRESSING STORY.
KLTTR
OH, AND YOU NEED TO LEARN HOW TO USE YOUR NAPKIN PROPERLY AT A RES-TAURANT.

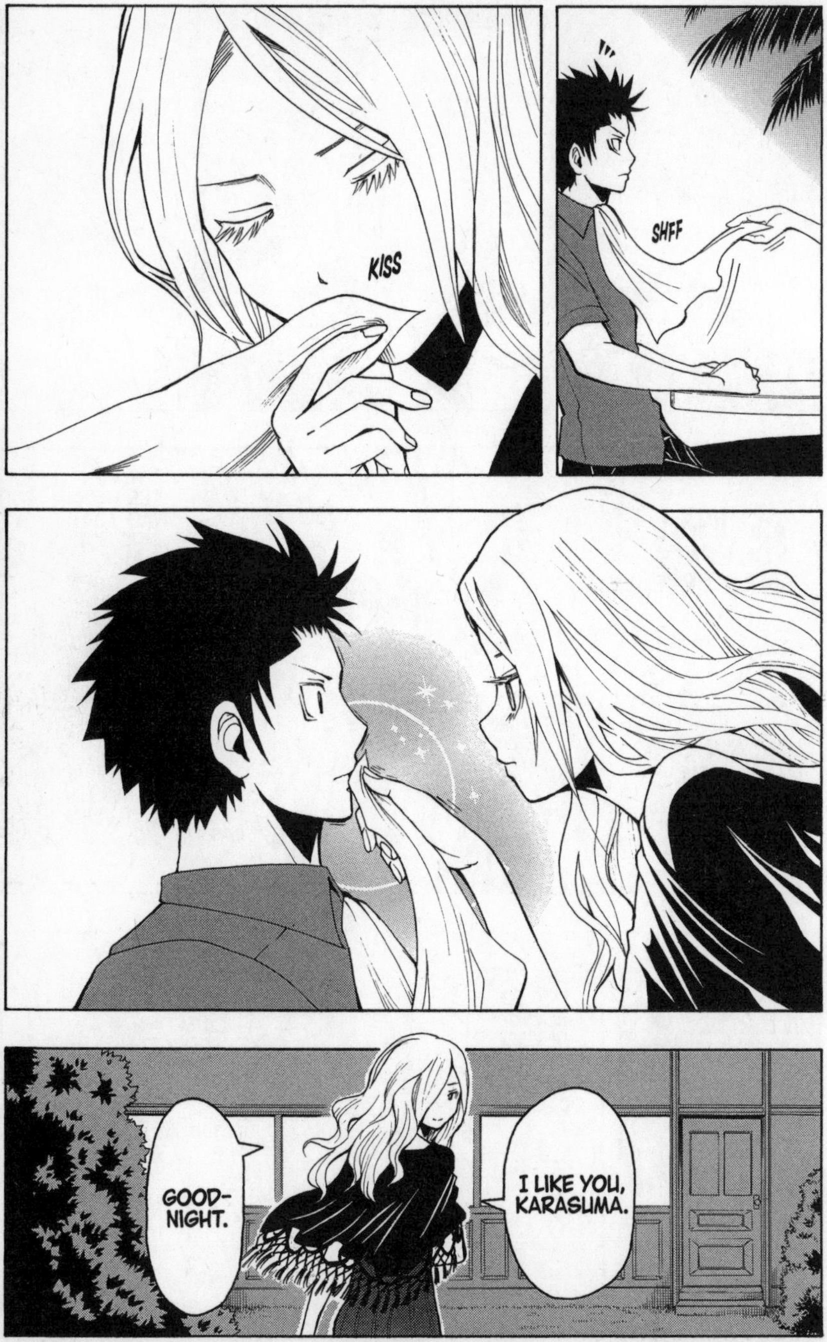
SHFF
KISS
I LIKE YOU, KARASUMA.
GOOD-NIGHT.

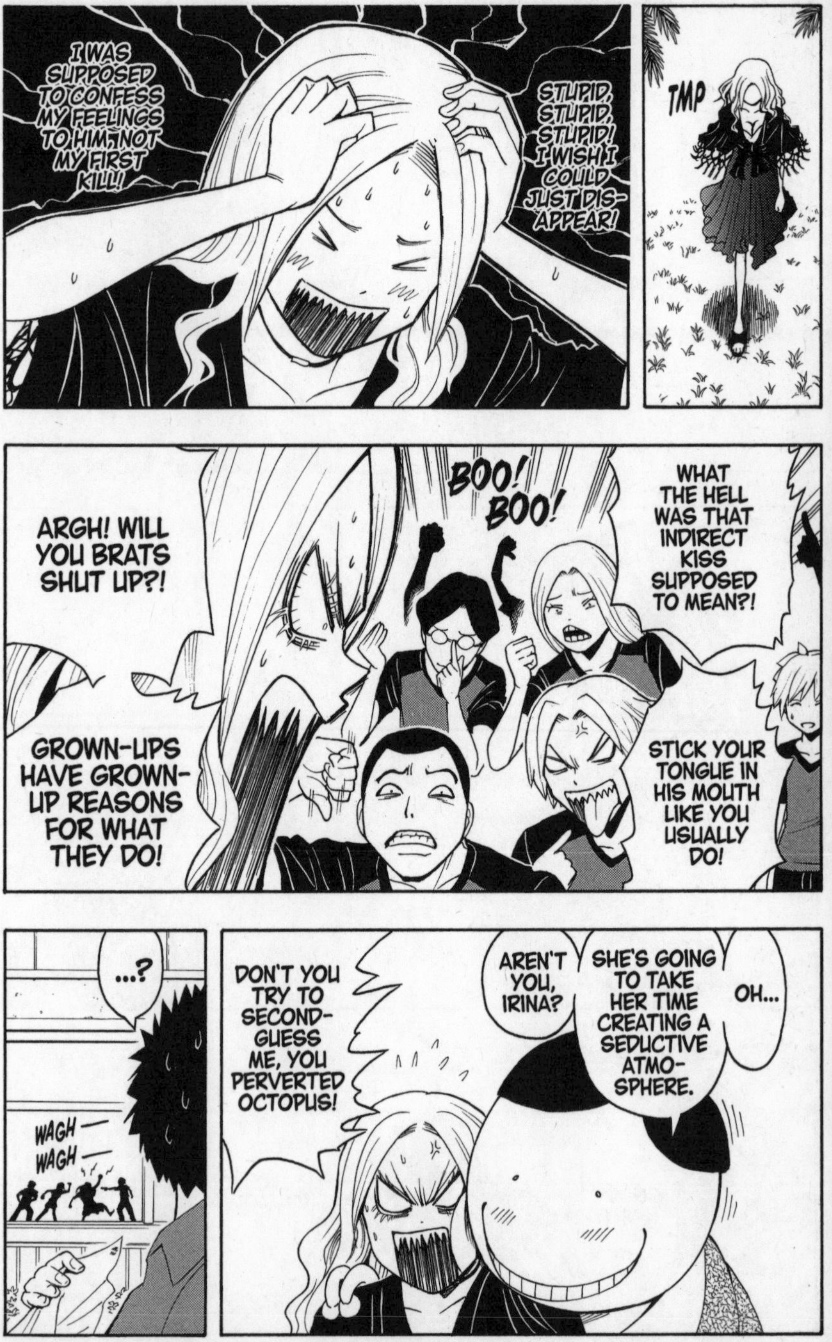
TMP
STUPID, STUPID, STUPID! I WISH I COULD JUST DIS-APPEAR!
I WAS SUPPOSED TO CONFESS MY FEELINGS TO HIM, NOT MY FIRST KILL!
WHAT THE HELL WAS THAT INDIRECT KISS SUPPOSED TO MEAN?!
BOO! BOO!
STICK YOUR TONGUE IN HIS MOUTH LIKE YOU USUALLY DO!
ARGH! WILL YOU BRATS SHUT UP?!
GROWN-UPS HAVE GROWN-UP REASONS FOR WHAT THEY DO!
OH...
SHE'S GOING TO TAKE HER TIME CREATING A SEDUCTIVE ATMO-SPHERE.
AREN'T YOU, IRINA?
DON'T YOU TRY TO SECOND-GUESS ME, YOU PERVERTED OCTOPUS!
...?
WAGH — WAGH —

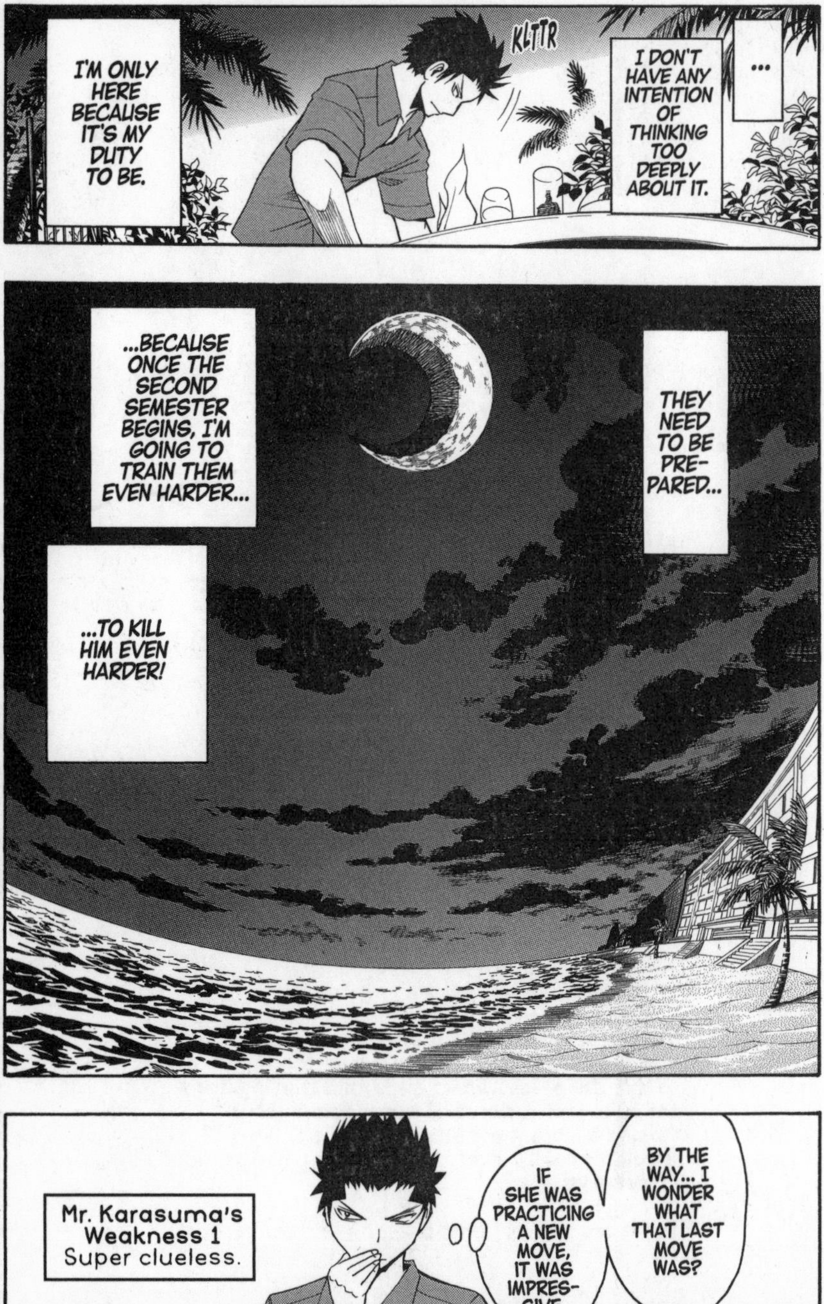
...
I DON'T HAVE ANY INTENTION OF THINKING TOO DEEPLY ABOUT IT.
KLTTR
I'M ONLY HERE BECAUSE IT'S MY DUTY TO BE.
THEY NEED TO BE PRE-PARED...
...BECAUSE ONCE THE SECOND SEMESTER BEGINS, I'M GOING TO TRAIN THEM EVEN HARDER...
...TO KILL HIM EVEN HARDER!
BY THE WAY... I WONDER WHAT THAT LAST MOVE WAS?
IF SHE WAS PRACTICING A NEW MOVE, IT WAS IMPRES-SIVE.
Mr. Karasuma's Weakness 1 Super clueless.

Ms. Vitch's Super Amazing Technique Series 2 -Mouth Model-Building-

If it's a simple plastic model like the ones that come with a candy, she only needs one minute to cut the pieces apart and build it using her tongue. This is proof of her incomparable kissing techniques. But honestly speaking, I wouldn't really want to touch the plastic model afterwards.

Don't try this at home because it's dangerous!

CLASS 76 A SHOCKING TIME

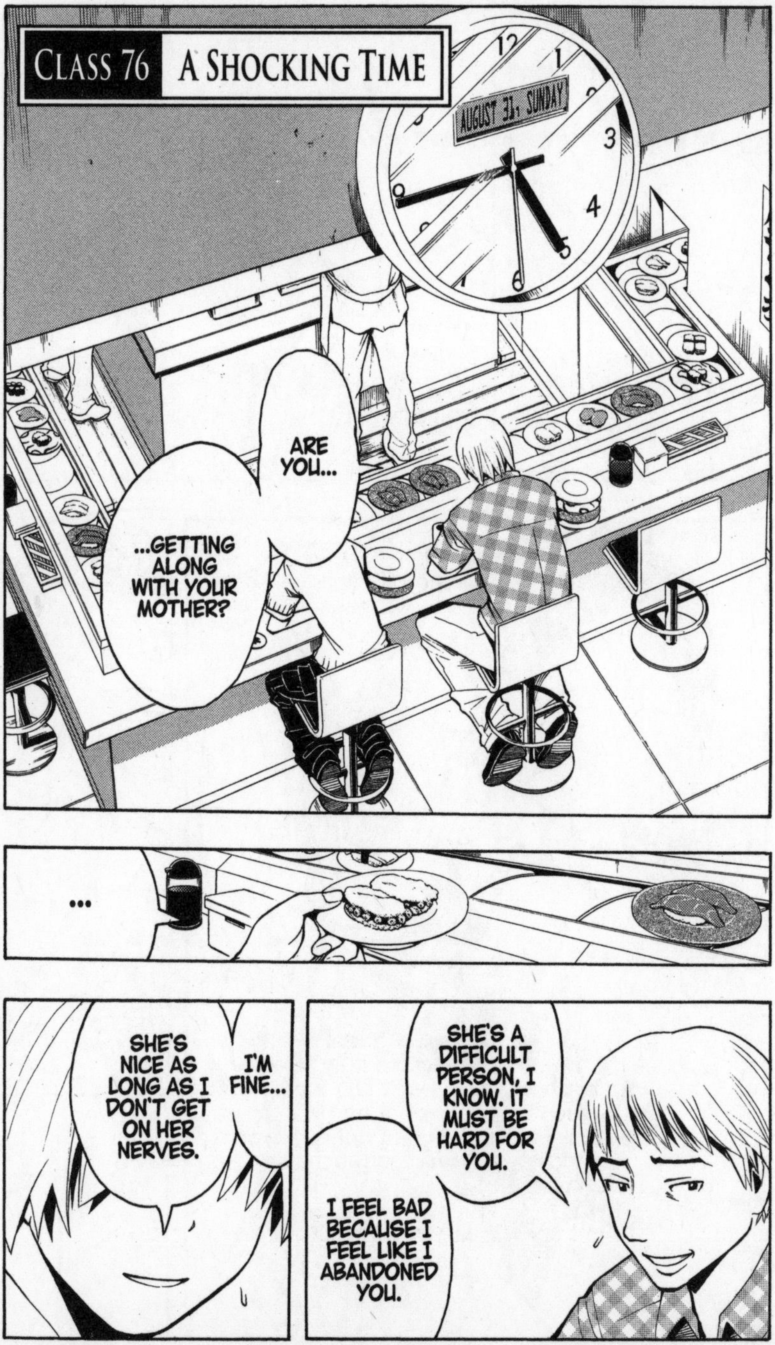
AUGUST 31, SUNDAY
ARE YOU...
...GETTING ALONG WITH YOUR MOTHER?
...
SHE'S A DIFFICULT PERSON, I KNOW. IT MUST BE HARD FOR YOU.
I FEEL BAD BECAUSE I FEEL LIKE I ABANDONED YOU.
I'M FINE...
SHE'S NICE AS LONG AS I DON'T GET ON HER NERVES.

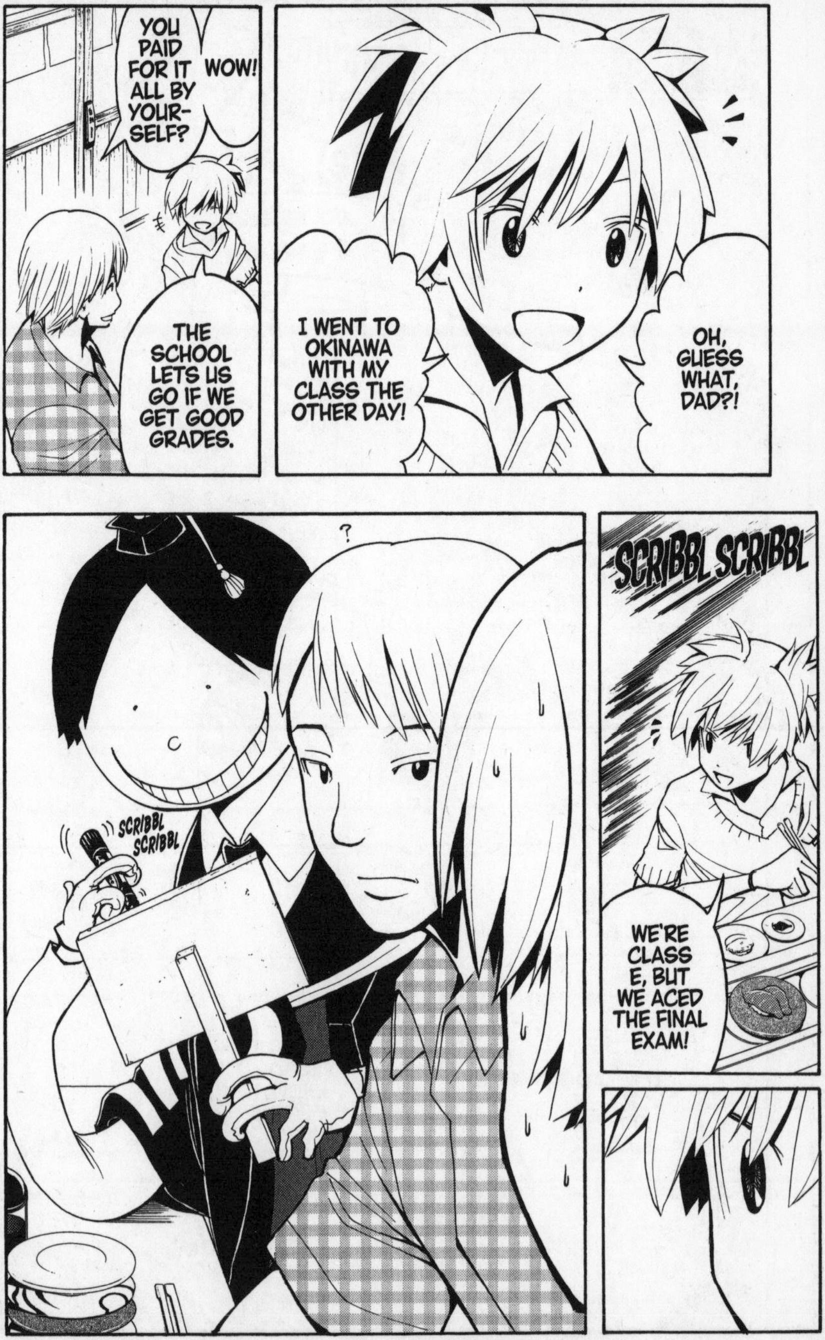
OH, GUESS WHAT, DAD?!
I WENT TO OKINAWA WITH MY CLASS THE OTHER DAY!
WOW!
YOU PAID FOR IT ALL BY YOURSELF?
THE SCHOOL LETS US GO IF WE GET GOOD GRADES.
SCRIBBL SCRIBBL
WE'RE CLASS E, BUT WE ACED THE FINAL EXAM!
?
SCRIBBL SCRIBBL

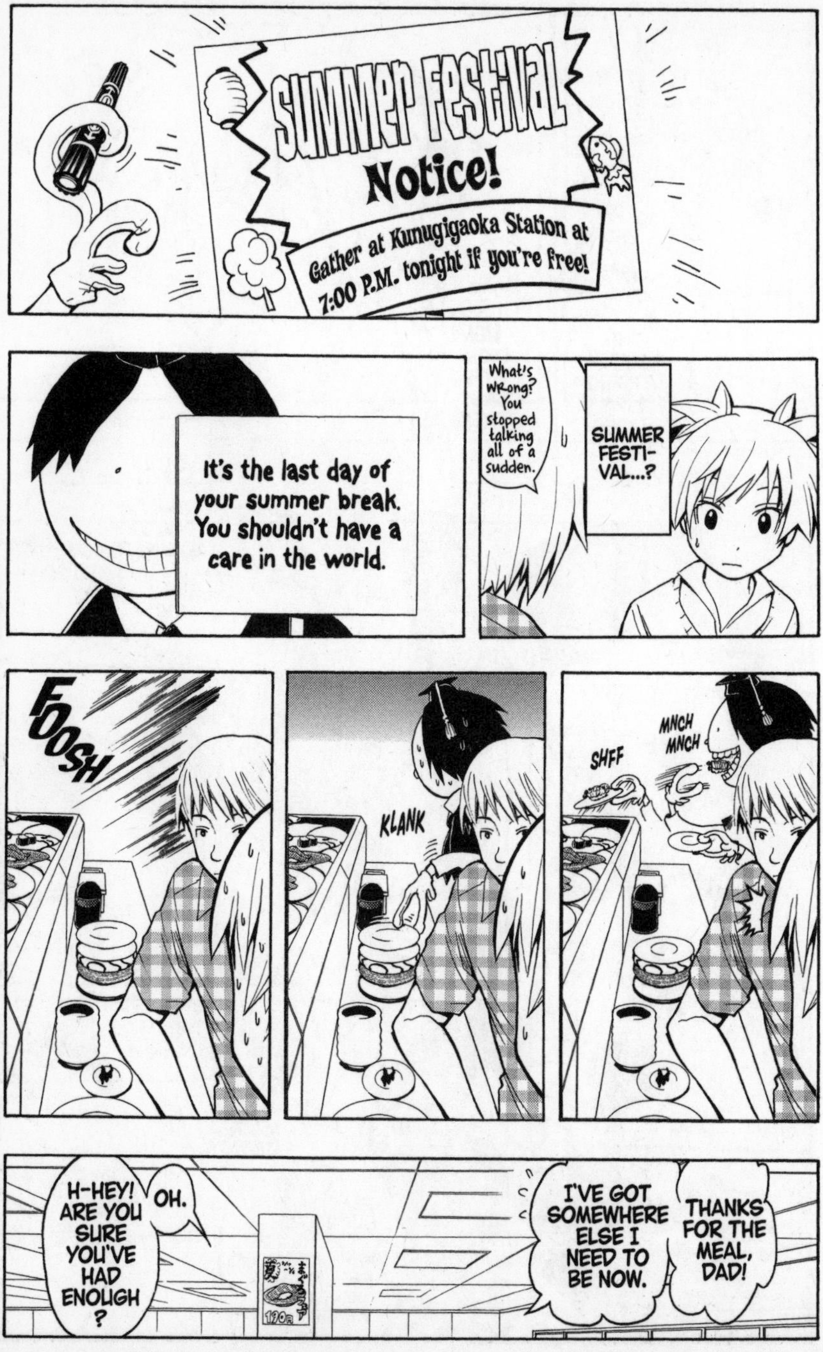
SUMMER FESTIVAL
Notice!
Gather at Kunugigaoka Station at 7:00 P.M. tonight if you're free!
SUMMER FESTI-VAL...?
What's wrong? You stopped talking all of a sudden.
It's the last day of your summer break. You shouldn't have a care in the world.
MNCH MNCH
SHFF
KLANK
FOOSH
THANKS FOR THE MEAL, DAD!
I'VE GOT SOMEWHERE ELSE I NEED TO BE NOW.
OH.
H-HEY! ARE YOU SURE YOU'VE HAD ENOUGH?

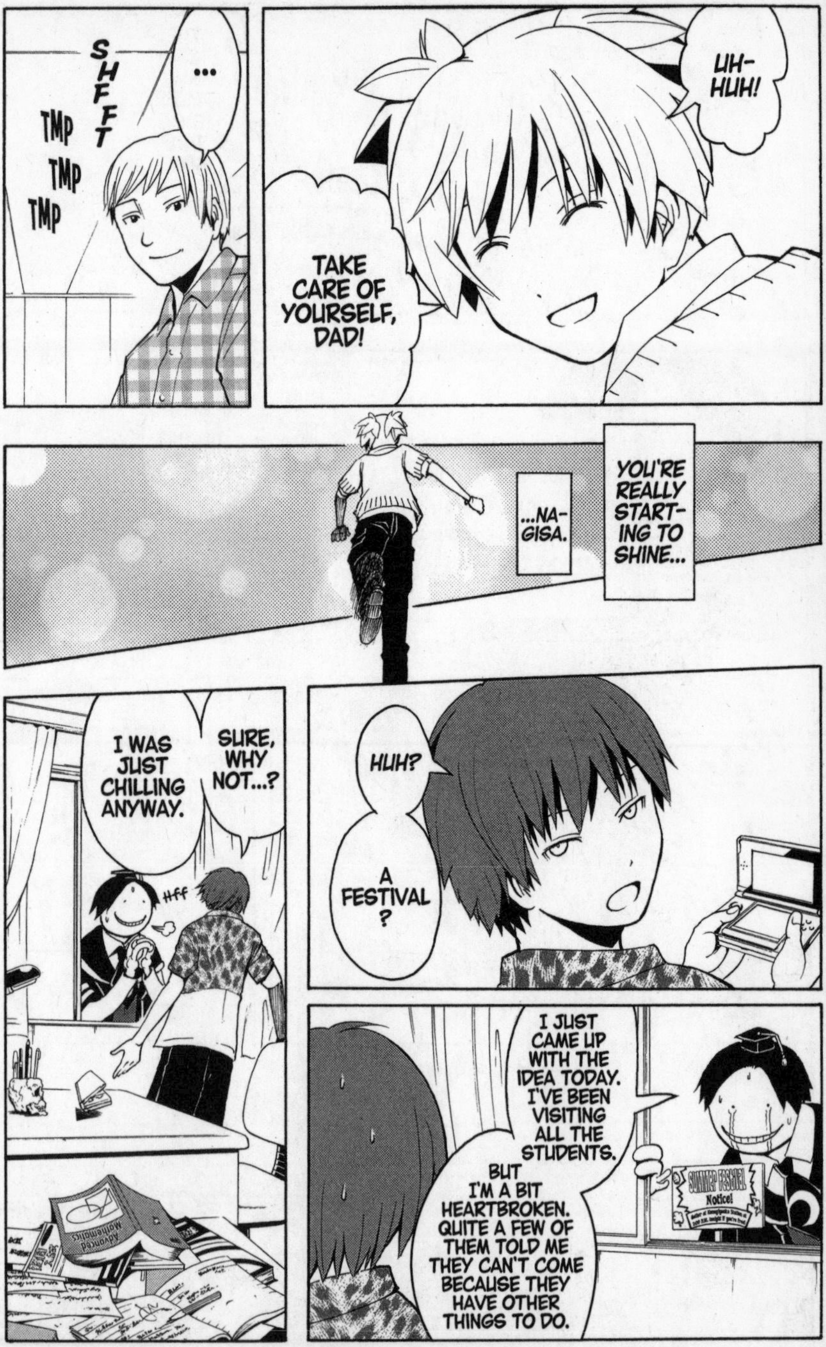
UH-HUH!
TAKE CARE OF YOURSELF, DAD!
SHFFT
TMP
TMP
TMP
...
YOU'RE REALLY START-ING TO SHINE...
...NA-GISA.
HUH?
A FESTIVAL?
I JUST CAME UP WITH THE IDEA TODAY. I'VE BEEN VISITING ALL THE STUDENTS.
BUT I'M A BIT HEARTBROKEN. QUITE A FEW OF THEM TOLD ME THEY CAN'T COME BECAUSE THEY HAVE OTHER THINGS TO DO.
Notice!
SURE, WHY NOT...?
I WAS JUST CHILLING ANYWAY.
Hff
Advanced Mathematics

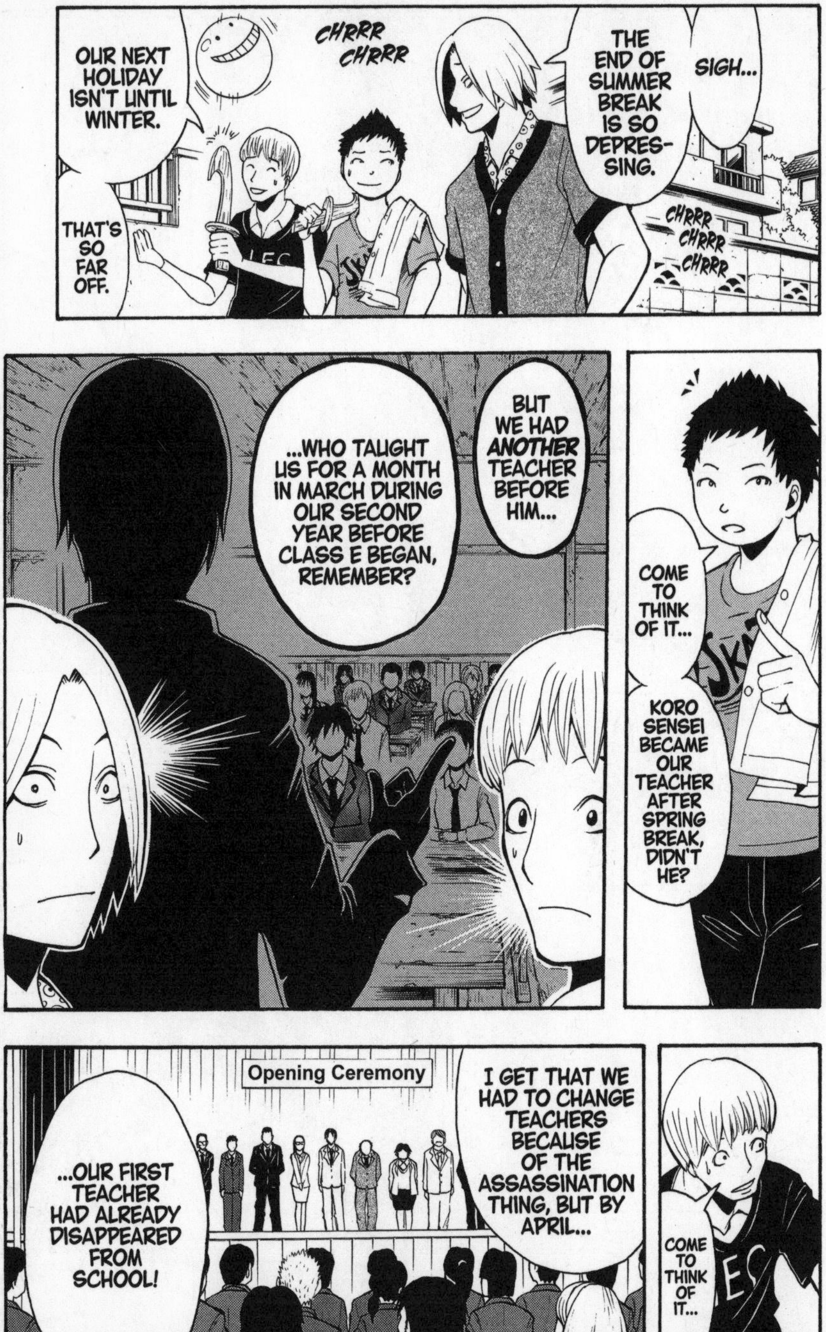
SIGH...
THE END OF SUMMER BREAK IS SO DEPRESSING.
CHRRR CHRRR
OUR NEXT HOLIDAY ISN'T UNTIL WINTER.
CHRRR CHRRR CHRRR
THAT'S SO FAR OFF.
COME TO THINK OF IT...
KORO SENSEI BECAME OUR TEACHER AFTER SPRING BREAK, DIDN'T HE?
BUT WE HAD ANOTHER TEACHER BEFORE HIM...
...WHO TAUGHT US FOR A MONTH IN MARCH DURING OUR SECOND YEAR BEFORE CLASS E BEGAN, REMEMBER?
COME TO THINK OF IT...
Opening Ceremony
I GET THAT WE HAD TO CHANGE TEACHERS BECAUSE OF THE ASSASSINATION THING, BUT BY APRIL...
...OUR FIRST TEACHER HAD ALREADY DISAPPEARED FROM SCHOOL!

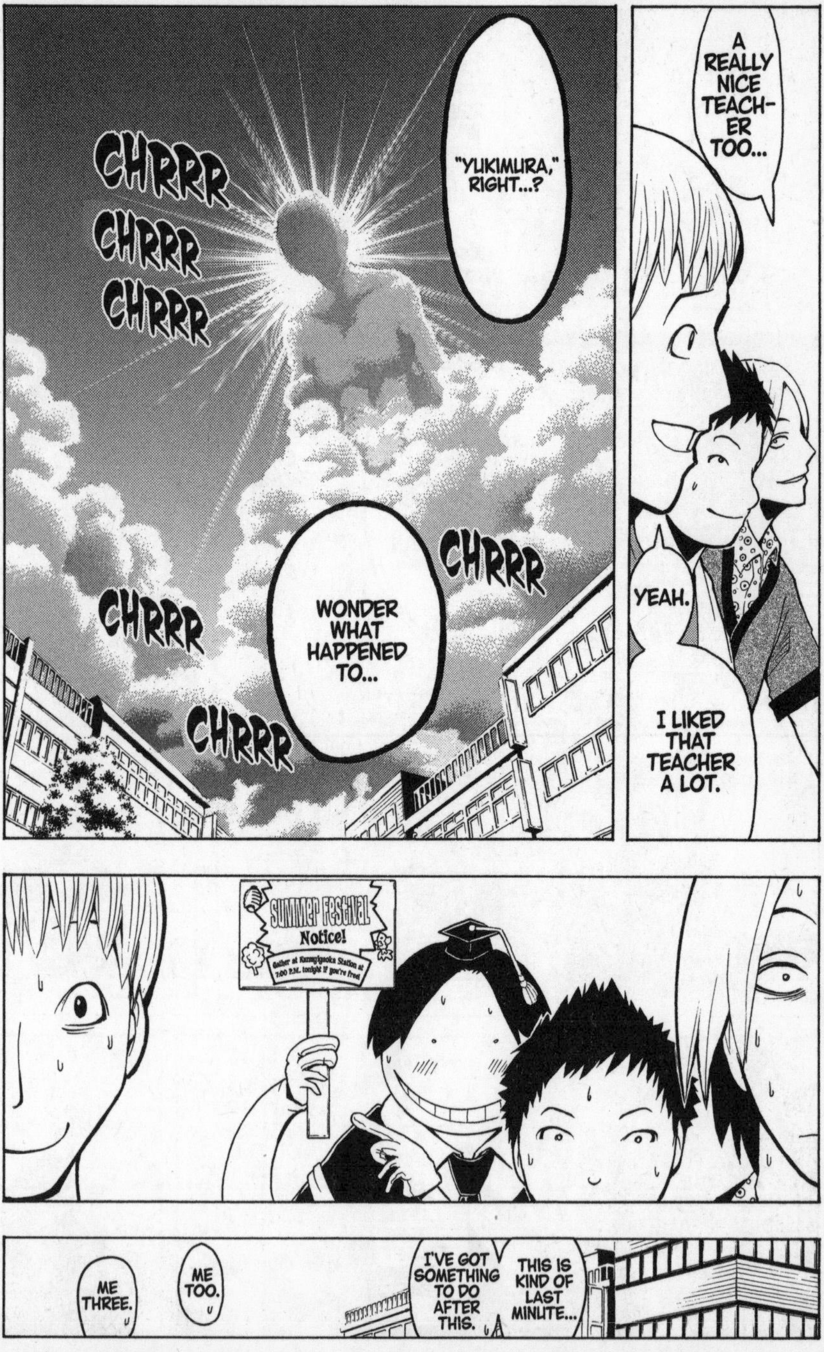
A REALLY NICE TEACHER TOO...
YEAH.
I LIKED THAT TEACHER A LOT.
"YUKIMURA," RIGHT...?
CHRRR
CHRRR
CHRRR
CHRRR
WONDER WHAT HAPPENED TO...
CHRRR
CHRRR
Summer Festival
Notice!
Gather at Kunugigaoka Station at 7:00 P.M. tonight if you're free!
THIS IS KIND OF LAST MINUTE...
I'VE GOT SOMETHING TO DO AFTER THIS.
ME TOO.
ME THREE.

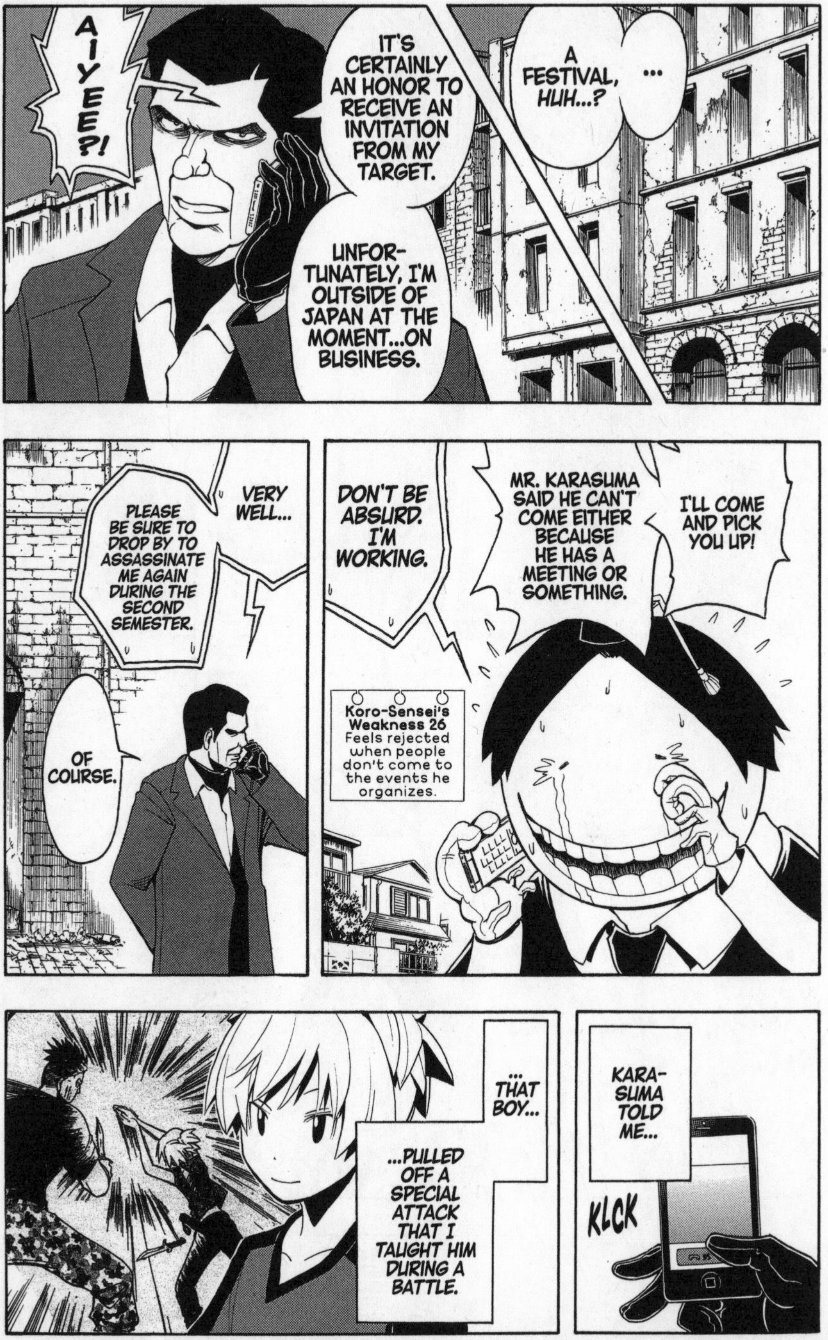
...
A FESTIVAL, HUH...?
IT'S CERTAINLY AN HONOR TO RECEIVE AN INVITATION FROM MY TARGET.
UNFORTUNATELY, I'M OUTSIDE OF JAPAN AT THE MOMENT...ON BUSINESS.
AIYEE?!
I'LL COME AND PICK YOU UP!
MR. KARASUMA SAID HE CAN'T COME EITHER BECAUSE HE HAS A MEETING OR SOMETHING.
DON'T BE ABSURD. I'M WORKING.
Koro-Sensei's Weakness 26
Feels rejected when people don't come to the events he organizes.
VERY WELL...
PLEASE BE SURE TO DROP BY TO ASSASSINATE ME AGAIN DURING THE SECOND SEMESTER.
OF COURSE.
KARA-SUMA TOLD ME...
KLCK
...THAT BOY...
...PULLED OFF A SPECIAL ATTACK THAT I TAUGHT HIM DURING A BATTLE.

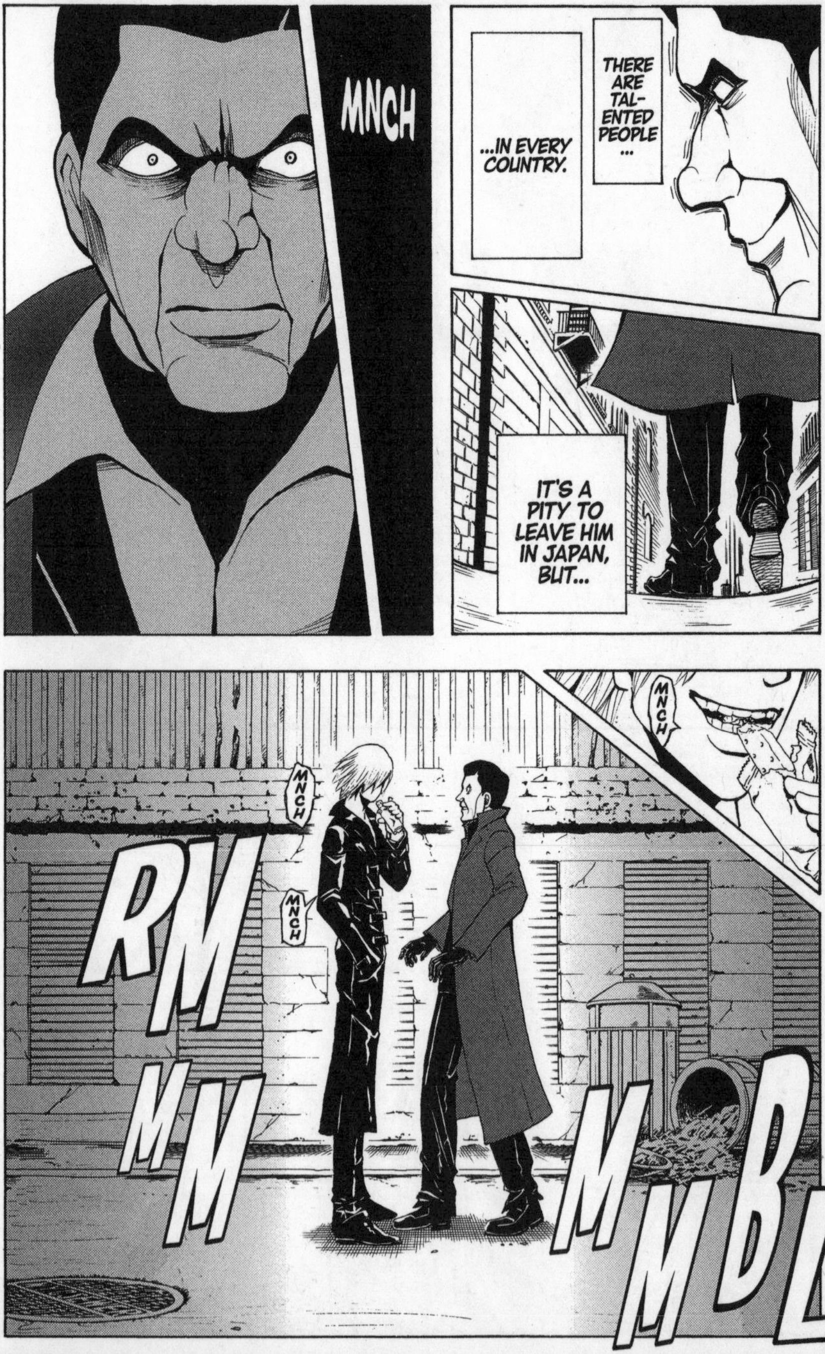
THERE ARE TAL-ENTED PEOPLE...
...IN EVERY COUNTRY.
IT'S A PITY TO LEAVE HIM IN JAPAN, BUT...
MNCH
MNCH
MNCH
MNCH
RMMM
MMBL

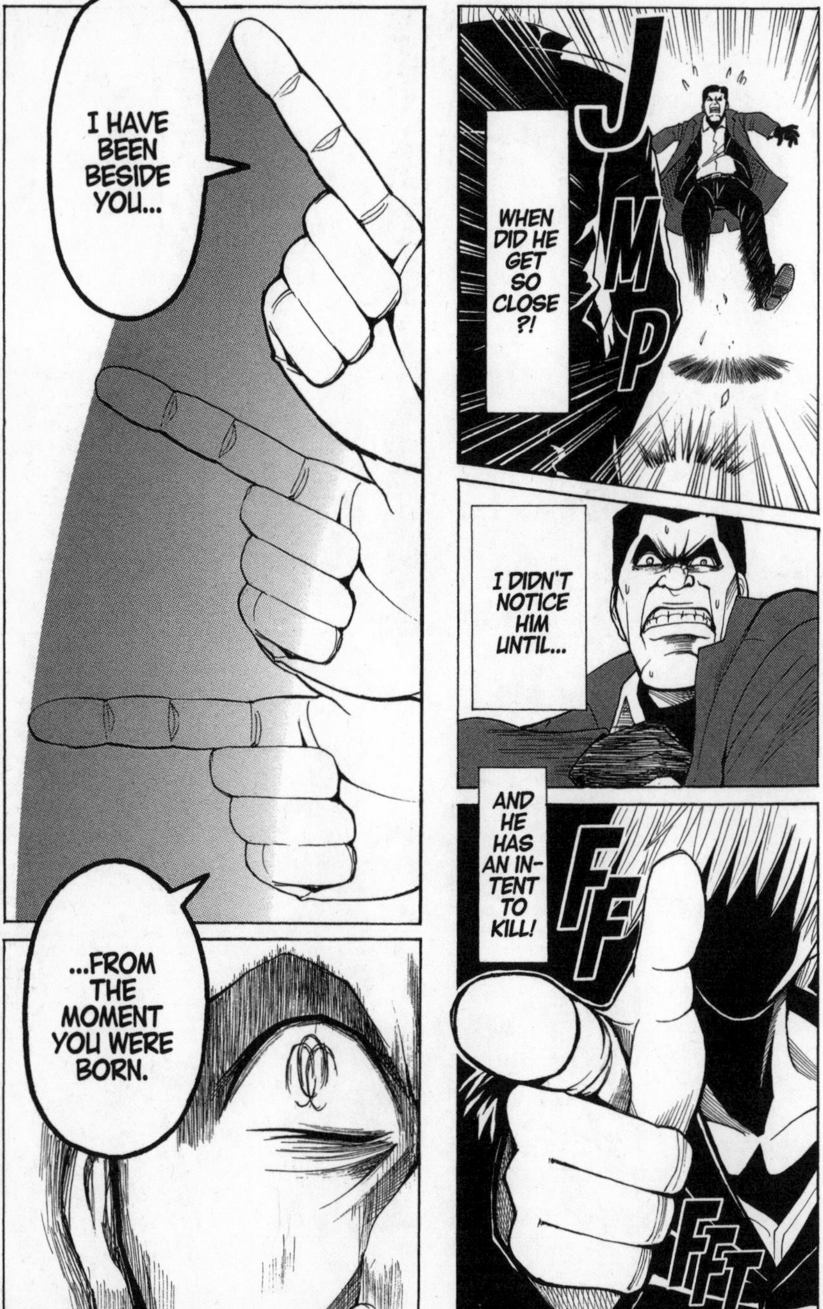
JMP
WHEN DID HE GET SO CLOSE?!
I DIDN'T NOTICE HIM UNTIL...
AND HE HAS AN IN-TENT TO KILL!
FF
FFFT
I HAVE BEEN BESIDE YOU...
...FROM THE MOMENT YOU WERE BORN.

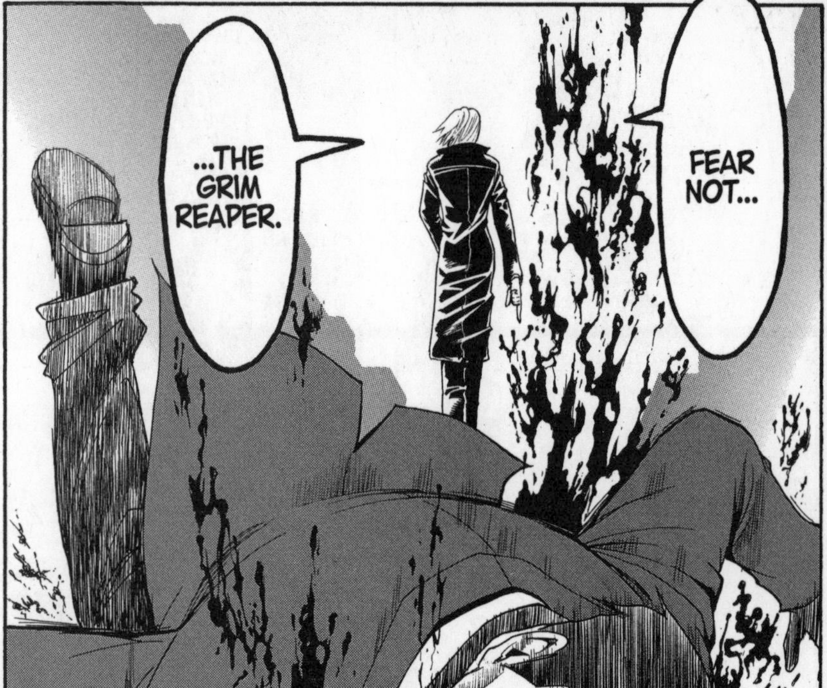
FEAR NOT...
...THE GRIM REAPER.

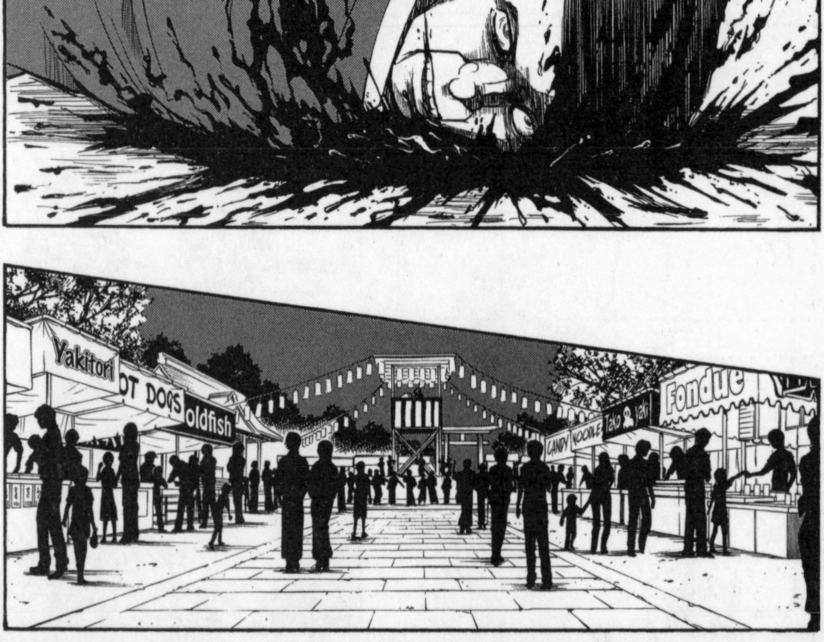
Fondue
CANDY
NOODLE
Yakitori
OT DOGS
oldfish

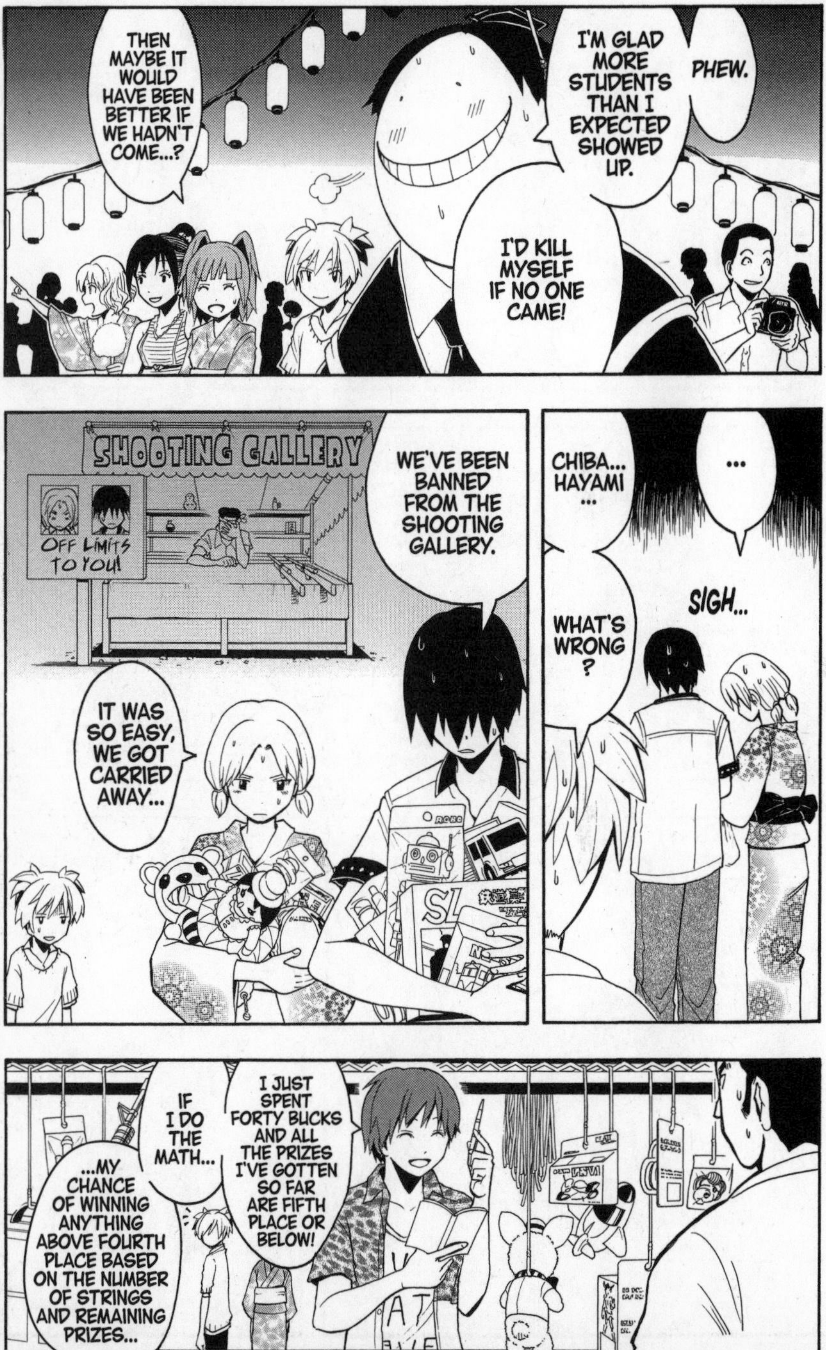
PHEW.
I'M GLAD MORE STUDENTS THAN I EXPECTED SHOWED UP.
I'D KILL MYSELF IF NO ONE CAME!
THEN MAYBE IT WOULD HAVE BEEN BETTER IF WE HADN'T COME...?
...
CHIBA... HAYAMI...
SIGH...
WHAT'S WRONG?
SHOOTING GALLERY
OFF LIMITS TO YOU!
WE'VE BEEN BANNED FROM THE SHOOTING GALLERY.
IT WAS SO EASY, WE GOT CARRIED AWAY...
I JUST SPENT FORTY BUCKS AND ALL THE PRIZES I'VE GOTTEN SO FAR ARE FIFTH PLACE OR BELOW!
IF I DO THE MATH...
...MY CHANCE OF WINNING ANYTHING ABOVE FOURTH PLACE BASED ON THE NUMBER OF STRINGS AND REMAINING PRIZES...

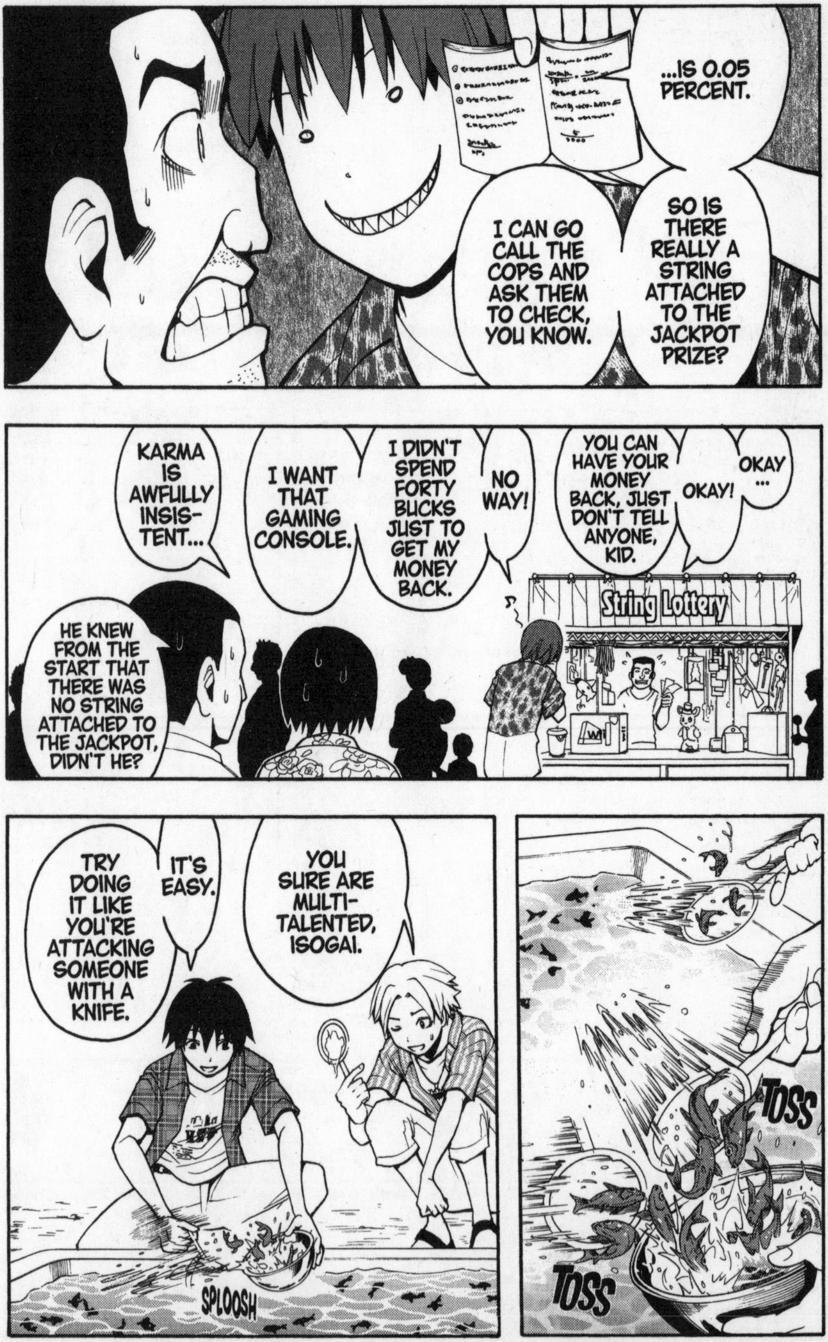

...IS 0.05 PERCENT.
SO IS THERE REALLY A STRING ATTACHED TO THE JACKPOT PRIZE?
I CAN GO CALL THE COPS AND ASK THEM TO CHECK, YOU KNOW.
OKAY ...
OKAY!
YOU CAN HAVE YOUR MONEY BACK, JUST DON'T TELL ANYONE, KID.
String Lottery
NO WAY!
I DIDN'T SPEND FORTY BUCKS JUST TO GET MY MONEY BACK.
I WANT THAT GAMING CONSOLE.
KARMA IS AWFULLY INSIS-TENT...
HE KNEW FROM THE START THAT THERE WAS NO STRING ATTACHED TO THE JACKPOT, DIDN'T HE?
TOSS
TOSS
YOU SURE ARE MULTI-TALENTED, ISOGAI.
IT'S EASY.
TRY DOING IT LIKE YOU'RE ATTACKING SOMEONE WITH A KNIFE.
SPLOOSH

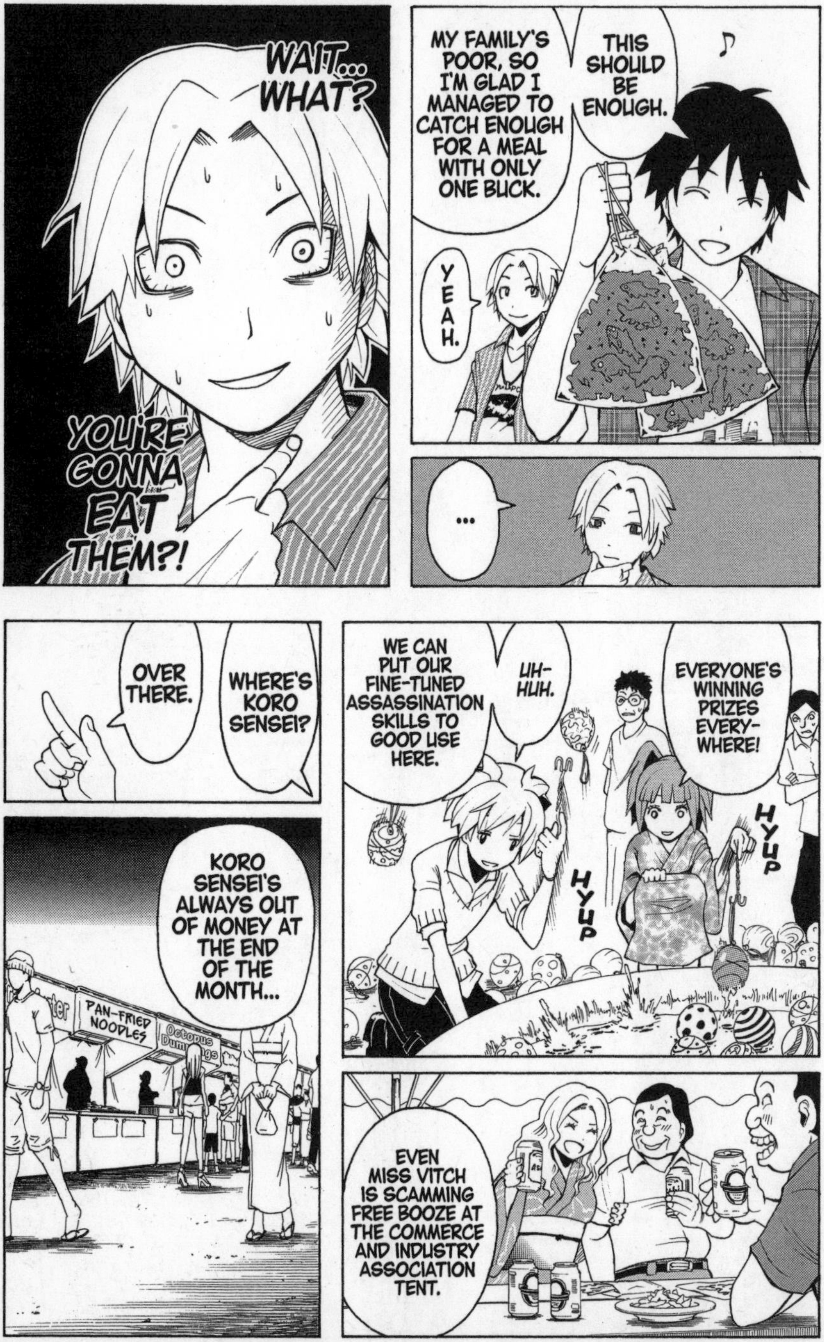
THIS SHOULD BE ENOUGH.
♪
MY FAMILY'S POOR, SO I'M GLAD I MANAGED TO CATCH ENOUGH FOR A MEAL WITH ONLY ONE BUCK.
YEAH.
...
WAIT... WHAT?
YOU'RE GONNA EAT THEM?!
EVERYONE'S WINNING PRIZES EVERYWHERE!
UH-HUH.
WE CAN PUT OUR FINE-TUNED ASSASSINATION SKILLS TO GOOD USE HERE.
HYUP
HYUP
WHERE'S KORO SENSEI?
OVER THERE.
KORO SENSEI'S ALWAYS OUT OF MONEY AT THE END OF THE MONTH...
PAN-FRIED NOODLES
EVEN MISS VITCH IS SCAMMING FREE BOOZE AT THE COMMERCE AND INDUSTRY ASSOCIATION TENT.

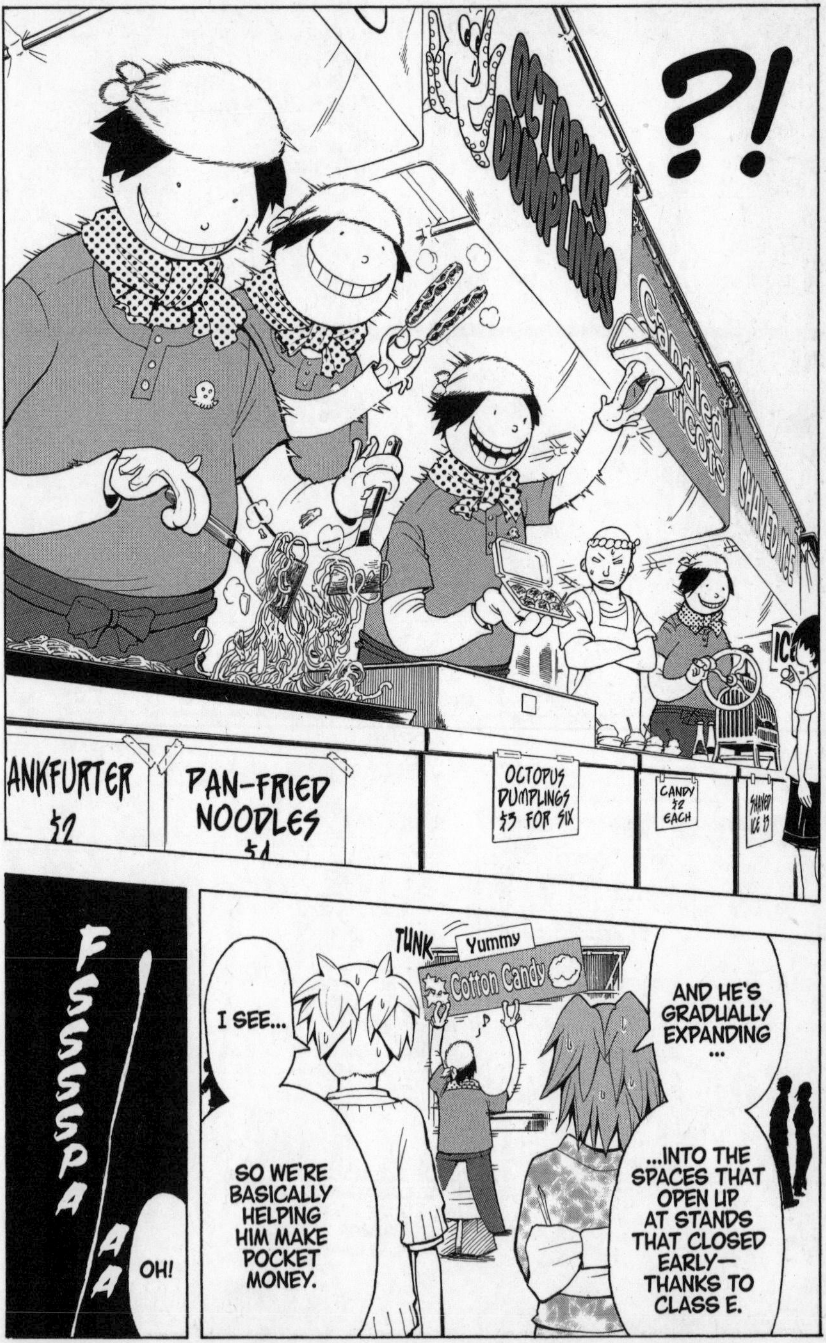
?!
OCTOPUS DUMPLINGS
Candied
ricots
SHAVED ICE
ICE
ANKFURTER ¥2
PAN-FRIED NOODLES
OCTOPUS DUMPLINGS ¥3 FOR SIX
CANDY ¥2 EACH
SHAVED ICE ¥3
AND HE'S GRADUALLY EXPANDING...
TUNK
Yummy
Cotton Candy
I SEE...
...INTO THE SPACES THAT OPEN UP AT STANDS THAT CLOSED EARLY— THANKS TO CLASS E.
SO WE'RE BASICALLY HELPING HIM MAKE POCKET MONEY.
FSSSSPAAA
OH!

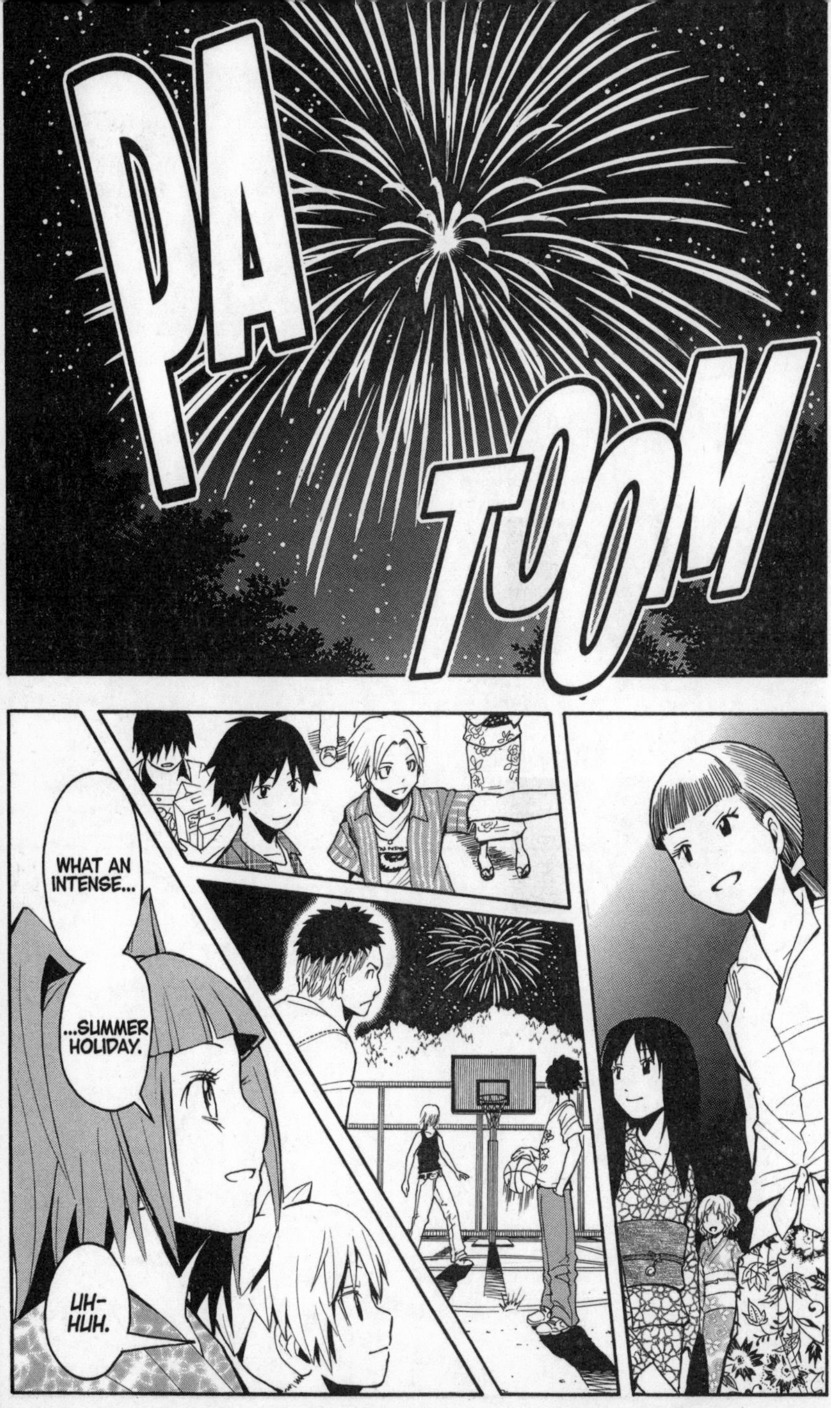
PA
TOOM
WHAT AN INTENSE...
...SUMMER HOLIDAY.
UH-HUH.

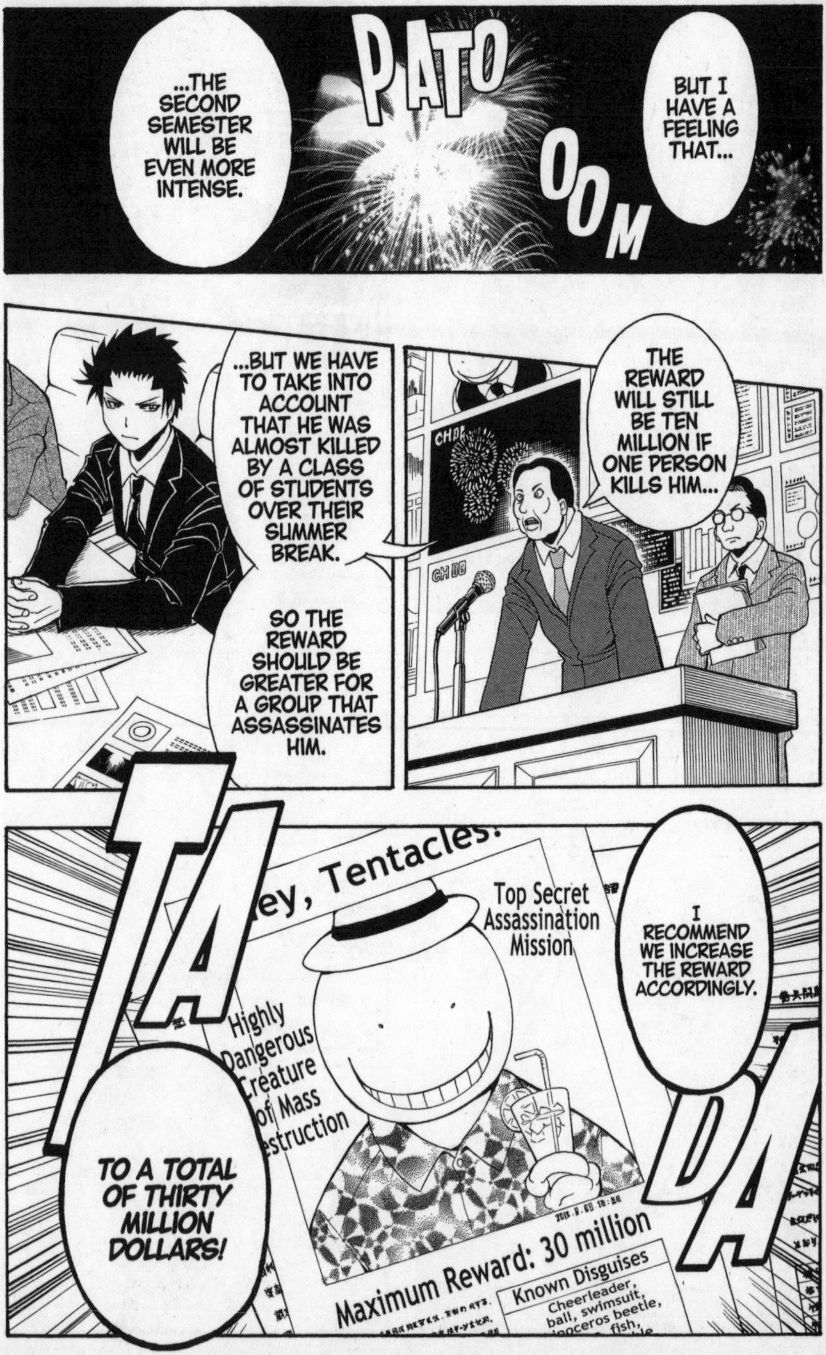
BUT I HAVE A FEELING THAT...
PATOOOM
...THE SECOND SEMESTER WILL BE EVEN MORE INTENSE.
THE REWARD WILL STILL BE TEN MILLION IF ONE PERSON KILLS HIM...
...BUT WE HAVE TO TAKE INTO ACCOUNT THAT HE WAS ALMOST KILLED BY A CLASS OF STUDENTS OVER THEIR SUMMER BREAK.
SO THE REWARD SHOULD BE GREATER FOR A GROUP THAT ASSASSINATES HIM.
I RECOMMEND WE INCREASE THE REWARD ACCORDINGLY.
TA DA
Top Secret Assassination Mission
Highly
TO A TOTAL OF THIRTY MILLION DOLLARS!
Maximum Reward: 30 million
Known Disguises
Cheerleader, ball, swimsuit,

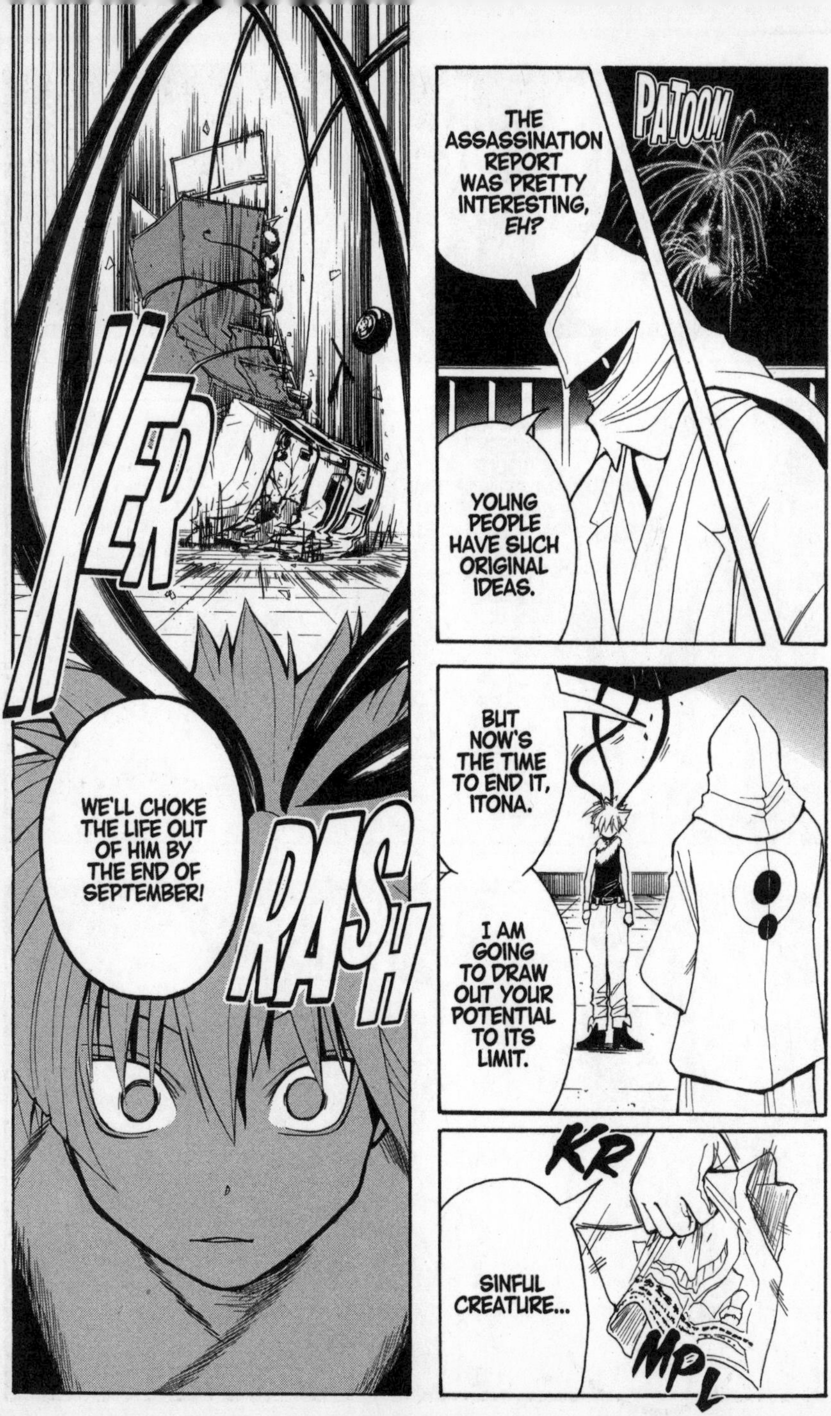
PATOOM
THE ASSASSINATION REPORT WAS PRETTY INTERESTING, EH?
YOUNG PEOPLE HAVE SUCH ORIGINAL IDEAS.
BUT NOW'S THE TIME TO END IT, ITONA.
I AM GOING TO DRAW OUT YOUR POTENTIAL TO ITS LIMIT.
KR
SINFUL CREATURE...
MPL
KER
WE'LL CHOKE THE LIFE OUT OF HIM BY THE END OF SEPTEMBER!
RASH

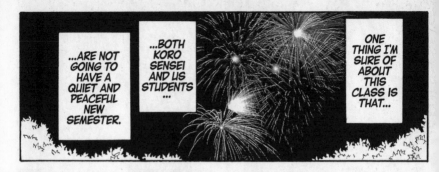

ONE THING I'M SURE OF ABOUT THIS CLASS IS THAT...
...BOTH KORO SENSEI AND US STUDENTS...
...ARE NOT GOING TO HAVE A QUIET AND PEACEFUL NEW SEMESTER.
PHEW! I MADE SO MUCH MONEY TODAY!
EVEN DEDUCTING THE COST OF THE INGREDIENTS, I STILL HAVE MORE THAN ENOUGH LEFT FOR MY SEPTEMBER SNACKS.
DID YOU ENJOY YOURSELVES TOO?
STUDYING BEGINS TOMORROW...
...SO YOU MIGHT AS WELL STRETCH YOUR WINGS TODAY...
....
....
W-WHAT...?
FSSSSPA

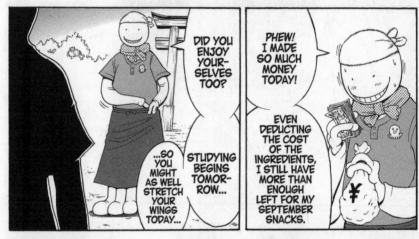

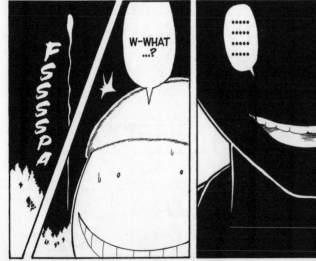

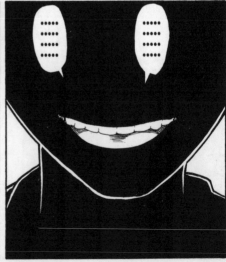

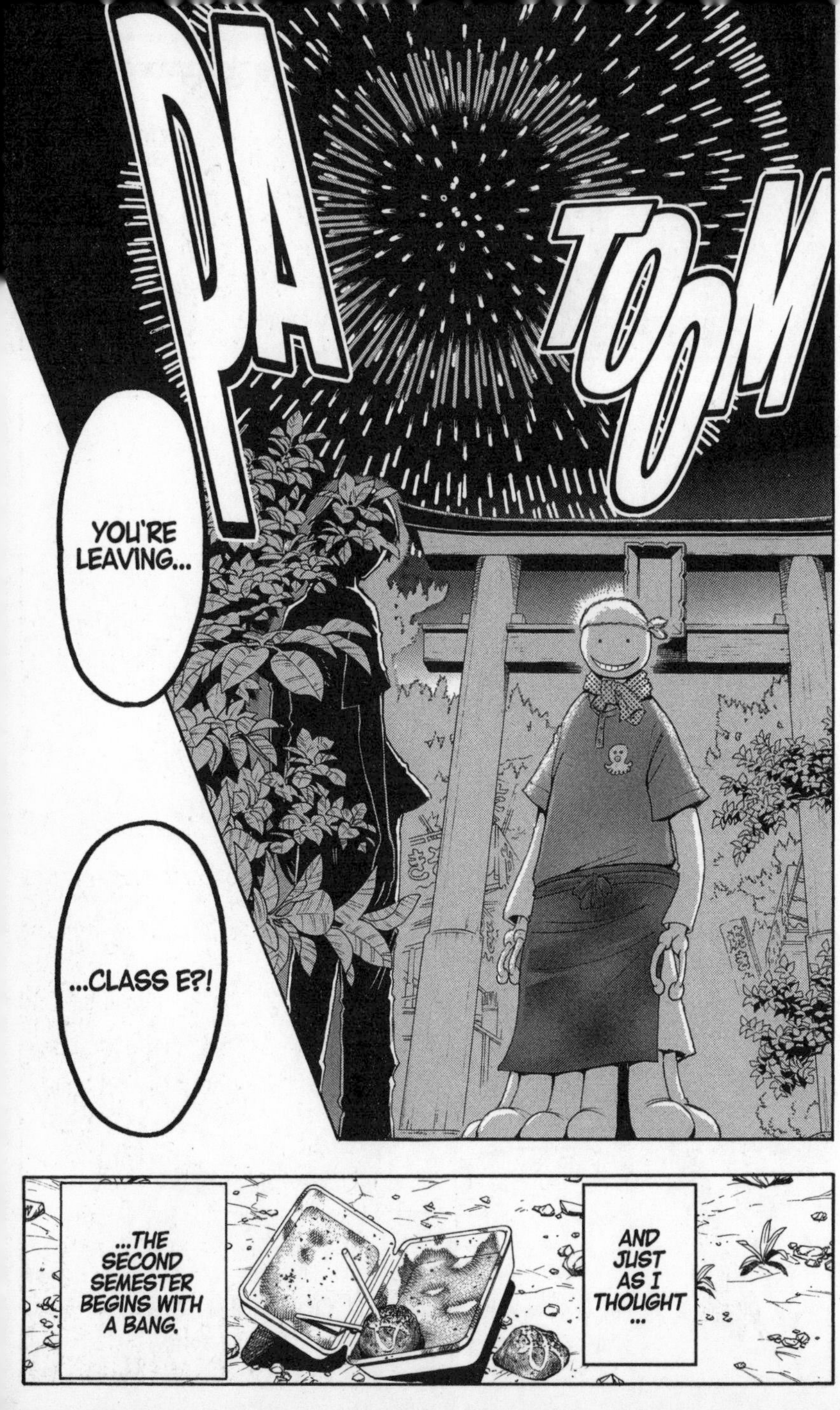
PA
TOOM
YOU'RE LEAVING...
...CLASS E?!
AND JUST AS I THOUGHT...
...THE SECOND SEMESTER BEGINS WITH A BANG.

Isogai Family Specialty: Goldfish Soup

① Fillet the goldfish and remove the small bones and skin.

② Marinate the fish in miso overnight.

③ In the garden, grill the fish until golden brown and then place them in miso soup.

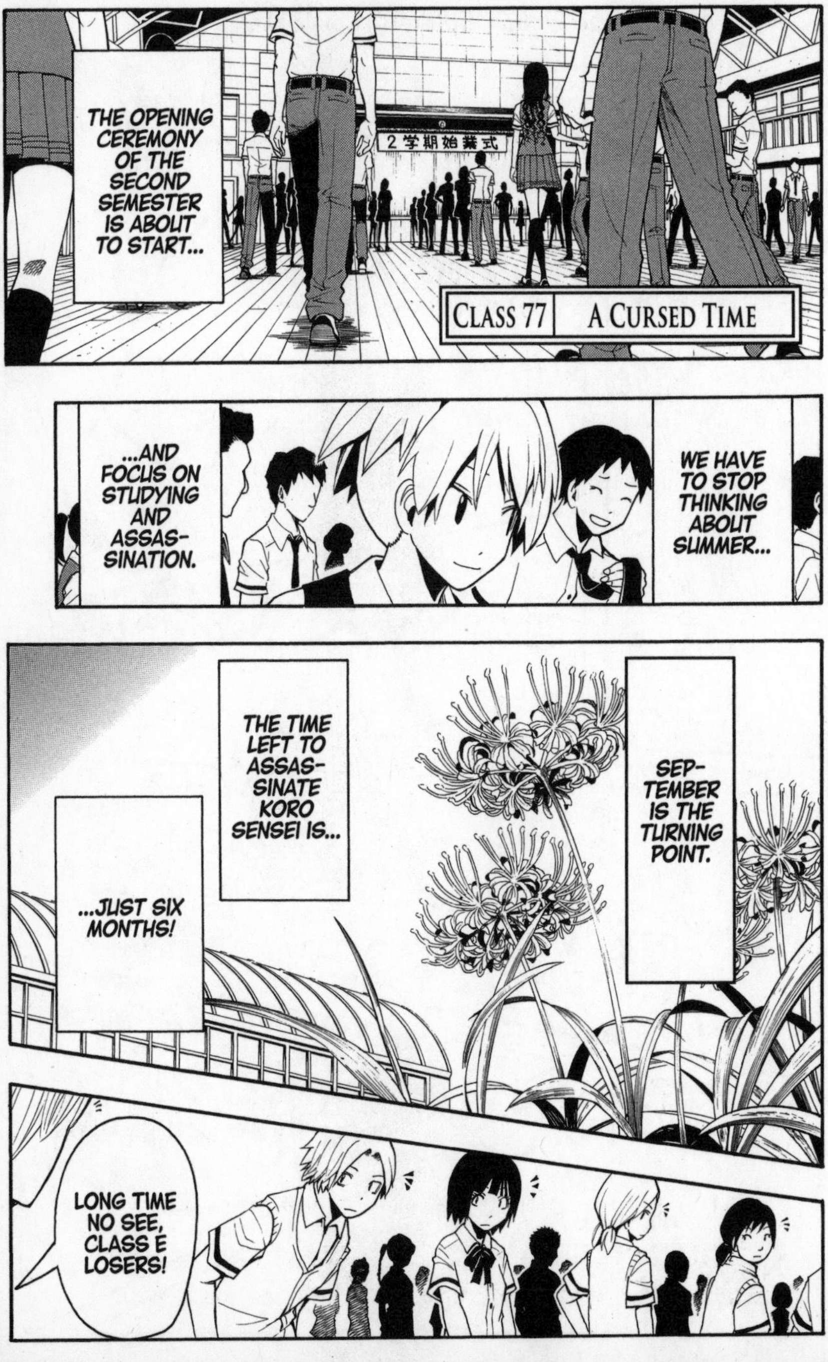
2学期始業式
THE OPENING CEREMONY OF THE SECOND SEMESTER IS ABOUT TO START...
CLASS 77 A CURSED TIME
WE HAVE TO STOP THINKING ABOUT SUMMER...
...AND FOCUS ON STUDYING AND ASSAS-SINATION.
SEP-TEMBER IS THE TURNING POINT.
THE TIME LEFT TO ASSAS-SINATE KORO SENSEI IS...
...JUST SIX MONTHS!
LONG TIME NO SEE, CLASS E LOSERS!

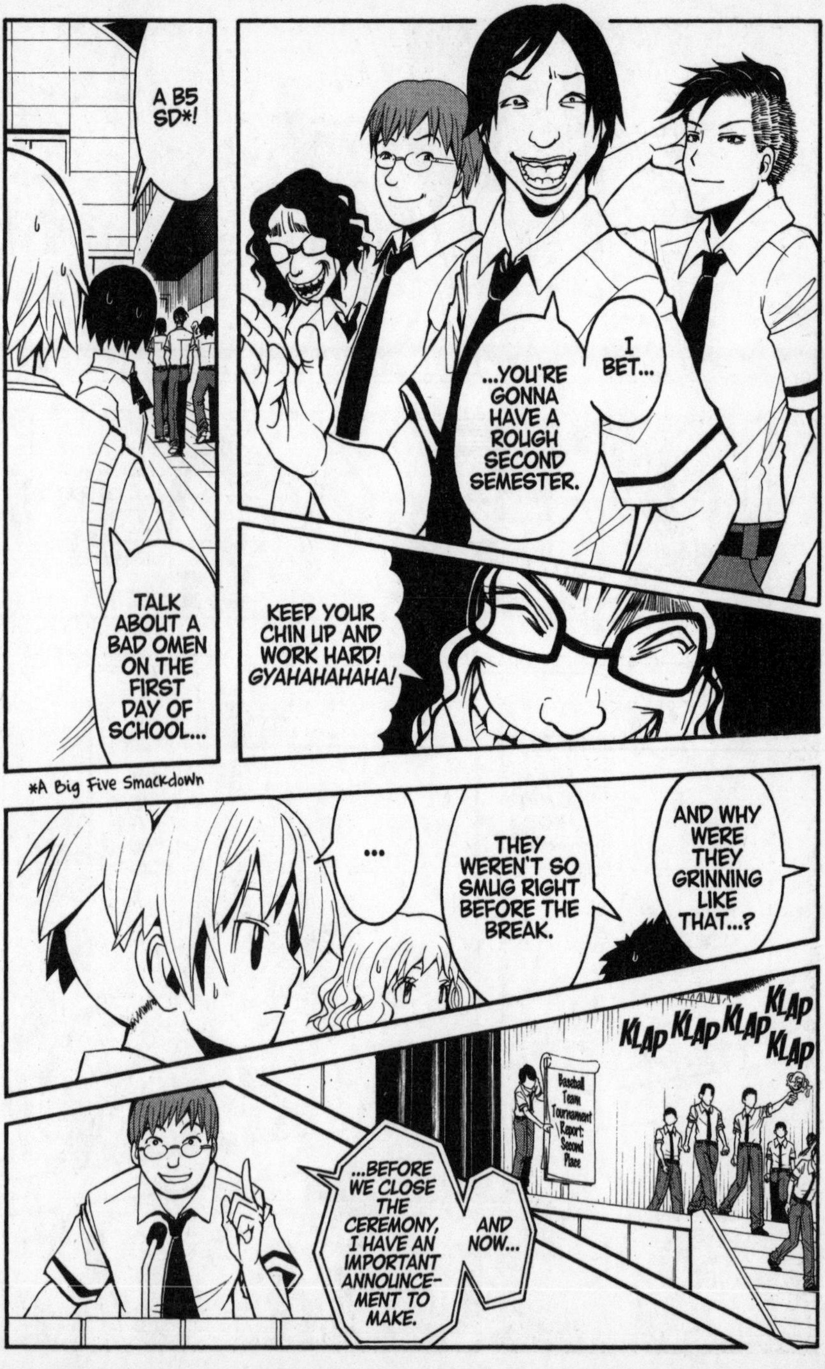
I BET...
...YOU'RE GONNA HAVE A ROUGH SECOND SEMESTER.
KEEP YOUR CHIN UP AND WORK HARD! GYAHAHAHAHA!
A B5 SD*!
TALK ABOUT A BAD OMEN ON THE FIRST DAY OF SCHOOL...
AND WHY WERE THEY GRINNING LIKE THAT...?
THEY WEREN'T SO SMUG RIGHT BEFORE THE BREAK.
...
KLAP KLAP KLAP KLAP KLAP
Baseball Team Tournament Report: Second Place
AND NOW...
...BEFORE WE CLOSE THE CEREMONY, I HAVE AN IMPORTANT ANNOUNCE-MENT TO MAKE.

*A Big Five Smackdown

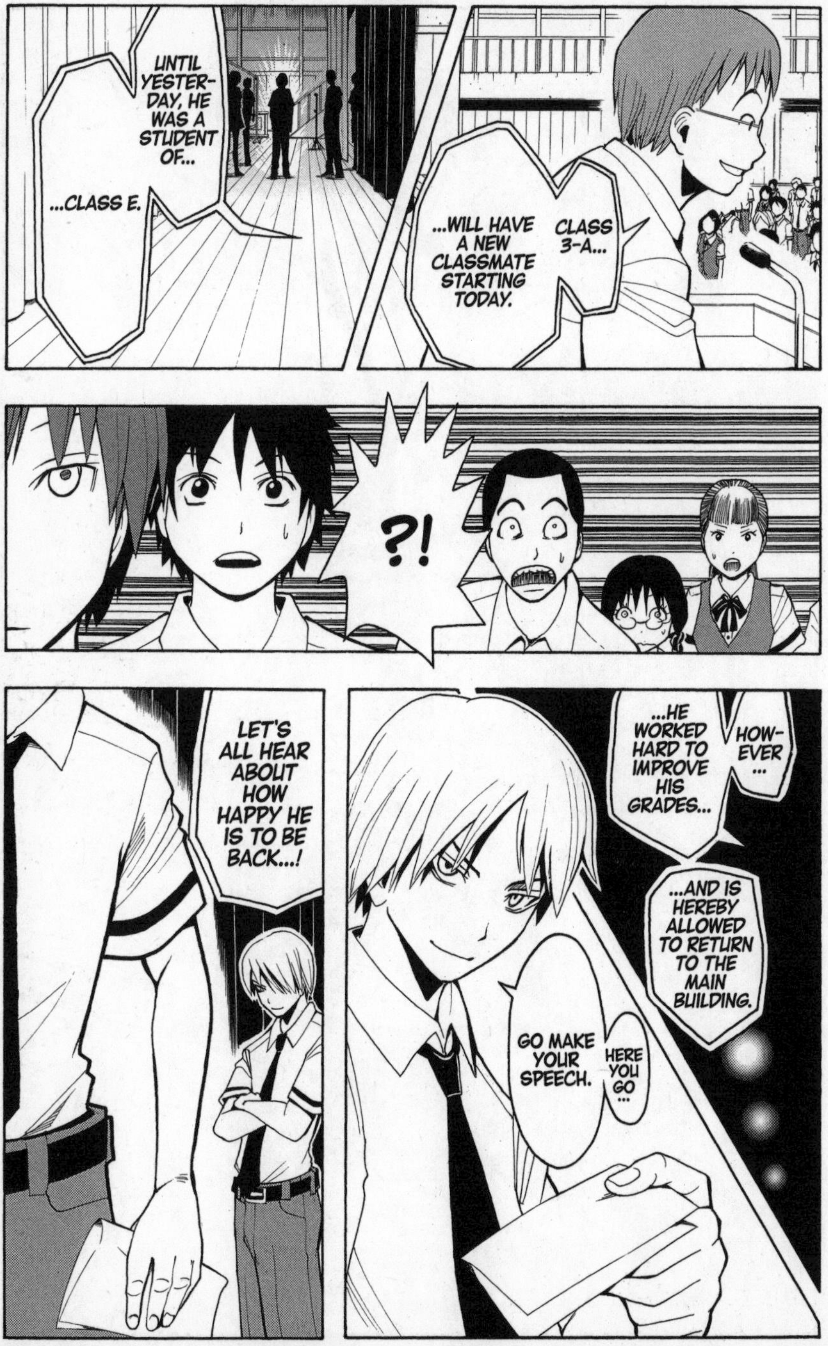
CLASS 3-A...
...WILL HAVE A NEW CLASSMATE STARTING TODAY.
UNTIL YESTER-DAY, HE WAS A STUDENT OF...
...CLASS E.
?!
HOW-EVER...
...HE WORKED HARD TO IMPROVE HIS GRADES...
...AND IS HEREBY ALLOWED TO RETURN TO THE MAIN BUILDING.
HERE YOU GO...
GO MAKE YOUR SPEECH.
LET'S ALL HEAR ABOUT HOW HAPPY HE IS TO BE BACK...!

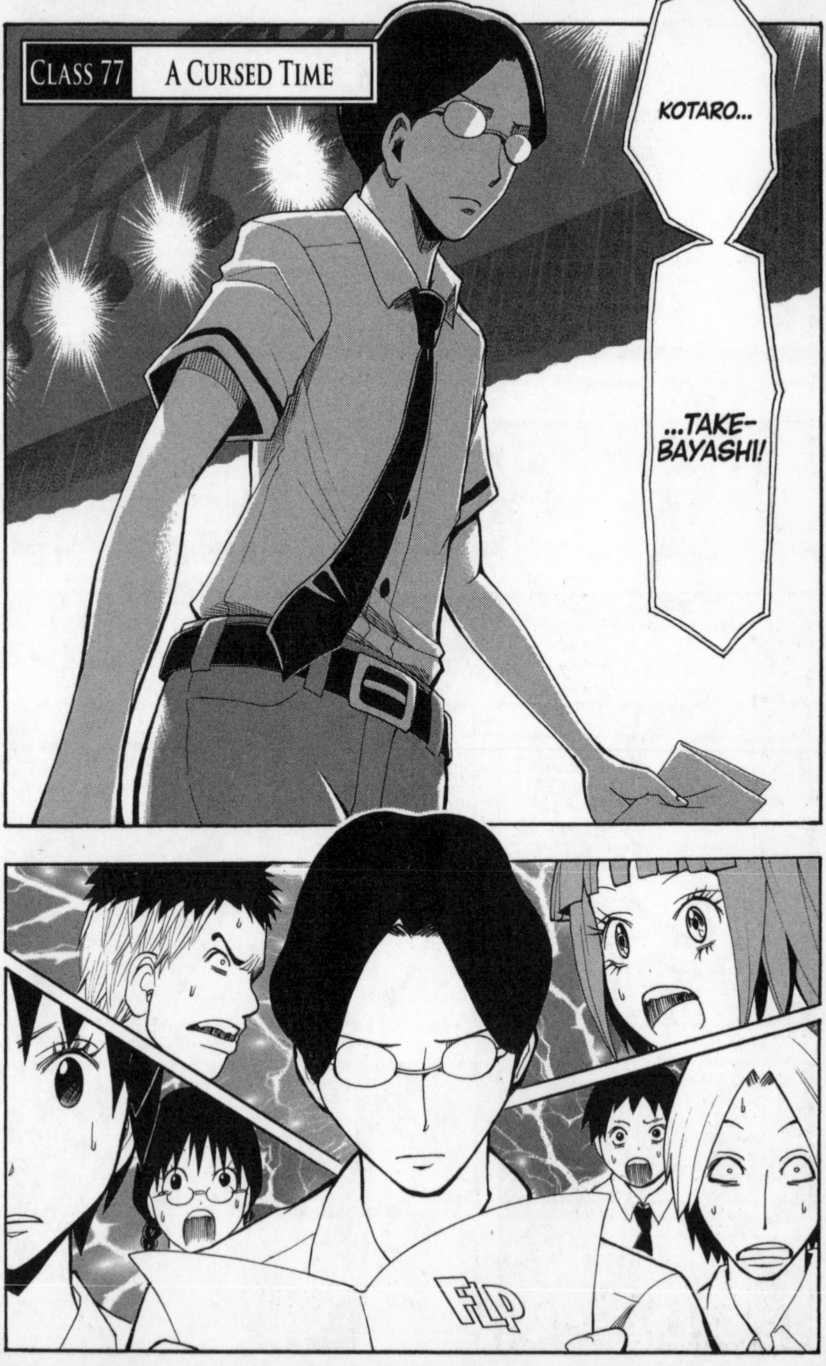
CLASS 77 A CURSED TIME
KOTARO...
...TAKE-BAYASHI!
FLP

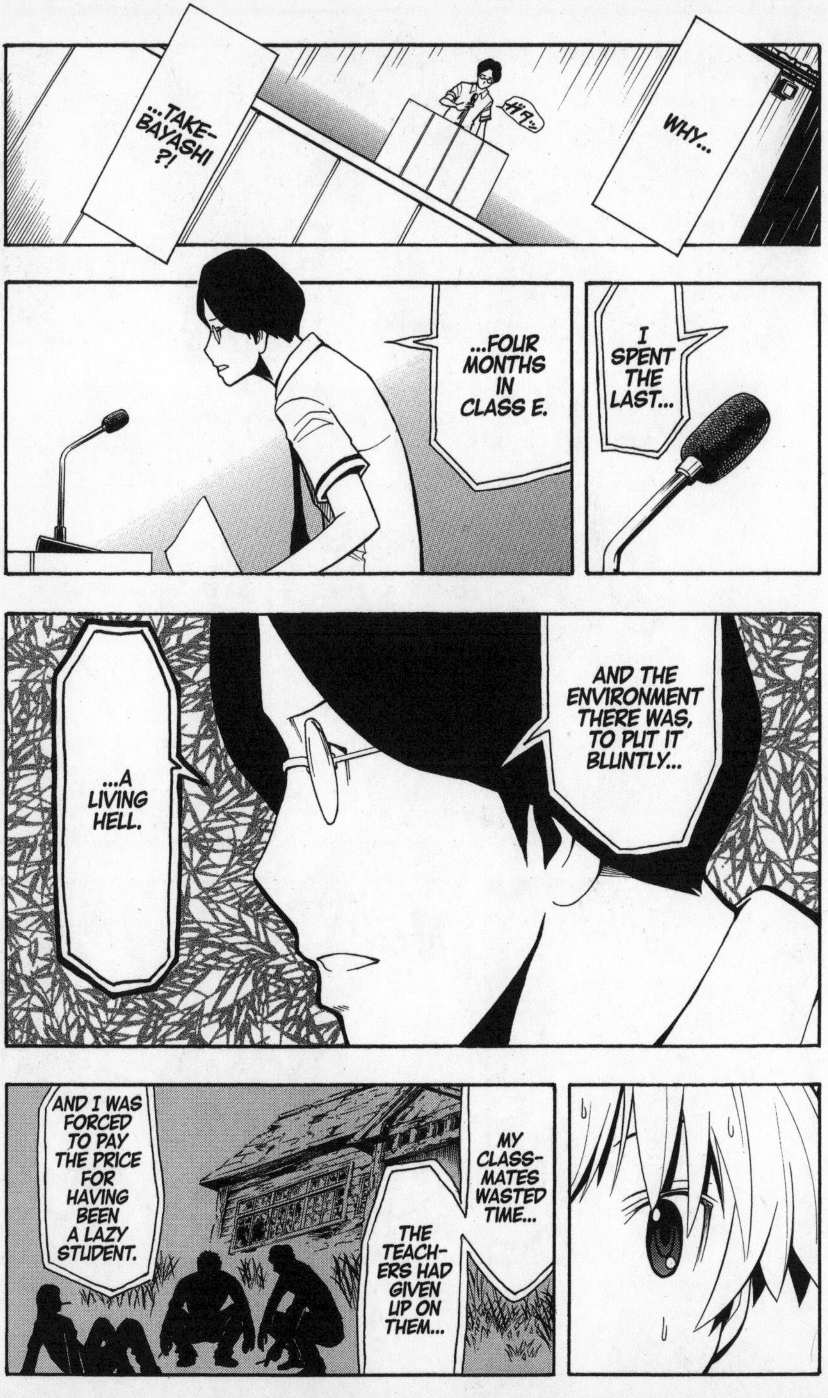
WHY...
...TAKE-BAYASHI?!
I SPENT THE LAST...
...FOUR MONTHS IN CLASS E.
AND THE ENVIRONMENT THERE WAS, TO PUT IT BLUNTLY...
...A LIVING HELL.
MY CLASS-MATES WASTED TIME...
THE TEACH-ERS HAD GIVEN UP ON THEM...
AND I WAS FORCED TO PAY THE PRICE FOR HAVING BEEN A LAZY STUDENT.

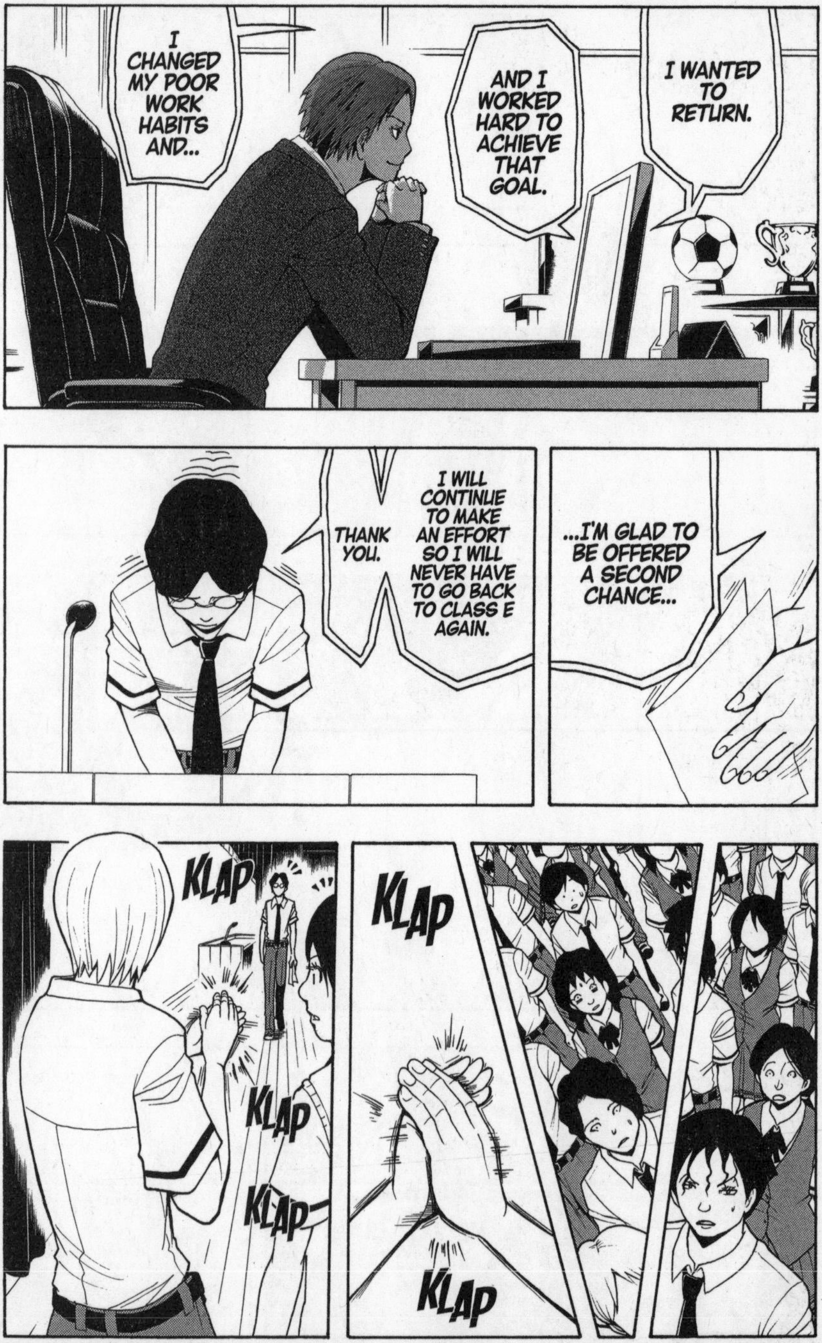
I WANTED TO RETURN.
AND I WORKED HARD TO ACHIEVE THAT GOAL.
I CHANGED MY POOR WORK HABITS AND...
...I'M GLAD TO BE OFFERED A SECOND CHANCE...
I WILL CONTINUE TO MAKE AN EFFORT SO I WILL NEVER HAVE TO GO BACK TO CLASS E AGAIN.
THANK YOU.
KLAP
KLAP
KLAP
KLAP
KLAP
KLAP

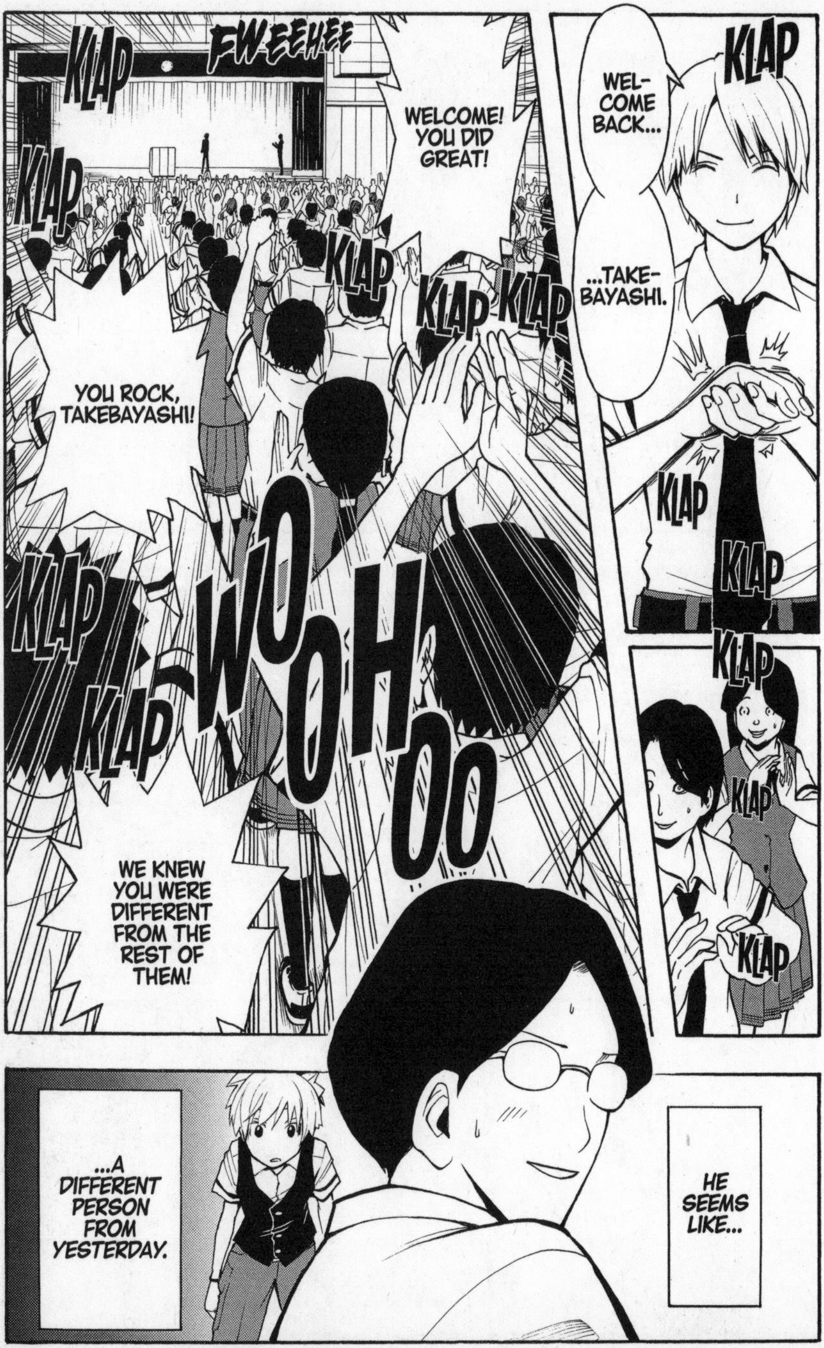
KLAP
WELCOME BACK...
...TAKEBAYASHI.
KLAP
KLAP
KLAP
KLAP
KLAP
FWEEHEE
KLAP
WELCOME! YOU DID GREAT!
KLAP
KLAP
KLAP-KLAP
YOU ROCK, TAKEBAYASHI!
WOOOHOOO
KLAP
KLAP
WE KNEW YOU WERE DIFFERENT FROM THE REST OF THEM!
HE SEEMS LIKE...
...A DIFFERENT PERSON FROM YESTERDAY.

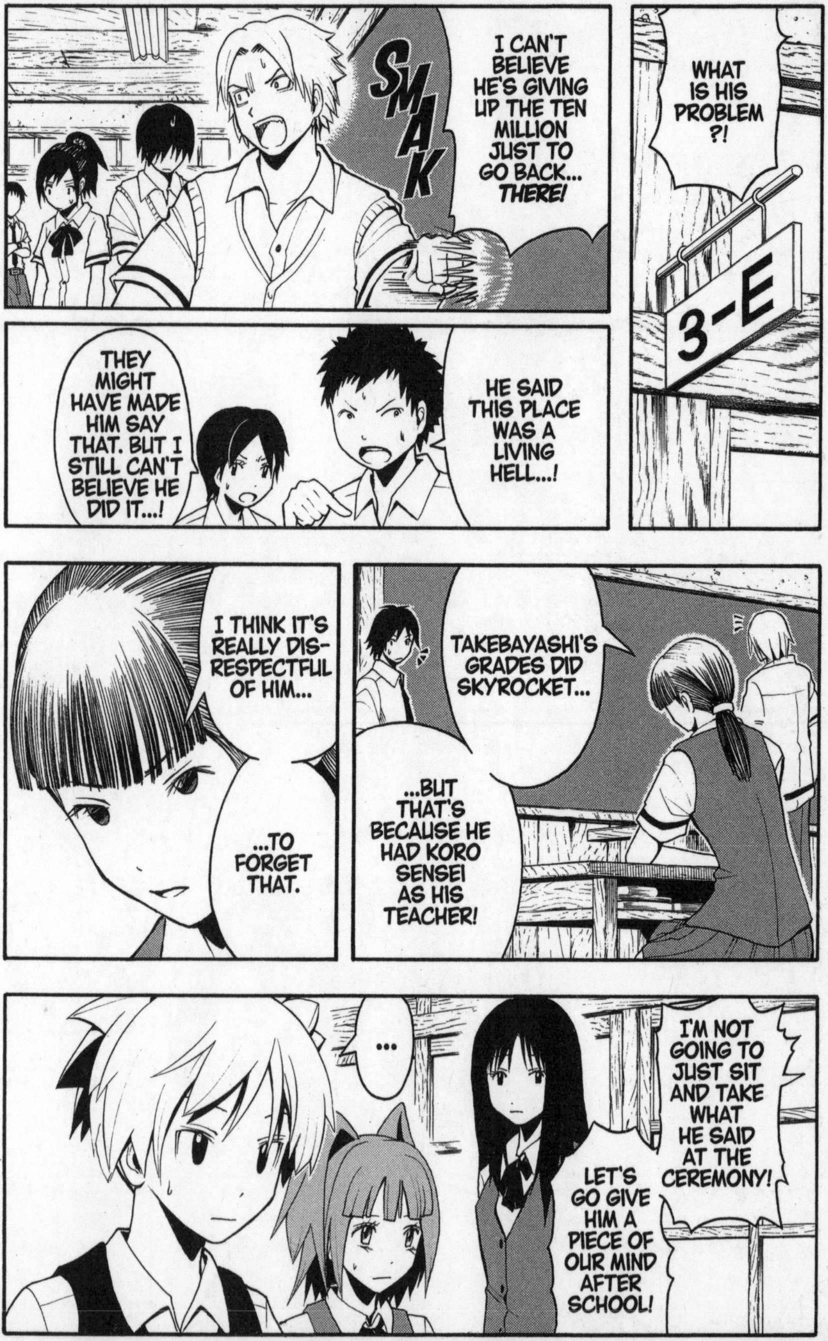
WHAT IS HIS PROBLEM?!
3-E
SMAK
I CAN'T BELIEVE HE'S GIVING UP THE TEN MILLION JUST TO GO BACK... THERE!
HE SAID THIS PLACE WAS A LIVING HELL...!
THEY MIGHT HAVE MADE HIM SAY THAT. BUT I STILL CAN'T BELIEVE HE DID IT...!
TAKEBAYASHI'S GRADES DID SKYROCKET...
...BUT THAT'S BECAUSE HE HAD KORO SENSEI AS HIS TEACHER!
I THINK IT'S REALLY DIS-RESPECTFUL OF HIM...
...TO FORGET THAT.
I'M NOT GOING TO JUST SIT AND TAKE WHAT HE SAID AT THE CEREMONY!
LET'S GO GIVE HIM A PIECE OF OUR MIND AFTER SCHOOL!
...

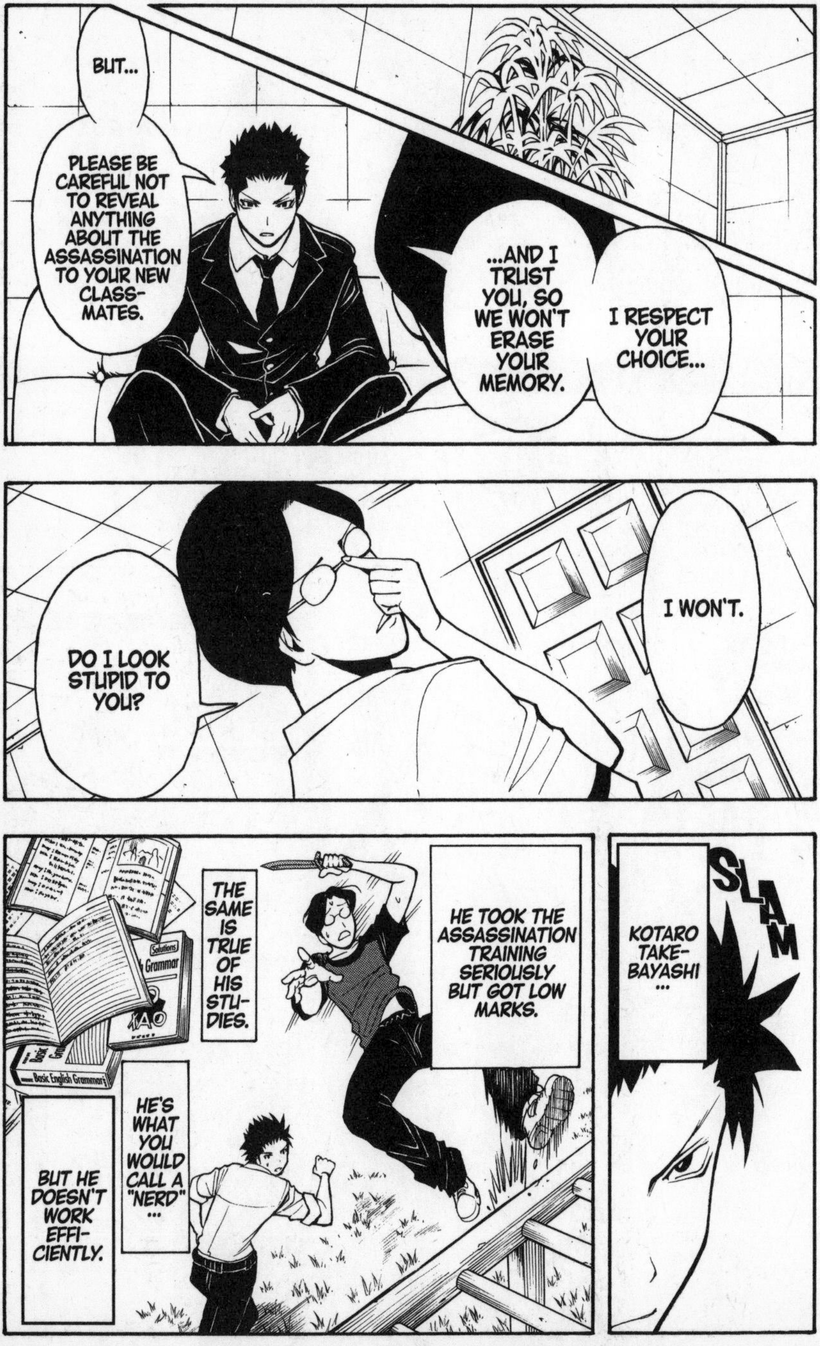
I RESPECT YOUR CHOICE...
...AND I TRUST YOU, SO WE WON'T ERASE YOUR MEMORY.
BUT...
PLEASE BE CAREFUL NOT TO REVEAL ANYTHING ABOUT THE ASSASSINATION TO YOUR NEW CLASS-MATES.
I WON'T.
DO I LOOK STUPID TO YOU?
SLAM
KOTARO TAKE-BAYASHI...
HE TOOK THE ASSASSINATION TRAINING SERIOUSLY BUT GOT LOW MARKS.
THE SAME IS TRUE OF HIS STU-DIES.
Solutions
Grammar
Basic English Grammar
HE'S WHAT YOU WOULD CALL A "NERD"...
BUT HE DOESN'T WORK EFFI-CIENTLY.

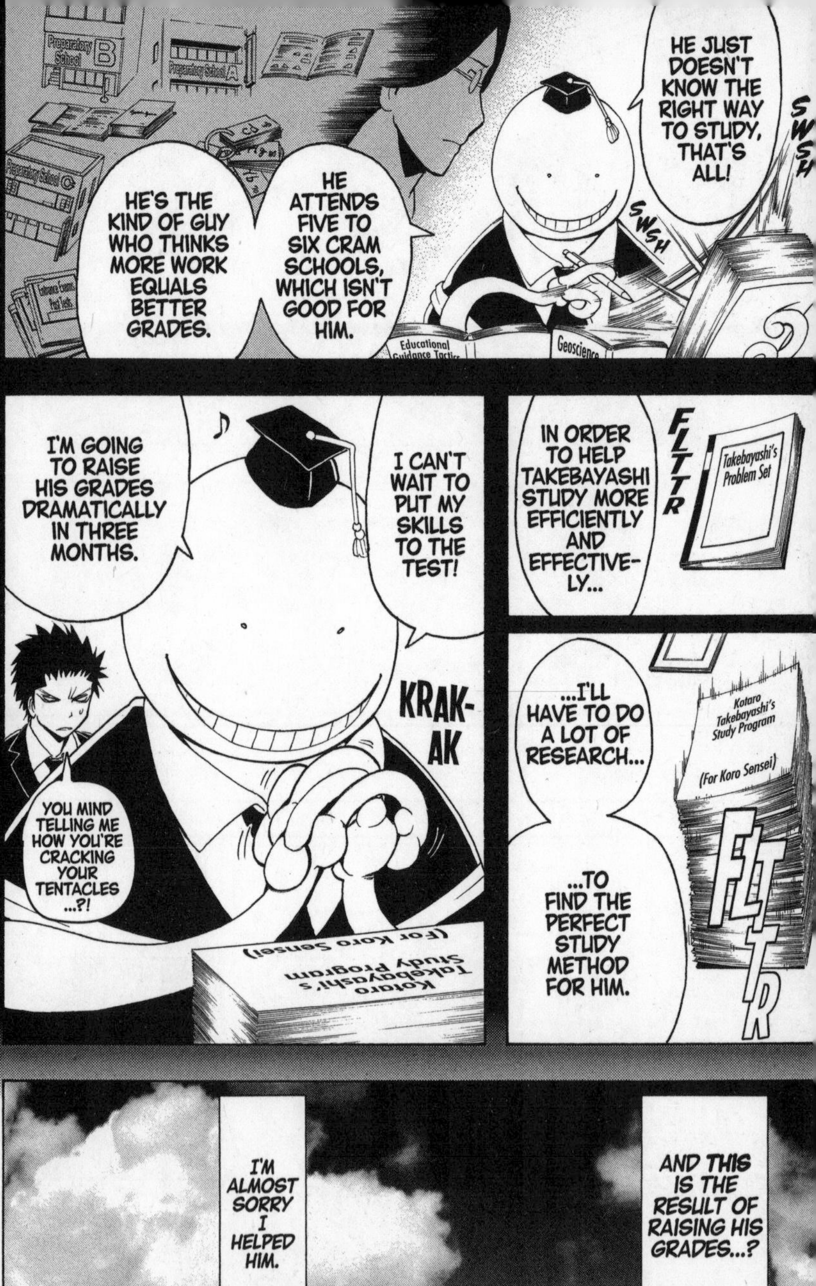
HE JUST DOESN'T KNOW THE RIGHT WAY TO STUDY, THAT'S ALL!
SWSH
SWSH
HE ATTENDS FIVE TO SIX CRAM SCHOOLS, WHICH ISN'T GOOD FOR HIM.
HE'S THE KIND OF GUY WHO THINKS MORE WORK EQUALS BETTER GRADES.
Preparatory School B
Preparatory School A
Preparatory School C
Entrance Exams Past Tests
Educational Guidance Tactics
Geoscience
IN ORDER TO HELP TAKEBAYASHI STUDY MORE EFFICIENTLY AND EFFECTIVE-LY...
FLTTR
Takebayashi's Problem Set
...I'LL HAVE TO DO A LOT OF RESEARCH...
...TO FIND THE PERFECT STUDY METHOD FOR HIM.
Kotaro Takebayashi's Study Program (For Koro Sensei)
FLTTR
I CAN'T WAIT TO PUT MY SKILLS TO THE TEST!
I'M GOING TO RAISE HIS GRADES DRAMATICALLY IN THREE MONTHS.
KRAK-AK
YOU MIND TELLING ME HOW YOU'RE CRACKING YOUR TENTACLES ...?!
Kotaro Takebayashi's Study Program (For Koro Sensei)
AND THIS IS THE RESULT OF RAISING HIS GRADES...?
I'M ALMOST SORRY I HELPED HIM.

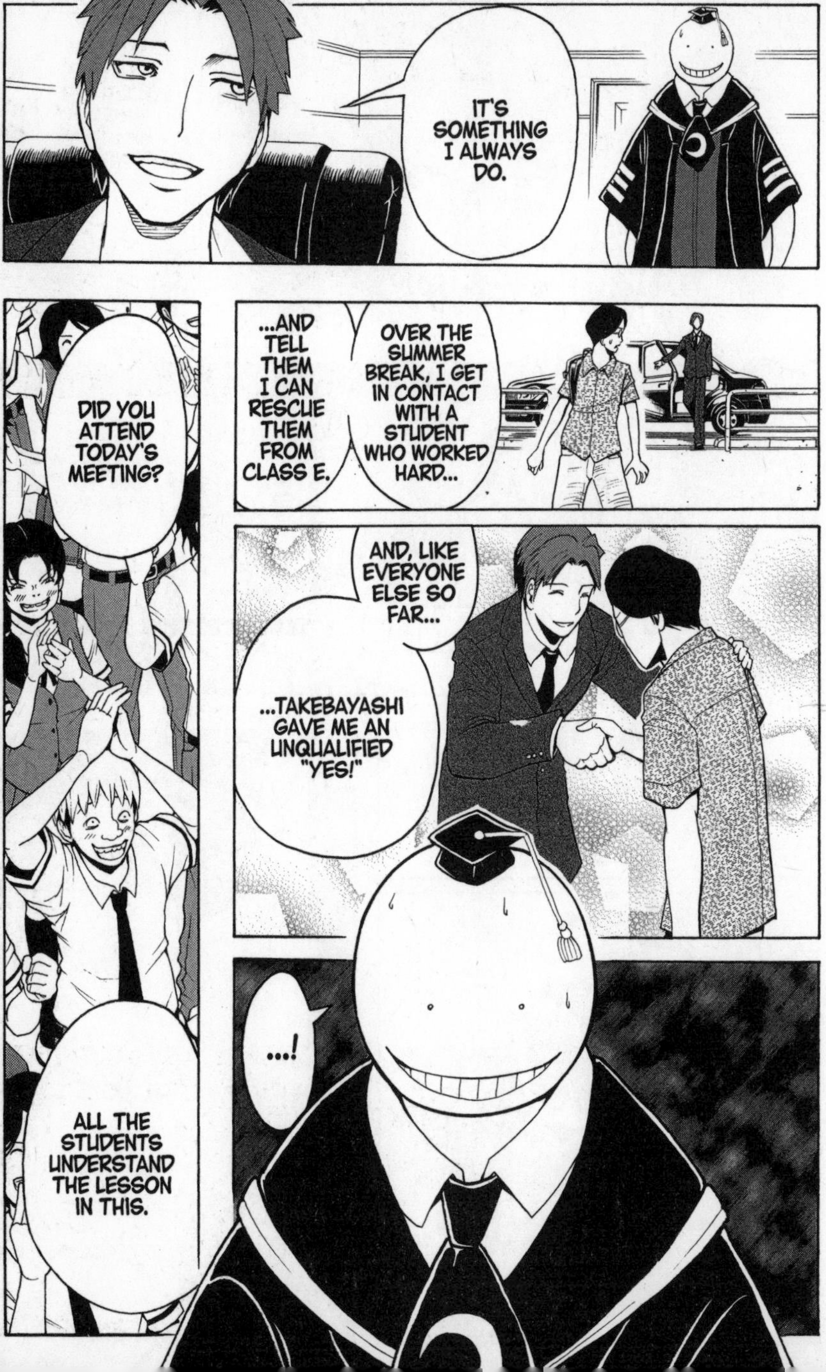
IT'S SOMETHING I ALWAYS DO.
OVER THE SUMMER BREAK, I GET IN CONTACT WITH A STUDENT WHO WORKED HARD...
...AND TELL THEM I CAN RESCUE THEM FROM CLASS E.
AND, LIKE EVERYONE ELSE SO FAR...
...TAKEBAYASHI GAVE ME AN UNQUALIFIED "YES!"
...!
DID YOU ATTEND TODAY'S MEETING?
ALL THE STUDENTS UNDERSTAND THE LESSON IN THIS.

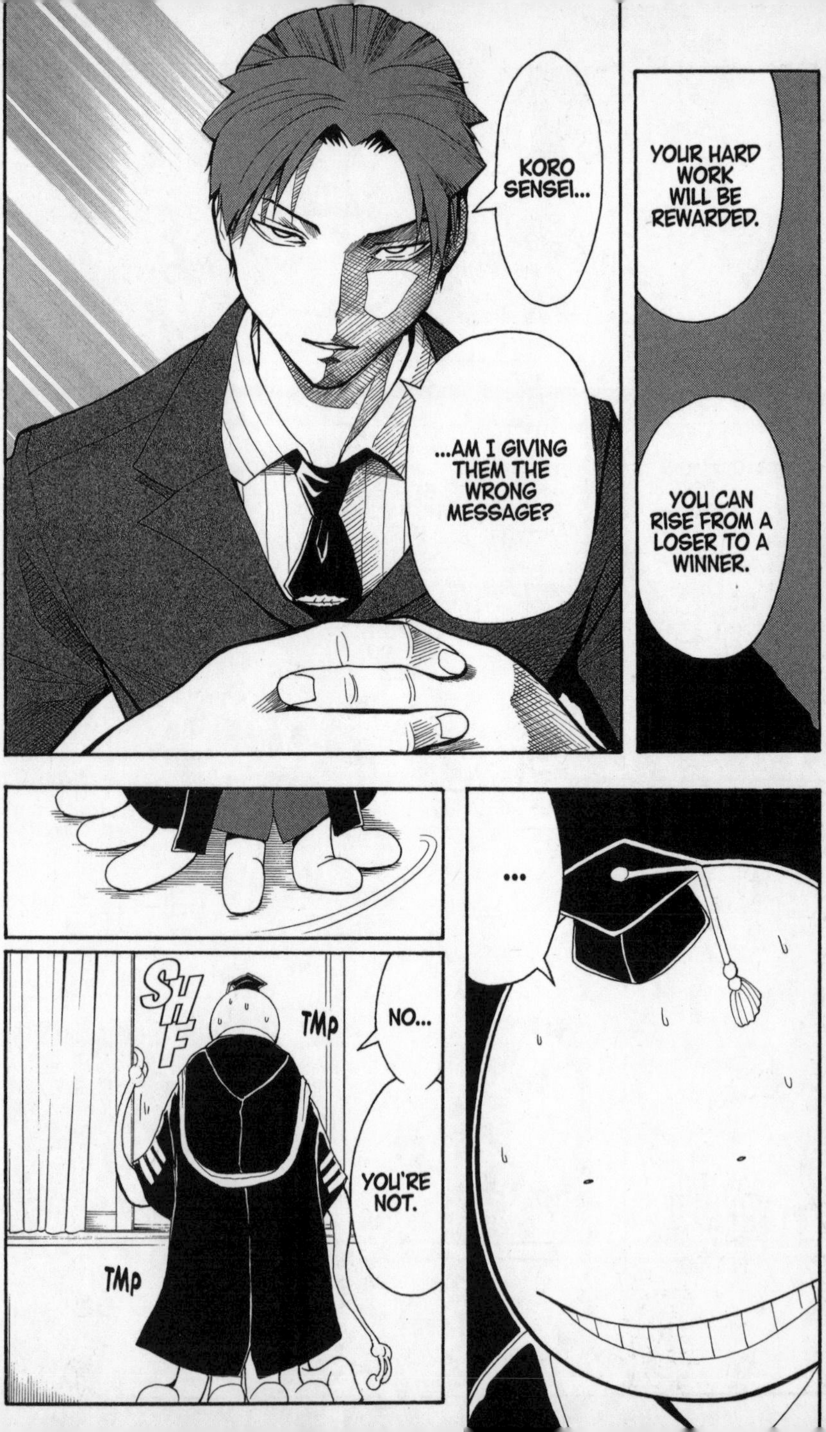

YOUR HARD WORK WILL BE REWARDED.
YOU CAN RISE FROM A LOSER TO A WINNER.
KORO SENSEI...
...AM I GIVING THEM THE WRONG MESSAGE?
...
NO...
YOU'RE NOT.
SHF
TMP
TMP

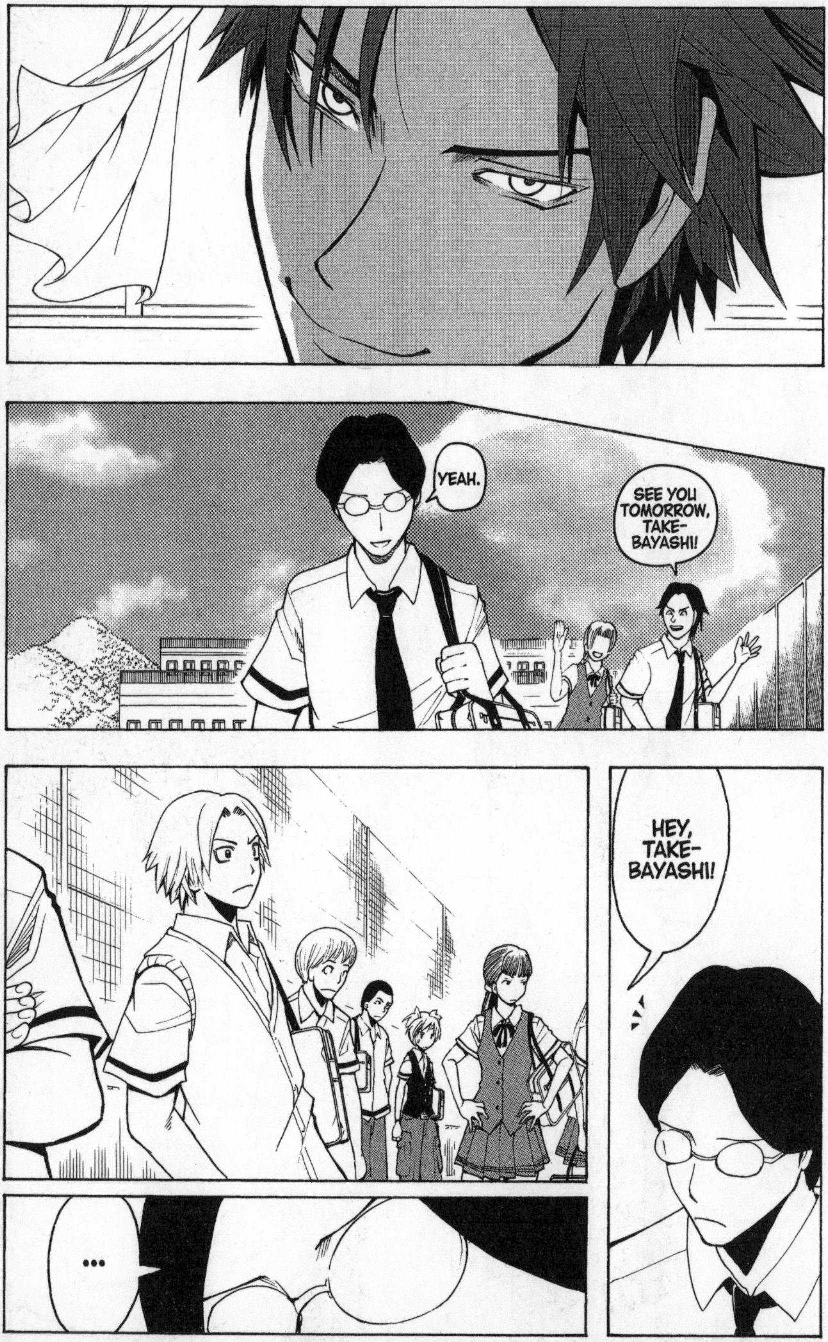
SEE YOU TOMORROW, TAKE-BAYASHI!
YEAH.
HEY, TAKE-BAYASHI!
...

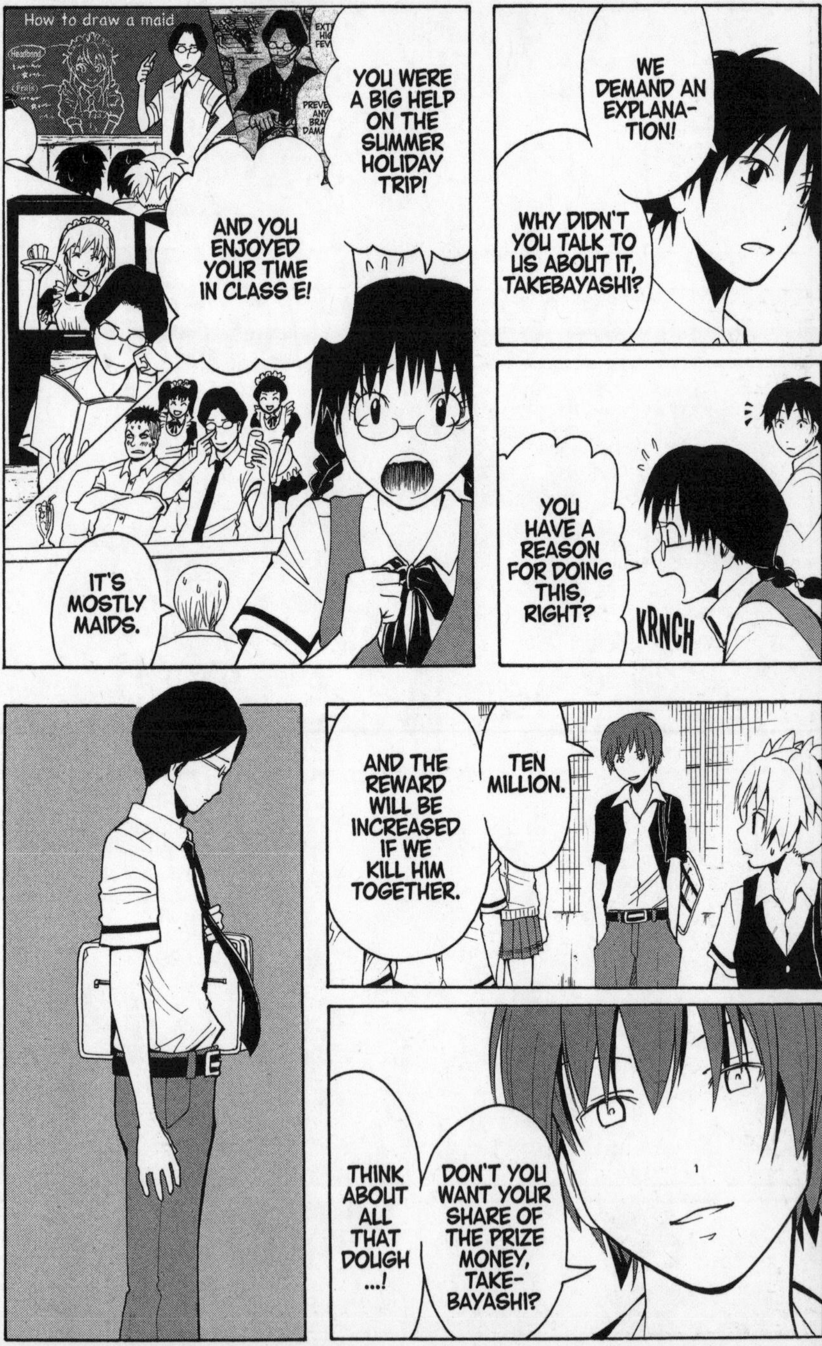
WE DEMAND AN EXPLANATION!
WHY DIDN'T YOU TALK TO US ABOUT IT, TAKEBAYASHI?
YOU HAVE A REASON FOR DOING THIS, RIGHT?
KRNCH
YOU WERE A BIG HELP ON THE SUMMER HOLIDAY TRIP!
How to draw a maid
Headband
Frills
AND YOU ENJOYED YOUR TIME IN CLASS E!
IT'S MOSTLY MAIDS.
TEN MILLION.
AND THE REWARD WILL BE INCREASED IF WE KILL HIM TOGETHER.
DON'T YOU WANT YOUR SHARE OF THE PRIZE MONEY, TAKE-BAYASHI?
THINK ABOUT ALL THAT DOUGH ...!

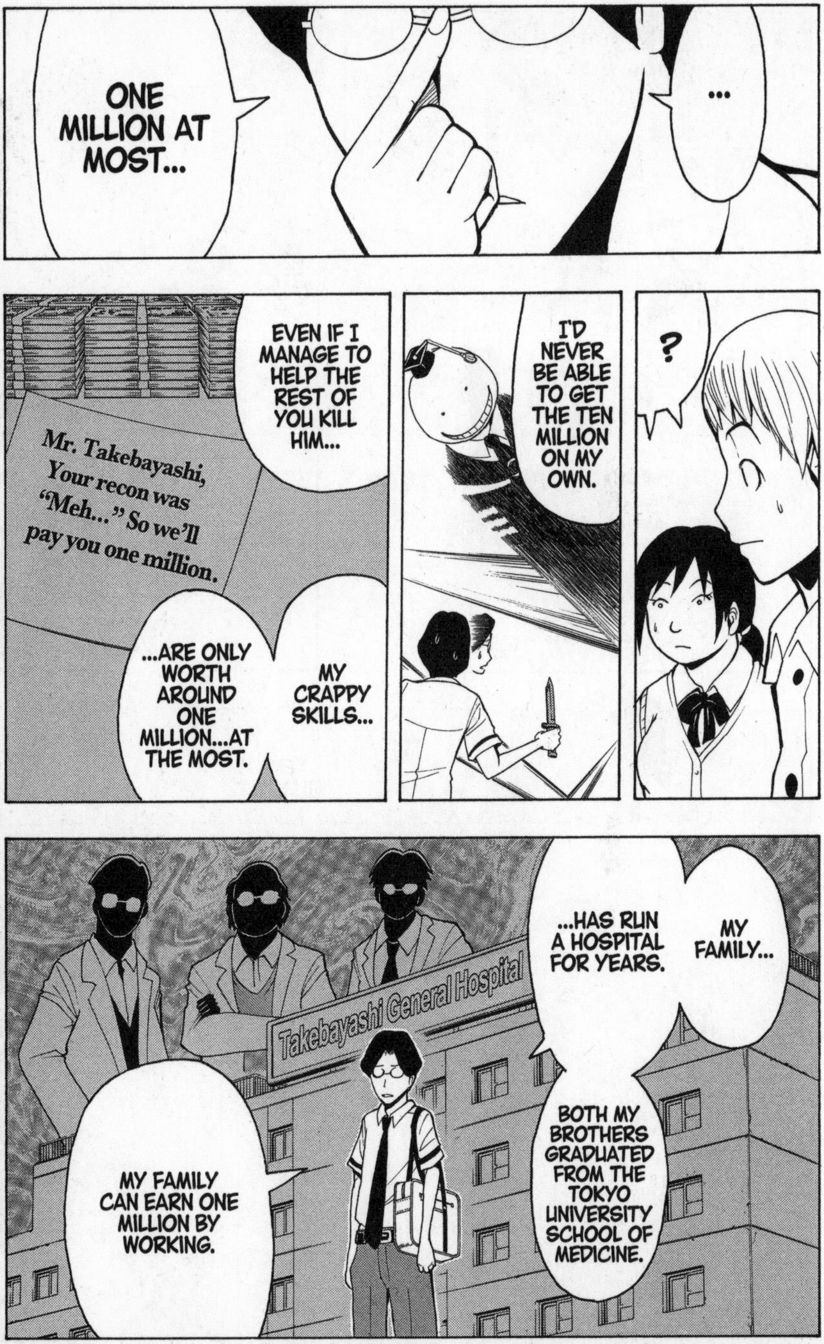
...
ONE MILLION AT MOST...
?
I'D NEVER BE ABLE TO GET THE TEN MILLION ON MY OWN.
EVEN IF I MANAGE TO HELP THE REST OF YOU KILL HIM...
Mr. Takebayashi, Your recon was "Meh..." So we'll pay you one million.
MY CRAPPY SKILLS...
...ARE ONLY WORTH AROUND ONE MILLION...AT THE MOST.
MY FAMILY...
...HAS RUN A HOSPITAL FOR YEARS.
Takebayashi General Hospital
BOTH MY BROTHERS GRADUATED FROM THE TOKYO UNIVERSITY SCHOOL OF MEDICINE.
MY FAMILY CAN EARN ONE MILLION BY WORKING.

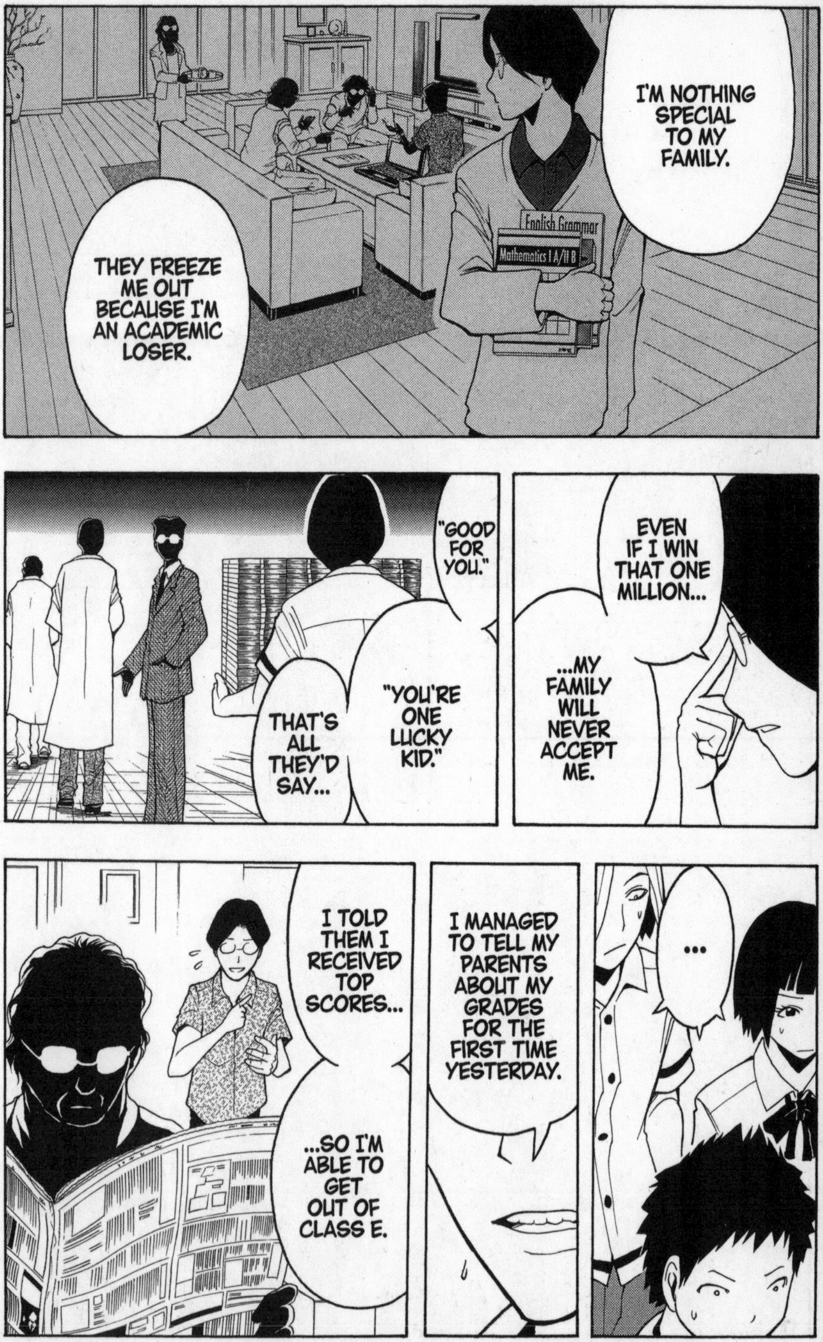
I'M NOTHING SPECIAL TO MY FAMILY.
English Grammar
Mathematics I A/II B
THEY FREEZE ME OUT BECAUSE I'M AN ACADEMIC LOSER.
EVEN IF I WIN THAT ONE MILLION...
...MY FAMILY WILL NEVER ACCEPT ME.
"GOOD FOR YOU."
"YOU'RE ONE LUCKY KID."
THAT'S ALL THEY'D SAY...
...
I MANAGED TO TELL MY PARENTS ABOUT MY GRADES FOR THE FIRST TIME YESTERDAY.
I TOLD THEM I RECEIVED TOP SCORES...
...SO I'M ABLE TO GET OUT OF CLASS E.

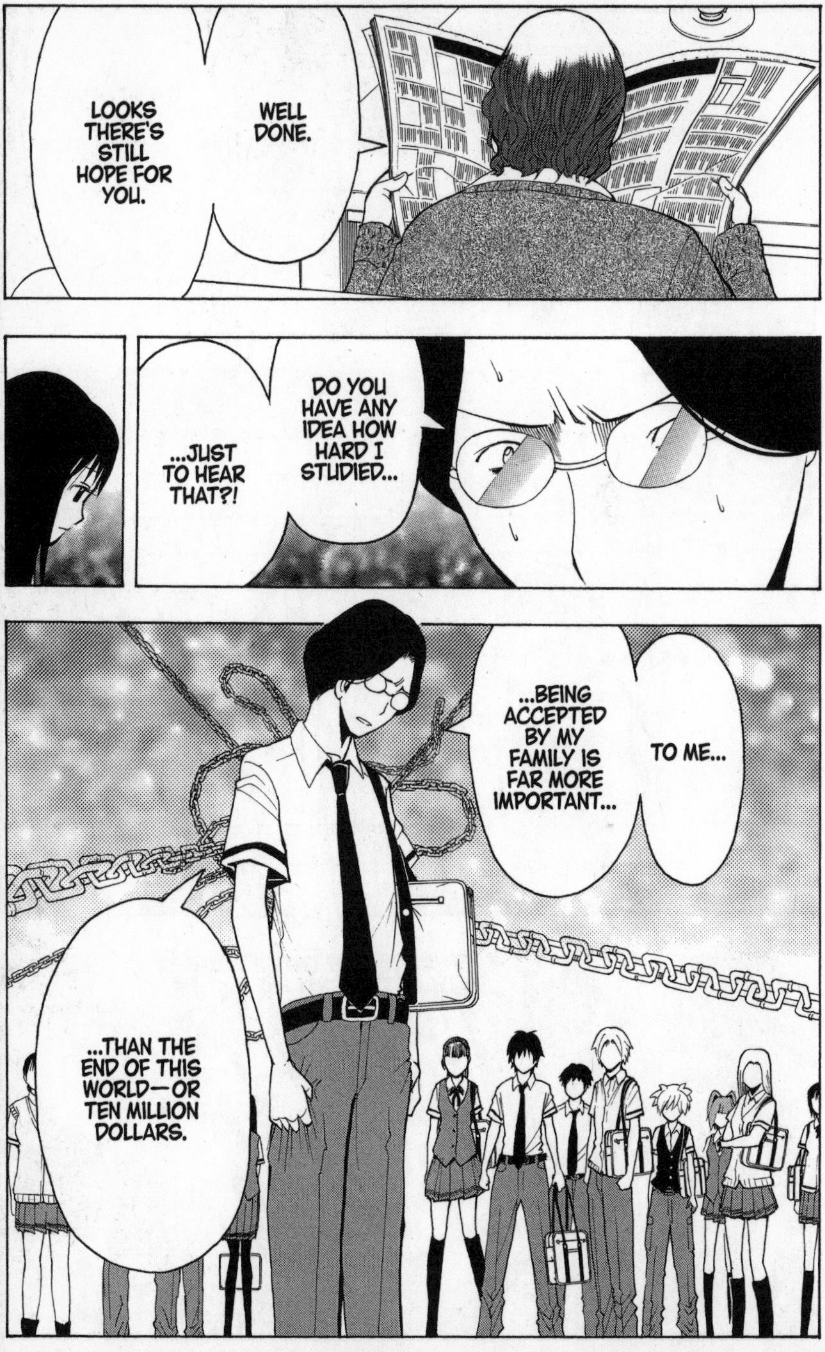
WELL DONE.
LOOKS THERE'S STILL HOPE FOR YOU.
DO YOU HAVE ANY IDEA HOW HARD I STUDIED...
...JUST TO HEAR THAT?!
TO ME...
...BEING ACCEPTED BY MY FAMILY IS FAR MORE IMPORTANT...
...THAN THE END OF THIS WORLD—OR TEN MILLION DOLLARS.

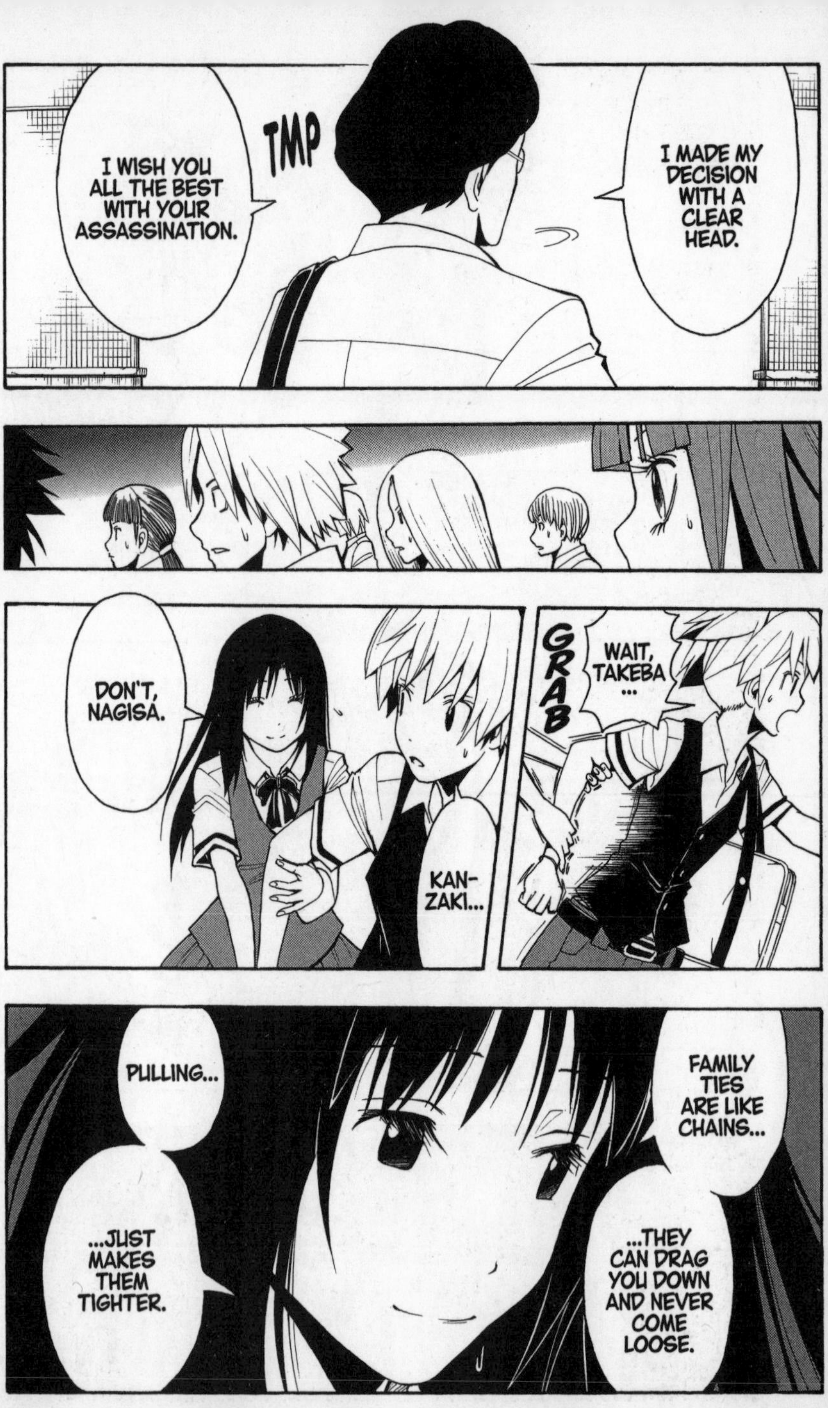
I MADE MY DECISION WITH A CLEAR HEAD.
TMP
I WISH YOU ALL THE BEST WITH YOUR ASSASSINATION.
GRAB
WAIT, TAKEBA...
DON'T, NAGISA.
KAN-ZAKI...
FAMILY TIES ARE LIKE CHAINS...
...THEY CAN DRAG YOU DOWN AND NEVER COME LOOSE.
PULLING...
...JUST MAKES THEM TIGHTER.

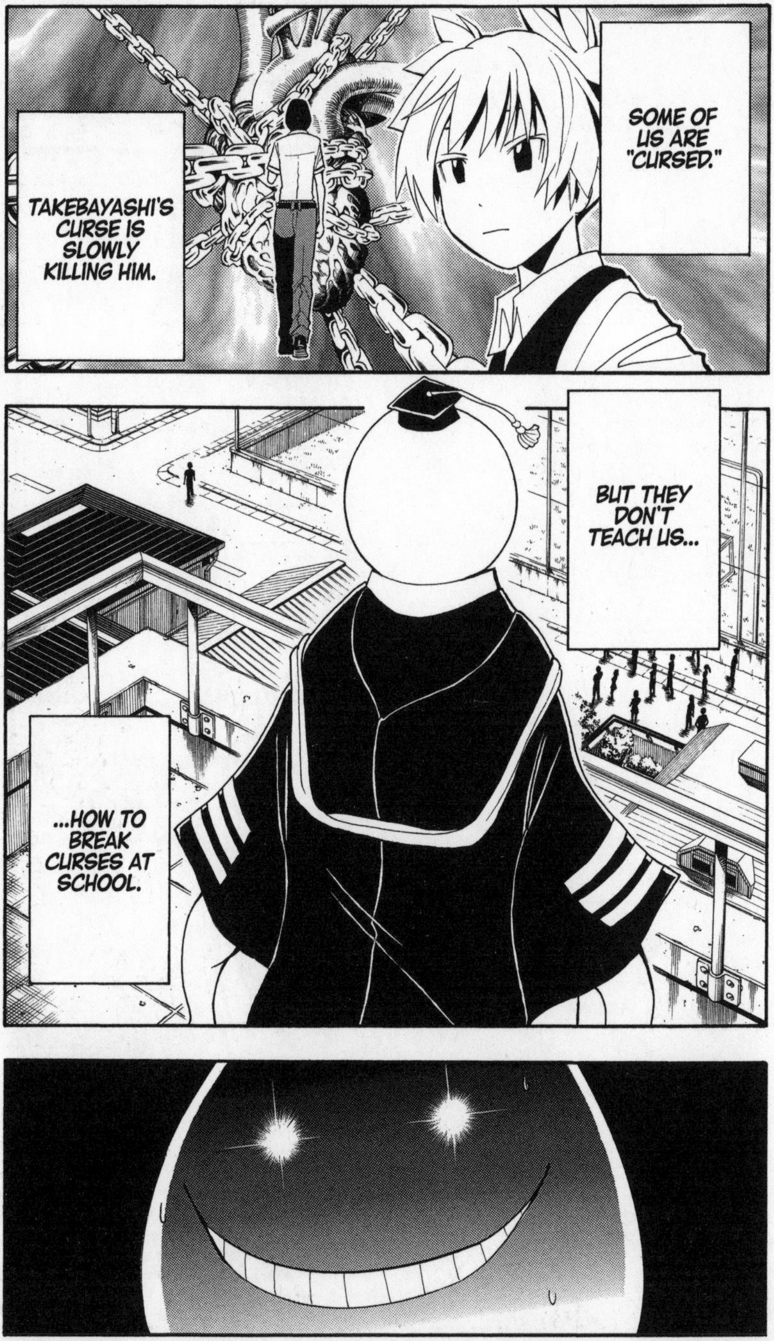
SOME OF US ARE "CURSED."
TAKEBAYASHI'S CURSE IS SLOWLY KILLING HIM.
BUT THEY DON'T TEACH US...
...HOW TO BREAK CURSES AT SCHOOL.

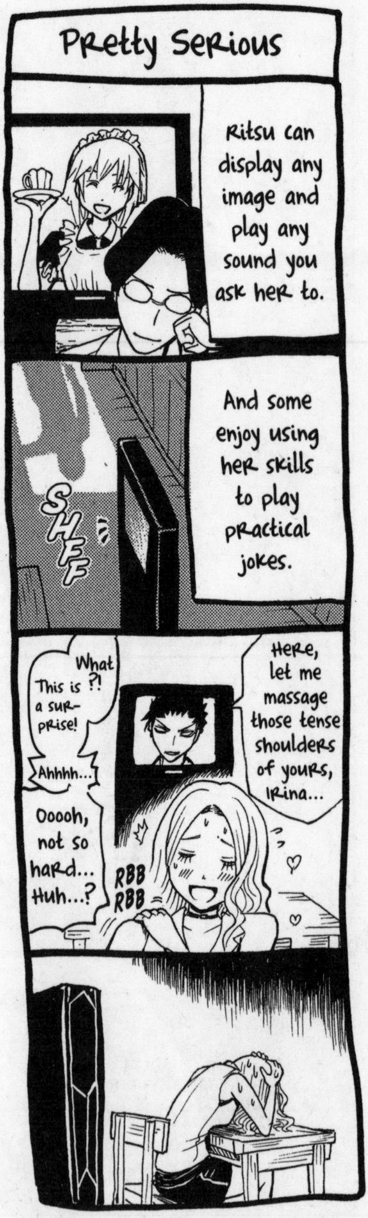
Pretty Serious
Ritsu can display any image and play any sound you ask her to.
And some enjoy using her skills to play practical jokes.
SHFF
Here, let me massage those tense shoulders of yours, Irina...
What?! This is a surprise!
Ahhhh...
Ooooh, not so hard... Huh...?
RBB RBB

Class 78 Time for Takebayashi

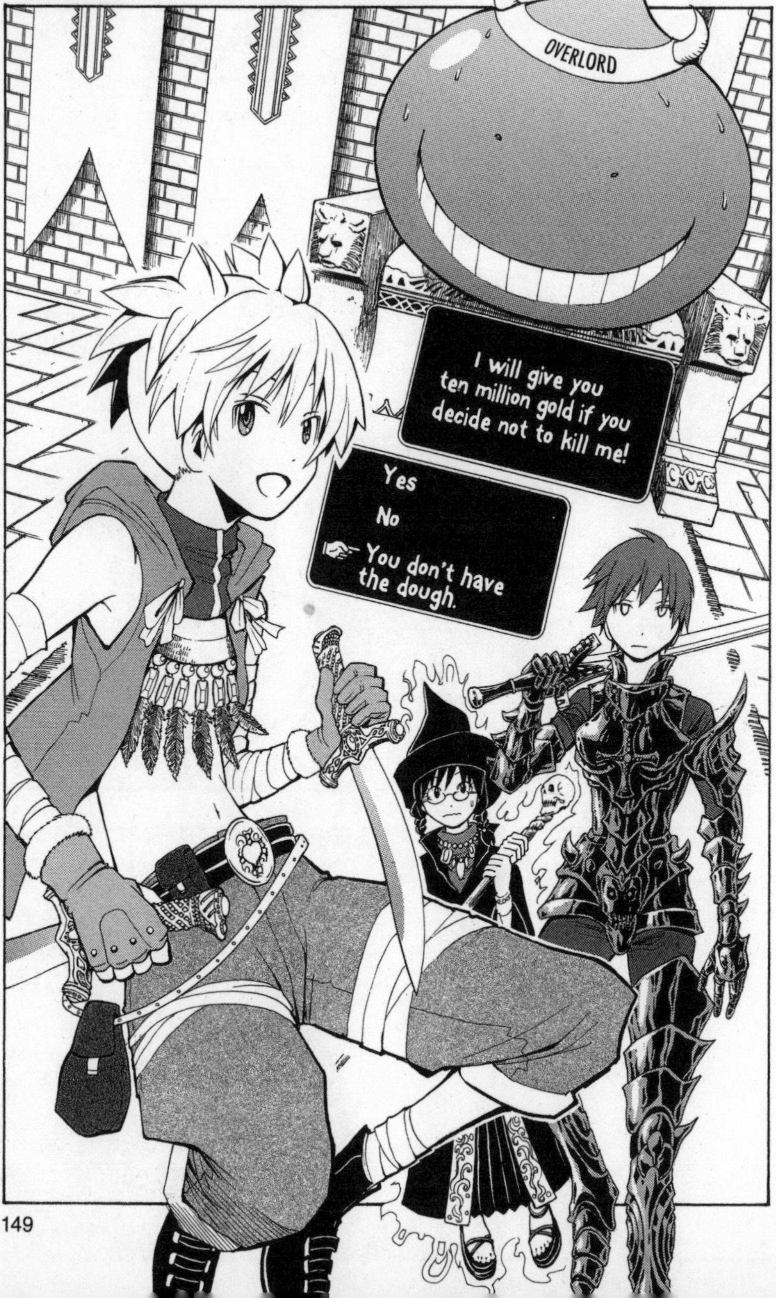
OVERLORD
I will give you ten million gold if you decide not to kill me!
Yes
No
You don't have the dough.

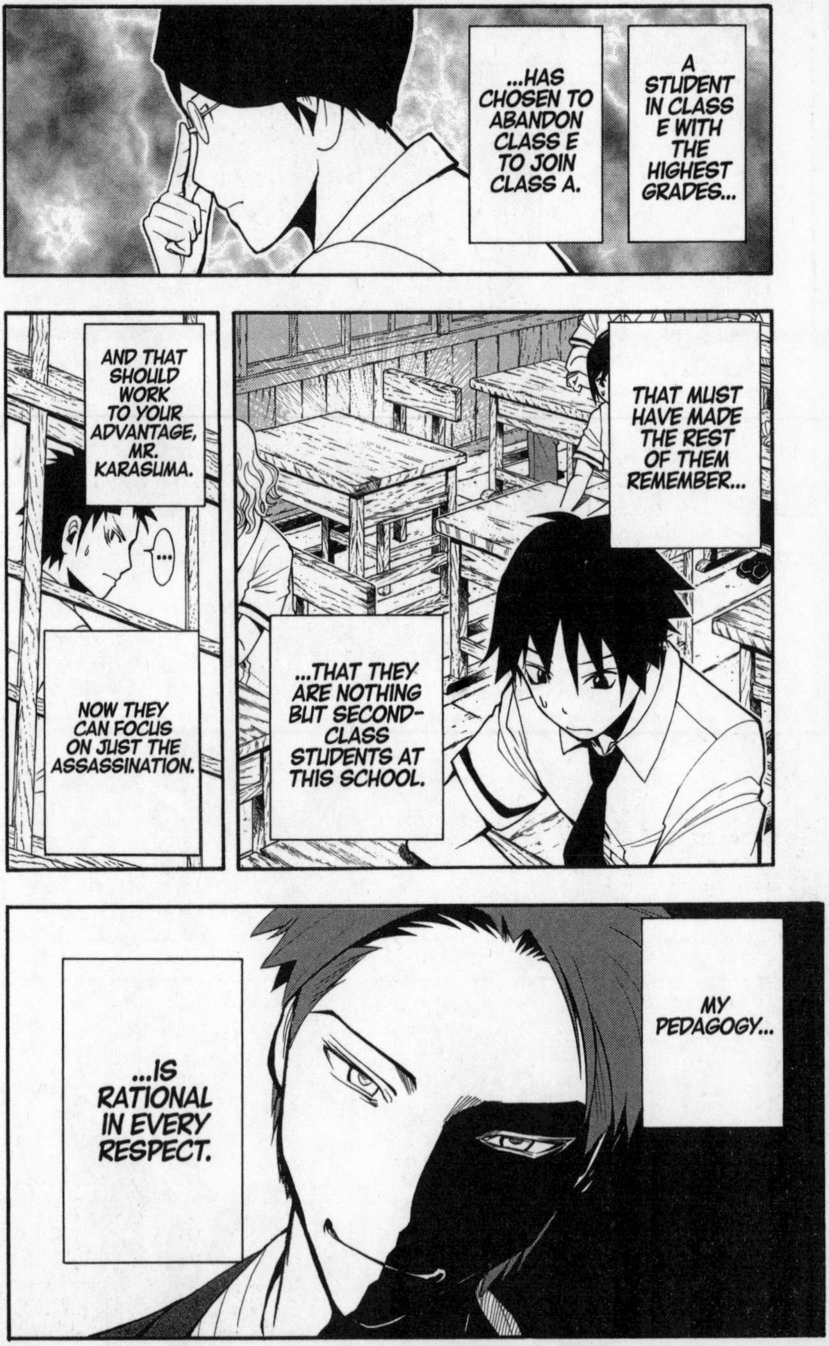
A STUDENT IN CLASS E WITH THE HIGHEST GRADES...
...HAS CHOSEN TO ABANDON CLASS E TO JOIN CLASS A.
THAT MUST HAVE MADE THE REST OF THEM REMEMBER...
...THAT THEY ARE NOTHING BUT SECOND-CLASS STUDENTS AT THIS SCHOOL.
AND THAT SHOULD WORK TO YOUR ADVANTAGE, MR. KARASUMA.
...
NOW THEY CAN FOCUS ON JUST THE ASSASSINATION.
MY PEDAGOGY...
...IS RATIONAL IN EVERY RESPECT.

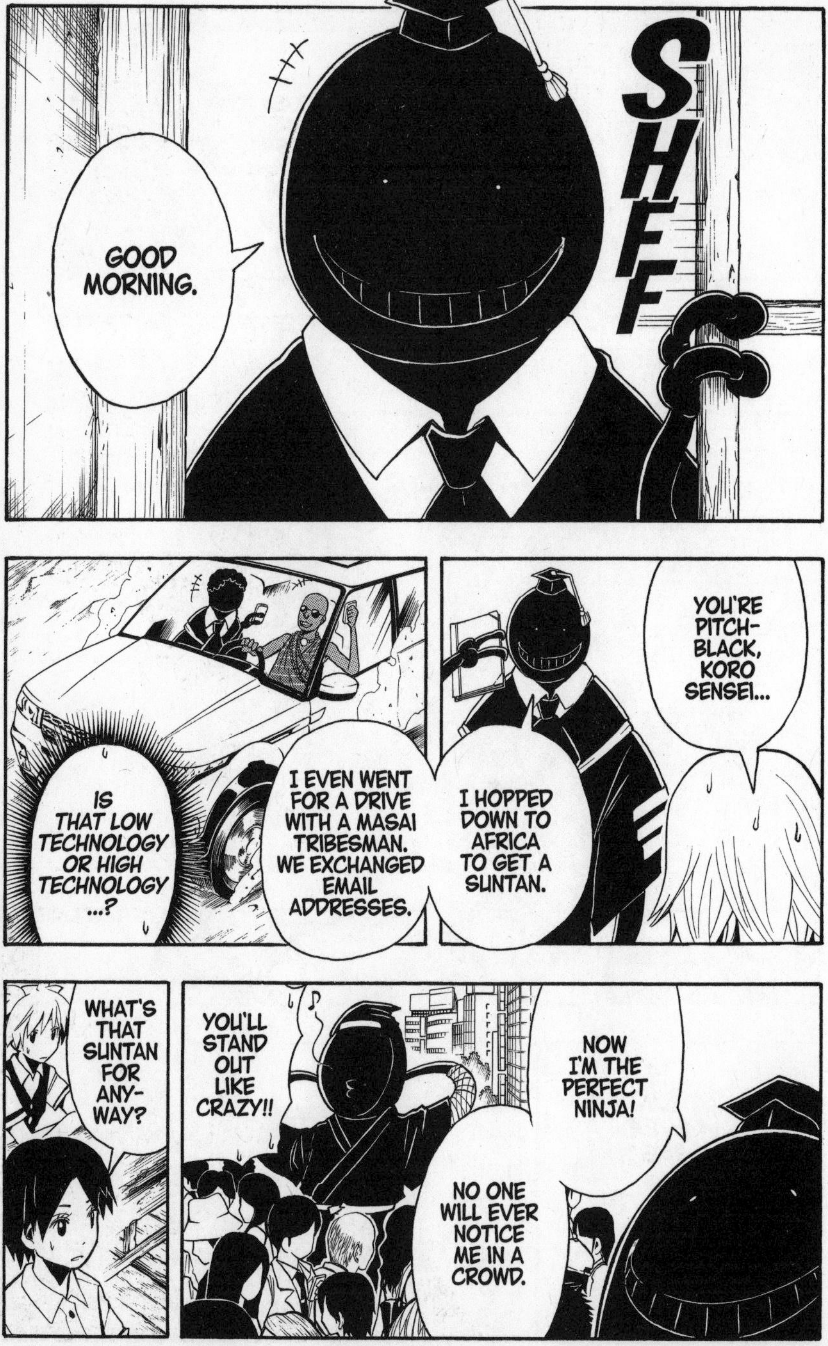
SHFF
GOOD MORNING.
YOU'RE PITCH-BLACK, KORO SENSEI...
I HOPPED DOWN TO AFRICA TO GET A SUNTAN.
I EVEN WENT FOR A DRIVE WITH A MASAI TRIBESMAN. WE EXCHANGED EMAIL ADDRESSES.
IS THAT LOW TECHNOLOGY OR HIGH TECHNOLOGY ...?
NOW I'M THE PERFECT NINJA!
NO ONE WILL EVER NOTICE ME IN A CROWD.
YOU'LL STAND OUT LIKE CRAZY!!
WHAT'S THAT SUNTAN FOR ANY-WAY?

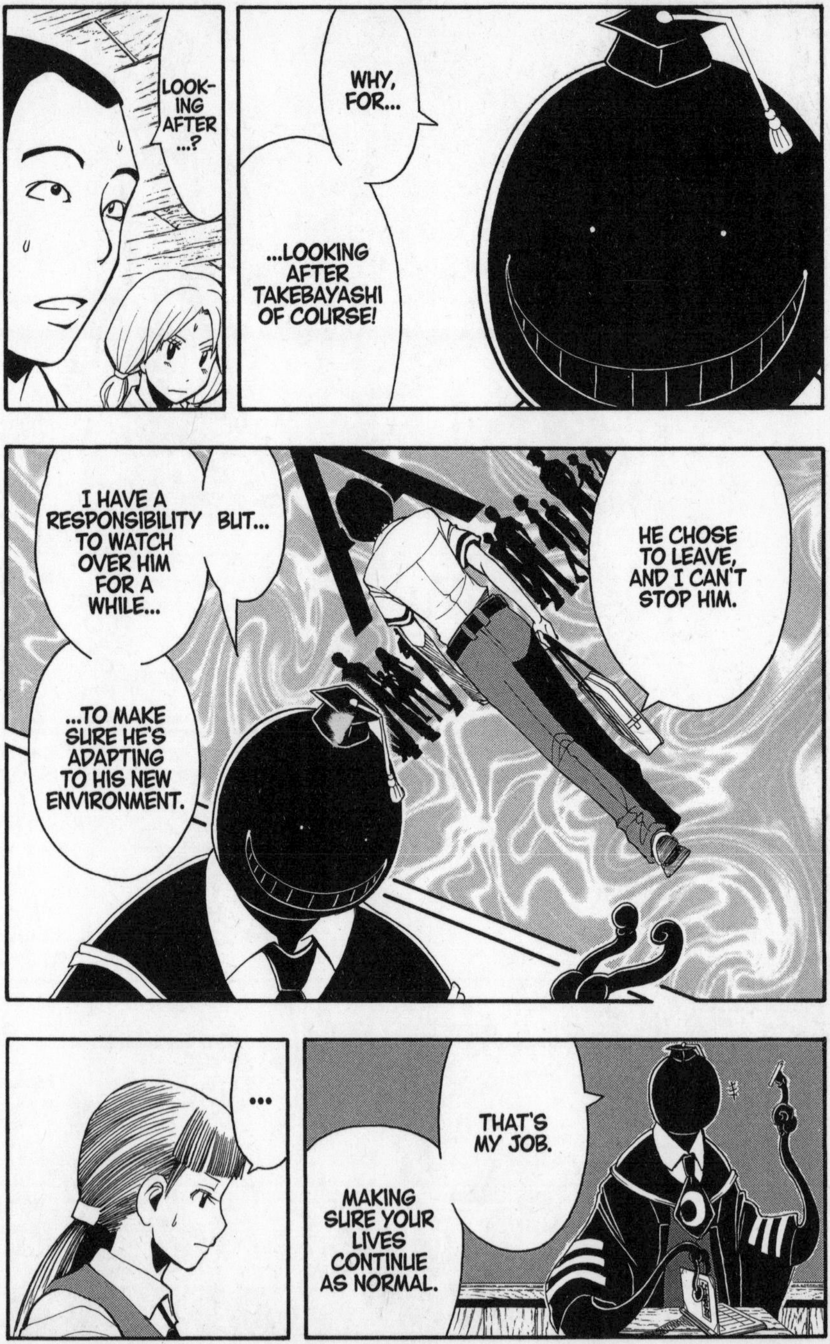
WHY, FOR...
...LOOKING AFTER TAKEBAYASHI OF COURSE!
LOOKING AFTER ...?
HE CHOSE TO LEAVE, AND I CAN'T STOP HIM.
BUT...
I HAVE A RESPONSIBILITY TO WATCH OVER HIM FOR A WHILE...
...TO MAKE SURE HE'S ADAPTING TO HIS NEW ENVIRONMENT.
THAT'S MY JOB.
MAKING SURE YOUR LIVES CONTINUE AS NORMAL.
...

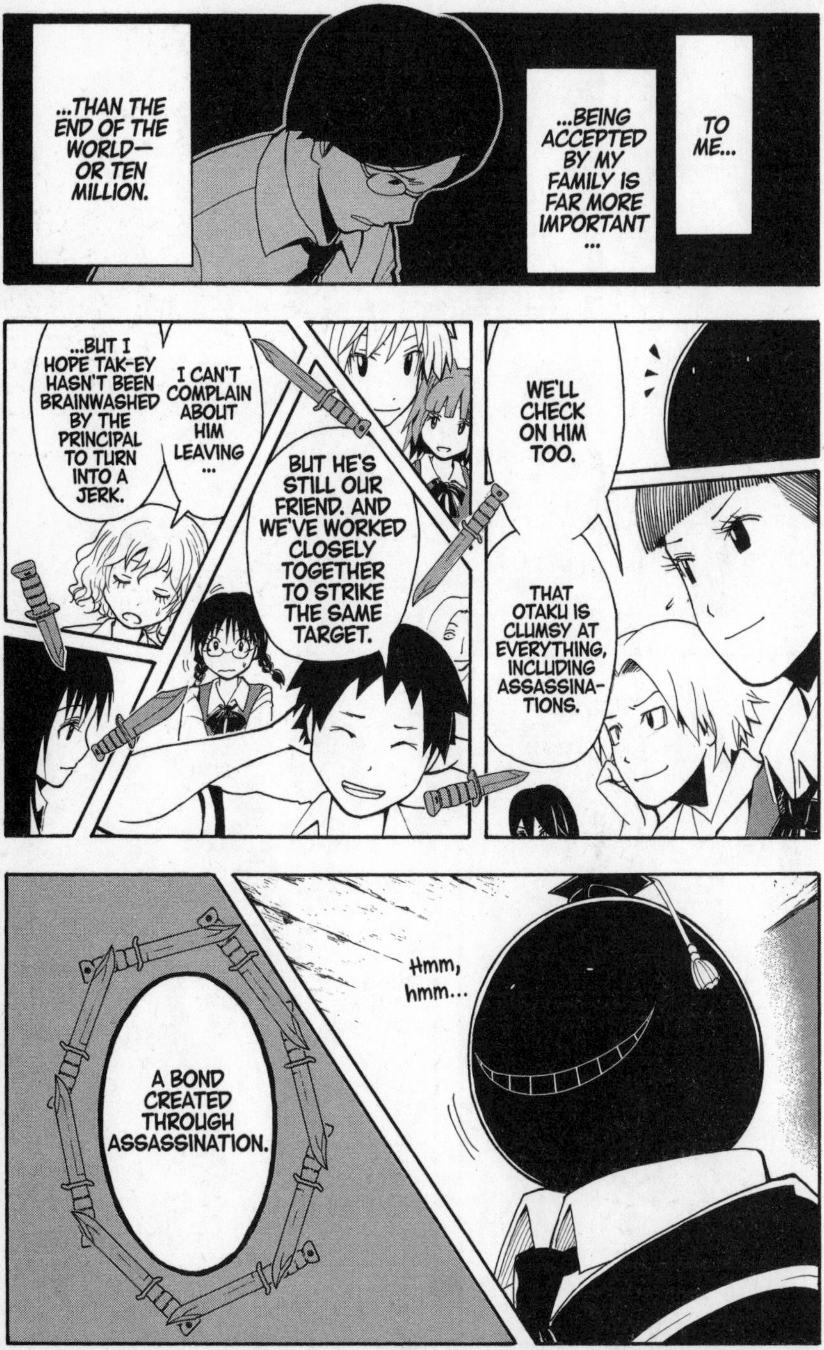
TO ME...
...BEING ACCEPTED BY MY FAMILY IS FAR MORE IMPORTANT...
...THAN THE END OF THE WORLD— OR TEN MILLION.
WE'LL CHECK ON HIM TOO.
THAT OTAKU IS CLUMSY AT EVERYTHING, INCLUDING ASSASSINATIONS.
I CAN'T COMPLAIN ABOUT HIM LEAVING...
...BUT I HOPE TAK-EY HASN'T BEEN BRAINWASHED BY THE PRINCIPAL TO TURN INTO A JERK.
BUT HE'S STILL OUR FRIEND. AND WE'VE WORKED CLOSELY TOGETHER TO STRIKE THE SAME TARGET.
Hmm, hmm...
A BOND CREATED THROUGH ASSASSINATION.

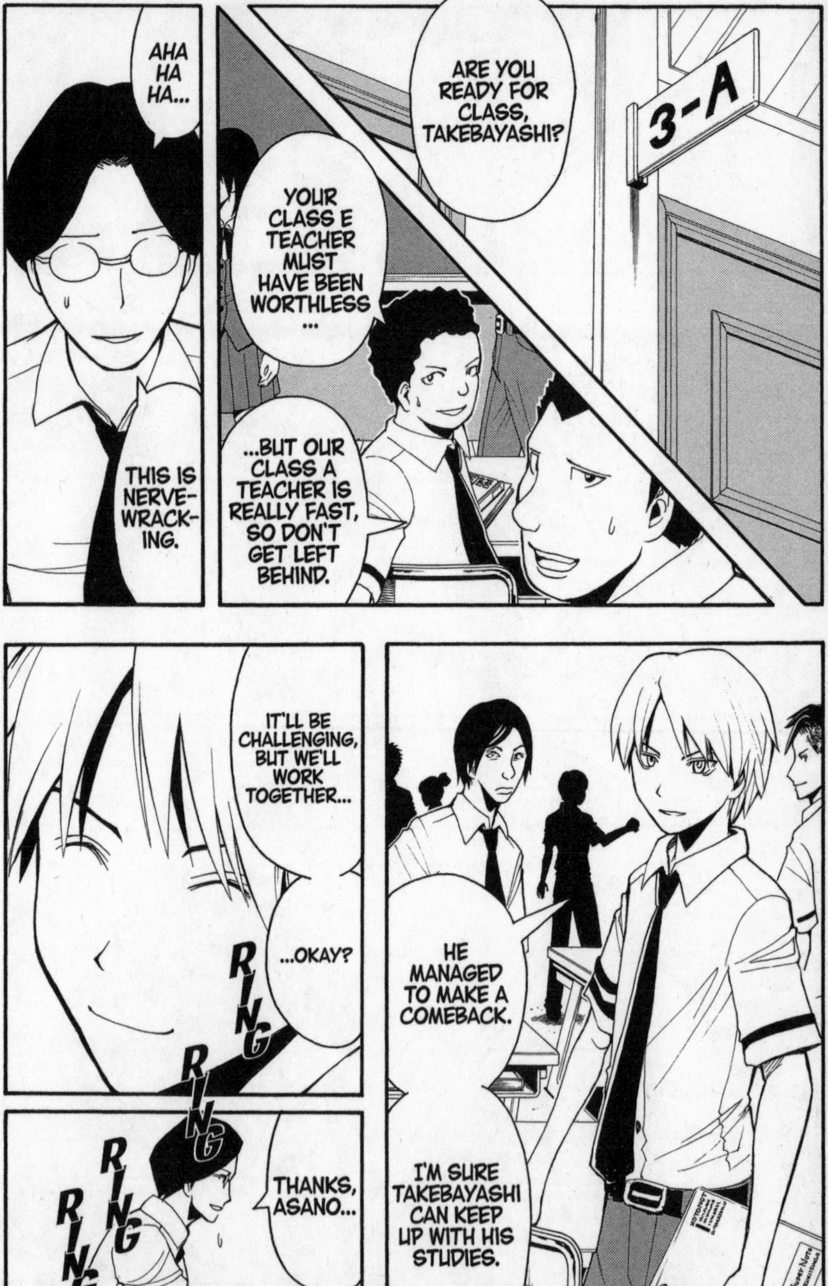
3-A
ARE YOU READY FOR CLASS, TAKEBAYASHI?
YOUR CLASS E TEACHER MUST HAVE BEEN WORTHLESS...
...BUT OUR CLASS A TEACHER IS REALLY FAST, SO DON'T GET LEFT BEHIND.
AHA HA HA...
THIS IS NERVE-WRACKING.
HE MANAGED TO MAKE A COMEBACK.
I'M SURE TAKEBAYASHI CAN KEEP UP WITH HIS STUDIES.
IT'LL BE CHALLENGING, BUT WE'LL WORK TOGETHER...
...OKAY?
RING
RING
THANKS, ASANO...
RING
RING

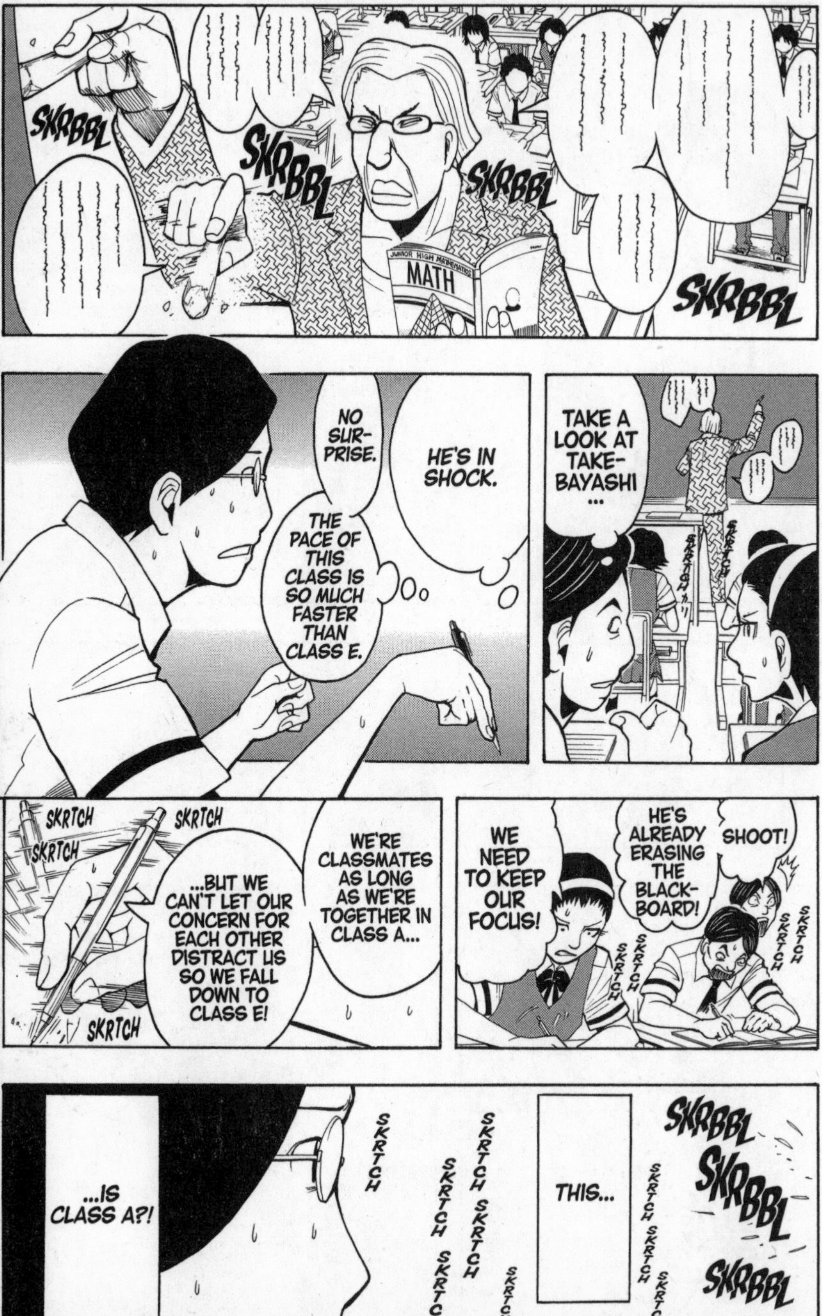
SKRBBL
SKRBBL
SKRBBL
SKRBBL
JUNIOR HIGH MATHEMATICS
MATH
TAKE A LOOK AT TAKE-BAYASHI...
SKRTCH
SKRTCH
NO SUR-PRISE.
HE'S IN SHOCK.
THE PACE OF THIS CLASS IS SO MUCH FASTER THAN CLASS E.
SHOOT!
HE'S ALREADY ERASING THE BLACK-BOARD!
WE NEED TO KEEP OUR FOCUS!
SKRTCH
SKRTCH
SKRTCH
SKRTCH
WE'RE CLASSMATES AS LONG AS WE'RE TOGETHER IN CLASS A...
...BUT WE CAN'T LET OUR CONCERN FOR EACH OTHER DISTRACT US SO WE FALL DOWN TO CLASS E!
SKRTCH
SKRTCH
SKRTCH
SKRTCH
SKRBBL
SKRBBL
SKRBBL
THIS...
SKRTCH
SKRTCH
SKRTCH
SKRTCH
SKRTCH
SKRTCH
SKRTCH
SKRTCH
...IS CLASS A?!

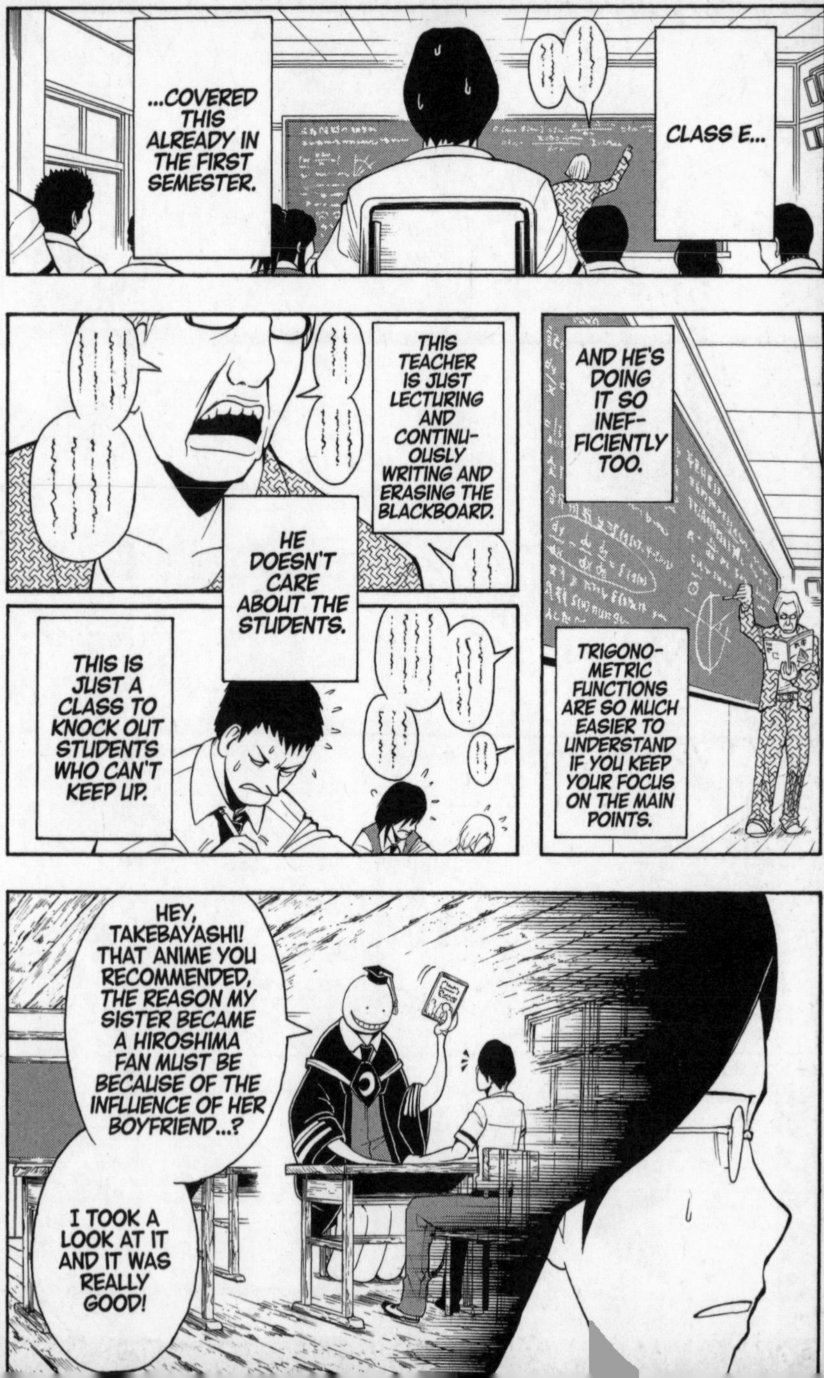
CLASS E...
...COVERED THIS ALREADY IN THE FIRST SEMESTER.
AND HE'S DOING IT SO INEFFICIENTLY TOO.
TRIGONOMETRIC FUNCTIONS ARE SO MUCH EASIER TO UNDERSTAND IF YOU KEEP YOUR FOCUS ON THE MAIN POINTS.
THIS TEACHER IS JUST LECTURING AND CONTINUOUSLY WRITING AND ERASING THE BLACKBOARD.
HE DOESN'T CARE ABOUT THE STUDENTS.
THIS IS JUST A CLASS TO KNOCK OUT STUDENTS WHO CAN'T KEEP UP.
HEY, TAKEBAYASHI! THAT ANIME YOU RECOMMENDED, THE REASON MY SISTER BECAME A HIROSHIMA FAN MUST BE BECAUSE OF THE INFLUENCE OF HER BOYFRIEND...?
I TOOK A LOOK AT IT AND IT WAS REALLY GOOD!

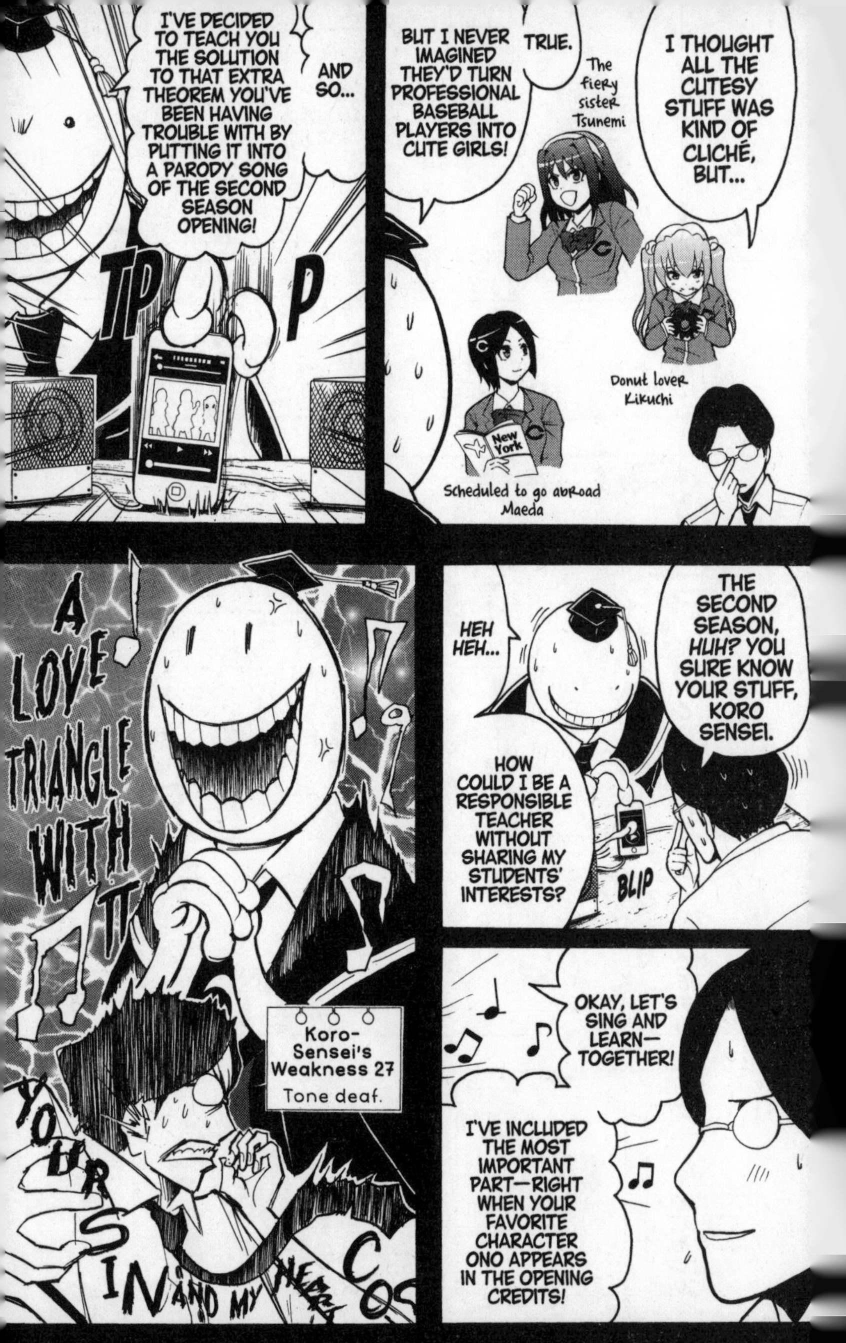
I THOUGHT ALL THE CUTESY STUFF WAS KIND OF CLICHÉ, BUT...
TRUE.
BUT I NEVER IMAGINED THEY'D TURN PROFESSIONAL BASEBALL PLAYERS INTO CUTE GIRLS!
The fiery sister Tsunemi
Donut lover Kikuchi
New York
Scheduled to go abroad Maeda
AND SO...
I'VE DECIDED TO TEACH YOU THE SOLUTION TO THAT EXTRA THEOREM YOU'VE BEEN HAVING TROUBLE WITH BY PUTTING IT INTO A PARODY SONG OF THE SECOND SEASON OPENING!
TP
P
THE SECOND SEASON, HUH? YOU SURE KNOW YOUR STUFF, KORO SENSEI.
HEH HEH...
HOW COULD I BE A RESPONSIBLE TEACHER WITHOUT SHARING MY STUDENTS' INTERESTS?
BLIP
OKAY, LET'S SING AND LEARN—TOGETHER!
I'VE INCLUDED THE MOST IMPORTANT PART—RIGHT WHEN YOUR FAVORITE CHARACTER ONO APPEARS IN THE OPENING CREDITS!
A LOVE TRIANGLE WITH IT
YOUR SINS
AND MY
COS
Koro-Sensei's Weakness 27
Tone deaf.

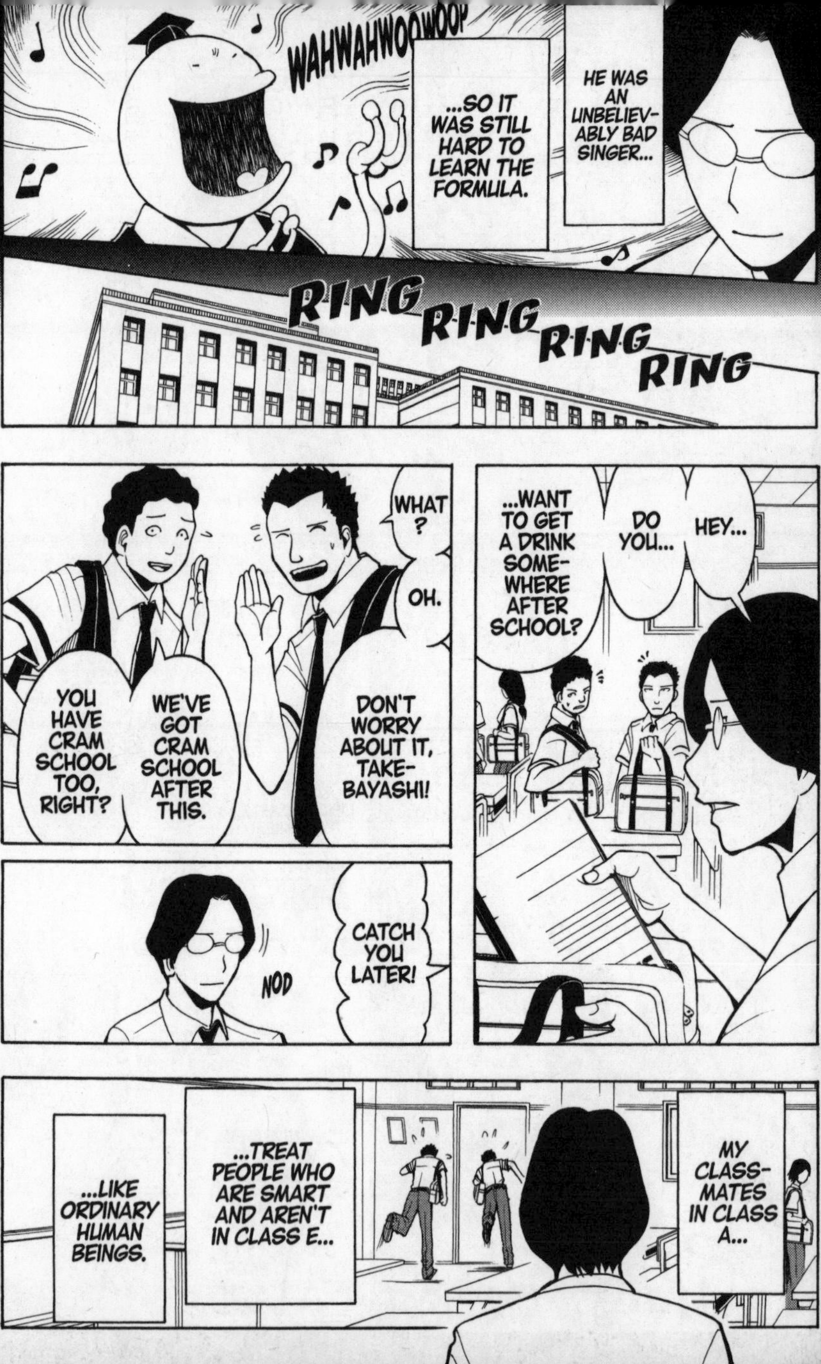
HE WAS AN UNBELIEVABLY BAD SINGER...
...SO IT WAS STILL HARD TO LEARN THE FORMULA.
WAHWAHWOOWOOP
RING RING RING RING
HEY...
DO YOU...
...WANT TO GET A DRINK SOMEWHERE AFTER SCHOOL?
WHAT?
OH.
DON'T WORRY ABOUT IT, TAKE-BAYASHI!
WE'VE GOT CRAM SCHOOL AFTER THIS.
YOU HAVE CRAM SCHOOL TOO, RIGHT?
CATCH YOU LATER!
NOD
MY CLASSMATES IN CLASS A...
...TREAT PEOPLE WHO ARE SMART AND AREN'T IN CLASS E...
...LIKE ORDINARY HUMAN BEINGS.

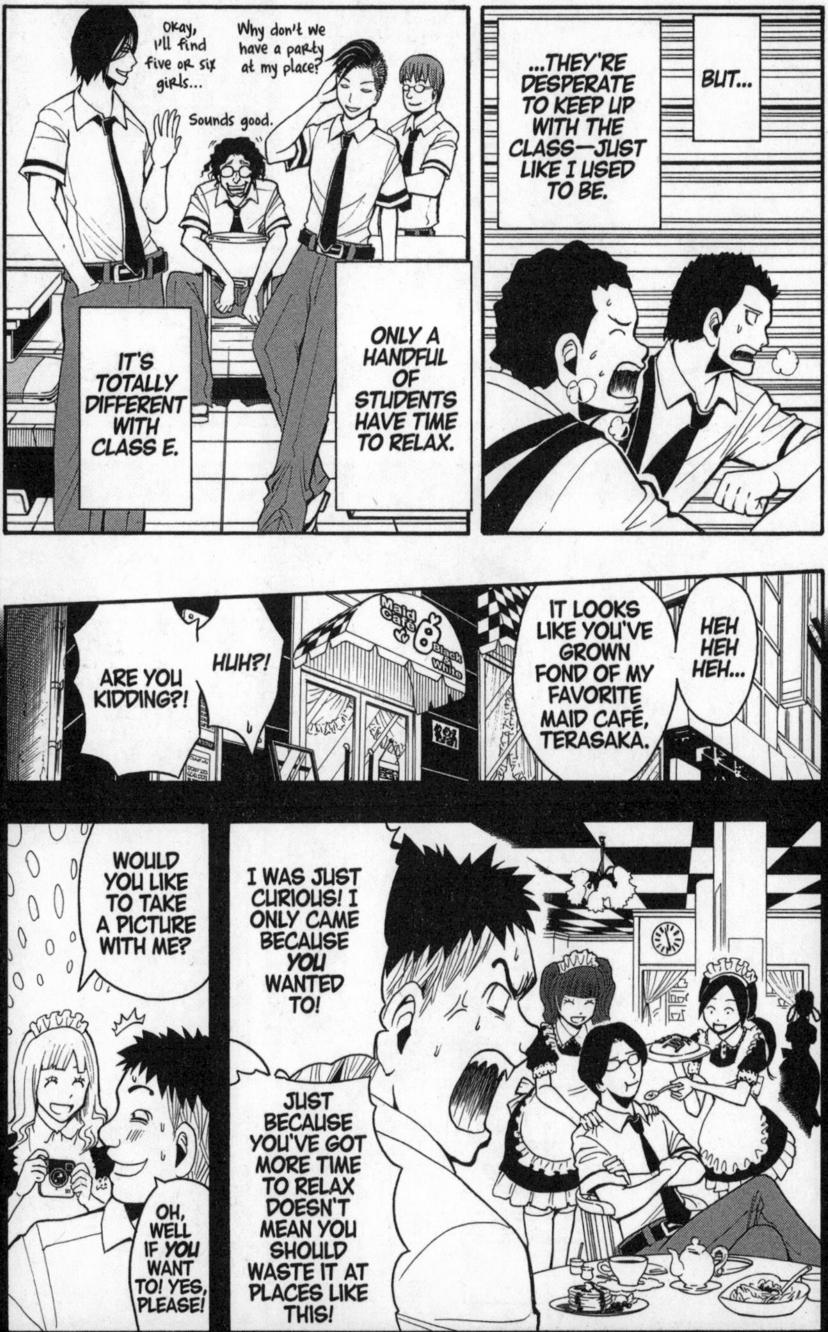
BUT...
...THEY'RE DESPERATE TO KEEP UP WITH THE CLASS—JUST LIKE I USED TO BE.
Why don't we have a party at my place?
Okay, I'll find five or six girls...
Sounds good.
ONLY A HANDFUL OF STUDENTS HAVE TIME TO RELAX.
IT'S TOTALLY DIFFERENT WITH CLASS E.
HEH HEH HEH...
IT LOOKS LIKE YOU'VE GROWN FOND OF MY FAVORITE MAID CAFÉ, TERASAKA.
Maid Café
Black & White
HUH?!
ARE YOU KIDDING?!
I WAS JUST CURIOUS! I ONLY CAME BECAUSE YOU WANTED TO!
JUST BECAUSE YOU'VE GOT MORE TIME TO RELAX DOESN'T MEAN YOU SHOULD WASTE IT AT PLACES LIKE THIS!
WOULD YOU LIKE TO TAKE A PICTURE WITH ME?
OH, WELL IF YOU WANT TO! YES, PLEASE!

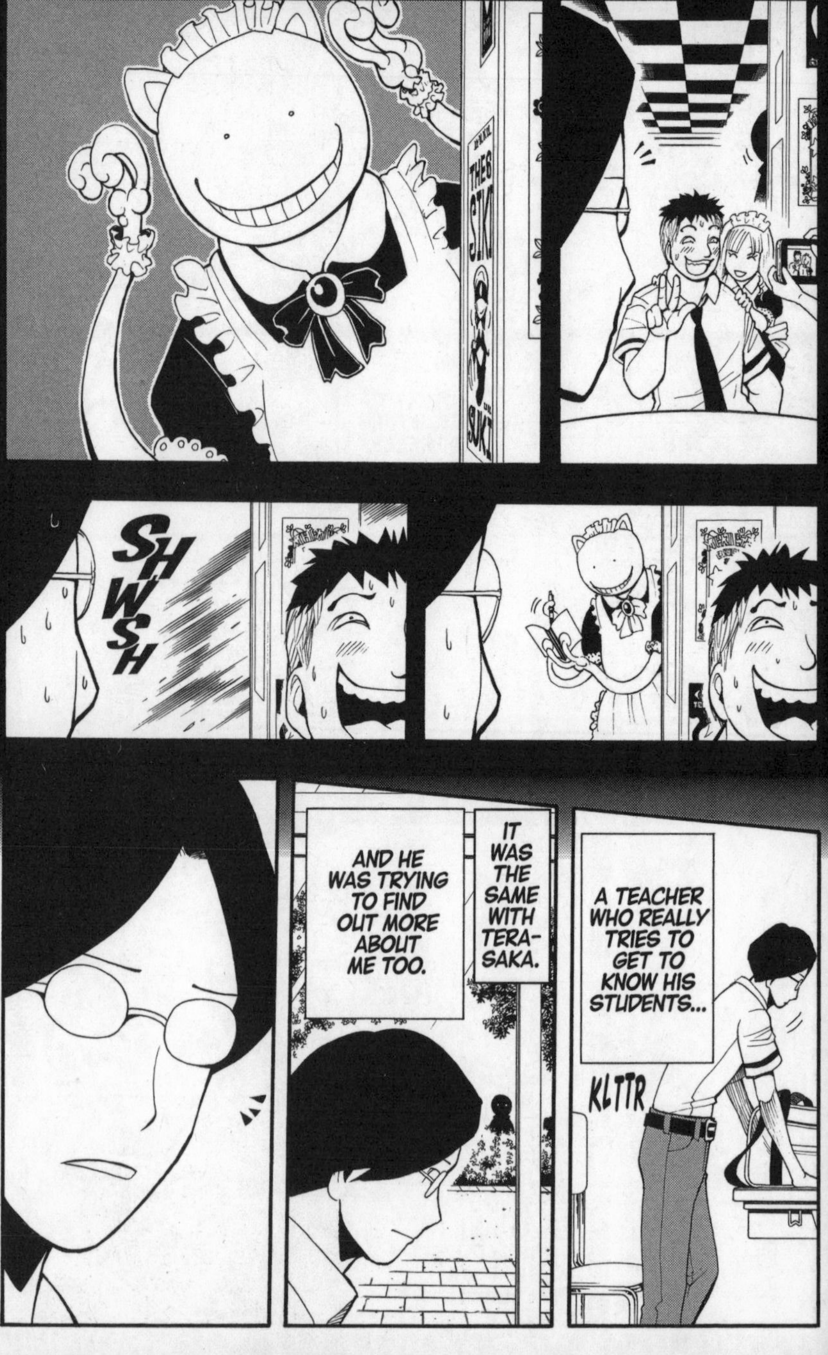
SHWSH
A TEACHER WHO REALLY TRIES TO GET TO KNOW HIS STUDENTS...
KLTTR
IT WAS THE SAME WITH TERA-SAKA.
AND HE WAS TRYING TO FIND OUT MORE ABOUT ME TOO.

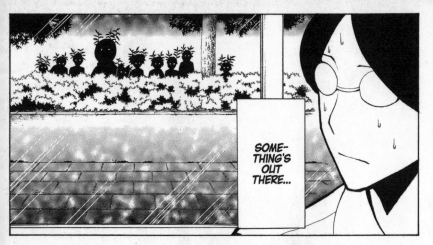

SOME-THING'S OUT THERE...
LOOKS LIKE HE'S DOING OKAY...
DOES HE SEEM FRIENDLIER THAN USUAL TO YOU?
HA!
THAT'S WHY I TOLD YOU TO FORGET ABOUT FOUR-EYES.
THAT'S A CAMOUFLAGE TECHNIQUE WE LEARNED FROM MR. KARASUMA...
...BUT THE SHRUBS AT THE MAIN SCHOOL BUILDING ARE DIFFERENT FROM THE ONES AT CLASS E, SO IT JUST MAKES THEM LOOK WEIRD.
ESPECIALLY THAT BLACK SHINY OBJECT!
WHY ARE THEY HERE?!

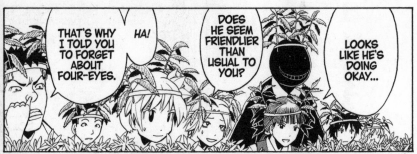

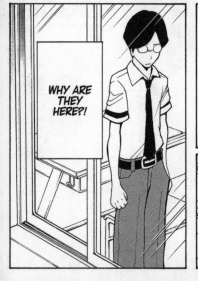

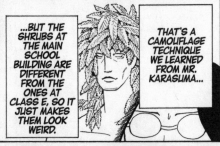

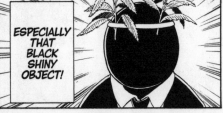

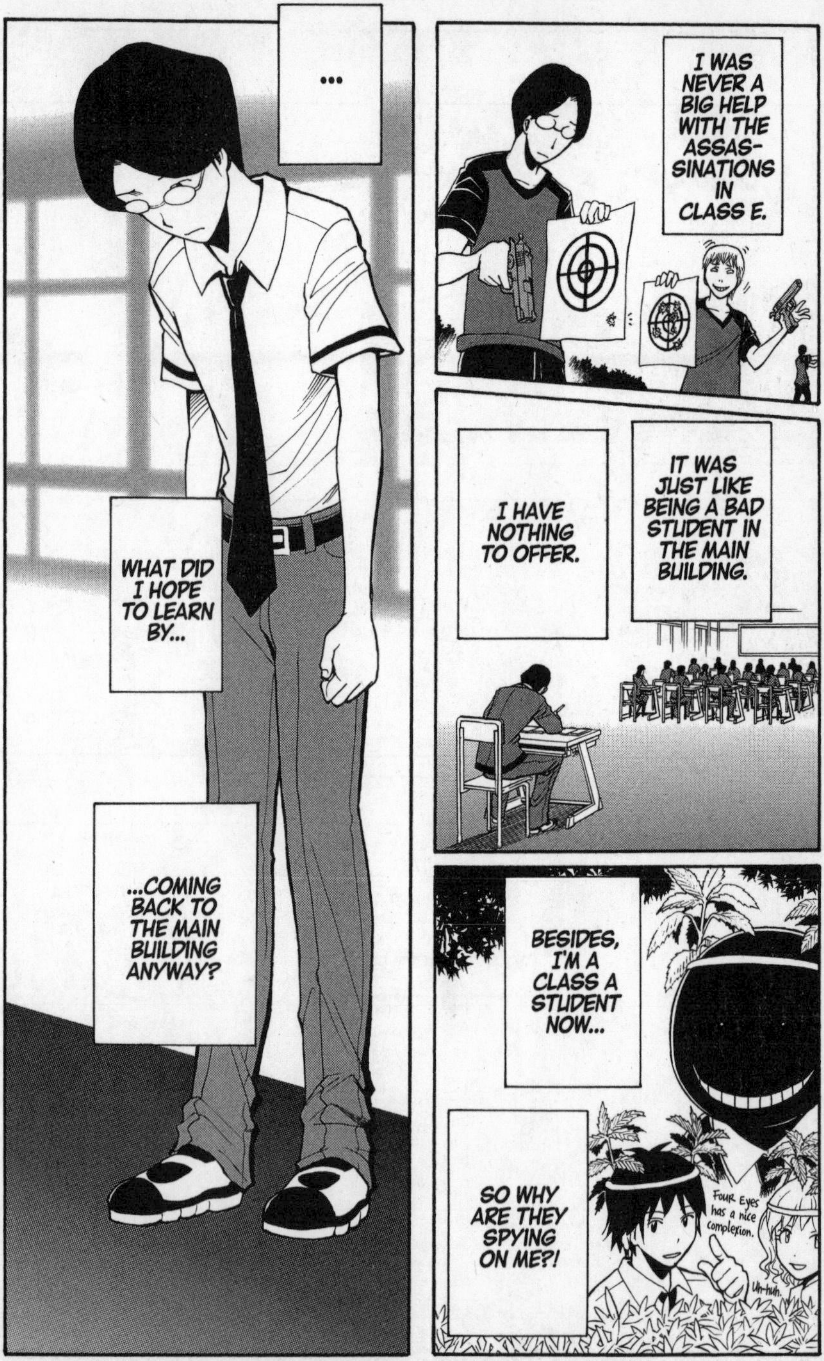
I WAS NEVER A BIG HELP WITH THE ASSASSINATIONS IN CLASS E.
IT WAS JUST LIKE BEING A BAD STUDENT IN THE MAIN BUILDING.
I HAVE NOTHING TO OFFER.
BESIDES, I'M A CLASS A STUDENT NOW...
SO WHY ARE THEY SPYING ON ME?!
Four Eyes has a nice complexion.
Uh-huh.
...
WHAT DID I HOPE TO LEARN BY...
...COMING BACK TO THE MAIN BUILDING ANYWAY?

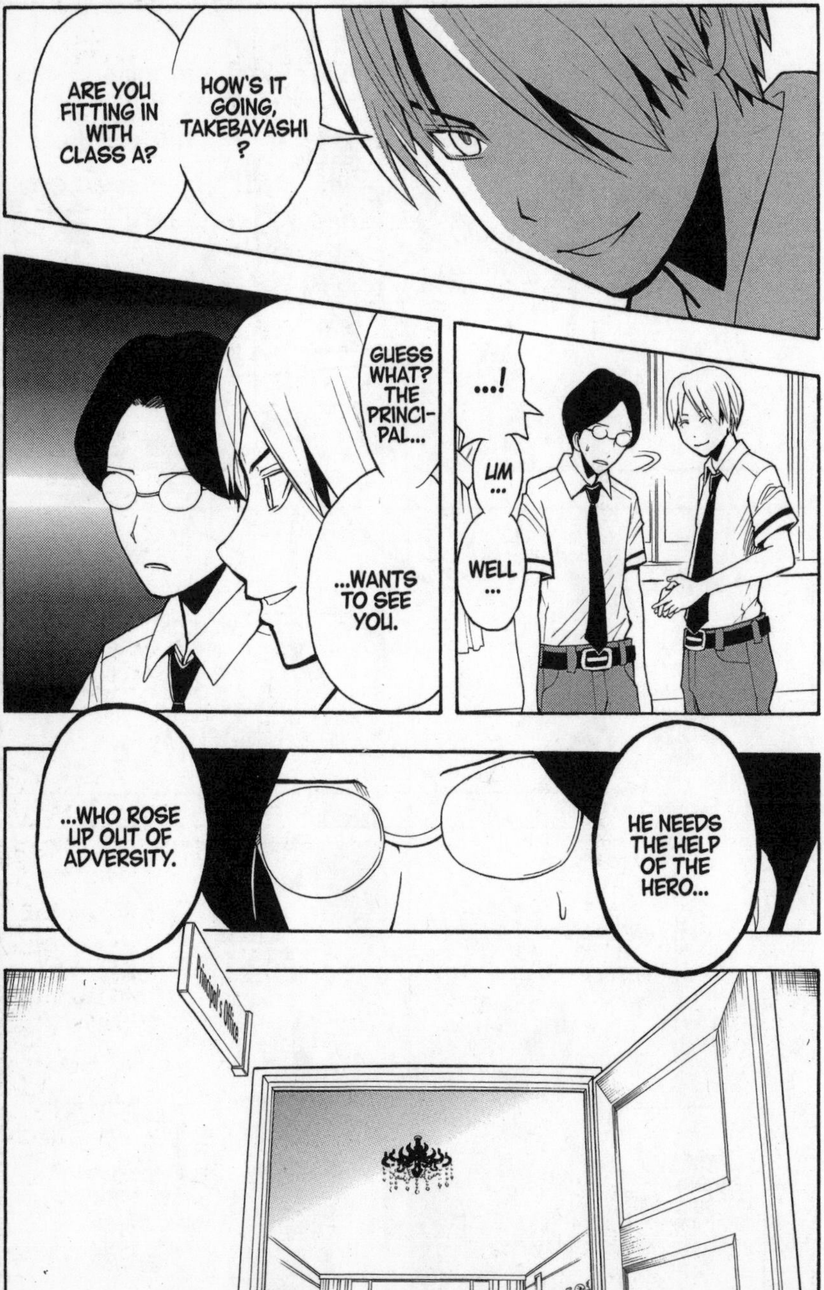
HOW'S IT GOING, TAKEBAYASHI ?
ARE YOU FITTING IN WITH CLASS A?
...!
UM ...
WELL ...
GUESS WHAT? THE PRINCI- PAL...
...WANTS TO SEE YOU.
HE NEEDS THE HELP OF THE HERO...
...WHO ROSE UP OUT OF ADVERSITY.
Principal's Office

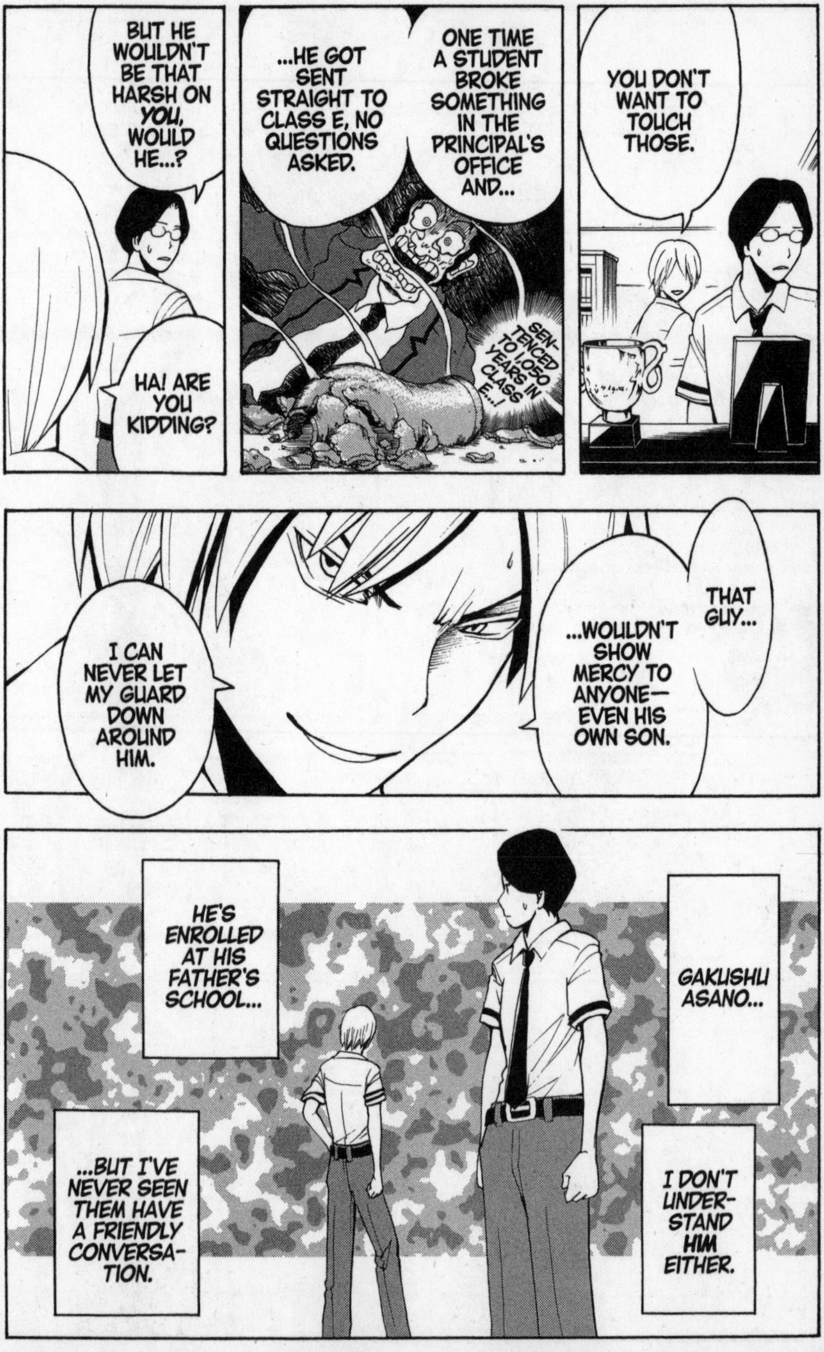
YOU DON'T WANT TO TOUCH THOSE.
ONE TIME A STUDENT BROKE SOMETHING IN THE PRINCIPAL'S OFFICE AND...
...HE GOT SENT STRAIGHT TO CLASS E, NO QUESTIONS ASKED.
SENTENCED TO 1,050 YEARS IN CLASS E...!
BUT HE WOULDN'T BE THAT HARSH ON *YOU*, WOULD HE...?
HA! ARE YOU KIDDING?
THAT GUY...
...WOULDN'T SHOW MERCY TO ANYONE—EVEN HIS OWN SON.
I CAN NEVER LET MY GUARD DOWN AROUND HIM.
GAKUSHU ASANO...
HE'S ENROLLED AT HIS FATHER'S SCHOOL...
...BUT I'VE NEVER SEEN THEM HAVE A FRIENDLY CONVERSATION.
I DON'T UNDERSTAND HIM EITHER.

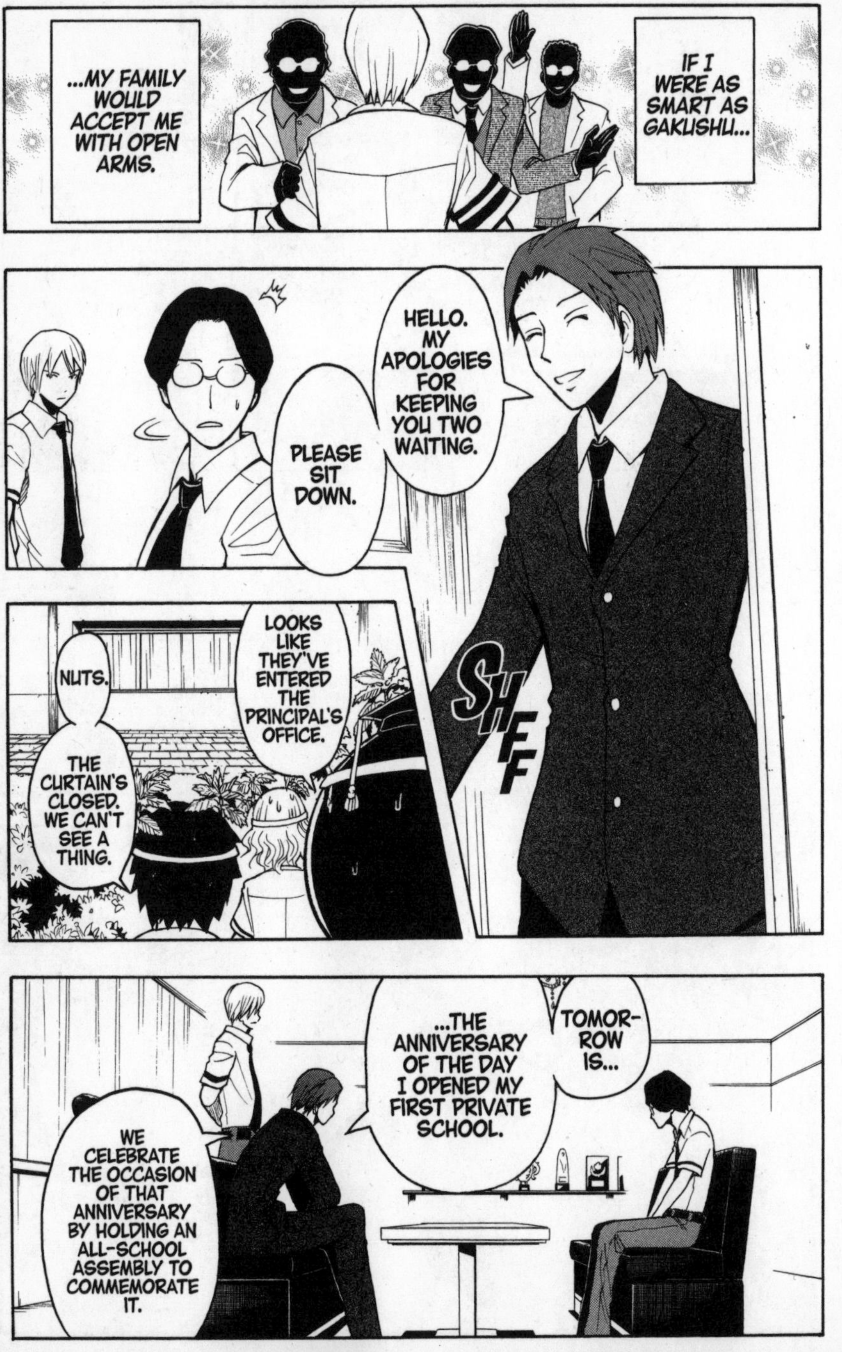
IF I WERE AS SMART AS GAKUSHU...
...MY FAMILY WOULD ACCEPT ME WITH OPEN ARMS.
HELLO. MY APOLOGIES FOR KEEPING YOU TWO WAITING.
PLEASE SIT DOWN.
SHFF
LOOKS LIKE THEY'VE ENTERED THE PRINCIPAL'S OFFICE.
NUTS.
THE CURTAIN'S CLOSED. WE CAN'T SEE A THING.
TOMORROW IS...
...THE ANNIVERSARY OF THE DAY I OPENED MY FIRST PRIVATE SCHOOL.
WE CELEBRATE THE OCCASION OF THAT ANNIVERSARY BY HOLDING AN ALL-SCHOOL ASSEMBLY TO COMMEMORATE IT.

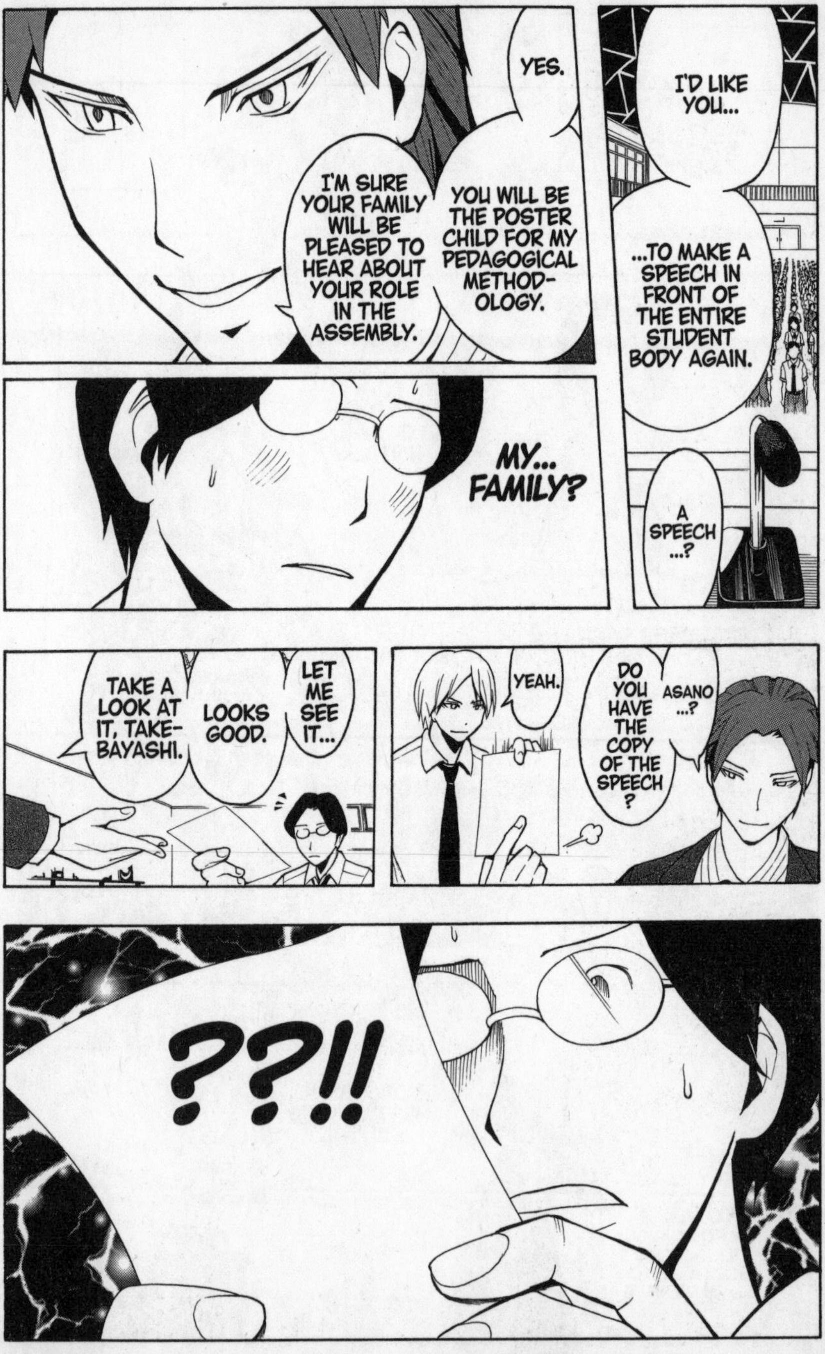
I'D LIKE YOU...
...TO MAKE A SPEECH IN FRONT OF THE ENTIRE STUDENT BODY AGAIN.
A SPEECH ...?
YES.
YOU WILL BE THE POSTER CHILD FOR MY PEDAGOGICAL METHOD-OLOGY.
I'M SURE YOUR FAMILY WILL BE PLEASED TO HEAR ABOUT YOUR ROLE IN THE ASSEMBLY.
MY... FAMILY?
ASANO ...?
DO YOU HAVE THE COPY OF THE SPEECH?
YEAH.
LET ME SEE IT...
LOOKS GOOD.
TAKE A LOOK AT IT, TAKE-BAYASHI.
??!!

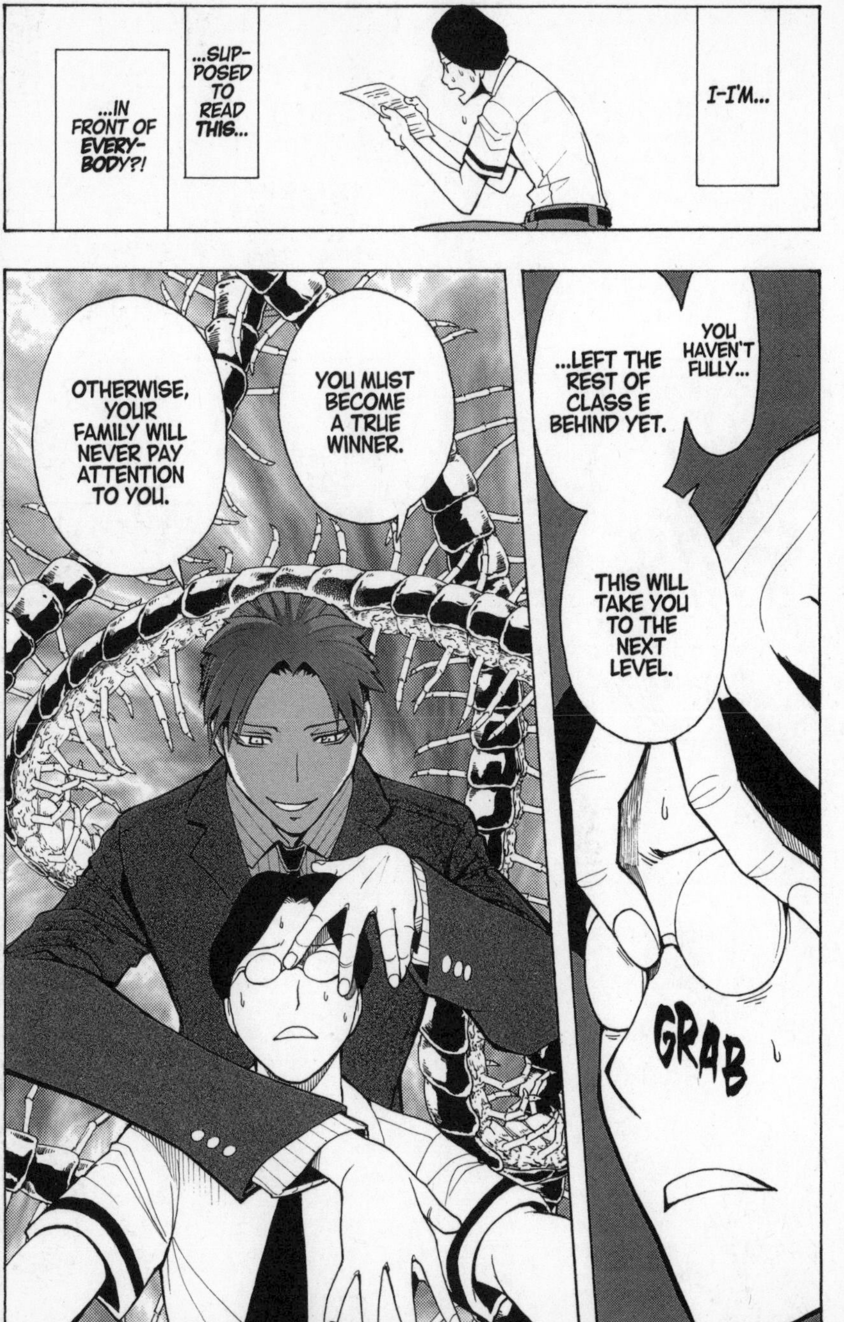
I-I'M...
...SUP-POSED TO READ THIS...
...IN FRONT OF EVERY-BODY?!
YOU HAVEN'T FULLY...
...LEFT THE REST OF CLASS E BEHIND YET.
THIS WILL TAKE YOU TO THE NEXT LEVEL.
GRAB
YOU MUST BECOME A TRUE WINNER.
OTHERWISE, YOUR FAMILY WILL NEVER PAY ATTENTION TO YOU.

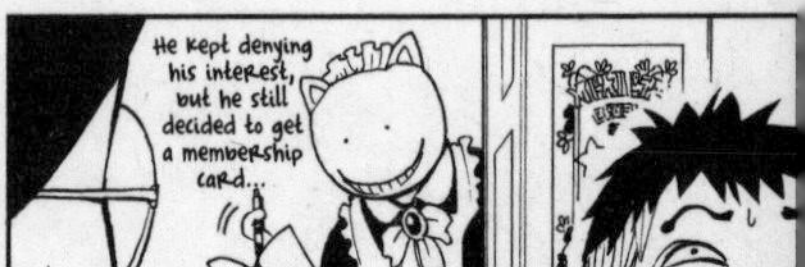
He kept denying his interest, but he still decided to get a membership card...
Maid Café Black & White
白黒
Member's Card

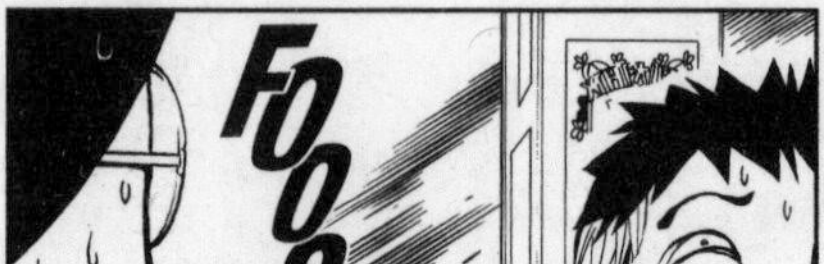
FOOSH
Maid Café Black & White
白黒
Member's Card

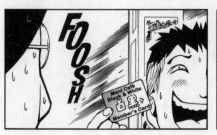

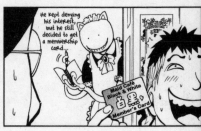

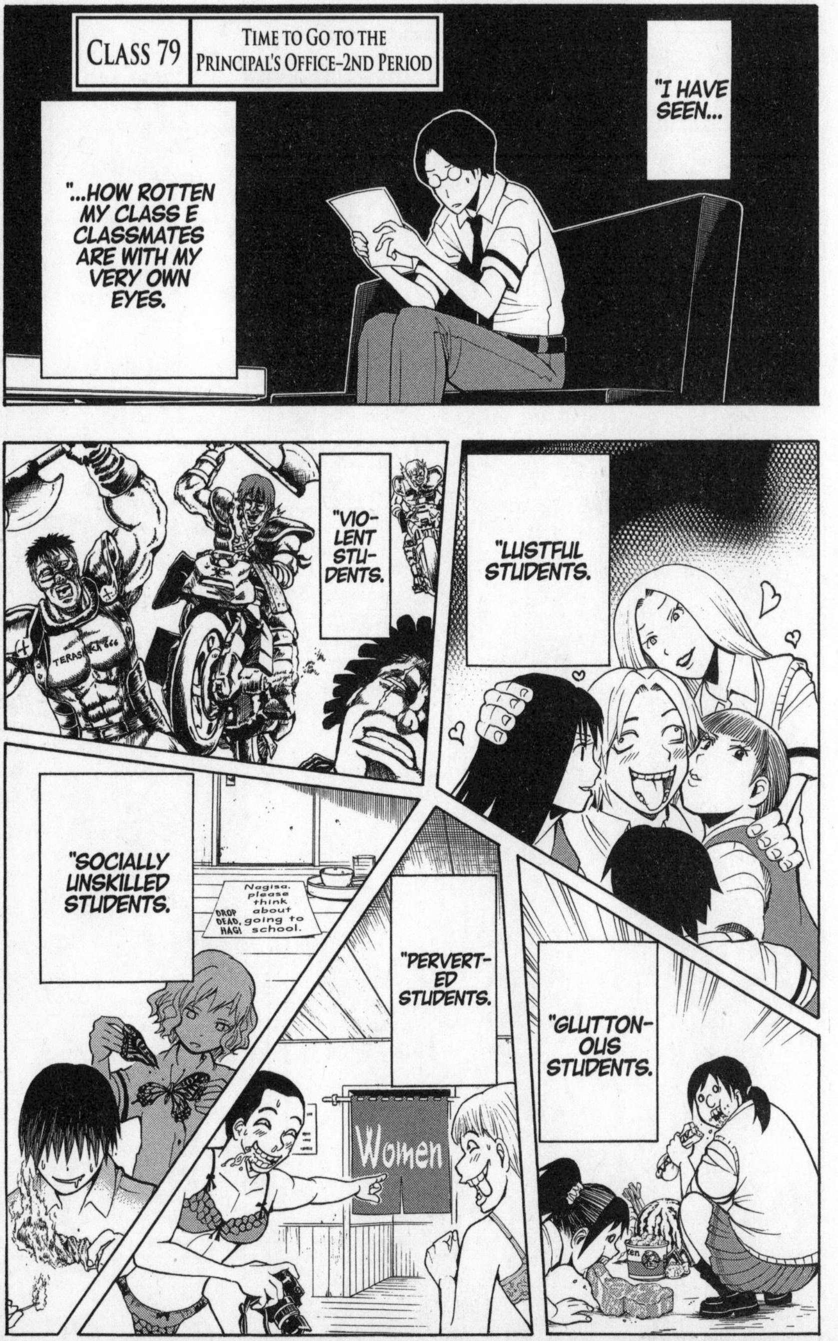
CLASS 79
TIME TO GO TO THE PRINCIPAL'S OFFICE–2ND PERIOD
"I HAVE SEEN...
"...HOW ROTTEN MY CLASS E CLASSMATES ARE WITH MY VERY OWN EYES.
"LUSTFUL STUDENTS.
"VIO-LENT STU-DENTS.
"GLUTTON-OUS STUDENTS.
"PERVERT-ED STUDENTS.
Women
"SOCIALLY UNSKILLED STUDENTS.
Nagisa, please think about going to school.
DROP DEAD, HAGI

CLASS 79 TIME TO GO TO THE PRINCIPAL'S OFFICE–2ND PERIOD

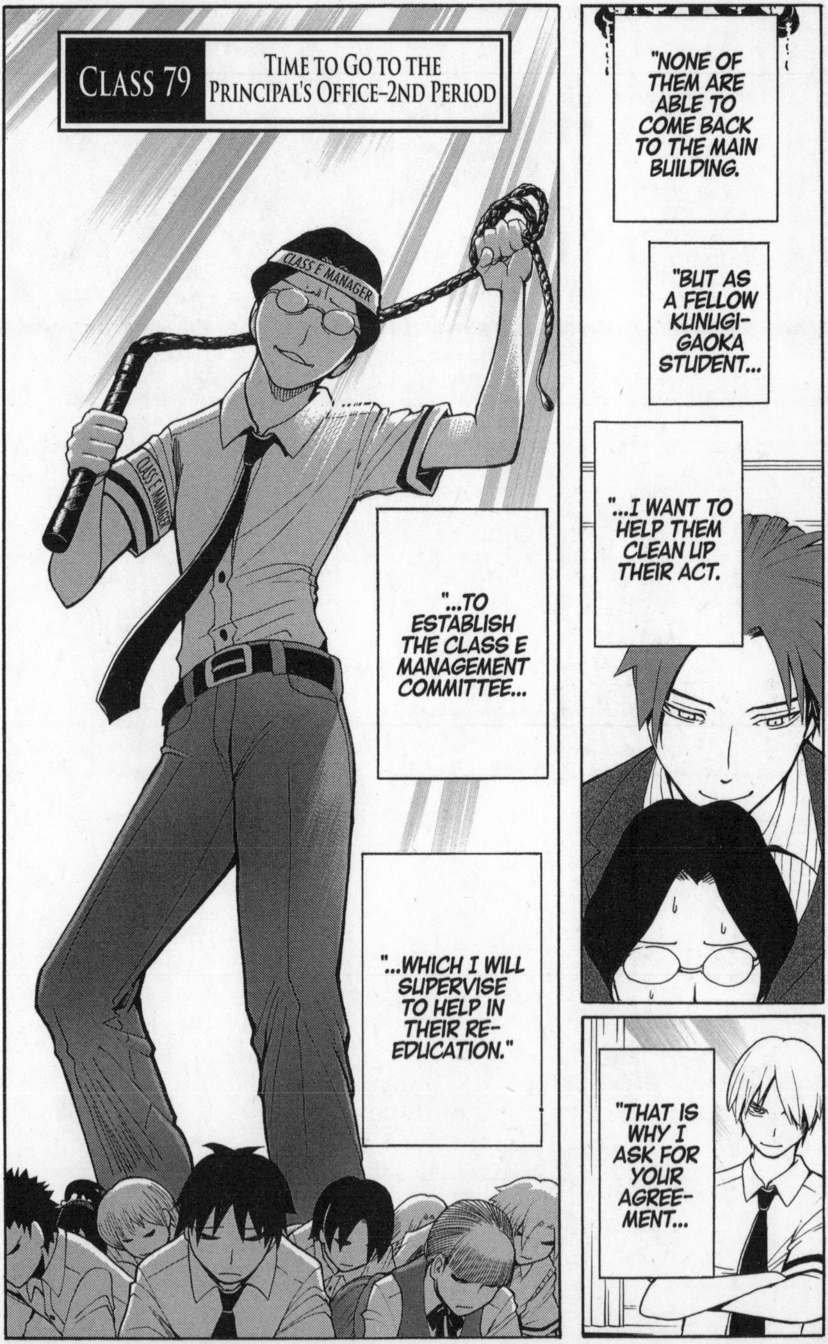
"NONE OF THEM ARE ABLE TO COME BACK TO THE MAIN BUILDING.
"BUT AS A FELLOW KUNUGI-GAOKA STUDENT...
"...I WANT TO HELP THEM CLEAN UP THEIR ACT.
"THAT IS WHY I ASK FOR YOUR AGREE-MENT...
CLASS E MANAGER
CLASS E MANAGER
"...TO ESTABLISH THE CLASS E MANAGEMENT COMMITTEE...
"...WHICH I WILL SUPERVISE TO HELP IN THEIR RE-EDUCATION."

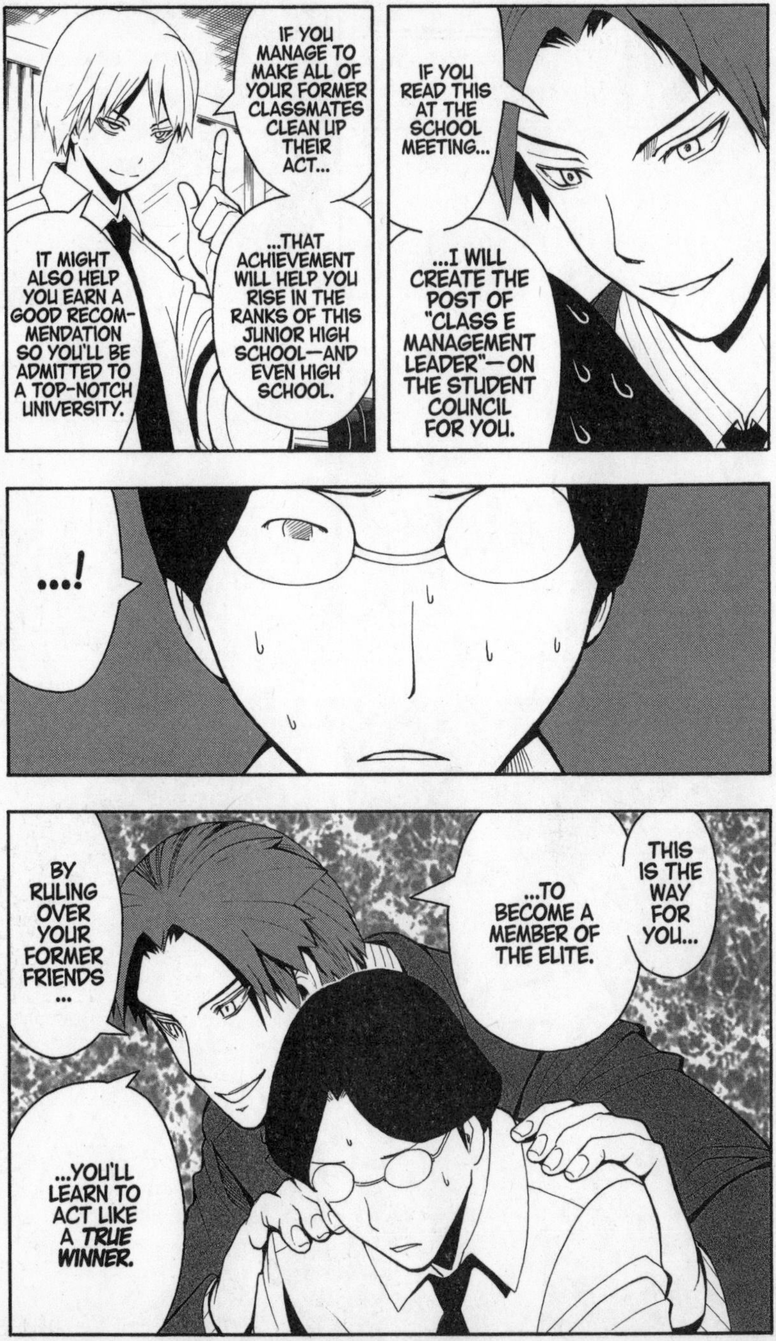
IF YOU READ THIS AT THE SCHOOL MEETING...
...I WILL CREATE THE POST OF "CLASS E MANAGEMENT LEADER"—ON THE STUDENT COUNCIL FOR YOU.
IF YOU MANAGE TO MAKE ALL OF YOUR FORMER CLASSMATES CLEAN UP THEIR ACT...
...THAT ACHIEVEMENT WILL HELP YOU RISE IN THE RANKS OF THIS JUNIOR HIGH SCHOOL—AND EVEN HIGH SCHOOL.
IT MIGHT ALSO HELP YOU EARN A GOOD RECOMMENDATION SO YOU'LL BE ADMITTED TO A TOP-NOTCH UNIVERSITY.
...!
THIS IS THE WAY FOR YOU...
...TO BECOME A MEMBER OF THE ELITE.
BY RULING OVER YOUR FORMER FRIENDS...
...YOU'LL LEARN TO ACT LIKE A *TRUE* WINNER.

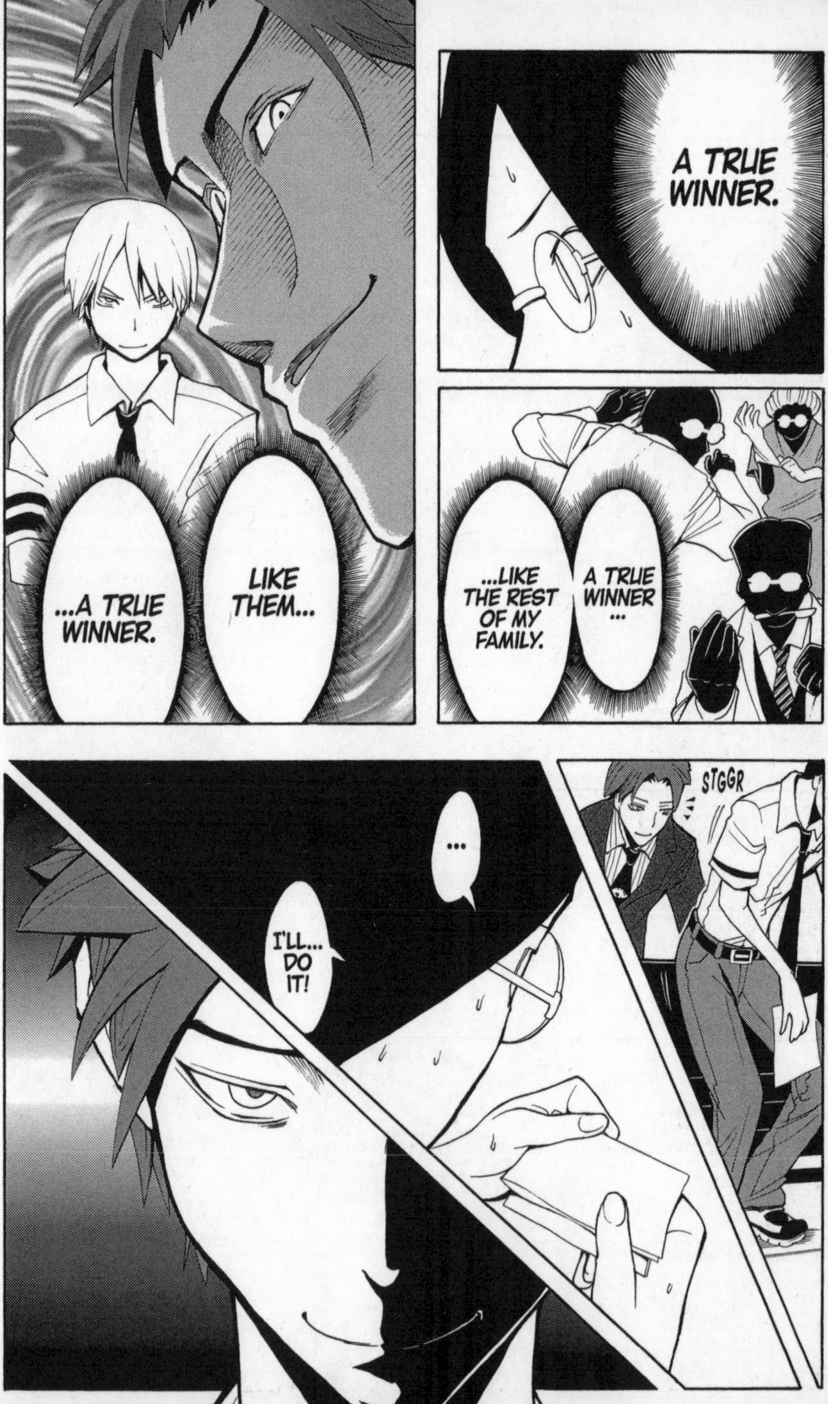
A TRUE WINNER.
A TRUE WINNER ...
...LIKE THE REST OF MY FAMILY.
LIKE THEM...
...A TRUE WINNER.
STGGR
...
I'LL... DO IT!

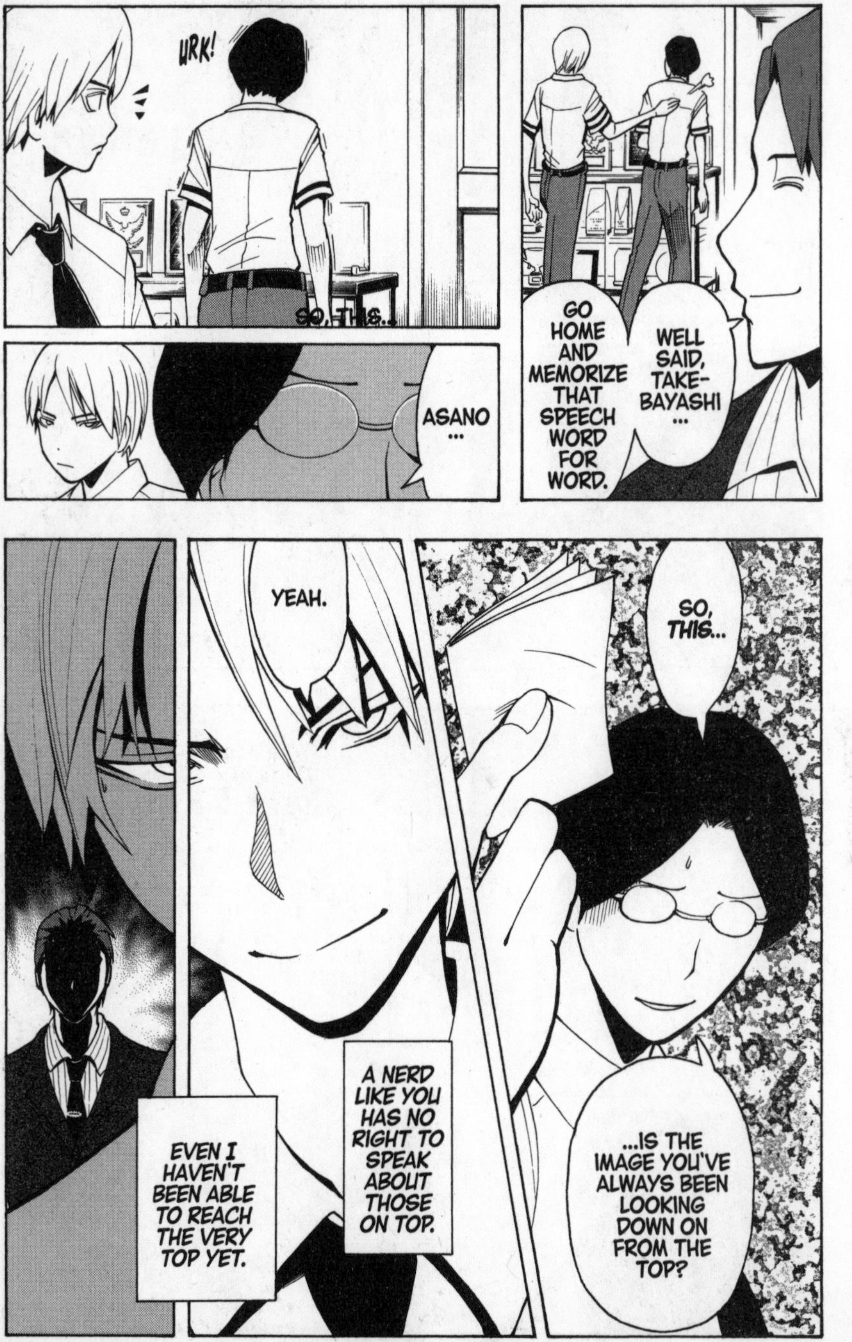
WELL SAID, TAKE-BAYASHI...
GO HOME AND MEMORIZE THAT SPEECH WORD FOR WORD.
URK!
SO, THIS..
ASANO...
SO, THIS...
...IS THE IMAGE YOU'VE ALWAYS BEEN LOOKING DOWN ON FROM THE TOP?
YEAH.
A NERD LIKE YOU HAS NO RIGHT TO SPEAK ABOUT THOSE ON TOP.
EVEN I HAVEN'T BEEN ABLE TO REACH THE VERY TOP YET.

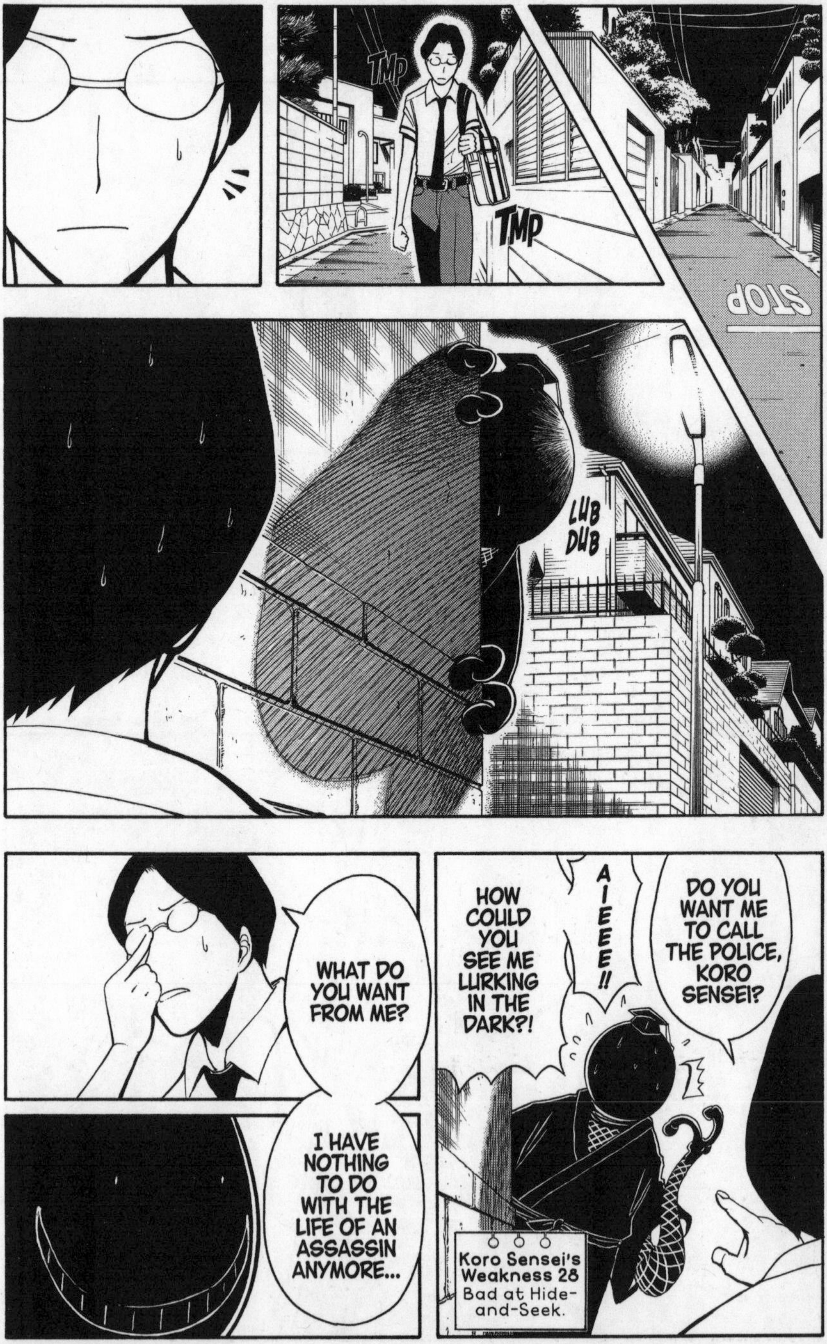
STOP
TMP
TMP
LUB DUB
DO YOU WANT ME TO CALL THE POLICE, KORO SENSEI?
AIEEEE!!
HOW COULD YOU SEE ME LURKING IN THE DARK?!
Koro Sensei's Weakness 28 Bad at Hide-and-Seek.
WHAT DO YOU WANT FROM ME?
I HAVE NOTHING TO DO WITH THE LIFE OF AN ASSASSIN ANYMORE...

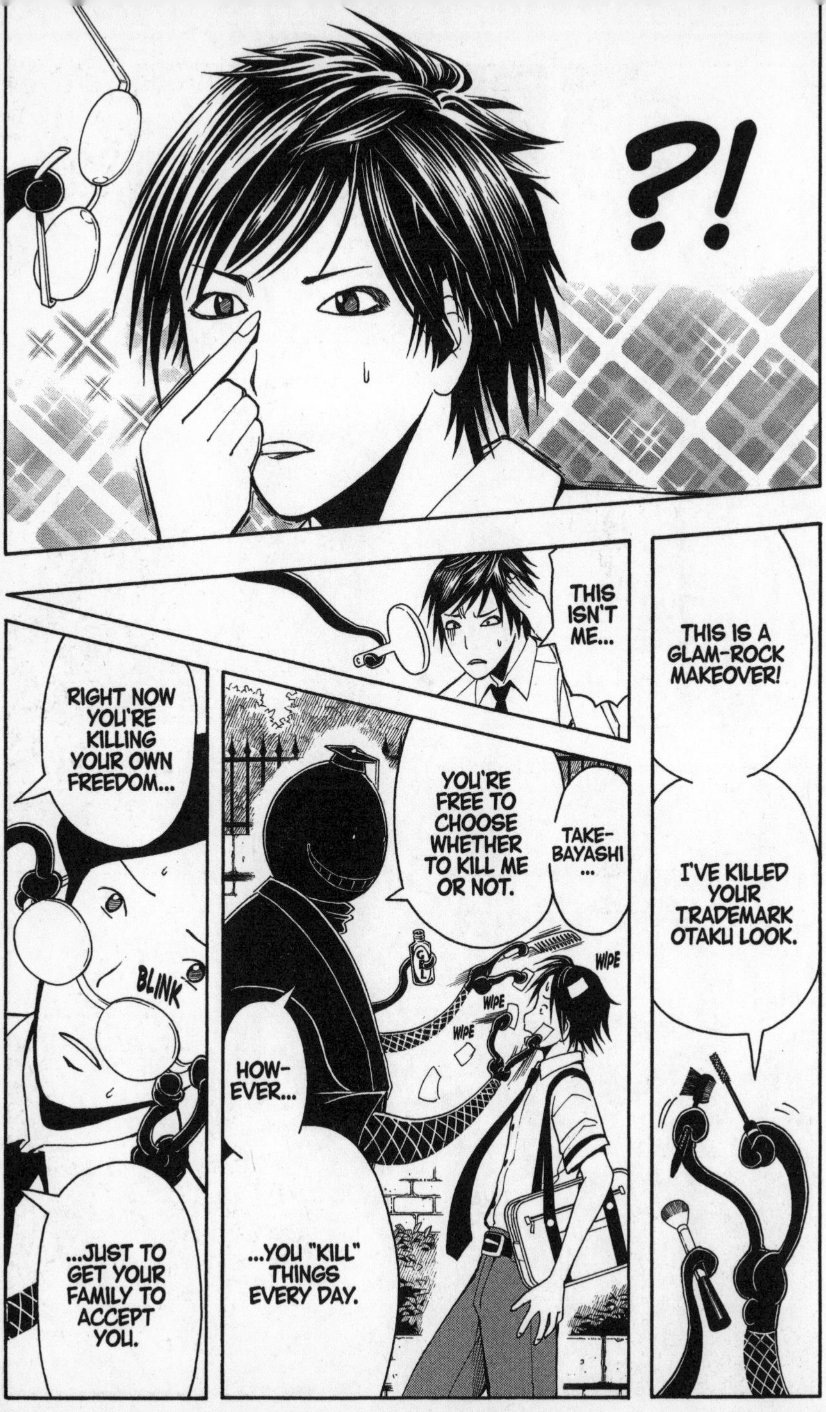
?!
THIS IS A GLAM-ROCK MAKEOVER!
I'VE KILLED YOUR TRADEMARK OTAKU LOOK.
THIS ISN'T ME...
TAKE-BAYASHI ...
YOU'RE FREE TO CHOOSE WHETHER TO KILL ME OR NOT.
WIPE
WIPE
WIPE
HOW-EVER...
...YOU "KILL" THINGS EVERY DAY.
RIGHT NOW YOU'RE KILLING YOUR OWN FREEDOM...
BLINK
...JUST TO GET YOUR FAMILY TO ACCEPT YOU.

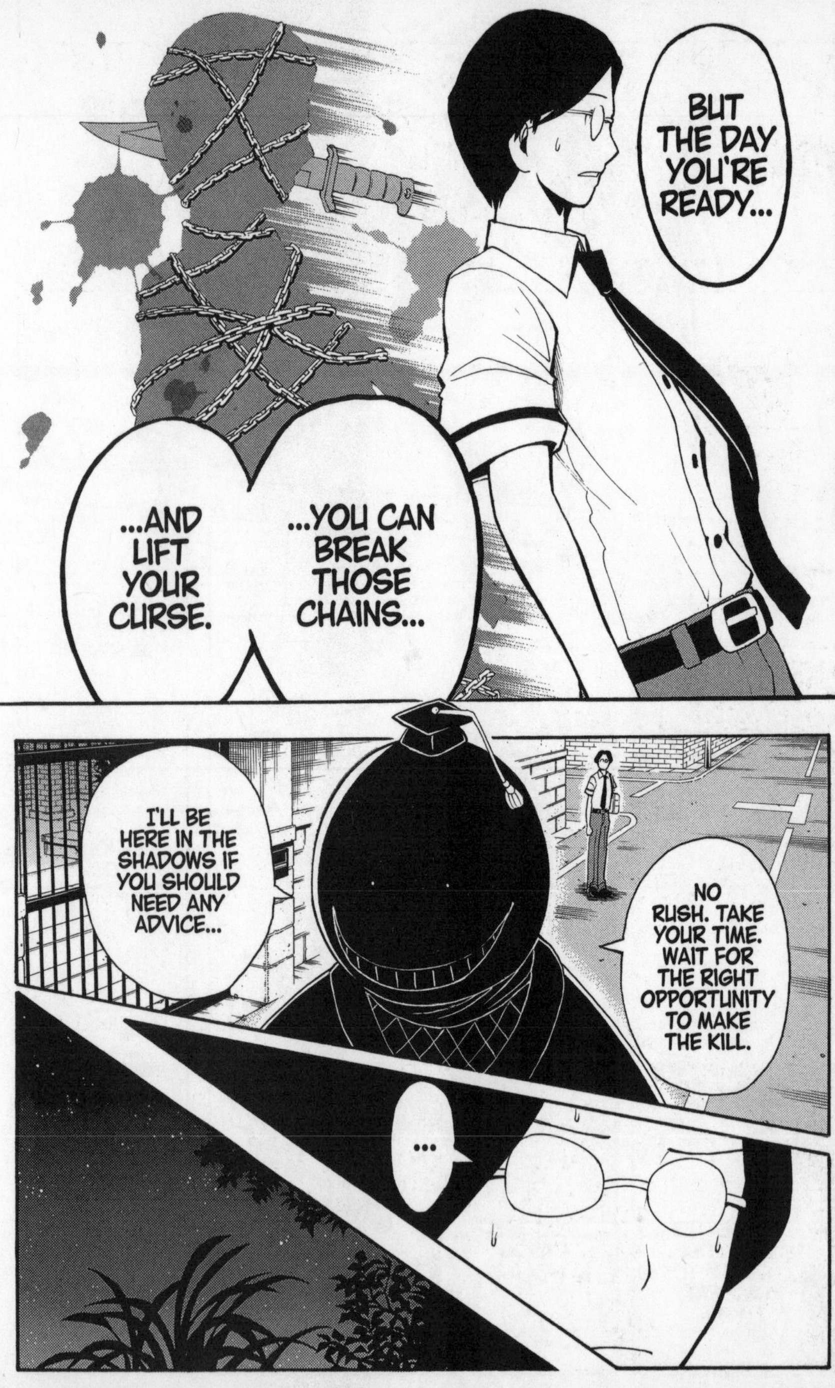
BUT THE DAY YOU'RE READY...
...YOU CAN BREAK THOSE CHAINS...
...AND LIFT YOUR CURSE.
NO RUSH. TAKE YOUR TIME. WAIT FOR THE RIGHT OPPORTUNITY TO MAKE THE KILL.
I'LL BE HERE IN THE SHADOWS IF YOU SHOULD NEED ANY ADVICE...
...

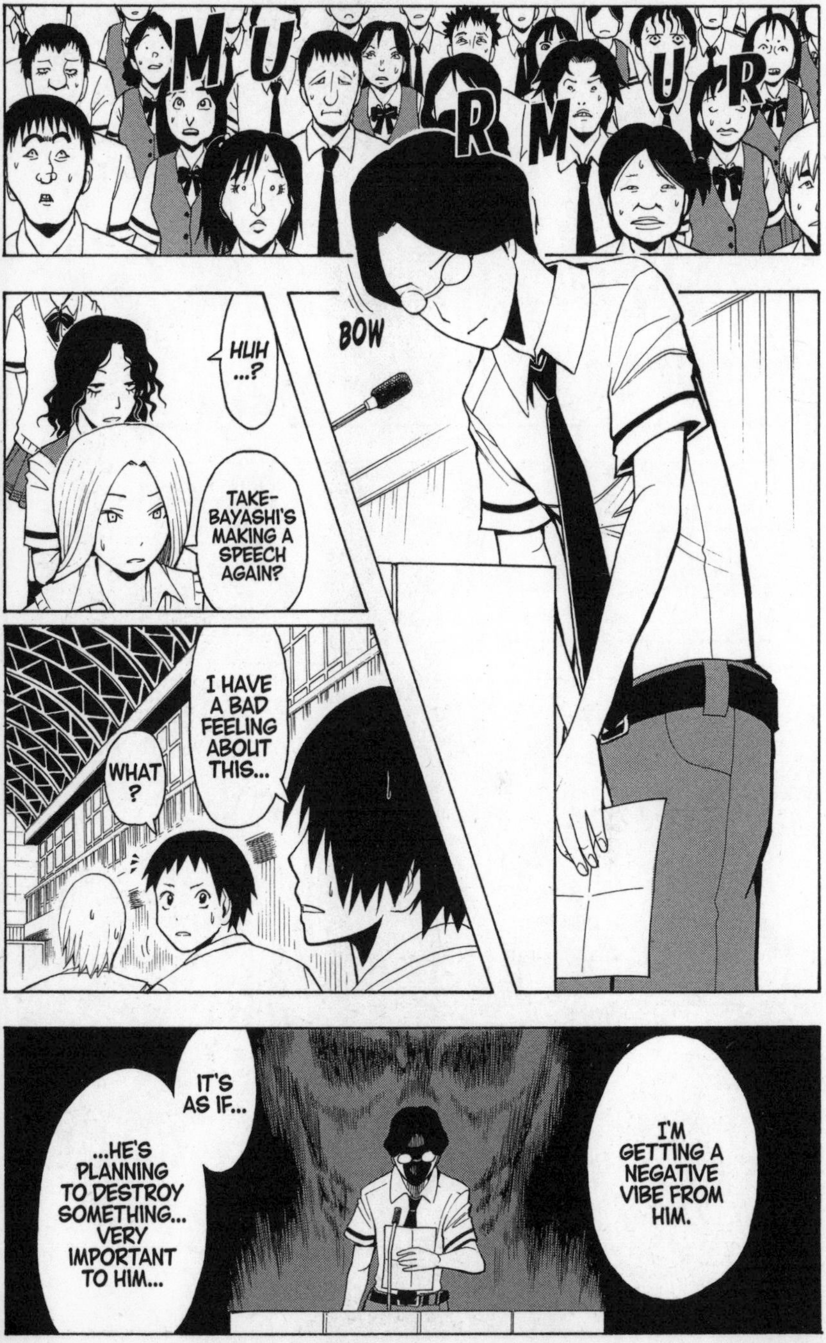
MURMUR
BOW
HUH ...?
TAKE-BAYASHI'S MAKING A SPEECH AGAIN?
I HAVE A BAD FEELING ABOUT THIS...
WHAT ?
I'M GETTING A NEGATIVE VIBE FROM HIM.
IT'S AS IF...
...HE'S PLANNING TO DESTROY SOMETHING... VERY IMPORTANT TO HIM...

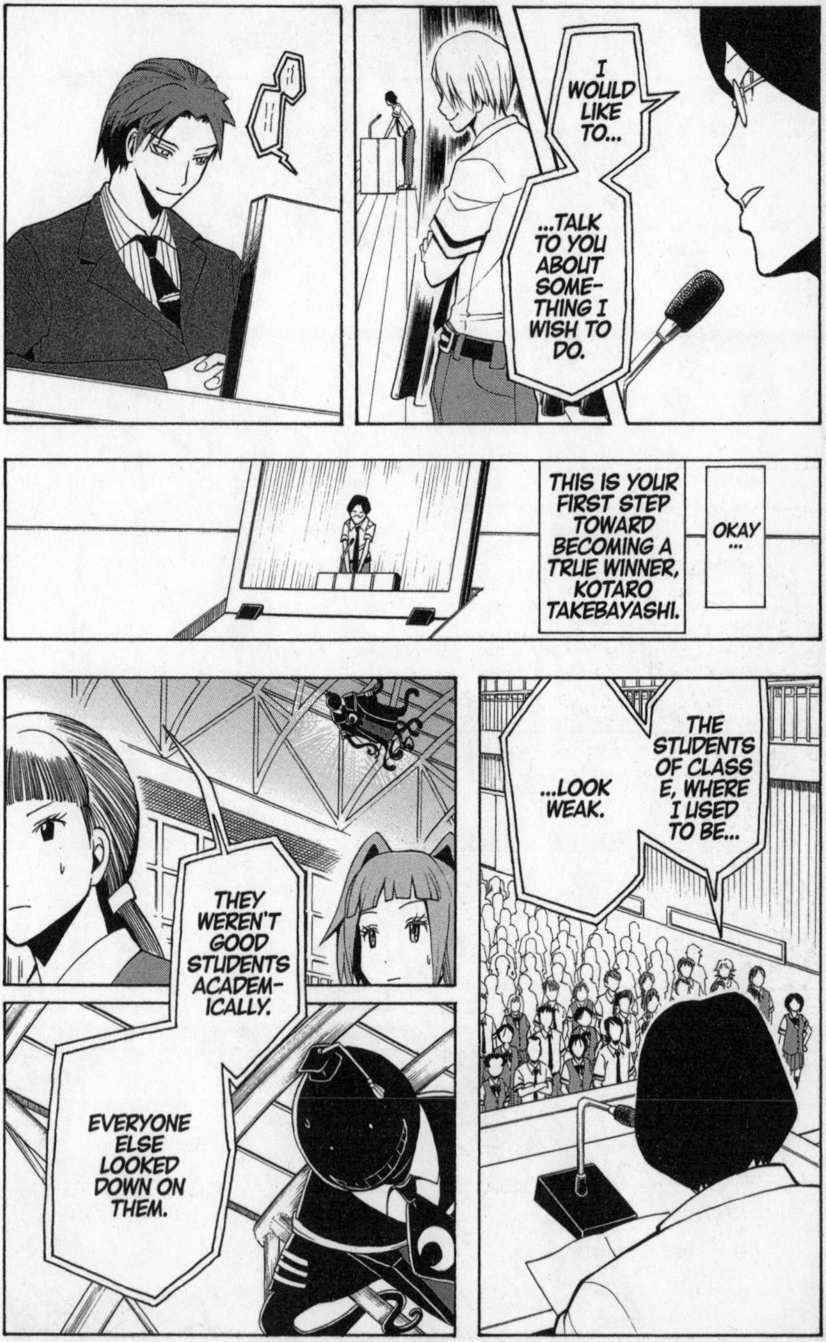
I WOULD LIKE TO...
...TALK TO YOU ABOUT SOME-THING I WISH TO DO.
OKAY ...
THIS IS YOUR FIRST STEP TOWARD BECOMING A TRUE WINNER, KOTARO TAKEBAYASHI.
THE STUDENTS OF CLASS E, WHERE I USED TO BE...
...LOOK WEAK.
THEY WEREN'T GOOD STUDENTS ACADEM-ICALLY.
EVERYONE ELSE LOOKED DOWN ON THEM.

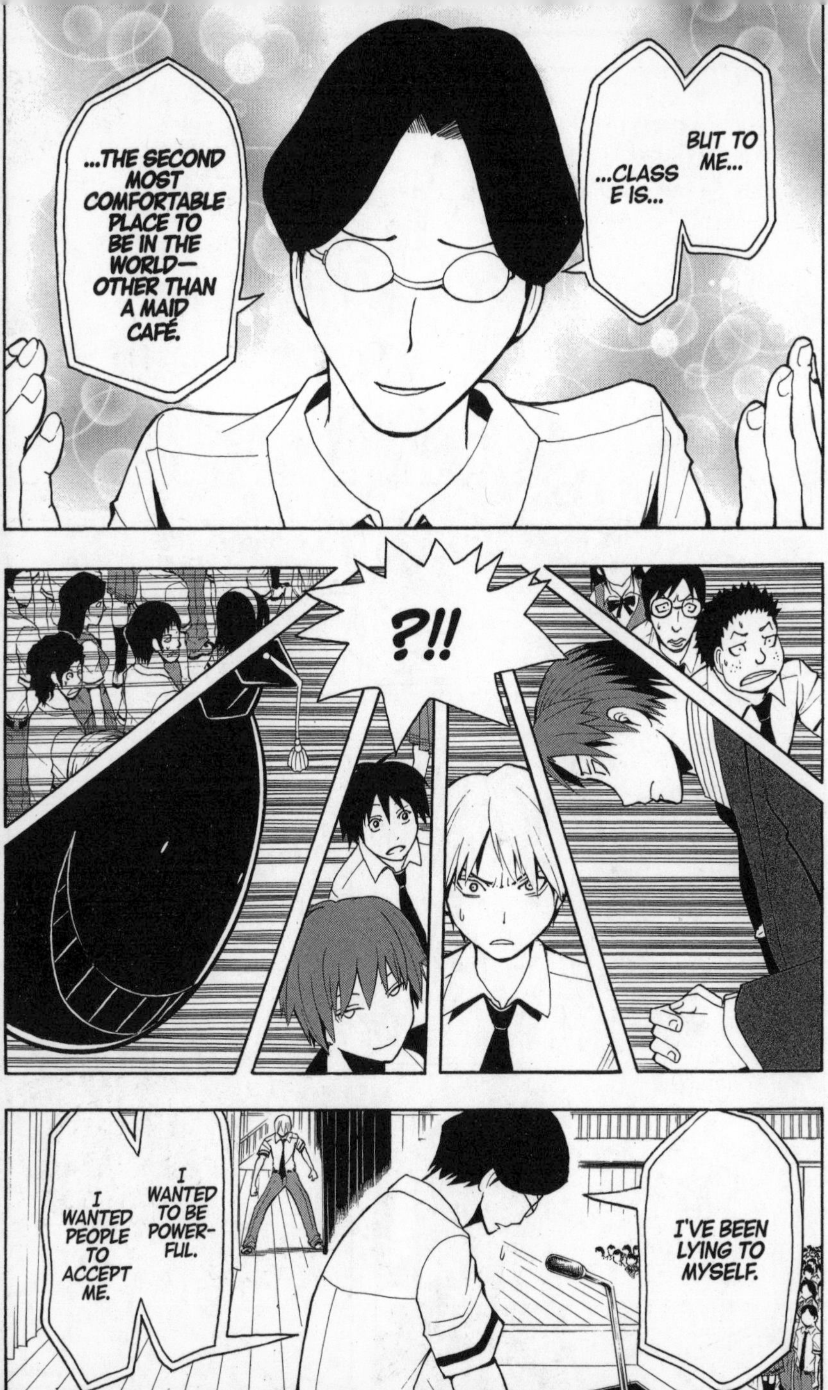
BUT TO ME...
...CLASS E IS...
...THE SECOND MOST COMFORTABLE PLACE TO BE IN THE WORLD—OTHER THAN A MAID CAFÉ.
?!!
I'VE BEEN LYING TO MYSELF.
I WANTED TO BE POWER-FUL.
I WANTED PEOPLE TO ACCEPT ME.

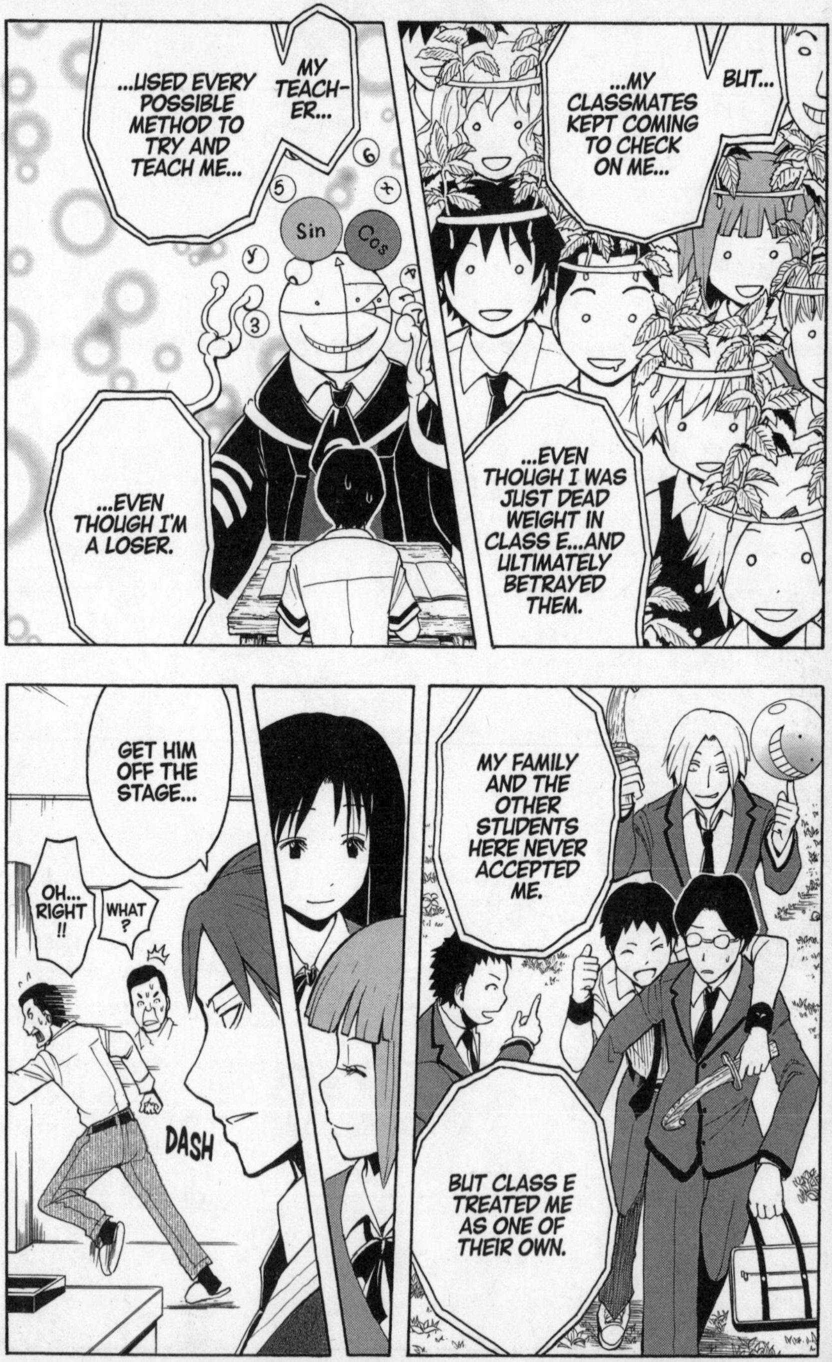
BUT...
...MY CLASSMATES KEPT COMING TO CHECK ON ME...
...EVEN THOUGH I WAS JUST DEAD WEIGHT IN CLASS E...AND ULTIMATELY BETRAYED THEM.
MY TEACHER...
...USED EVERY POSSIBLE METHOD TO TRY AND TEACH ME...
Sin
Cos
...EVEN THOUGH I'M A LOSER.
MY FAMILY AND THE OTHER STUDENTS HERE NEVER ACCEPTED ME.
BUT CLASS E TREATED ME AS ONE OF THEIR OWN.
GET HIM OFF THE STAGE...
WHAT?
OH... RIGHT!!
DASH

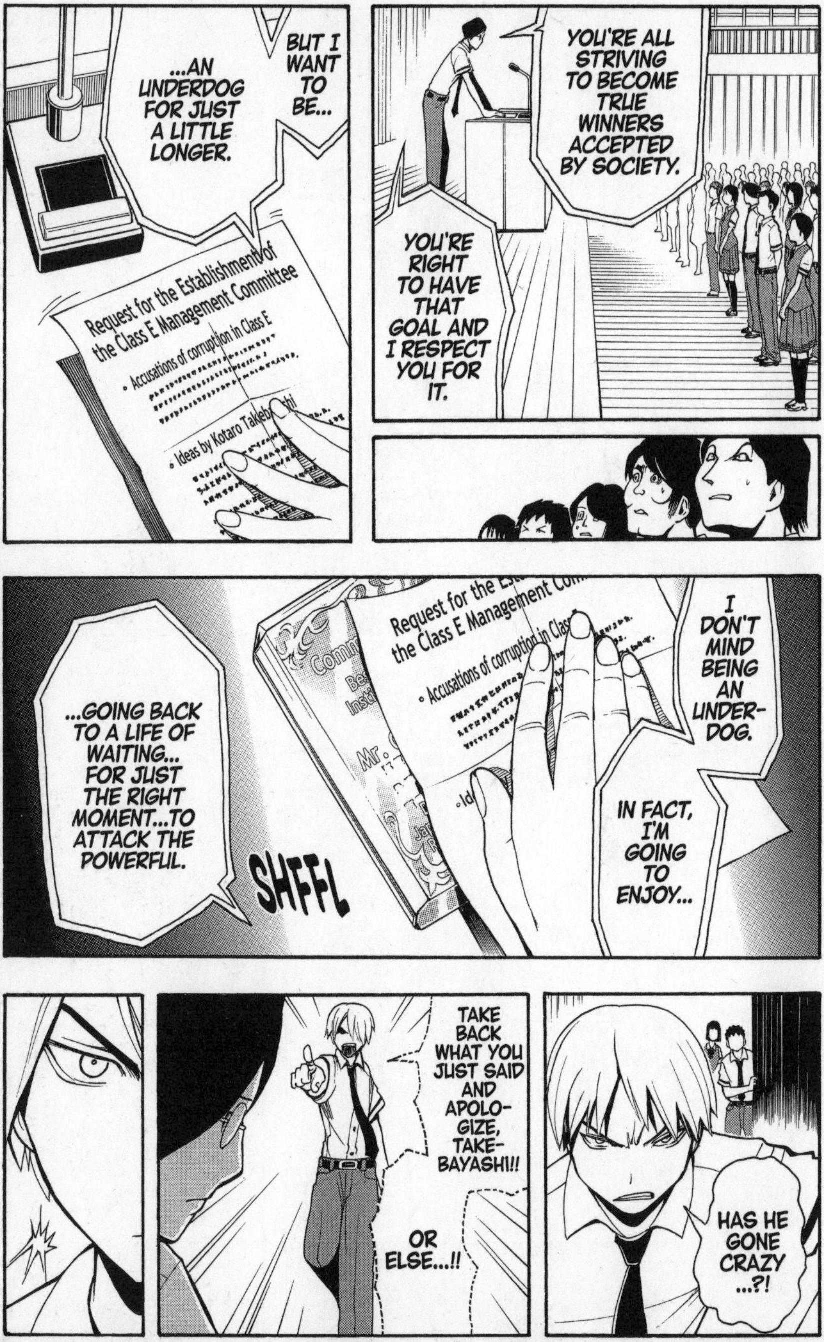
YOU'RE ALL STRIVING TO BECOME TRUE WINNERS ACCEPTED BY SOCIETY.
YOU'RE RIGHT TO HAVE THAT GOAL AND I RESPECT YOU FOR IT.
BUT I WANT TO BE...
...AN UNDERDOG FOR JUST A LITTLE LONGER.
Request for the Establishment of the Class E Management Committee
Accusations of corruption in Class E
I DON'T MIND BEING AN UNDER-DOG.
IN FACT, I'M GOING TO ENJOY...
SHFFL
...GOING BACK TO A LIFE OF WAITING... FOR JUST THE RIGHT MOMENT...TO ATTACK THE POWERFUL.
Request for the Establishment of the Class E Management Committee
HAS HE GONE CRAZY ...?!
TAKE BACK WHAT YOU JUST SAID AND APOLOGIZE, TAKE-BAYASHI!!
OR ELSE...!!

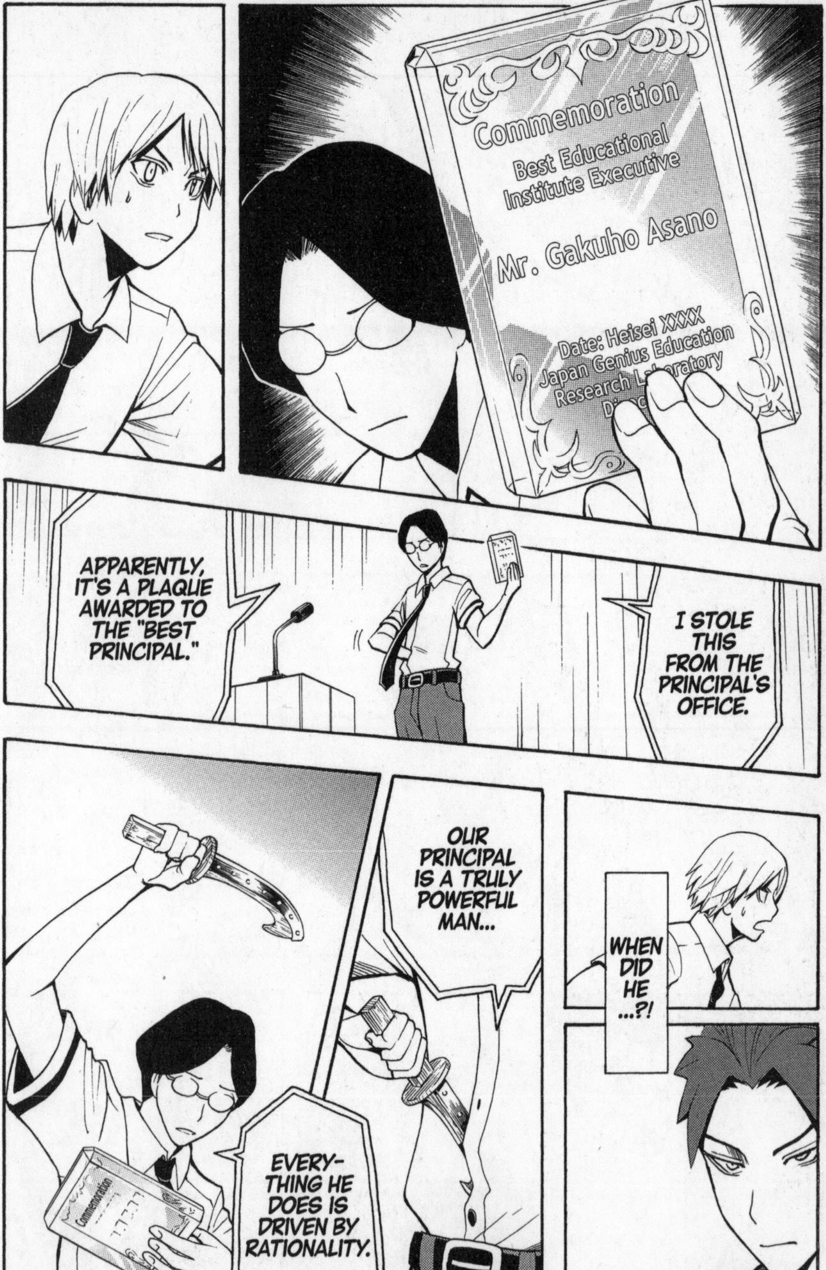
Commemoration
Best Educational Institute Executive
Mr. Gakuho Asano
Date: Heisei XXXX
Japan Genius Education
Research Laboratory
I STOLE THIS FROM THE PRINCIPAL'S OFFICE.
APPARENTLY, IT'S A PLAQUE AWARDED TO THE "BEST PRINCIPAL."
WHEN DID HE ...?!
OUR PRINCIPAL IS A TRULY POWERFUL MAN...
EVERYTHING HE DOES IS DRIVEN BY RATIONALITY.
Commemoration

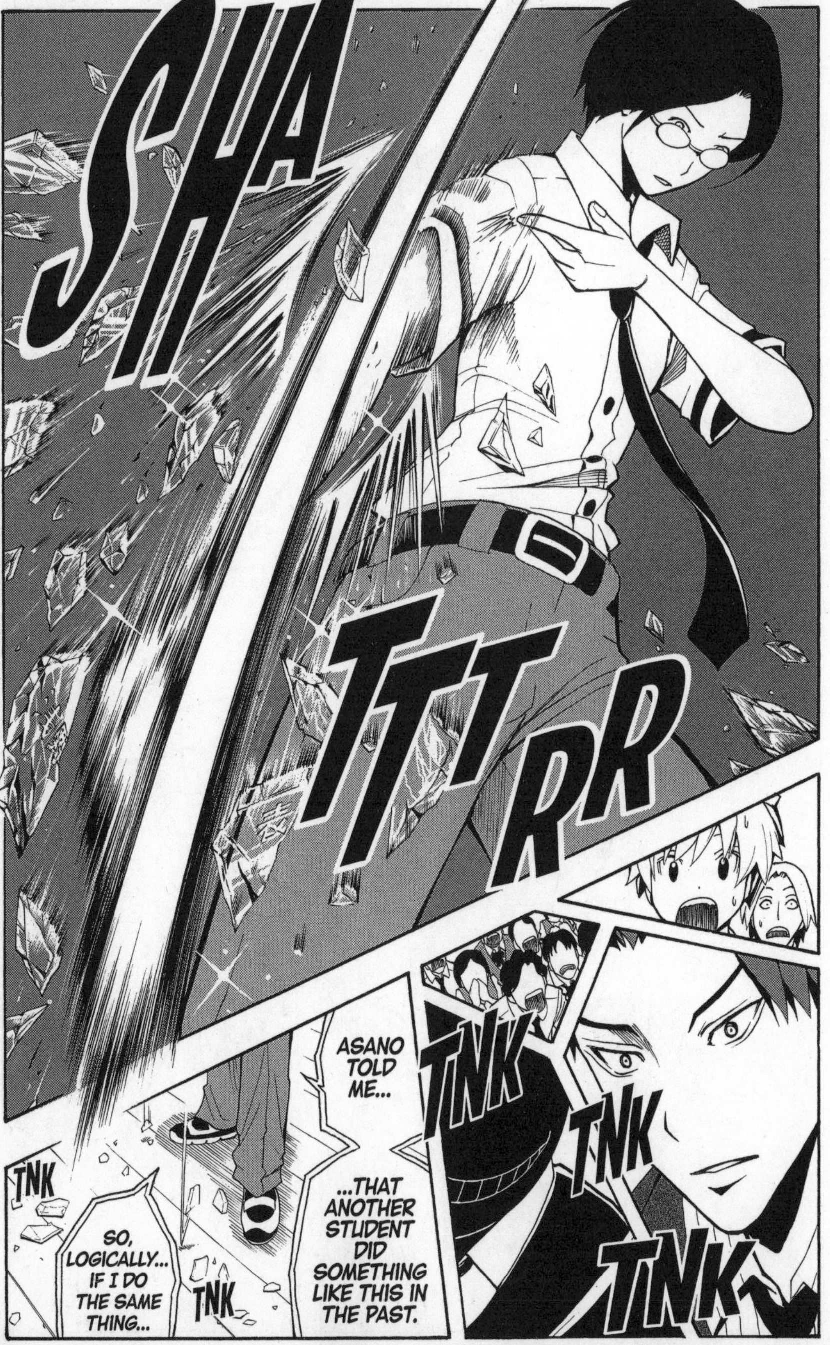
SHA
TTTRR
TNK
TNK
TNK
ASANO TOLD ME...
...THAT ANOTHER STUDENT DID SOMETHING LIKE THIS IN THE PAST.
SO, LOGICALLY... IF I DO THE SAME THING...
TNK
TNK

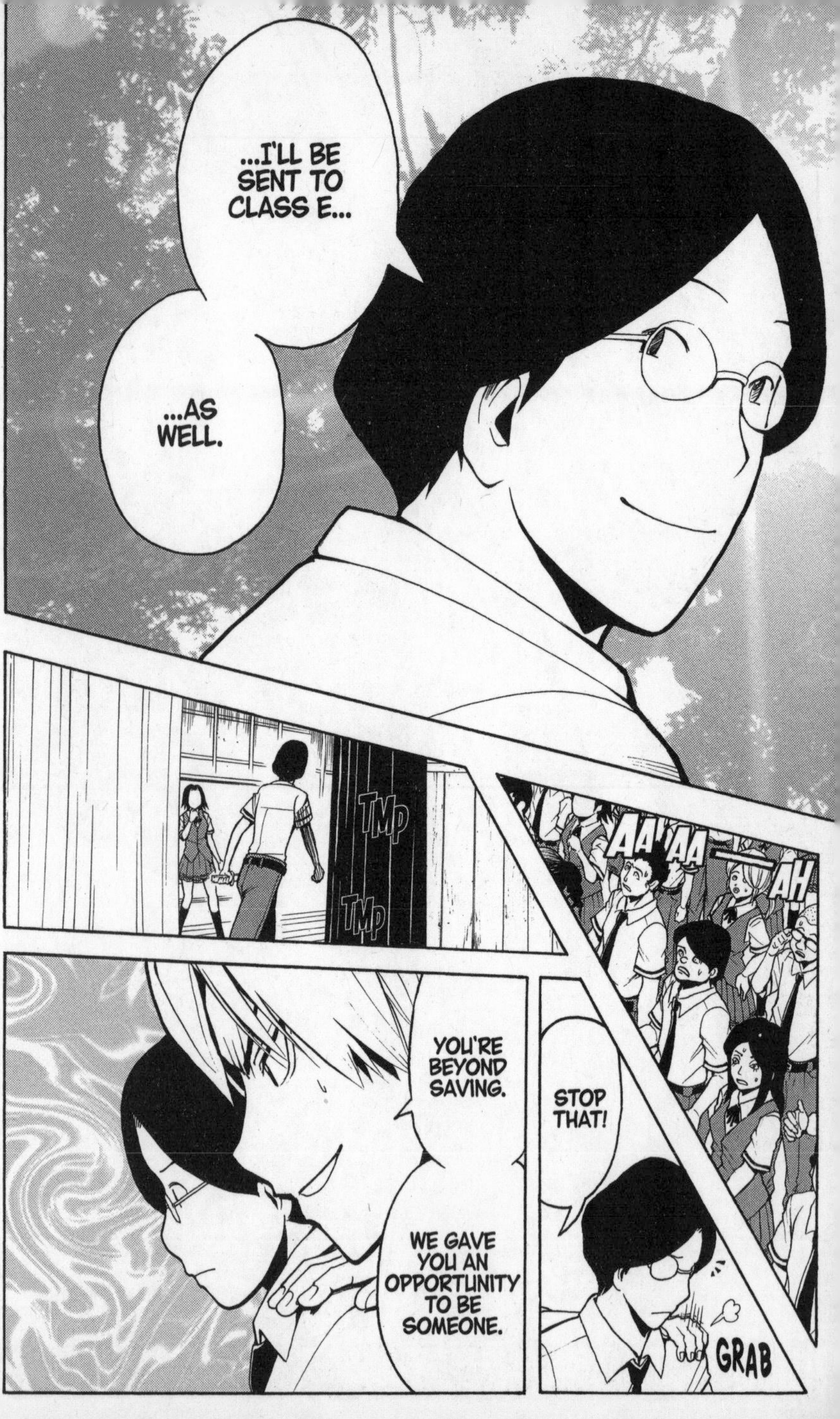
...I'LL BE SENT TO CLASS E...
...AS WELL.
AAAAA—AH
TMP
TMP
STOP THAT!
GRAB
YOU'RE BEYOND SAVING.
WE GAVE YOU AN OPPORTUNITY TO BE SOMEONE.

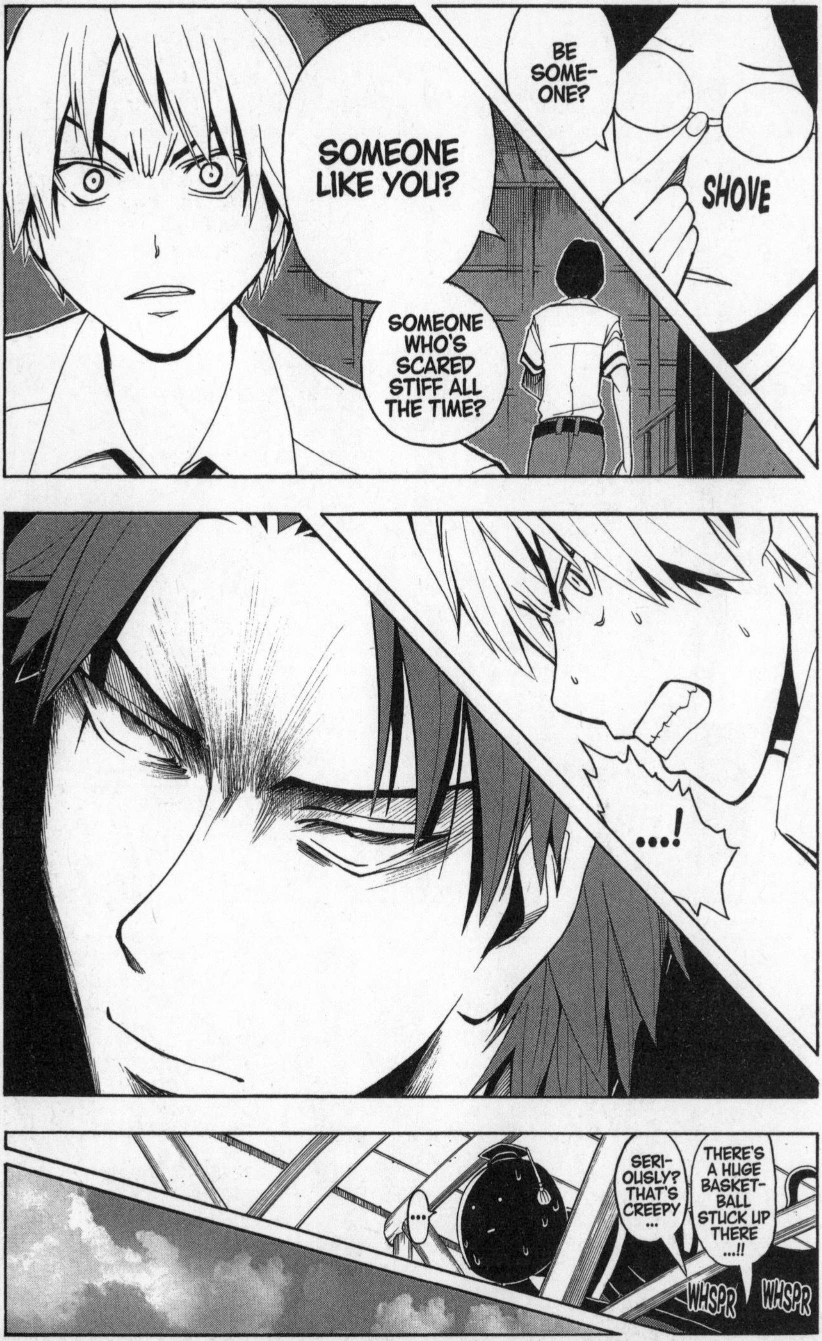
BE SOME-ONE?
SHOVE
SOMEONE LIKE YOU?
SOMEONE WHO'S SCARED STIFF ALL THE TIME?
...!
THERE'S A HUGE BASKET-BALL STUCK UP THERE ...!!
WHSPR
SERI-OUSLY? THAT'S CREEPY ...
WHSPR
...

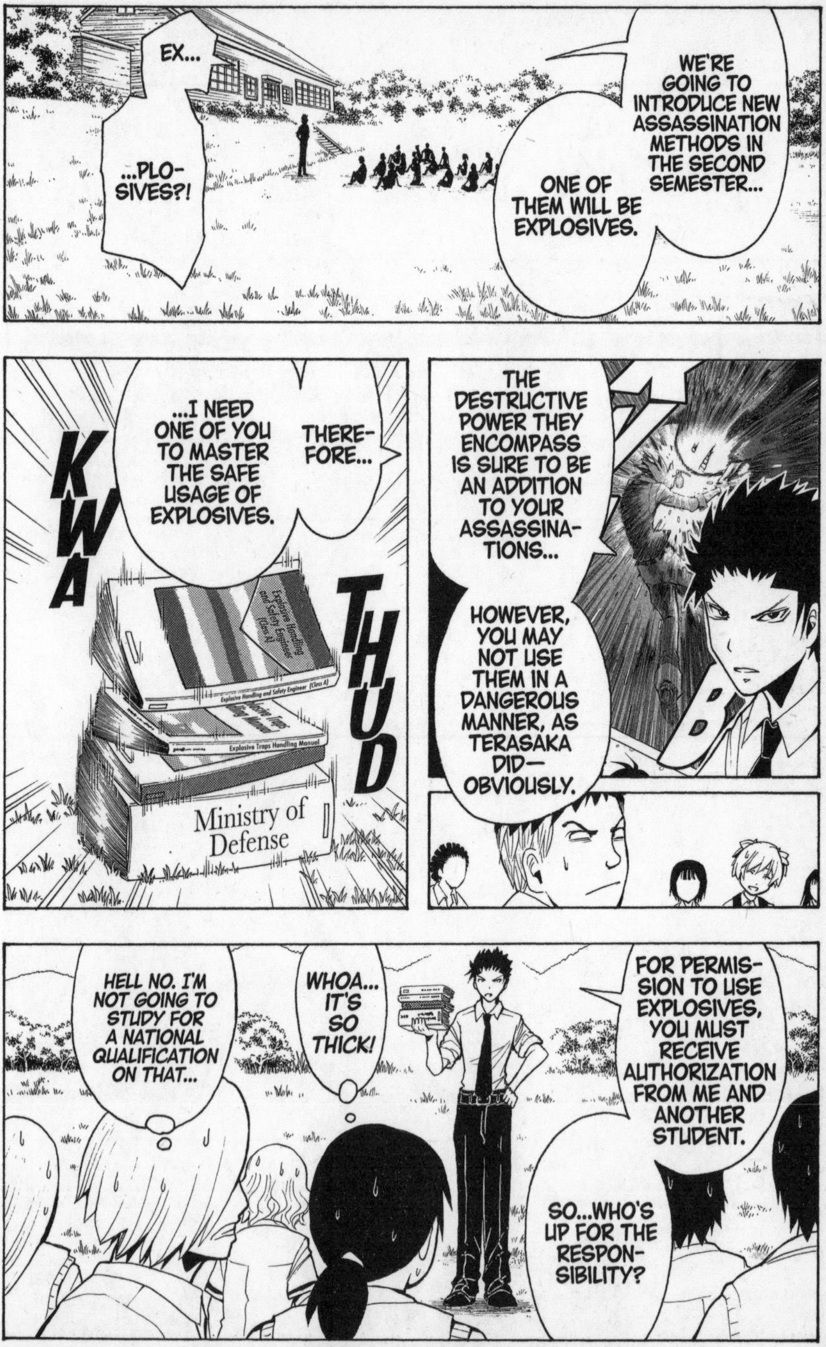
WE'RE GOING TO INTRODUCE NEW ASSASSINATION METHODS IN THE SECOND SEMESTER...
ONE OF THEM WILL BE EXPLOSIVES.
EX...
...PLO-SIVES?!
THE DESTRUCTIVE POWER THEY ENCOMPASS IS SURE TO BE AN ADDITION TO YOUR ASSASSINA-TIONS...
HOWEVER, YOU MAY NOT USE THEM IN A DANGEROUS MANNER, AS TERASAKA DID—OBVIOUSLY.
THERE-FORE...
...I NEED ONE OF YOU TO MASTER THE SAFE USAGE OF EXPLOSIVES.
KWA
THUD
Explosive Handling and Safety Engineer (Class A)
Explosive Traps Handling Manual
Ministry of Defense
FOR PERMIS-SION TO USE EXPLOSIVES, YOU MUST RECEIVE AUTHORIZATION FROM ME AND ANOTHER STUDENT.
SO...WHO'S UP FOR THE RESPON-SIBILITY?
WHOA... IT'S SO THICK!
HELL NO. I'M NOT GOING TO STUDY FOR A NATIONAL QUALIFICATION ON THAT...

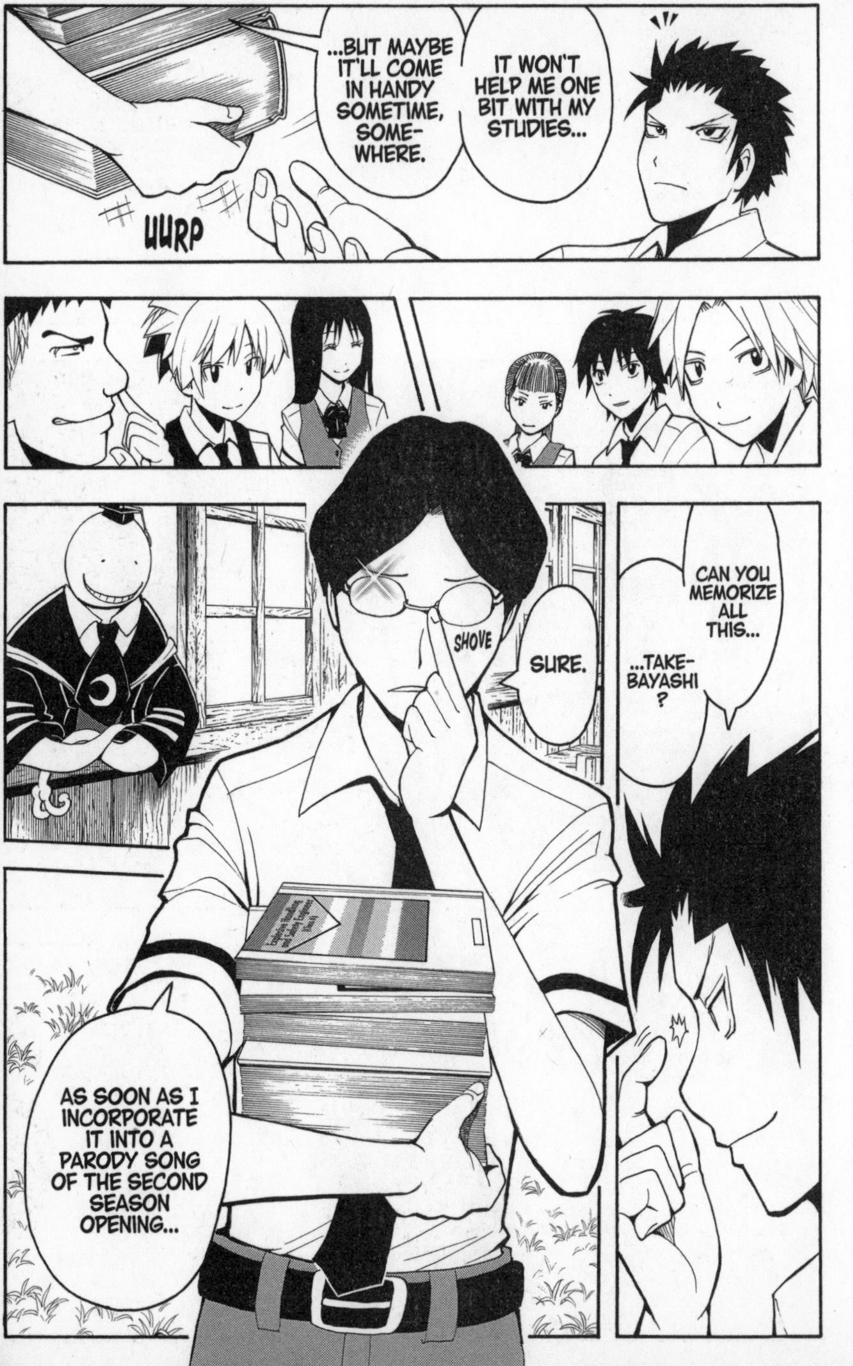
IT WON'T HELP ME ONE BIT WITH MY STUDIES...
...BUT MAYBE IT'LL COME IN HANDY SOMETIME, SOME-WHERE.
UURP
CAN YOU MEMORIZE ALL THIS...
...TAKE-BAYASHI?
SURE.
SHOVE
AS SOON AS I INCORPORATE IT INTO A PARODY SONG OF THE SECOND SEASON OPENING...

to be continued♡

Whenever the popularity of a series is low, the story takes a sharp turn or a new character who was never meant to appear is suddenly introduced. We often refer to this as pandering. Luckily for me, I've never had to pander in my manga artist life so far.

That is to say, thankfully I've never been in that position. But even if I do work on a series that isn't that popular, I probably wouldn't consider pandering to readers.

People might think that means I'm not trying hard enough, but I want to build a trusting relationship with my readers as a manga artist who wraps up the story properly even if the series isn't super popular.

...that should cover any problems in the future. (laugh)

—Yusei Matsui

Yusei Matsui was born on the last day of January in Saitama Prefecture, Japan. He has been drawing manga since elementary school. Some of his favorite manga series are *Bobobo-bo Bo-bobo*, *JoJo's Bizarre Adventure* and *Ultimate Muscle*. Matsui learned his trade working as an assistant to manga artist Yoshio Sawai, creator of *Bobobo-bo Bo-bobo*. In 2005, Matsui debuted his original manga *Neuro: Supernatural Detective* in *Weekly Shonen Jump*. In 2007, *Neuro* was adapted into an anime. In 2012, *Assassination Classroom* began serialization in *Weekly Shonen Jump*.

light

heavy

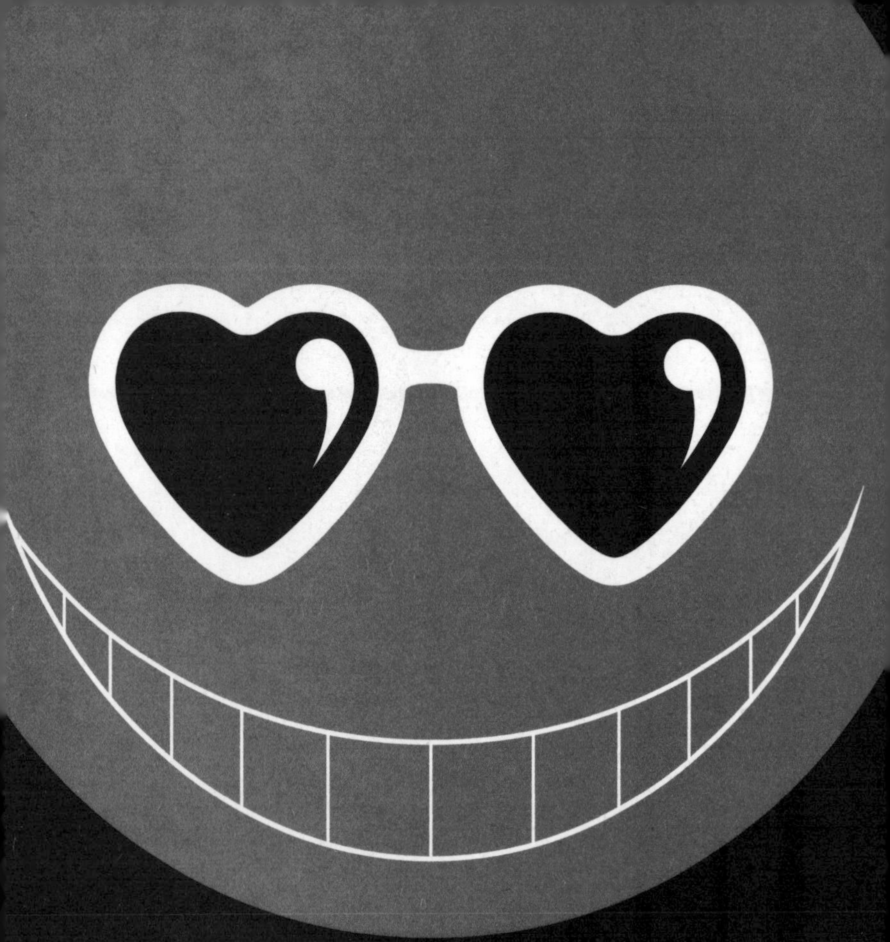

Koro Sensei's suntanned face is so dark brown it's almost black. It will go back to normal in a couple of days, but until then, you can't tell if he's crying or angry. How confusing.

ASSASSINATION CLASSROOM

YUSEI MATSUI

9

A SHOCKING TIME

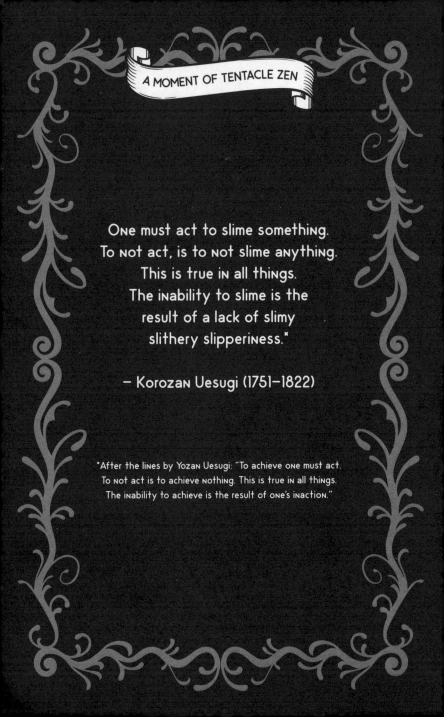

A MOMENT OF TENTACLE ZEN

One must act to slime something.
To not act, is to not slime anything.
This is true in all things.
The inability to slime is the
result of a lack of slimy
slithery slipperiness.*

– Korozan Uesugi (1751–1822)

*After the lines by Yozan Uesugi: "To achieve one must act.
To not act is to achieve nothing. This is true in all things.
The inability to achieve is the result of one's inaction."

ASSASSINATION CLASSROOM

Volume 9
SHONEN JUMP ADVANCED Manga Edition

Story and Art by YUSEI MATSUI

Translation/Tetsuichiro Miyaki
English Adaptation/Bryant Turnage
Touch-up Art & Lettering/Stephen Dutro
Cover & Interior Design/Sam Elzway
Editor/Annette Roman

ANSATSU KYOSHITSU © 2012 by Yusei Matsui
All rights reserved.
First published in Japan in 2012 by SHUEISHA Inc., Tokyo.
English translation rights arranged by SHUEISHA Inc.

The stories, characters and incidents mentioned in this
publication are entirely fictional.

Printed in the U.S.A.

Published by VIZ Media, LLC
P.O. Box 77010
San Francisco, CA 94107

10 9 8 7 6 5 4 3 2
First printing, April 2016
Second printing, August 2017

www.shonenjump.com

www.viz.com

Syllabus for Assassination Classroom, Vol. 10

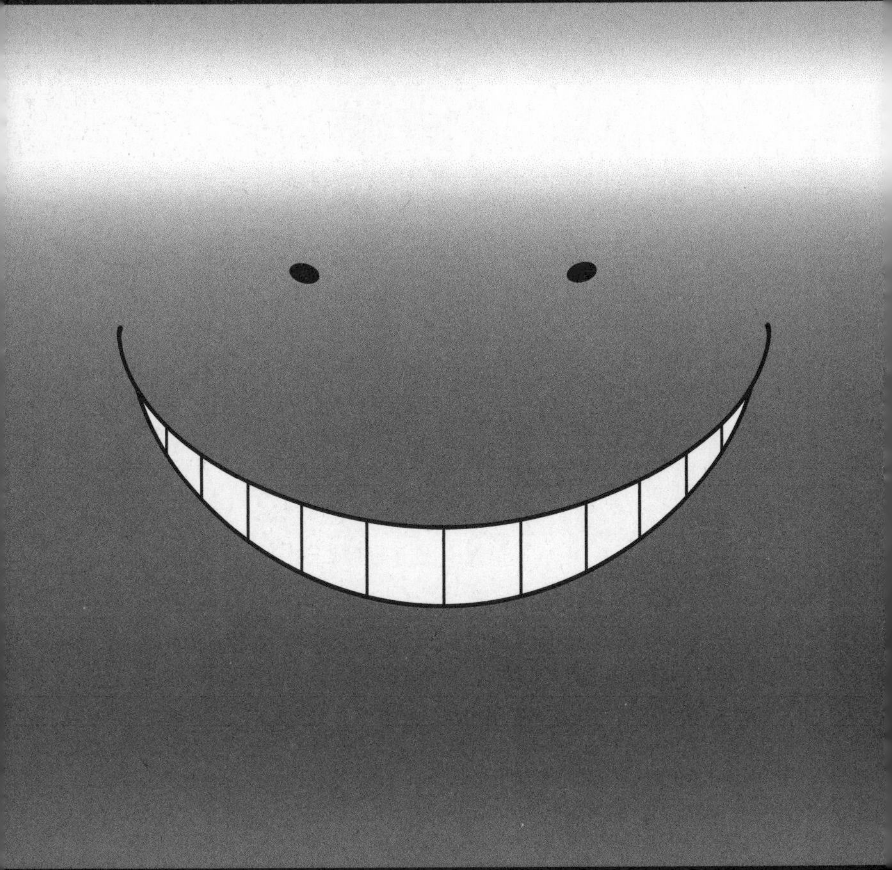

The students of 3-E turn a surplus of eggs to good use—in pursuit of their usual goal. Karasuma teaches them the art of parkour while Koro Sensei teaches them the game of cops and robbers. Then, someone is stealing lingerie, and naturally Koro Sensei is the prime suspect! But is he being framed...and if so, by whom? Lastly, biologically modified Itona discovers that sometimes tentacles can be a burden rather than a gift. He puts everything he's got into his latest assassination attempt on Koro Sensei...but who will save Itona from himself?!

Available Now!

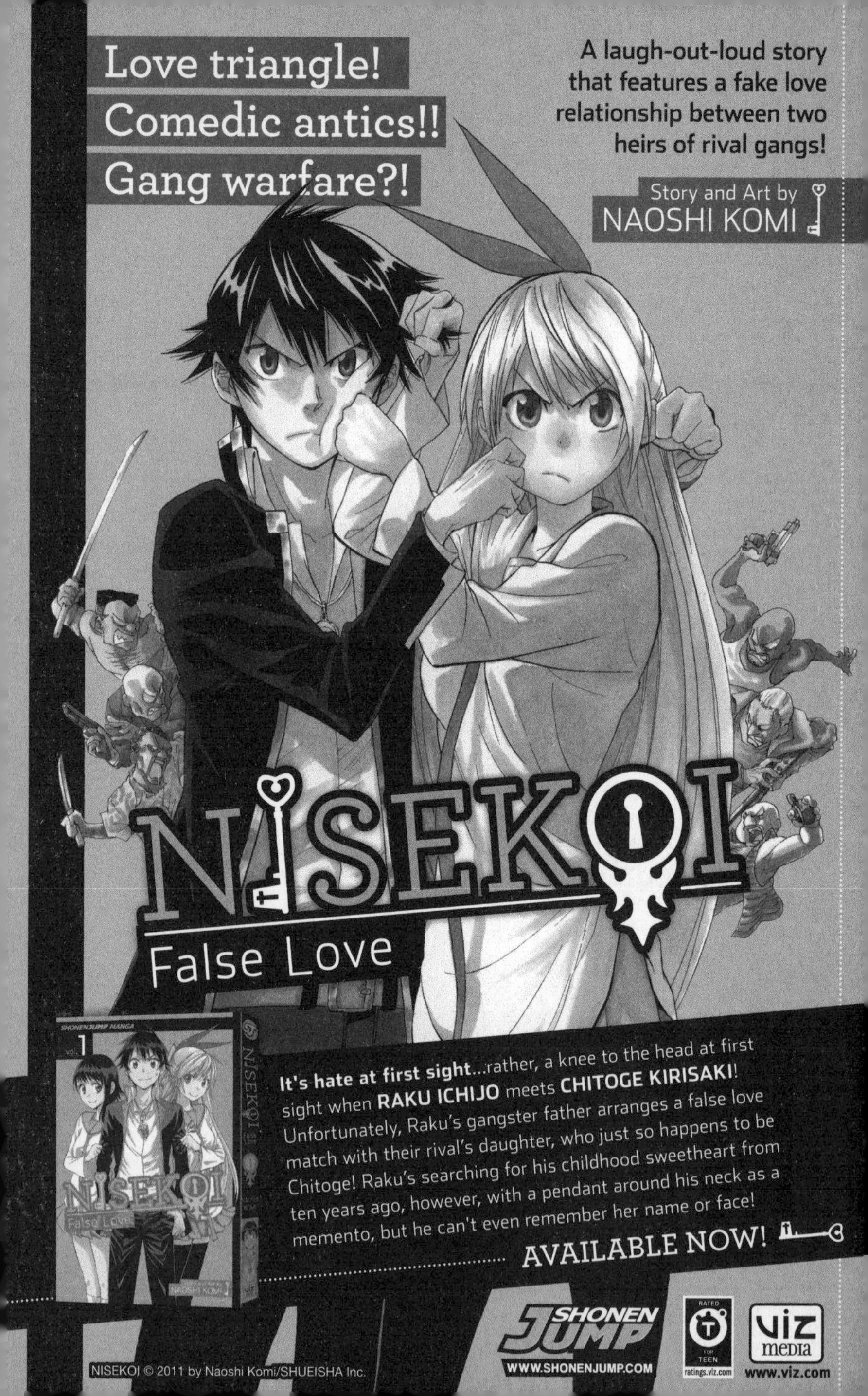
Love triangle!
Comedic antics!!
Gang warfare?!
A laugh-out-loud story that features a fake love relationship between two heirs of rival gangs!
Story and Art by NAOSHI KOMI
NISEKOI
False Love
It's hate at first sight...rather, a knee to the head at first sight when RAKU ICHIJO meets CHITOGE KIRISAKI! Unfortunately, Raku's gangster father arranges a false love match with their rival's daughter, who just so happens to be Chitoge! Raku's searching for his childhood sweetheart from ten years ago, however, with a pendant around his neck as a memento, but he can't even remember her name or face!
AVAILABLE NOW!
SHONEN JUMP
WWW.SHONENJUMP.COM
RATED T TEEN
ratings.viz.com
viz media
www.viz.com
NISEKOI © 2011 by Naoshi Komi/SHUEISHA Inc.

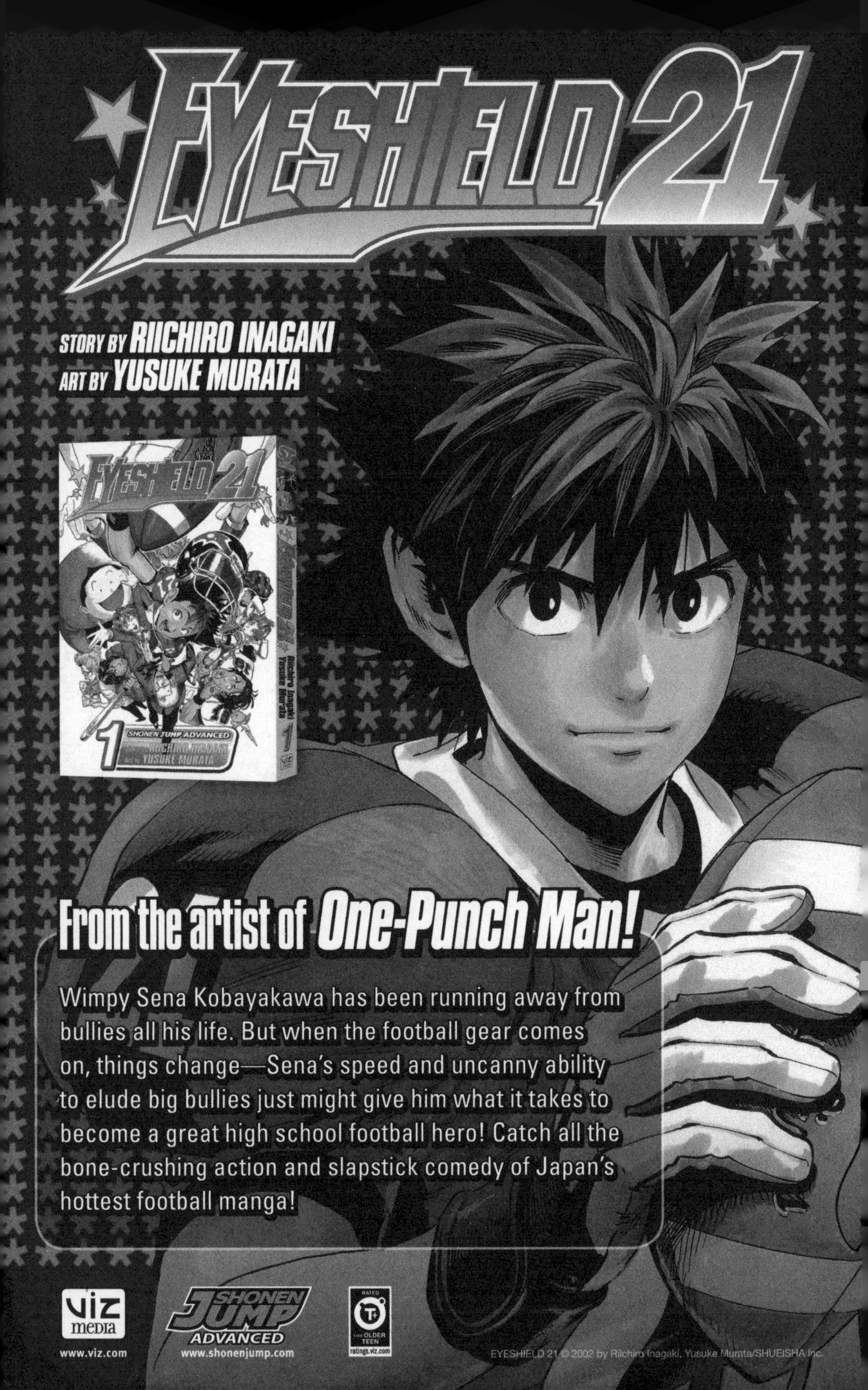
EYESHIELD 21
STORY BY RIICHIRO INAGAKI
ART BY YUSUKE MURATA
From the artist of One-Punch Man!
Wimpy Sena Kobayakawa has been running away from bullies all his life. But when the football gear comes on, things change—Sena's speed and uncanny ability to elude big bullies just might give him what it takes to become a great high school football hero! Catch all the bone-crushing action and slapstick comedy of Japan's hottest football manga!
viz media
www.viz.com
SHONEN JUMP ADVANCED
www.shonenjump.com
RATED T+ FOR OLDER TEEN
ratings.viz.com
EYESHIELD 21 © 2002 by Riichiro Inagaki, Yusuke Murata/SHUEISHA Inc.

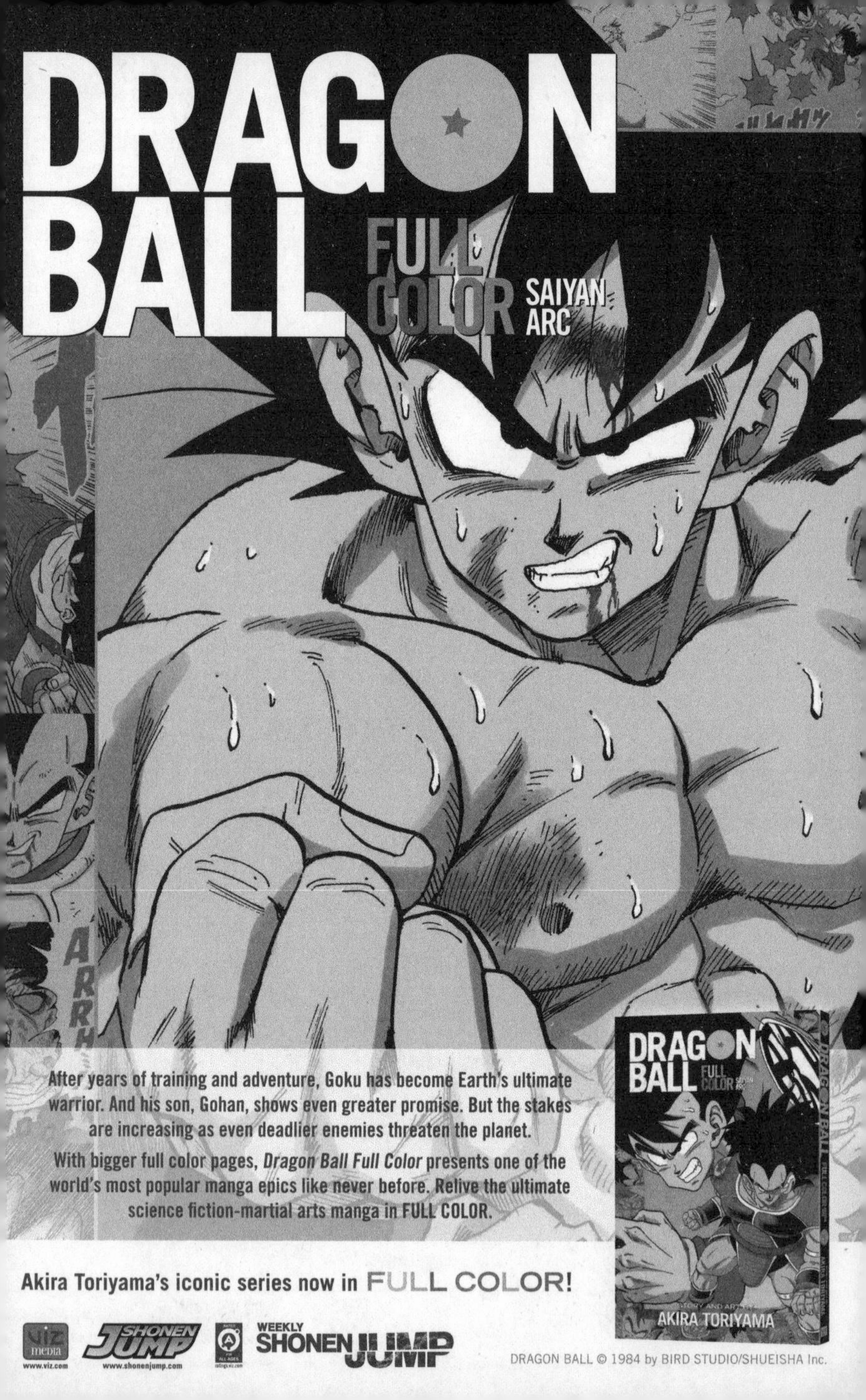
DRAGON BALL
FULL COLOR
SAIYAN ARC
ARRH
After years of training and adventure, Goku has become Earth's ultimate warrior. And his son, Gohan, shows even greater promise. But the stakes are increasing as even deadlier enemies threaten the planet.
With bigger full color pages, *Dragon Ball Full Color* presents one of the world's most popular manga epics like never before. Relive the ultimate science fiction-martial arts manga in FULL COLOR.
DRAGON BALL
FULL COLOR
STORY AND ART BY
AKIRA TORIYAMA
Akira Toriyama's iconic series now in FULL COLOR!
viz media
www.viz.com
SHONEN JUMP
www.shonenjump.com
RATED A FOR ALL AGES
ratings.viz.com
WEEKLY SHONEN JUMP
DRAGON BALL © 1984 by BIRD STUDIO/SHUEISHA Inc.

You're Reading in the Wrong Direction!!

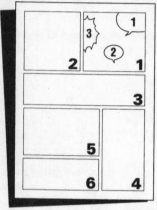

Whoops! Guess what? You're starting at the wrong end of the comic!

...It's true! In keeping with the original Japanese format, **Assassination Classroom** is meant to be read from right to left, starting in the upper-right corner.

Unlike English, which is read from left to right, Japanese is read from right to left, meaning that action, sound effects and word-balloon order are completely reversed... something which can make readers unfamiliar with Japanese feel pretty backwards themselves. For this reason, manga or Japanese comics published in the U.S. in English have sometimes been published "flopped"—that is, printed in exact reverse order, as though seen from the other side of a mirror.

By flopping pages, U.S. publishers can avoid confusing readers, but the compromise is not without its downside. For one thing, a character in a flopped manga series who once wore in the original Japanese version a T-shirt emblazoned with "M A Y" (as in "the merry month of") now wears one which reads "Y A M"! Additionally, many manga creators in Japan are themselves unhappy with the process, as some feel the mirror-imaging of their art skews their original intentions.

We are proud to bring you Yusei Matsui's **Assassination Classroom** in the original unflopped format.
For now, though, turn to the other side of the book and let the adventure begin...!

—Editor